Kathinka Zitz-Halein
and
Female Civic Activism
in Mid-Nineteenth-Century
Germany

Stanley Zucker

Southern Illinois University Press
Carbondale and Edwardsville

Library of Congress Cataloging-in-Publication Data

Zucker, Stanley, 1936–1988.
    Kathinka Zita-Halein and female civic activism in mid-nineteenth-
century Germany / Stanley Zucker.
        p.   cm.
    Includes bibliographical references and index.
    ISBN 0-8093-1674-9
    1. Zitz-Halein, Kathinka—Biography.   2. Authors, German—19th
century—Biography.   3. Feminists—Germany—Biography.   4. Zitz-
Halein, Kathinka—Political and social views.   5. Women in
politics—Germany—History—19th century.   I. Title.
PT2377.K32Z98   1991
838'.709—dc20
[B]   90-36156
                                                                              CIP

Frontispiece: Kathinka Zitz-Halein at 33. Courtesy, Hessische
Landesbibliothek, Wiesbaden, West Germany.

The paper used in this publication meets the minimum requirements of
American National Standard for Information Sciences—Permanence
of Paper for Printed Library Materials, ANSI Z39.48-1984. ∞

Contents

Acknowledgments

*E*ven if the individual scholar is solely responsible for the finished work, every research project requires the assistance of archivists, librarians, colleagues, friends, and family. Among the first two groups I wish to thank especially the staffs of the Hessische Landesbibliothek in Wiesbaden and the Stadtarchiv and Stadtbibliothek of Mainz for their willingness to make available their holdings and for permitting extensive copying of the Zitz-Halein papers. I am also indebted to the staff of Morris Library, Southern Illinois University at Carbondale, for their never-tiring efforts to procure books for me through the interlibrary loan network. Southern Illinois University at Carbondale also deserves my thanks for its financial support of this project.

Stanley Zucker

Though the author finished the text of this book, he was unable to completely express his gratitude to those who fostered his research. Stanley Zucker's widow, Barbara Fleisher Zucker, has attempted to complete Professor Zucker's personal acknowledgments as he would have written them. Barbara Zucker would like to thank Joan Wallach Scott, Margaret Lavinia Anderson, and James F. Harris for their close reading of and helpful suggestions concerning Professor Zucker's manuscript.

In addition to Southern Illinois University, grant support was received from the American Philosophical Society, the National Endowment for the Humanities Travel to Collections program, and the Deutscher Akademischer Austauschdienst. Also, the opportunity to present papers at meetings of the German Studies Association, the Consortium on Revolutionary Europe, the Berkshire Conference on the History of Women, a conference on autobiography and biography sponsored by Stanford University's Center for Research on Women, and a conference of interdisciplinary nineteenth-century studies all directly influenced this manuscript.

Since the mid 1960s, when a portion of the author's dissertation research was completed in Mainz, access to resources and professional courtesy was graciously given by the city library, archive, and the university library. Special thanks are to extended to Dr. Ludwig Falck and Herr Friedrich Schütz of the Mainz city archive, Johannes Gutenberg University, and to Professor Dr. Winfried Baumgart of its history department. Gratitude also to Professor Donald Mattheisen of the University of Lowell in Massachusetts for sharing his knowledge of the resources of the Bundesarchiv Aussenstelle in Frankfurt and to Dr. Schenk of this respository. Many others who contributed their scholarly expertise have been credited throughout the chapter notes and bibliography.

Advice and assistance relevant to publication were given by Theodore S. Hamerow and H. Arnold Barton, professors of history at the University of Wisconsin, Madison, and Southern Illinois University at Carbondale, respectively. In addition, the manuscript would have not made it beyond the typescript stage without the support of the Department of History at Southern Illinois University at Carbondale. Special thanks to the departmental chair, Dr. David P. Werlich, for access to the department's computer resources and to Angie Calcaterra for her cheerful secretarial support. The author is responsible for all the translations.

Introduction

Writing a biography of a "missed" historical figure can be a daunting task, and more so if that person is a mid-nineteenth-century female. Biographies of women normally cannot be approached in the same way as those of men. Women's history, especially before the end of the nineteenth century, presents some of the problems that one encounters researching the lives of working-class individuals: a difficulty in identifying the most significant women and their achievements. Gerda Lerner asks whether women are noteworthy only when their achievements fall into the categories established for men. "Obviously not," she replies. But if we need another scale, it is not clear how that scale should be calibrated. Women usually did not have the same kind of public life as men. And it is public involvement that is the stuff from which biographical history is written. Jelinek's study of women's autobiographies reveals that they generally focused on domestic and personal activities, not professional, philosophical, or political ones. For women the dividing line between public and private spheres is much less sharply defined than for men. Cooking, cleaning, marital relations, and child rearing, although they appeared less significant than writing a political essay and participating in a political organization, were integrally related to the latter activities. Unfortunately, one can rarely sufficiently document the former.[1]

Furthermore, there is the question of sources. Before the second half of the nineteenth century, as Kay Goodman has demonstrated, women only occasionally wrote memoirs or autobiographies, kept diaries, or left behind substantial letter collections. Letters from women were usually not considered important enough to retain, especially if written to men.[2]

Given the obstacles that the historian of women faces, it should not be surprising that the first works on early and mid-nineteenth-century

Introduction

females have focused on literary figures. Recent work on German women of the period 1800–1870 has highlighted writers, even if renowned in other areas, such as Mathilde Francis Anneke, Bettina von Arnim, Louise Aston, Louise Dittmar, Ida Hahn-Hahn, Louise Otto, Malwida von Meysenbug, Fanny Lewald Stahr, and Rahel Varnhagen von Ense. Literary activity provided the most convenient means for a woman to become a noted individual whose configuration was distinguishable from the mass. Researchers have the corpus of published material to exploit, and they can use it for clues to an individual's private life, especially if diaries and letters are lacking. This research, which has been done both by historians and scholars in German literature, has pushed back the beginnings of women's civic activity and the initial efforts toward emancipation to the 1840s.

The life of Kathinka Zitz (born Halein) provides several new perspectives on women's activities and their history in nineteenth-century Germany. As a professional writer she had a fifty-year career of publications that included poems, translations, novellas, fairy tales, children's stories, journalistic work, and biographical novels. An impressive body of material, it reflects in part the mass production-like publishing pressures of the literary profession to which she was subjected. In addition to the published works she left a significant body of unpublished material, most important of which are her memoirs and diary. Her memoirs, among the earliest by a German woman and entitled "Skizzen aus meinem Leben," are in the Hessische Landesbibliothek in Wiesbaden. Written in the early 1850s they recount the first fifty years of her life. She composed two drafts, the longer containing more intimate details. They were apparently to be used as the basis for a biography that never came to fruition. Nevertheless, they remain significant sources not only for the details of her life but equally for the manners and mores of her contemporaries. She continued her life's story in the form of a diary, or "Tagebuch,"[3] which covers the period 1854–1874 and chronicles her social life, medical problems, and psychological moods. These two sources are supplemented by hundreds of letters, mostly to her, from female and male friends. The earlier letters are in the Stadtarchiv in Mainz and those from her later life in the Wiesbaden library. The letters often serve as a means to test the accuracy of her memoirs and diary and generally have corroborated them.

The material offers insights into women's status within the literary field. We learn about Zitz-Halein's difficulties in becoming established as a writer and her struggles for recognition and fair treatment by publishers and critics. Her papers also detail her relations with the two men in her life, one to whom she was engaged for eleven years and the other whom she married then separated from after eighteen months, whose legal wife she fought to remain. A third major area covered by her published and unpublished works involves her efforts on behalf of German democratization and unification and demonstrates how women could make a contribution to Germany's political and social progress.

What follows is not primarily a study of Kathinka Zitz-Halein's literary activities or a critical analysis of her work, but rather a biographical history of her life and work. Biographies must integrate the public and private spheres, and the sources that Zitz-Halein left behind make this possible. Moreover, in her own view her literary work could not be divorced from her private life, which it often revealed, or from the civic issues of the day, in which she was passionately interested. Her literary work was the connecting link between her public and private existences. Throughout this study I will attempt to illuminate the latter two by the former.

In writing a biography of Kathinka Zitz-Halein the historian must begin with a blank slate and literally create her life. She has not attracted scholars, and except for brief entries in biographical dictionaries her life and accomplishments have been unrecorded and unevaluated. Why this is so derives in part from her gender: she was an example of the general neglect of women's accomplishments that was even more pronounced in Germany than in Anglo-Saxon countries. There is also the question of the quality of her work. No one would claim that she was one of the great German writers of the nineteenth century. Financial necessity may have driven her to write faster than was wise and forced her to follow literary modes regardless of her talent for them. Failure to have been a great writer, Elaine Showalter stresses, should not lead to neglect by historians, for then we "miss the connecting links" within a literary tradition. The principle is true, one might add, for every area of human endeavor. Zitz-Halein was also outspoken, had a troubled private life, and exhibited strong democratic and anticlerical leanings, all of which alienated certain groups in her hometown of Mainz. Not even a local historian has found her worthy of a biographical sketch. Only a twenty-minute radio program in 1964 brought her before the public.[4]

Retrieving her life and work from the dust of archives and libraries is worth the effort. Of the German women who had an impact on her contemporaries probably none was more influential than Kathinka

Introduction

Zitz-Halein. Through her literary and organizational work, the latter of unprecedented scope, she was one of the few women who played a leadership role in the political reform movement of the first half of the nineteenth century. A knowledge of her life also tells us about the educational opportunities available to girls; illuminates certain aspects of marital relations, including the issues of separation and divorce; and informs us of the employment opportunities open to middle-class women. Her civic activities and her contacts broaden our view of the role of women in the pre-1848 and 1848 reform effort. And finally her life intersects the emerging feminist movement. To what degree she shared and opposed its goals should make us rethink or redefine the concept of female emancipation.

She was not an ordinary woman in terms of social origin, education, or literary talent, and her life remains uniquely her own. Nevertheless, it touches the lives of a variety of other women and thus by this limited ripple effect broadens our view of human development.

The book is organized as follows. The first four chapters delineate the influences that helped shape Kathinka Zitz-Halein's outlook. Chapter 1 examines the first thirty-two years of her life: her familial problems, education, and work experience. Chapter 2 covers her turbulent relationship with her husband. Chapter 3 deals with her emerging literary activity, the obstacles that women writers had to face, and her views on women's role in society. Chapter 4 describes the political and social influences on Zitz-Halein and her efforts on behalf of reform before 1848. Chapters 5, 6, and 7 treat her many-sided roles during the Revolution of 1848 as a writer and a political organizer. Chapters 8 through 10 follow her post-1850 personal, literary, and political activities. The emphasis throughout this work will be on the civic impulse that Kathinka Zitz-Halein possessed and how this was related to and influenced by her private life and reflected in her writings.

*Kathinka Zitz-Halein
and
Female Civic Activism
in Mid-Nineteenth-Century
Germany*

1
Early Life

*O*ngoing research into the history of German female activism in the nineteenth century is demonstrating that the decade from 1840 to 1850 was rich in individual and organizational efforts by German women.[1] Of these women Kathinka Zitz-Halein was one of the most important. No other woman was more involved in the political and social events of her day than she. Her midcentury roles, to be fully understood and evaluated, must be viewed against the backdrop of her early life. We must also explore the social and political world in which she was raised to understand how she could step outside the social parameters in which women typically operated.[2] The most useful keys to Kathinka Zitz-Halein's mid-nineteenth-century initiatives are provided by an investigation of her family life, education, work experience, marriage, development as a writer, religious beliefs, and attitude toward women's role in society and the influence of her hometown, Mainz.

Born on November 4, 1801, into the prominent Mainz business family of Anton Victor and Anna Marie Markowitzka Halein, Kathinka was the eldest of three children, the survivors of at least twelve live births. The Haleins had extensive business operations, including a powder and starch factory and a shipping concern, and a business as suppliers of English china. Kathinka's father was educated in Switzerland and trained at the Wedgewood factory in England. He was apparently a talented man, fluent in eight languages and an accomplished artist and musician, whose home was the scene of frequent concerts, or so his daughter remembered. The family was also well connected socially, especially with the military. Kathinka's paternal aunts both married aristocratic army officers, one Austrian and one English; her uncle, Heinrich, became an officer, and her maternal aunts married French army officers. Many of her friends seemed to be either military personnel or the wives, widows, and children of soldiers. Given the fact that Mainz was a major military fortress where, at various times, French, Prussian, Austrian, and Hessian troops were stationed, the Halein experience was not so unusual. The family was also related by blood or marriage to many of the leading families in Mainz, having connections to the business, governmental, and clerical establishments.

Although she was favored by a patrician birth, Kathinka Halein's first twenty-three years were marked by increasing misfortune. One problem was economic. The Napoleonic wars, which resulted in Mainz's annexation to France, had damaged the family's business operations by destroying the shipping activities and the trade in English china. Changes in fashion caused by the French Revolution (the rejection of powdered wigs) undermined the powder and starch factory. By the time Kathinka was three these businesses had been given up, and the family was forced to sell its house and move in with Kathinka's maternal grandmother. Still resourceful and well connected, the Haleins made their way. The paternal grandmother, Felicitas Halein, who had been the legal owner of the family business ventures, started the first important lending library in Mainz, in which Kathinka would be able to satisfy her budding literary interests. Kathinka's parents opened a store that specialized in rugs, wall hangings, and stationery. It prospered as they became the official suppliers for the French military and civilian administration in Mainz. The father, sometime later, took a position managing the business operations of an uncle, Georg Ludwig Kaiser, one of the twelve largest taxpayers in Mainz, which brought in a significant income.[3] The still satisfactory economic position could not be maintained. After the defeat of Napoleon in 1814 Mainz was annexed by the Grand Duchy of Hesse, "becoming German" in Kathinka Halein's words, which hurt the family's economic situation, probably because of the loss of government contracts. By 1820 the Haleins were not listed among the 1,049 taxpayers (20 percent of the total) who paid sufficient taxes to qualify as electors (*Wahlmänner*).[4]

The main problem for the Haleins, however, was not economic but human: the mental and physical deterioration of Kathinka's parents. There is little reason to doubt the picture of them drawn by their daughter. Married at twenty-two in 1799 to escape military service, Anton Halein made his marriage of convenience scarcely a happy one. The businessman was, apparently like his father, a domestic tyrant full of unpredictable moods and with a streak of cruelty. His daughter never remembered hearing an encouraging word from him, with the exception of compliments about her poetry. Instead, she was a frequent victim of his outbursts, examples of which included being chained to a woodpile in the cellar and forced to subsist on bread and water, being whipped several times until bloody, and being required to watch public executions. He also restricted her social life so that only with the connivance of her mother could she attend masked balls.

Since her childhood, she recalled, it had been painful to be in his presence. Fortunately this was not often required, given her father's life-style. A normal day would see him at his uncle's business firm, home only for meals, and after the evening meal he would repair to a wine house until bedtime. When he did sit down at the table it was, according to his daughter, as if the sultriness that precedes a thunderstorm had appeared in their midst. Either silence or insults emanated from him. One example that she relates suggests the domestic tension but also the intellectual interests of father and daughter. Anton Halein, implying he was King Lear, referred to his two daughters, Kathinka and Julia, as Lear's disloyal children, Goneril and Regan. Kathinka wrote that her sister, Julia, understood "nothing of this. She was of another nature. But I, who had devoured Shakespeare with reverence, almost died of mortification." Kathinka was thoroughly alienated from her father by the time she was nineteen.[5]

Her mood is captured in one of her early poems, "Klagen" (Lamentations)[6]:

> My fate I saw reflected in the future,
> Nothing happy blossoms for me on this earth,
> Love will not crown me.
> Instead of hope I will always find deception
> And painfully I feel life's emptiness.
> O God loosen the chains which bind me, . . .
> O lead me to a better life
> Where one finds what one has lost down here.

In 1821 she tried to escape this increasingly intolerable situation by writing to the grand duke of Hesse to request a position with the court theater in Darmstadt, which was highly regarded. It was the first of several attempts to find a position in the Hessian capital. In her letter to the monarch she described herself as talented in writing and singing, pointing out that she had published several poems that had not "gone unpraised," and that she had acted on the private stage in Mainz. She claimed that as a daughter of a good family she could not appear on the public stage in Mainz but would accept a position with an out-of-town company where good "morals ruled." This rather bold as well as desperate attempt by the nineteen-year-old was unsuccessful, but it illustrates the independence that she would display throughout her life.[7]

Starting around 1819 her father's behavior was marked by growing alcoholism and increased mental instability. He left his position with the uncle for unexplained reasons, giving up what had been the major part of the family income. He now spent most of his time in taverns or in an upstairs room drinking and took no part in the family's life or business. His condition deteriorated to the extent that when the mother became ill in the early 1820s it was Kathinka who was given the power of attorney for the business and ran it herself. She realized at this time just how much of her parents' wealth, especially her mother's share, had been dissipated by her father so that the liabilities could not always be covered. This period, which lasted nearly two years, was among the most difficult of her life. She not only had to manage the business by herself but to take care of the household; look after her younger brother and sister; minister to her mother, who was slowly dying of dropsy; and try to deal with her father's unpredictable behavior. To make matters worse, several journals in which she had begun to publish her poetry went out of business, robbing her of the emotional satisfaction that she needed.

The climax occurred a few months after her mother's death (May 26, 1825) as her father's actions became increasingly irrational. A bitter dispute between the two broke out over who should be guardian of the underage children. According to Napoleonic law a guardianship council had to be appointed. Anton Halein accused his daughter of trying to have a deputy guardian appointed in order to limit his powers. When a deputy was selected, relations between father and daughter quickly reached the breaking point. His behavior became menacing. He nailed the doors and windows of their house shut; he burned his wife's clothing and, using an axe, chopped up a picture of her. Through all of these scenes Kathinka never seemed to lose control or ceased to bring his food and drink to his room, where he spent most of his time. Finally her father threatened her with a knife. Here too she showed her coolness, evading her father's attack, maneuvering him out the door, and then rejoining her company. Nevertheless, she could no longer stay in the same house with him. After consulting the prominent judge Franz Aull, who had been the family's lawyer, she decided to leave home and support herself. Before she left she arranged for her sister and brother to be provided for and tried one last time to bring her father to his senses. She wrote to Anton Halein, calling upon him to put his affairs in order and resume the running of the business. It was believed that a shock treatment of this kind would bring the father out of his depression. It did not; his condition worsened as he continued to drink, and eventually he was committed to a mental institution, where he died in 1830. While Kathinka was away the business collapsed, and the creditors seized all of the assets, including their house. The lawyer estimated that her father had managed to squander an estate worth eighty thousand to one hundred thousand gulden.[8] The significance of this sum can be appreciated by Kathinka's need to support herself for most of her life on five hundred to six hundred gulden per year.

In contrast to the portrait of Kathinka's father, that of her mother, Anna Markowitzka Halein, is drawn in more flattering colors as the long-suffering spouse of an unfeeling man. Her mother, she recalled, required the "patience of an angel to bear her husband's injustices." Mother and daughter were one, according to Kathinka, their hearts "intertwined to their very capillaries." The older woman is depicted as embodying the essence of femininity: loving and caring for her children and being willing to help the less fortunate. Especially impressed on Kathinka's mind was her mother's activity during the allied blockade of Mainz in 1813–1814 as the anti-French coalition was driving the Napoleonic forces back to France. The blockade was quite severe, causing the deaths of about 10 percent of the city's population, in part because of the outbreak of a plague spread by the retreating French soldiers. The twelve-year-old Kathinka saw the dead and dying French soldiers, witnessed amputations, stepped over decaying bodies of horses, and dodged shell fire. She later regarded the experience as a test of her willpower under adverse conditions. Her mother transformed their house into a hospital as she took in, fed, and cared for the sick and wounded without any thought to her own safety. This is the image that remained in Kathinka Halein's mind: her mother as "an angel of mercy," a "Christian in the truest sense of the word," who looked after all the needy "without regard to religion and class." She also never forgot that even when their income was reduced her mother was ready to open her door to homeless children of friends and relatives and treat them as her own.[9]

There was another, more practical side to her mother's character. Anna too, Kathinka tells us, married for convenience: to escape an uncongenial household and unsympathetic stepfather. For Mrs. Halein the bond of marriage became not love but concern for the children. At the same time she must have been a competent business person, and perhaps concerned about protecting her dowry, because it was she who managed the family store for about twenty years until her illness. She was apparently involved in the previously owned powder and starch business as well. Kathinka, from the child's perspective, could not help pointing out that her mother, because of business commitments, had little time for her elder daughter, and she was left free to wander through Mainz.[10] The Halein household at this time appears to conform to the social model of the "entire house" *(ganzes Haus),* which remained the common domestic arrangement until replaced by the bourgeois household later in the nineteenth century. The store was attached to the living quarters, and running it was a family operation. There was little distinction between domestic and occupational functions. In the absence of the male the female would act on his behalf. When the father took his position with G. L. Kaiser it was Kathinka's mother who assumed responsibility for the business. Gradually Kathinka participated by keeping the books and taking care of business correspondence. The servants were part of the household and were indistinguishable from the wards of friends and relatives who also lived with the Haleins.[11]

When Franz Aull advised Kathinka Halein to leave home after the knife attack, he supposedly told her, "With your talent you will get along anywhere in the world."[12] Although effectively on her own at the age of twenty-three and without financial support, Kathinka was well prepared for her independent existence. Her schooling was probably as good as could be obtained in Germany by a women. It was primarily French, because of the French origins of her father's family and her parents' sympathies. Her education was entirely private, befitting someone of her social station. After having a French governess, from whom she acquired her fluency in the language, Kathinka was sent to the educational institute of Madam Pianet, where most of the pupils were the daughters of French officials. The directress of the school was described as "enlightened" and well educated; at the school "intellectual stimulation and a humanistic atmosphere reigned." There remained firmly etched in the memoirist's mind that in spite of her youth she was permitted to attend the advanced classes, where one did not use textbooks but read the French classics in the original. She recalls studying Corneille and Racine as well as Voltaire. She was also attracted to the study of history, which meant a secular and progressive interpretation culminating in the French Revolution. The influence on her of Voltaire and the Enlightenment was strong, and throughout her life she remained their spiritual heiress. Kathinka's education was not complete without extensive training in needlework, which was a major part of the curriculum in every girls' school. She became very proficient, and it would enable her to survive later difficult times.[13]

After the French defeat at the Battle of Leipzig in October 1813 Kathinka's parents transferred her to a Catholic school run by the Order of English Ladies. They may have done so because of their fear of a blockade, since the school was located outside the Mainz city walls, or because it was impolitic to have a child in a French educational institute. Founded in 1807, the new school was one element of the reestablishment of a Catholic presence in Mainz after the Concordat with Napoleon in 1801. The year's experience in the parochial school was painful for the secularly oriented Kathinka, causing her to criticize the quality of instruction, as barely at the level of the "3 Rs." She believed, even in her later years, that as a twelve-year-old, she knew more than her teachers. From her secular and practical perspective it seemed that one learned only "praying and idle chattering but not how one gets along in the world." She was also unsympathetic to what she regarded as the mechanical emphasis on religious practices and recalled that she composed scatological poems about clergymen, for which she was punished. Already demonstrating a strong streak of independence, she refused to kiss the bishop's hand and answered no when asked whether she wanted to become a nun. Not even the offer of sweets could make her change her mind. While still at Madam Pianet's, she remembered, she once left the confessional booth without absolution when the priest objected to a book she was reading. There seems little doubt that her Voltairean spirit was already well entrenched.

In May 1814 after the return of Mainz to German control she transferred to a private school in Strasbourg, where the young Mainzer spent two happy years, pleased by the education she received. When Kathinka was fourteen or fifteen, her formal education was considered complete and she was regarded as a young woman. Years later, when being courted by Franz Zitz, Kathinka was surprised that although he was a university graduate, he was less familiar with the French and German classics than she was.[14] In Kathinka Halein's educational experience there are some similarities to that of her contemporary, Louise Otto, who was fortunate to have a stimulating and enlightened history instructor, who even included material about women. Louise attended school until fifteen, one year longer than normal, but she complained as other women did that her education ended just when it should have begun.[15]

Although the breakdown of Kathinka Halein's family existence threw her back on her own resources, her education made it possible for her to survive economically. As a middle-class woman she was extremely limited in her employment opportunities, and given her training she fell into the most obvious profession open to educated women: teaching. Her first position upon leaving home was in Darmstadt as a governess in the family of Louis Cavalli, who was the official banker of the Hessian grand ducal family. How she obtained this job is not known, but she stressed that as soon as it was known that she was looking for a place as an educator, the Cavalli offer came. By 1825 she had published a number of poems and was beginning to develop a reputation, being included in Carl von Schindel's biographical dictionary of female writers, which was published in 1823 and 1825.[16]

The two years that Kathinka Halein spent in the Cavalli household were among the most enjoyable of her life and had a long-term impact on her, although not always positive. She stresses that she was "highly placed" in the Cavalli abode and "not treated like a usual governess" but as an "honored member of the family." Her salary was 220 gulden annually, part of which she had to use to pay for the support of her younger sister. She was given responsibility for Cavalli's six-year-old daughter, Leontine, by his second wife. However, Kathinka also struck up lifelong friendships with his older children, Nanni and Hugo, and the former became one of her closest friends. What made her stay even more satisfying were the opportunities to expand her cultural, social, and educational horizons. Louis Cavalli was remembered as a person of wide cultural interests and contacts. He collected paintings; had an impressive natural history collection, "better than the Grand Duke's," and also a significant coin collection, according to the young governess. She spent many hours, since she had relatively little to do, arranging and cataloguing his holdings. Her time was divided between Darmstadt and Cavalli's country estate near Heidelberg, and at the latter location Kathinka met a wide variety of interesting individuals, including scholars such as Friedrich Leuckart (1794–1843) and K. E. Moorstadt (1792–1850); the writer August Nodnagel (1803–1856), who had composed a book about women; and stage performers, such as the actress Luise Frank and the singer Auguste Kruger-Aschenbrenner (1791–1874). Regular contact with scholars and other interesting people permitted her to enlarge her knowledge.

The idyllic existence, however, came quickly to an end but continued to cast a long shadow over the young governess's life. When she had arrived at the Cavallis' she noticed that his wife, his second, was not present. Only later did she learn that the pair was in the process of formally separating, later to divorce. When the divorce was final, Cavalli not only had to pay his former spouse a large sum of money but surrender Kathinka's young charge, Leontine, to her as well. This made the governess's presence no longer necessary, but in addition the experience shaped her relationship with her future husband, Franz Zitz, and perhaps even her attitude toward women.[17]

Not one to wait on events, even before she was released by Cavalli, Kathinka again tried to find employment with the grand duke of Hesse-Darmstadt. In a sycophantic but cleverly written letter, she described herself as an "orphan," "once rich and happy, now poor and parentless," and she presented him with a copy of her recent poem in praise of the Hessian ruler (it was published under a female pseudonym, Auguste Pauline, she pointed out, because she wanted it known that a woman had written it). She also sent him a short play of hers "for his evaluation," since it was the "prerogative of princes" to protect the arts, she added flatteringly. She also offered to do translations of French and English works and tried to convince him that she could be of use to the superintendent of the theater. Her attempt to devote herself to the royal house was once again unsuccessful.[18]

When her relationship with the Cavallis ended, the twenty-five-year-old governess accepted an invitation to go to Kaiserslautern to be the head of a newly established elementary school. It was organized by civil servants and well-to-do business families who wished to provide their daughters with a better education than was available at the city's elementary school *(Volksschule)*. She was supposed to be the directress and to teach French, receiving an annual salary of 400 gulden plus free housing, which appears to have been spartan, and fuel. A number of other teachers, both male and female, were to be hired to teach the other subjects. The reality of the situation proved otherwise. Because a lack of financial support the projected number of teachers was never hired. Only one teacher for the lower levels and one to teach embroidery were added, forcing her to teach a variety of subjects at the higher levels. She taught about seven hours per day and found the work load monotonous and oppressive. Additional problems occurred over religious instruction, which she was expected to give, as the families divided into Catholic and Protestant groups. To avoid antagonizing either side she refused, forcing the board to engage clergy for instruction. It was her only triumph. Also unforeseen was friction between the bureaucratic and business families over the content of the course plan as their different educational expectations came to the fore.

Although disappointed by her teaching responsibilities, Kathinka Halein felt partially compensated by the active social life that she led. She was accepted into the social circles of the leading judicial, administrative, and business families of the area and participated in a steady round of parties, picnics, and evenings playing whist at the casino. Moreover, she received a marriage proposal from a wealthy factory owner, which for reasons that will become clear in the next chapter she rejected.

In spite of her social life the burden of teaching was too great. She was not made for the "treadmill," as she expressed it, and once more wrote to the grand duke, now pleading for a position at the court theater because she was at the end of her "physical powers." Again she stressed her linguistic ability, growing literary reputation, and friendship with Cavalli. Trying to forestall any objections on the grounds of sex, she added, "Talent is not the property of one gender." When this renewed request failed, she eventually resigned her position in order to become a traveling companion. However, before this intention could be carried out, her sister Julie's declining health and psychological problems, typical of several Haleins, forced Kathinka to return to Mainz in January 1829.[19]

Now the second and harder phase of her employment began. Unable to obtain a teaching job in Mainz because of the need to care for her sister, and unable to support herself by her literary work, she fell back on the other major money-making activity open to middle-class women: needlework. That plus the income from private lessons in French provided the margin for a minimal standard standard of living during these years (1829–1833). The once-wealthy woman describes surrendering the only bed to her sister; rising at 4:00 A.M.; living on little more than bread, butter, fruit, and coffee; and gratefully receiving presents of food from her students and occasional financial assistance from her relatives. At the same time many of her former friends now avoided her since she had to earn money from her needlework and private instruction. The plight of middle-class women forced to support themselves is evident from her comments about former friends who no longer addressed her with the friendly *du* but instead used the cold *Sie*. Furthermore, there were the difficulties in persuading her needlework customers to pay promptly or not to demand unreasonable labor. The number of women who engaged in this sub-terranean economy cannot be ascertained, but at least two of her friends had much the same experiences.

After the first desperate year the "time of scarcity" was overcome as sales improved because of the quality of the sisters' work. Soon they could begin to live "very respectably." Then Julia's illness worsened and necessitated three operations, leaving the younger woman bedridden and misanthropic. Again forced to the edge of poverty until Julie's death in 1833, Kathinka did not even possess enough money to bury her. Twenty years later Kathinka believed it had been miraculous that she had been able to provide for both of them. After her sister's death it became possible for Kathinka to regain financial stability, and she proudly noted that by the time of her marriage to Franz Zitz in 1837 she owned personal property worth twelve hundred gulden. She attributed it to her "industry, sense of order and frugality." During the hard first year, she stressed, she made it a firm principle not to use for food purchases money set aside for rent and utilities, to avoid contracting debts. Such practices would serve her well in later years.[20]

The first thirty-two years of Kathinka Halein's life had been a testing time for her. She had overcome a difficult family situation, had demonstrated her ability to support herself, and, as will be seen, was developing a literary reputation. These experiences molded and reflected her character and affected her political and social outlook. Plagued by adversity, she fought against it and overcame it. Through it all she demonstrated a firmness of will, personal courage, an overriding sense of duty to family and friends regardless of her own situation, and of course an extraordinary capacity for work. Many of these characteristics she would need and exhibit during her long and turbulent relationship with Franz Zitz.

2
Love and Marriage

*L*ove and marriage were facts of life about which Kathinka Halein ought not to have had any illusions. She admitted frankly that her parents' marriage had been one of convenience on both sides and remained a loveless relationship. Her maternal grandmother had been divorced twice, and her father for a time supported in his household his brother's illegitimate daughter. One of her friends was seduced by an army officer and bore a child out of wedlock. She also knew the history of several Mainz families in which divorce, adultery, and illegitimacy were common. Moreover, as a governess with the Cavalli family she became privy to its somewhat sordid marital history. Cavalli, while married to his first wife, fell in love with his cousin and carried on an affair with her for five years, during which time two children were born. Increasingly frustrated by the arrangement, he plotted to divorce his faithful wife by hiring a friend to "compromise" her. Now married to his lover, Cavalli could not prevent his second wife from falling in love with someone else. She was able to win a divorce on very favorable financial terms, an experience that would not be lost on the young governess.[1]

Kathinka Halein's early poetry and other writings also show an awareness of the relationships that can develop between men and women. The poems, which she called a "diary of my life," are an especially good source for her attitudes.[2] In them she often dealt with the subjects of men, male-female relationships, marriage, and women's place in society. The themes of deceit, tyranny, and exploitation, which women supposedly suffer at the hands of men, appear frequently. In "To Rosalie," one of her earliest poems (1820) but typical of many, she advises:

> Never, weak girl, trust a man
> Honey on his lips, poison in his heart . . .

Love and Marriage

Respecting his own sex, deceiving ours . . .
Our tears are witness to his victory.
Arrogantly he says to himself, "I am
The lord of creation. Woman is
Subject to my wishes." With the
Pride of the victor he robs us of our rights,
Chains of slavery he puts on the free woman.

Although men were not to be trusted, Zitz-Halein maintained, women had few options. Society and woman's nature combined to make her a victim. In 1827 she bemoaned her sex: "Woman is such a weak creature, so completely reared to obedience, that the smallest resistance appears to be tantamount to rebellion. Determined for one's whole life to obey a foreign will, she doubts her own independence. It is a requirement that she subordinate and sacrifice herself. And if there are no real obligations to fulfill, it is necessary to create and impose outrageous laws" [upon her]. Society did not even permit women's natural sexuality to emerge. A woman's love, she observed, must be like "the light of the moon rather than the scorching rays of the sun." Moreover, men did not commit themselves to women. For a man love was only a "pastime, a fragrant flower which pleases him, stimulates him, and when the color disappears is cruelly flung in the dust." These views made her skeptical of marriage: "One part, and indeed the larger, marries for money, rank or protection. . . . The man sees in his wife at most his chief maid, the wife sees in the man only a means of protection against want, and in later years against disrespect and ridicule. Only with few does one heart yearn for another, and these bloom like aloes only once every hundred years."[3]

Some of these attitudes derived from her first love affair, which began when at sixteen she met Lieutenant Karl Wild, a Prussian officer. She was not reluctant to describe herself as attractive, calling attention to her "graceful, delicate figure, pleasing mouth, a high forehead, expressive eyes, dark brown hair, rosy cheeks, and a well-shaped neck." The earliest picture we have of her bears this out. Wild, too, was physically attractive, and after the lieutenant fought a duel on her behalf, she fell in love with him. It was difficult to obtain parental approval of their relationship, however, because Wild lacked financial resources. According to Prussian regulations officers below the rank of captain could marry only if they proved possession or control of the interest on wealth equal to twelve thousand taler (eighteen thousand gulden). A second lieutenant's pay was only eleven taler per month, far too little to support a family. To Kathinka's father Wild was "Lt.

Have Nothing" *(Habenichts)*. Nevertheless, through the intervention of her mother, Anton Halein agreed to finance the marriage, and the engagement was formalized.

Their joy was short-lived. Soon thereafter Kathinka's father left his uncle's business and surrendered himself to drink, causing the family income to decline sharply and making an eighteen-thousand-gulden dowry impossible. The only other alternative was to wait until Wild was promoted to captain, when one could marry without proof of solvency. Unfortunately Wild was living proof that the militarily peaceful period from 1815 to 1848 was a time of desperation for young officers seeking promotion. During the approximately eleven years of their engagement (1819–1830) Wild was never promoted. Despite the prospects of a long wait they remained committed to each other.[4]

Not until Kathinka had left Mainz in 1825 did she begin to have doubts about her engagement to Wild. Her wider contacts in Darmstadt and Kaiserslautern made her more and more aware of his deficiencies and the fact that he was not the man to make her happy. Moreover, in Kaiserslautern another suitor presented himself, a wealthy and cultured factory owner. Believing that she could learn to love the new candidate while doubting that her feelings for Wild were those of real love, she wrote to the army officer and asked him to release her from her vow. Wild refused. The now-envious fiancé assured her of his imminent promotion to first lieutenant, from which it would be a short step to a captaincy. Unreleased by Wild, Kathinka rejected the new suitor and returned to Mainz in 1829 still bound to the officer.

Kathinka Halein's uneasy feeling that Wild no longer was a suitable future mate was now strengthened by new evidence of a more tangible nature. She discovered that she had been deceived about Wild's fidelity. When his escapades were virtually public knowledge she broke with him. On his death in 1865 she remarked only that it was a shame that she had thrown away her love "on a completely insignifcant man." Why the intelligent woman did is difficult to say. Engagements were serious affairs in the mid-nineteenth century, and a damage suit could result from a broken betrothal. But with her parents dead or incompetent and she independent and without a substantial estate, this was unlikely to happen. Her stories of acquaintances' liaisons indicate that a broken engagement was no bar to respectability. Instead she had a strong sense of honor, which made her feel obligated to Wild regardless of the provocation. Her apparent naïveté or toleration regarding Wild's sexual transgressions was due to her belief that Wild's behavior was normal for men, perhaps because of her sexual restraint. In her memoirs and even in a public statement she emphasized that her long relationship with Wild was always entirely proper, at least on her part. The same attitude would reappear in her connection with Franz Zitz.[5]

By the time she became involved with Zitz in February 1833 she could scarcely be called innocent of the real world. Their relationship provides an insight into early nineteenth-century attitudes toward courtship and marriage. Franz Zitz, two years younger than Kathinka Halein, also came from a prominent business family in Mainz. Nevertheless, Franz could scarcely have been said to have had a settled childhood. His mother was the widow of an army officer, by whom she had three surviving children. By her second husband she bore Franz and a sister before she died when Franz was eight. The father remarried and had three children by his new wife. Thus there were three sets of partially related children, who would have a long history of personal, financial, and legal problems. Franz grew up undisciplined and given to the pursuit of pleasure. According to Kathinka his unhappy childhood had made him moody and cynical as an adult. Nevertheless, he was intelligent, trained in law, and ultimately a prosperous attorney. Zitz was also an accomplished orator, having a talent that would propel him to prominence in Mainz and then make him a national figure. He was a man who seemed to enjoy public adulation and need flattery. He was also, by all accounts, handsome and known as a man who had an eye for the opposite sex.[6]

Why this thirty-year-old, well-to-do, ambitious man, with a promising career ahead of him, should be drawn to a woman two years his senior and without significant financial resources is not clear. Perhaps, as Kathinka claimed, Franz believed she could bring culture and stability into his life. She, too, was surprised that Franz was attracted to her, but she was so taken with him that by the end of 1833 she was writing to him of her "unreserved confidence and childish submission. . . . Only by you do I want to be recognized and understood." In her thoughts, she informed him, she smothered his "mouth with kisses."[7]

They became engaged in May 1834,[8] and the joy Kathinka exuded between betrothal and marriage suggested future happiness. Zitz, in her words, was a "beautiful, gifted man"; he was the "personification of excellence," the ideal of "what a man should be."[9] Her poetry, again reflecting her current moods, bubbles with a blissful enthusiasm that before and after is absent from her verses. In it she celebrates her newly found joy. Where previously her days "passed sadly," her existence "only a vegetating," her first love (Wild) only "an emotion" and her life "like Herculaneum covered with debris," now Franz had raised her up from the depths, "more beautiful than before and taught her love." He was her "salvation," her "bliss," her "hope," her "life—completely, unconditionally, without reservation." "That I love you above everything is not subject to doubt," she wrote to him at the time of their engagement.[10]

In spite of her emotions three years passed between engagement and marriage, since Zitz's expected appointment as a lawyer did not materialize. The Hessian government strictly regulated the licensing of lawyers, especially those from Mainz, who might be associated with the political opposition, and prescribed where they could practice. Finally in 1837 Franz received a license to practice in Alzey, a commercial center about thirty miles southwest of Mainz, and on June 3, 1837 they were married.[11]

In a sense the honeymoon ended with the wedding ceremony. Their cohabitation of eighteen months was only half as long as their engagement. Although there had been intimations of problems before the marriage, nothing could have prepared Kathinka for the request that Franz purportedly made to her as they were riding to Alzey a few days after the wedding. He could not, Franz revealed, be satisfied with only one woman. Unfortunately, he continued, Alzey was a small, gossipy town where one could not take a step without being observed; thus he expected her from time to time to invite a "pretty seamstress" to the town and close her eyes to his marital indiscretions. Given this statement, it is not clear why Franz Zitz went through with the marriage. It does lend credence to his later charge that their marriage was not without an element of compulsion. Perhaps he thought that she would accept any indiscretion of his without objection.[12]

Even though Zitz quickly assured her that he had been joking about the seamstress, she learned soon enough that he had been serious, though he did not limit himself to seamstresses. His first extramarital activity involved the wife of the Protestant pastor in Alzey. According to Kathinka the woman had a checkered past that included time in a house of prostitution before she married the clergyman. Their marriage eventually ended in divorce, and it is a story that again raises questions about standards of morality in Biedermeier Germany. Kathinka caught the woman and Franz in a state of "disarray," after already surmising that he was carrying on with her under the guise of giving her advice about her pending divorce action. The two spent hours in his office, which Kathinka was forbidden to enter. Franz maintained his own social and business life, of which Kathinka shared only a small part. Most of his evenings were spent at the "Casino," which she did not visit, and he often went on trips with his friends. All of this she would have accepted, she tells us, as inevitable without asking "presumptuous questions," if only her "rights" at home were respected and Franz did not flaunt his "immorality in front of me." Years later it was still her basic belief as she defended a recently deceased male friend who had a reputation for womanizing. Even if the man did not take his marriage vows all too seriously, she opined, at least he never "let his wife feel it."[13]

Zitz was not so considerate, as Kathinka described in detail the "moral mistreatment" that she received at his hands. Probably even her discovery of Franz and his lover together, in Franz's view, indicated that she did not respect his honor. Yet he showed his disrespect for her honor in a variety of ways. He could not refrain from attempting to seduce his wife's friends. He taunted her about his past, present, and intended conquests. He informed Kathinka that his friend's wife laughingly accepted her husband's liaisons, and he told her he would not be angry if she were unfaithful to him. Franz accused her of having a "novelistic sensitivity which contradicted reality." Not even his trip to a whorehouse was concealed. He also spread the story that their marriage was never consummated, which seems to be contradicted by his wife's intimation that she suffered a miscarriage.[14]

Again her poetry best portrays her feelings. In "Calpurnia" Caesar's rejected wife laments[15]:

> Great Zeus, O do you hear my call?
> O hear my bloody tears.
> All buds, all young blooms
> Which bloomed for me in the empire of hope
> Have become white roses of pain
> Which the storms of life toss about.
> And the prince of pain, the hater of joy
> Squeezes bitter tears from me.

The cascade of incidents and insults climaxed toward the end of 1838, when Franz began an affair with a former pupil of Kathinka's from Kaiserslautern, and then with her older sister. In December 1838 Kathinka agreed to a separation and returned to Mainz. It had been a tempestuous eighteen months.[16]

Although Kathinka Zitz-Halein's version of their marriage portrays her as infinitely patient and Franz as irrational, considering any wife as an infringement on his freedom, there was probably more to it than that. A letter from Kathinka's friend J. G. Kaufmann, written at the end of the divorce proceedings gives us another perspective on their relationship. "I feared right from the beginning," he told her, "that two proud souls would not be good for each other. The lion tolerates only a tender being around him. Didn't you lament so unconsolably about your lost freedom even during your honeymoon. . . . I said to my children, if this Kathinka, this proud soul, is happy how I'll praise her." Her intense pride and her lack of submissiveness, two of her most pronounced characteristics, made it intolerable for her to accept a subordinate position. And without it there was no chance of being happy with Franz Zitz. She claimed on one occasion that by marrying him she had "raised him above his entire sex." On another, when Kathinka took him to task for consorting with a notoriously promiscuous woman, he criticized her for being presumptuous, wishing to "show off," and treating him like a "showpiece." By contrast, the attitude of J. G. Kaufmann's daughter, Marie, would have served Kathinka's marriage better. Marie made allowances for the fact that her husband had lived alone for fourteen years and deferred to his "crazy ideas." She remarked that her "submissive" mother was surprised how quickly she had "bowed to the marriage yoke" and how she accepted the small dissonances that "as a girl I would have thought impossible to bear." "So it goes . . . that the problems of life can be solved." Not for her friend, Kathinka.[17]

The first issue to be decided on separating was that of financial support. Although Kathinka Zitz-Halein had been self-supporting before marriage, she had no desire to return to that situation but wished to be supported as the wife of a well-to-do lawyer. She requested an alimony based on their marriage contract, which provided for her support in the event of Zitz's death. According to her she was to receive either seven hundred gulden per year, or, if Zitz's estate after marriage increased by at least fourteen thousand gulden, she would get half. Using the marriage contract stipulations as a basis of discussion, it was agreed that Zitz-Halein would get six hundred gulden yearly.[18]

However, this was only the opening gambit in lengthy negotiations over where she would reside and whether the separation would lead to a divorce. Zitz was not prepared to pay her six hundred gulden to stay in Mainz, especially after it became clear that she would not agree to a divorce. He wanted her as far away as possible and for as long a period as possible. He had in mind that she take up residence in Paris, where, he advised her, a friend of his would find accommodations for her. He tried to convince her of the correctness of such a move. Residence in Paris, he told her, would give her a "comfortable entry into an active and productive life" until she could accustom herself to her new situation. "Not in idleness, flirtations and day dreams," he warned this energetic and experienced woman, "is the seriousness of life satisfied, neither intellectually nor morally." He encouraged her to become active, to earn money, to put some aside for later years. This would be "better nourishment" for her inner disposition than reading novels and daydreaming. Paris offered her a future as a teacher, translator, or companion. He concluded this strange letter by stressing that she should not mistake his advice for concern or think that by following it she would satisfy him. "Your life," he grandly informed her, "lies outside the borders of my wishes."[19]

Predictably his letter failed to convince her, and a tug-of-war began, as she sought to gain more alimony. She informed him that she did not think she could function any longer as a teacher or governess. Instead she threatened to stay in Mainz and return to her earlier occupation of needlework and, if that failed, to apply for poor relief. This was one of the few means of pressure that she possessed, and she would use the threat repeatedly. She realized that as a prominent lawyer he could not permit his wife to live in such a way.[20] Not even pressure from the judicial establishment could convince her to accept less than she thought necessary. Judge Weiss of Alzey, who served as an intermediary in the negotiations about her future, soothingly advised her to give in: "Rise up, honored woman through the power of your intellect, to tragic nobility, to Christian submission."[21]

Kathinka Zitz-Halein was hardly the person to be influenced by such sentiments. As she wrote to Weiss: "My 'immoderate' demands appear to have been completely misunderstood by Zitz." To her husband's claim that she used to get along on relatively little she responded: "True, at that time I was Miss Halein who lived from the work of her hands, and . . . could feed myself for eight groschen per day." Now she was six years older and again accustomed to a better way of life. "What I had to put up with then would be unfitting for the wife of . . . Dr. Zitz." Also unacceptable to her was his demand that she remain four to five years in Paris. How long she would stay there would depend on circumstances. In her strongest tone she explained to Weiss:

> I am the sovereign mistress of my will. Moreover, I know of no law which can forbid me to live in my husband's place of residence

> if it pleases me. . . . Mr. Zitz appears to have forgotten completely
> that I have not been stripped of the right to return to him any
> day. It was not for nothing that I was the wife of a lawyer; and
> also you had the goodness to lend me the codes des femmes which
> I read not entirely without benefit.[22]

Finally she obtained a relatively favorable compromise. Zitz granted her an additional one hundred gulden alimony, giving her seven hundred gulden or about fifteen hundred francs per year. She in turn would reside in Paris for at least one year.[23]

After more than two months of wrangling, and apparently on her own terms, Kathinka Zitz-Halein left for Paris around the middle of February. The Paris of the July monarchy was the intellectual and cultural center of Europe, and with her fluency in French and her familiarity with French culture she was well suited to take advantage of the European metropolis. She also had a number of friends and relatives in the city and came armed with recommendations. Judge Weiss, for example, provided her with introductions to his legal colleagues, especially those with an interest in German literature. He also commissioned her to obtain reference works for a book he was writing. Weiss's daughter, Henriette, struck the right tone when she praised Zitz-Halein: "You have always lived for scholarship and will find in the metropolis opportunity through your intelligence to improve your life."[24]

Not that she needed much encouragement. As she wrote of this period of her life: "Believing in the basic principle that activity is the most effective antidote against mental depression," she immediately sought to derive literary gain from her Parisian sojourn. She compiled a French-German dictionary of French idioms, which was published in 1841 and reissued nineteen years later. To complete it she gained permission to work at the Royal (National) Library, which was not normally granted to women. She also attended meetings of the Chamber of Deputies.[25]

More than the opportunities that Paris offered, the continued cold war with her husband marked Kathinka Zitz-Halein's life there. The accommodations that he had arranged for her proved to be inadequate and she moved. She heard that Zitz continued to malign her. He also sent her first quarterly alimony payment made out in her maiden name. Moreover, her initial efforts to find employment were fruitless. She eventually found a job as a bookkeeper for fifty francs per month but apparently had to give it up after a few weeks.[26]

Love and Marriage

Kathinka Zitz-Halein's sense of being in exile was intensified by an illness during the summer of 1839, which required nursing care and suddenly made her budgetary problems more difficult. Instead of assistance Zitz sent threats. He simply did not take her illness seriously nor believe that she managed her money well. How much she needed in order to live a middle-class existence in Paris cannot be accurately gauged. Heinrich Heine found it difficult to get by on a minimum of 4,800 francs while the average working-class female earned 500 francs annually. When she first settled in Paris George Sand had 1,500 francs as "pin money." Later she had to support herself on 250 francs per month, twice as much as Zitz-Halein was receiving, and could only afford an apartment five flights up. Judging by the price Zitz-Halein paid for her apartment (1,200 francs per year, 200 more than her first lodging), it was probably one of the best in the boardinghouse and sounds similar to those described in Balzac's *Père Goriot*. Nevertheless Zitz-Halein complained that with her income it was impossible to live in Paris if one did not want to "belong to the scum of the earth." She also knew that her husband was able to take pleasure trips to Switzerland and cultivate new affairs. Franz, however, was in no doubt; he referred to her "mania" for spending and her financial "excesses." It was "dissipation or folly." In August, he complained, he sent her 400 francs, and by September she was "broke." She received the exact sum that was sufficient for living, and all her "poesie" would not convince him to pay her more than the agreed-upon 1,500 francs.[27] Later, fearing that she might return to Mainz, he threatened to reduce her alimony to 1,000 francs. He ordered her never to come within fifty miles of his place of residence and implied that a divorce might be the best resolution of their relationship.[28]

Already by April Zitz-Halein had had enough. "If I live to see February 16, 1840 [the end of the promised one year stay in Paris]," she wrote to her supposed friend, Bertha Henrich, "on this day I return to Mainz. . . ." She now doubted she had taken the right step in going to Paris and claimed she had been tricked. In an outburst of self-pity and moral outrage against Zitz she condemned all men

> who in their lust to serve themselves nurture us, flatter us, make us feel proud of the attentiveness of an excellent man. They disturb the repose of a woman in order to involve her in a love which she does not seek. . . . one arouses her, intoxicates her and after a short marriage one is tired of her without cause, leaving her with a horrible feeling and confusion which she cannot fathom

> because she does not know her misdeed. Her only certainty is her
> rejection. . . . nothing remains but the rogue, who beats her in her
> weakness, . . . who dishonors everything good in order to excuse
> his misdeed.

But her tenacity again came through. "Precisely out of weakness do I draw my strength. My death would be a too beautiful triumph for him."[29]

One of Zitz-Halein's main contacts in Mainz was Bertha Röslin Henrich and her physician husband. They, too, illustrate the lives of middle-class people in Biedermeier Germany. Dr. Henrich became adept at the new technique of mesmerism pioneered by the Franco-German physician, Franz A. Mesmer. However, Henrich used his hypnotic talent to seduce and impregnate a patient, for which he was held up to public ridicule (*Pasquillen*), and for a time could not find a respectable position.[30] It eventually blew over and he married Bertha Röslin, a young actress. Bertha Henrich, increasingly sympathetic to Franz Zitz, tried to explain to Kathinka the reality of her position. The former actress regretted that the latter's stay in Paris was going so poorly. But, she advised, Zitz-Halein must accept the situation, which could not be changed. Further, she warned Kathinka not "to *claim* your *rights* [*sic*], for believe me the wife never has rights, and even the laws are too weak for the weak woman. Consider that your future could become even worse, for a passionate man when he is aroused no longer knows any limits."[31]

Not one to be intimidated, Zitz-Halein responded in kind. "I should tremble before him," she wrote to Bertha Henrich, "does he think I am a wild animal who can be hunted." She would oppose his "tyranny" with all the "strength of my character." "I swear by God and by my belief in a just retribution that I will not let myself be suppressed to this degree. If he pushes me to the extreme he will experience '*this proud soul*' [*sic*], as he used to call me, in all her pride."[32]

The realistic Bertha Henrich made one final effort to keep her from Mainz, combining calls for Kathinka to use her good sense with threats of dire consequences if she did not. Her letter again highlights the subordinate position that women occupied in society and the prevalence of the double standard in sexual relations. She revealed to Kathinka that she had shown Zitz all her letters, in some of which Kathinka had reviewed her husband's past indiscretions. The letters would be important pieces of evidence at the divorce trial, since the truth of Zitz-Halein's accusations would not be at issue but simply whether she was publicizing them, and thus, holding her husband up to ridicule. Bertha described Zitz's agitation and his unwillingness to let the matter rest. "I fear," she continued, "that you can only lose; I do not know which ground for a divorce Zitz will find," but "trust him to have enough prudence and intelligence not to begin a case where the probability is not present that he will win it." If she were Kathinka, she stressed, "I would act more cautiously and prudently; what you say about supporting yourself and [entering a] poor house are things which, after some reflection, are not practicable. If you were again eighteen years old it might work but at our age it won't." Bertha further advised Kathinka that if she would not contest a divorce suit, she could later return to Mainz with a pension of six hundred gulden. And in a concluding admonition Zitz's friend wrote:

> If you come here to oppose him I foresee only pain for you. You have fewer friends than you believe, and Zitz will gradually win them all over. . . . Due to your sensitivity you must fear a trial. For a woman to say such things openly [about Zitz] in court will be thought worse than a man who did them secretly. The judgement of [letter torn] which for the most part is still led by women would probably be directed against you if you wish to raise yourself [letter torn] your sex. Your already reduced strength would break down, or I have completely deceived myself about the knowledge of the feminine condition.

Bertha, who hoped that Kathinka's reason would triumph over her passions, did not understand that Kathinka's passions rarely overshadowed her reason.[33]

By the time Kathinka Zitz-Halein received Bertha's letter she was departing Paris for Mainz, where she arrived on November 23, 1839. Unintimidated by her friend's warnings, she now set forth her terms for settlement of the dispute. Zitz could have his divorce but only if he were willing to give her an independent capital of fourteen thousand gulden. If Zitz did not accept her terms they could remain married and he could continue paying her six hundred gulden annually.[34]

The pressure and counterpressure continued. Zitz reduced her support payment to four hundred gulden per year. She threatened to resume her embroidery or open a millinery shop. He proposed cutting off all her alimony. She in turn asked her lawyer to institute legal action to force Zitz to pay her an appropriate alimony based on their marriage contract.[35] Her lawyer during these negotiations as well as during the initial phase of the divorce proceedings was Eduard Lehne (1805–1857). Lehne sought to act as an intermediary betweeen the warring couple, but like Judge Weiss, he tried to convince her that a divorce was the best solution. He told her, in phrases that suggested his later partiality, if not dishonesty, that he hoped she did not have the "ignoble intention" of thinking too highly of herself and using the impossibility of dissolving the marriage without her consent to punish and avenge herself on Zitz. He then advised her that on the basis of discussions with Zitz, the latter would, if she accepted a divorce, pay her at least six hundred gulden in such a way that she would be free to receive and dispose of the money without being exposed to his arbitrariness. She would be free from a man, he cautioned her, "who has the power and the legal right to force you to be exposed to his hate." Even if she received a judgment against him, he predicted accurately, it would still be in his power to plague her through chicanery. "You know," he echoed Bertha Henrich's warning, "what Zitz is capable of when he is angered." When all of the above was compared to the "serenity of a secure income and peaceful future," he did not think she would want him to proceed with the case.[36]

He was wrong. She again demanded as the price of a divorce sufficient capital to provide a satisfactory income. Perhaps decisive in her calculations was her experience as a governess with the Cavalli family. She remembered the difficulties Cavalli's innocent first wife had in forcing her former husband to pay the agreed-upon alimony and her descent into penury when his estate was later reduced to virtually nothing as a result of his second divorce. Moreover, there was the example of Cavalli's second wife, who, as part of her divorce arrangement, received a large sum of independent capital and lived comfortably ever after. In place of independent capital Zitz-Halein believed it legally better to remain his wife. She assumed that Franz would not always be a lawyer but eventually become a judge. Indeed that seemed to be the usual route among her lawyer friends. As a divorcee she would not be entitled to his pension if he died or retired as a state official. Thus as she put it, "Besides the point of honor, it was also in my material interests not to accept a divorce." Therefore, she opposed him with "a will of iron."[37]

Zitz struck first. On January 14, 1840, he instituted divorce proceedings against her.[38] Divorces were relatively infrequent in mid-nineteenth-century Europe, although they were more available in the German states than elsewhere. Many of the German law codes were revised during the Enlightenment and reflected the progressive ideas of that era. Statistics for Prussia from 1836 to 1841 show an annual average of 3,321 divorces for a population of 12 million, while Saxony with one-fourth the population had an annual rate of 440. The spotty figures for Mainz between 1839 and 1847 yield from one to three divorces per year.[39] Mainz and the Rhenish area of Germany used the Napoleonic code, which, although clearly establishing the legal superiority of the adult male, provided a detailed procedure for divorce and gave the wife significant protection. Besides the grounds of adultery or concubinage divorce could be granted for outrageous conduct, ill usage, or grievous injuries or by mutual consent. According to the procedure, the petitioner presented his statement, and the judge attempted a reconciliation at a private hearing. The petitioner then presented his evidence, to which the defendent could respond. The judge then decided whether to admit or reject the petition. If he admitted it, after hearing further witnesses and examining additional evidence, the court gave a final ruling. There was a right of appeal after both the decision on the admissibility of the petition and the final judgment.[40]

The divorce action was especially painful for Kathinka Zitz-Halein because her correspondent, Bertha Henrich, was a witness against her; and the letters she had written to Henrich were used as evidence against her. Franz Zitz hoped to establish that his wife's conduct was outrageous and that he had suffered ill usage at her hands, specifically that she had defamed him before friends and the public. She was confident that he had no legal basis for divorce.[41] The key phase in the divorce procedure involved the decision on whether to admit Zitz's suit. Here Zitz's legal contacts seemed to have helped. She asked her lawyer, Lehne, whether she ought to appear for the hearings, but he indicated that it was unnecessary and that he expected a favorable decision without her presence. She continued to discuss strategy with him and provided him with information about the details of her marriage and the names of people who could testify on her behalf.[42] Great was her surprise when the court accepted Franz Zitz's petition for a divorce. Lehne strained to explain the court's decision, claiming that certain pieces of evidence had not been taken into account by the judge and admitting that he too may have overlooked several aspects of the case. When she read the basis of the court's decision she was not only dissatisfied with the decision but clearly suspicious of Lehne's handling of the case. She now regretted accepting his advice not to attend the hearing and took him to task for not calling various witnesses. She also thought it unfair that the court put so much stress on the specific contents of her letters to Bertha Henrich without concerning itself about the "psychological situation" that called forth these outbursts. Her analysis of the decision was worthy of a lawyer and superior to Lehne's.[43]

Filled with doubts about the degree of Lehne's commitment to her case, she took the court documents to an old family friend, the retired Appeals Court justice, Philipp Heinrich Hadamar. After reviewing the file he advised her not to trust her lawyer. He did not see how an impartial court could have found in Zitz's favor if her case had been presented properly. On the basis of her talk with Hadamar she decided to appeal the decision. Almost gleefully she described how Zitz had held a premature "victory party," how he saw her already "lying in the dust," how she "quietly" waited until the end of the three-month period before she announced her appeal, how astonished Lehne was when he learned she intended to appeal, and finally, how "shattered" her husband was when she announced she would appeal the court's decision because it was based on a "misrepresentation of the facts." Even allowing for some poetic license in her rendition it must have been quite a triumph for her to see the the astonishment of Lehne and the consternation of her husband. To handle the appeal she selected a new lawyer, Paul Krämer.[44]

It was not until January 21, 1841, that the appeal hearing began in Mainz, but this time she was present. Zitz, apparently worried that his weak case might not hold up, accused her of a variety of additional transgressions, including improper behavior in Paris and generally having a bad character. These referred to two experiences in Paris. She had been caught up in the major historical event of 1839 in the French capital, the uprising of May led by Louis Auguste Blanqui. Walking by the Palace of Justice she suddenly found herself in the midst of the cross fire, was thrown to the ground, and with torn and blood-spattered clothing finally made her way back to her boarding-house. At the time she related her adventure to Henriette Weiss, who in turn relayed it to Zitz. He now used it in their divorce trial as evidence that she invented things or was a liar. A similar example was provided by her relationship with the Hessian ambassador to France, Count Pappenheim. After helping her in the matter of utilizing the Royal Library, Pappenheim unsuccessfully sought to borrow money from her. Again she wrote to friends in Mainz about the affair and later discovered that this information, too, was passed on to Zitz who used it to show how she could malign a respected government official. In both these examples the burden of proof would be on her to demonstrate the falseness of her husband's accusations.[45] Expecting this onslaught, she had procured letters from acquaintances who testified to the veracity of her statements. Her lifelong concern for proper behavior now served her well. All of Zitz's "ranting and raving," she recalled, did not prevent the systematic refutation of his charges.[46]

In spite of her likely success in the proceedings her lawyer again raised the question of a divorce, emphasizing Franz Zitz's honorable position in the legal profession and his standing within the community. She responded with all of her ingrained pride that a divorce would signify the loss of her honor either by indicating that her case was weak or by permitting her husband to brag about his supposed generosity. This was true. Divorce by mutual consent, which may have provided a way out, was not a neutral procedure but usually meant that some embarrassing information was being suppressed. Although Krämer could view the situation dispassionately, she could not forget, she continued, "the thousand varieties of torture which I had to endure from this man. For that reason it is doubly important to me to leave this affair with my honor intact."[47]

She did. In April 1841 the Mainz appeals court overturned the decision of the Alzey district court and ruled in her favor. It decided that the key piece of evidence against Kathinka Zitz-Halein, a letter to Bertha Henrich, had been provoked, and further that it had been a breach of trust to pass on the letter to Franz Zitz. The court ordered him to take his wife back or pay her a yearly alimony of six hundred gulden. He did neither but took his case to the superior appeals court in Darmstadt. In December 1841 this court upheld the verdict of the Mainz tribunal. Not only proud of her victory, she seemed even prouder of her ability to retain the friendship of the lawyers and judges involved in the case. This male approval seemed to confirm in her eyes the propriety of her actions and the spotlessness of her reputation.[48]

Triumphant in the legal arena, two years after her return from Paris, she learned that it was more difficult to force her husband to pay her the prescribed alimony. The most he would give her was four hundred gulden per year, claiming that she could earn a significant sum from her writing. Ever proud of her independence, she had not refrained from mentioning at the time of her marriage that she paid for her trousseau with the money she had earned from a translation of a play by Victor Hugo. This may have been why her husband believed she needed less from him to live on. An eight-month struggle ensued, during which her money ran out, she contracted various debts, and she complained of having to forgo meals. A striking picture of Kathinka Zitz-Halein's situation during the first half of 1842 is given in her bitter letter of May 19 to her lawyer.

> True one can live on 400 gulden and many a woman would be happy to possess so much. But why should I stuff myself on potatoes while my husband gives splendid banquets. He, the single man, lives in a series of beautifully appointed rooms . . . while I reside in a pigeon loft under the roof in the scarcely fashionable society of bugs and mice; he gathers to his soirees and parties witty men and women while I have my evening meal with a roll and a glass of water. He lacks no pleasurable diversion, but . . . when has it been possible for me to spend even a penny for my enjoyments. . . . He has money to make presents to others while more than once I have been bitterly embarrassed by having to pay the postage of an unexpected letter. . . . If he now seems to be of the belief that I could earn a significant income through my literary work, that is a colossal error. Germany, which lets its greatest poets half starve, makes no exception with us insignificant lesser lights. Most of the periodicals, particularly the local ones, pay at best with a thank you, . . . and the thanks of an editor cannot be credited to your savings account. Only the *Didaskalia* pays an honorarium, 8 gulden for 960 lines, . . . and you will concede that the lowest of your clerks earns as much with copying work without straining his brain. My literary income goes almost penny for penny for writing materials, and I would consider myself highly fortunate if someone would want to underwrite me with fifty gulden per year. If one is lucky today to make something, one can also sniff around for years in vain . . . for the roasted corpse of an honorarium. Believe me the existence of a writer is the most precarious of any.

She submitted her budget of 527 gulden, which showed 8 percent for linen and 24 percent for wardrobe. The latter figure, she noted, was high because she had purchased very little in the previous years and had accumulated various debts for the few items of wearing apparel that she had bought. Perhaps it was purchases such as these that so infuriated her husband. Her debts totaled 161 gulden. She expected to continue to lead a middle-class existence.[49]

Zitz-Halein resorted to a variety of devices to compel Zitz to pay: lodging a complaint with the district court in Mainz charging nonpayment of alimony, applying to the city government to receive poor relief, threatening to accept embroidery work, and even confronting him in his own house to demand support. She finally appealed to the masonic lodge to which Zitz belonged, requesting it bring him before a court of honor. This last step seems to have persuaded Zitz to negotiate. A basis for a settlement was found when Zitz offered her an annual payment of five hundred gulden and agreed to be responsible for her medical bills. In order, as she put it revealingly, to demonstrate to the court that she was not led by a "malicious intent" she accepted the compromise.[50]

In the nearly four turbulent years since their separation Kathinka Zitz-Halein had demonstrated anew her capacity to persevere and to defend her rights. Her experiences also indicate that it was possible for a woman to obtain justice but at a relatively high price. Would another woman without her strong character and wide contacts, without her education and professional experience, who had not been the wife of a lawyer and who had not led a life that was entirely free of social blemish have been able to end the matter successfully, at least according to her standards? Her desire to remain attached to Zitz was motivated by honor and pecuniary advantage. Unable to become completely independent of him because of his refusal to grant her a lump sum payment, Zitz-Halein preferred dependency as his wife. Her fight to remain married may be difficult to accept in the twentieth century. However, it made good sense by her analysis and experience. She had a clear sense of where her financial advantage lay. Nevertheless, she seemed obsessed by a love-hate attitude toward Zitz and appeared to hope that at some point he would come to his senses, recognize her admirable qualities, and agree to live with her again.[51]

Her years of struggle with Zitz left her bitter but not beaten. They reinforced her previously expressed views on love and marriage. "The country of marriage," she explained, "has the peculiarity that strangers have the desire to settle down there and the natives would like to be expelled from it. One claims love reaches beyond the grave but for many it seldom reaches beyond the marriage (ceremony)."[52] Her bitterness about marriage, however, did not destroy her will to resist, best expressed in her "Not so Dumb or the Philosophy of a Young Woman"[53]:

> When the spouse denies us love,
> Silly is the one who is consumed by sorrow;
> When he plagues us with stupid moods,
> Silly is the one who does not fight and dare.

In her notes written during the divorce proceedings she tried to convince herself not to fall prey to apathy or discouragement but to give courage to others "even when ours scarcely suffices to suppress the shreik from our fear of death." Indeed, during the final phase of her struggle with Zitz she became involved in the campaign to raise money for the victims of the Hamburg fire in spring 1842. Nowhere is her tenacious instinct to survive stated more directly than in her comments about a friend's suicide. Impoverished by the death of the father, the daughter was forced to find employment as a teacher, a future for which she was unprepared and would not accept. In Kathinka's view her friend, Tina, had been unable to "raise herself above her destiny." The tragic experiences of other similarly placed women are a measure of Kathinka Zitz-Halein's accomplishment.[54]

3

Becoming a Political Activist

*T*he six years from the conclusion of her separation struggle with Franz Zitz to the outbreak of the Revolution of 1848 were a
time of relative repose for Kathinka Zitz-Halein. She believed she had
foiled the efforts of her enemies to ruin her while discovering who her
true friends were. There is no indication that she suffered significant
prejudice as a separated woman, which is supported by her comments
about other such women and by Phillip's study of France. As for her
enemies, she wrote disarmingly at the end of her "Skizzen," she never
tried to harm them. "The only revenge which I took on them was that
I let them surface in my writings, in one guise or another." That was
probably enough. She was now able to devote the major portion of
her efforts to her literary work, and the publication of her *Herbstrosen
in Poesie und Prosa* (Autumn Roses in Poesie and Prose) in 1846 en-
hanced her reputation. She also became increasingly involved in the
campaign for political reform in Germany, belonging to that small
group of women who, as a result of being financially secure and/or
being single, separated, divorced, or widowed, had sufficient freedom
to participate in civic affairs. Nevertheless, she continued to regret the
absence of "traditional domesticity," refusing to believe that she would
find true happiness outside it.[1]

Although her legal battle against Franz Zitz gave her publicity, the
main reason for the public's awareness of Kathinka Zitz-Halein was
her literary activities. The first half of the nineteenth century witnessed
a steady increase in literary publications in the German states, with
book production rising from about forty-two hundred in 1820 to about
thirteen thousand in 1843, even if it fell to ten thousand by 1847.
Furthermore, by 1832 there were more than seven hundred book
dealers in the German Confederation, including sixteen in the Grand
Duchy of Hesse, and there was an increase in the number of literary

31

journals. It became possible for a handful of writers such as Heinrich Heine, Ludwig Börne, Heinrich Laube, and Berthold Auerbach to live from the proceeds of their literary work. New publishing houses emerged, such as Reclam, Sauerländer, and Hoffmann and Campe, which brought out the works of progressive writers.[2]

Female writers were no longer rarities by 1820. Schindel lists more than five hundred in the German states for the first quarter of the nineteenth century, and Schenda, whose list is probably more discriminating, records 229 for 1871. Nevertheless, women continued to be criticized for engaging in literary work. One had not advanced much beyond the experiences of previous generations. The French writer and feminist, Olympe de Gouges, complained in 1788 that men claim, "We are useful for nothing but running a house. However, women who strive after intellectual things and devote themselves diligently to literature are unbearable to society." Some ten years later Friedrich Schlegel wrote of his sister-in-law, Caroline Schlegel, that she could write a book if she wished, but then "It is all over with femininity." In the 1820s Schindel saw a hundred men who "lie in wait to make a female writer laughable," and Honore Daumier's sketches of female writers in the 1830s verify this claim. On the eve of the Revolution of 1848 the *Fliegende Blätter* satirized a "poetess" as an "emancipated woman" who wrote while her husband came home with the groceries and the children ran to him. Not to be outdone, the *Mainzer Tagblatt*, a progressive newspaper, quoted approvingly a Persian saying, "Better a bearded woman than a poetess." Even as late as 1863 the respected *Blätter für literarische Unterhaltung* wrote almost mockingly about the woman writer: "Later she gets a trifling honorarium; she dares to approach another newspaper; she's fortunate to place one or more short tales and now she is firmly convinced that a genius slumbers in her and that it is her calling to write." This success, the article continued, would be followed up by collected stories for which she finds a publisher because she accepts a smaller honorarium than most authors would; and so the woman writer made her way selling secondhand merchandise cheaply.[3]

This attitude was present not only in Germany and France but also in England. Showalter, in her study of British women writers of the nineteenth century, describes the condescension of male critics, who charged that female writers had a taste for the trivial and for gossip, and that only unhappy, frustrated, masculine, and ugly women wrote books. Male reviewers pounced on female intellectual pretentiousness with "malicious gusto," and for them literary women remained women first and writers, at best, second. Only women writers who knew their places, writing morally acceptable, sentimental romances, could win praise. This was the advice that *Didaskalia* gave female writers in 1858, that prejudice against them would cease when they "limit themselves to their own area," that is, to the nature of femininity. The criticism of women writers probably accounts for the fact that they showed pride in their domestic accomplishments, as did Zitz-Halein. According to Showalter, by working in the home and flaunting their femininity, female writers could atone for their will to write. Even so pronounced a feminist as Olympe de Gouges announced that women could combine domestic responsibilities with intellectual activity.[4]

Kathinka Zitz-Halein directly experienced the criticism aimed at female writers, relating how more than once the term *poetess* was flung in her face as a term of ridicule and how she was depicted as an "eccentric fool, as an inept, lazy heroine right out of a novel, against whose contact all mothers were to warn their daughters." She stresses, in contrast to others, that men were more willing to accept her as a writer, whereas women exhibited jealousy and tried to cut her down.[5] Her literary works often refer to the plight of the female writer. In "Ulrike" Zitz-Halein depicts a typical caricature of a poetess who makes verses while the roast burns, the child falls into the washtub, and the husband lacks fresh clothing. Ulrike gives the entire family a cold when she opens the window to view the moon; she curses like a trooper and smokes like a locomotive: "in short the woman writer is no longer a woman but an inkwell." In *Magdalene Horix* a female writer bemoans the fact that intellectual talent almost always leads a woman to ruin. A woman who thinks acutely and says what she thinks or has it printed, the character stresses, is tarred with the insulting name of female philosopher. On the contrary, she continues, a woman might do much evil and get away with it, if it is done in the customary form. But, when she offends this form, even if she does something good, "she is mercilessly damned, and most horribly of all one damns the writer." And not even the use of a male alias would insulate the female writer. In "Harpar and Tulisant," Zitz-Halein warns that although her literary sister may win fame under the cloak of anonymity, she will ultimately have to swallow the bitter pills of criticism for "one finds her humor too biting, her mournful passages too gloomy, her depictions of love and passion unsuitable for her sex; in short she should publish what is thoroughly insignificant." It appeared to her everyone wanted to scare promising young women away from literary activities. But the social intimidation would not work, Zitz-Halein concluded, because once the "demon of poesie has been awakened it no longer falls asleep so easily again." And female writers, she emphasized, represented the "most excellent women of this century." Surprisingly, the Mainz writer praised George Sand as a "phenomenon" among women, who was to female writers what Michelangelo was to painters. Sand, in spite of her unorthodox life-style, was generally admired by women of whatever persuasion.[6]

These insights are echoes of the age. Zitz-Halein's contemporary and friend, Louise Otto, explained her initial use of the alias Otto Stern by stressing how the literary and journalistic establishment was controlled by men and that she wished to write about "real issues of the day" and not just women's novels or articles for women's journals. With a woman's byline what man would read her articles on politics, she wondered. Rogers's study supports Zitz-Halein's comments about the difficulties women who tried to depict love and passion faced, as does Clemens von Brentano's reaction to his sister's (Bettina von Arnim) publication of her disarmingly frank *Goethes Briefwechsel mit einem Kind* (Goethe's Correspondence with a Child). Bettina had to defend herself against the charge of being immoral and accused her brother of not recognizing the innocence in her writings, which was the natural product of her desire for self-expression. If once he read the whole book, she told him pointedly, he would either share her view or "faint from shock."[7] Only in the late 1850s did Kathinka Zitz-Halein begin to detect a new attitude toward women writers. The gothic age was past, she wrote; one no longer believed the female writer neglected her family. She portrayed two women, one nursing a child, the other with a "thinker's brow," alone from morning until evening in a small study, which "lets in only a tiny piece of sky because thinking and writing are her profession. Each works in a different way. Both are understood and accepted by the spirit of the age." She was somewhat premature, as she herself would later discover.[8]

Kathinka Zitz-Halein belonged to the earliest generation of professional writers, corresponding to what Showalter defines as the feminine stage (1840–1880) of women's writing. It is marked by the imitation of the prevailing modes of the dominant (male) tradition and the acceptance of its standards. Zitz-Halein was a member of the upper middle class, which Schenda sees as the chief recruiting ground for this first generation of female writers. Her literary talent, which developed early, may have been stimulated by the superior education as well as the greater degree of leisure that these young women generally had. Surprisingly she did not encounter the familial opposition to her literary ambitions that Showalter suggests was typical. Expecting her father's hostility she kept her writing a secret from him; nevertheless, he found out when he poked around her room. The strange man said nothing to her but gave her written assignments involving translations or poems to be written on themes he suggested. She did the work and, again without a word exchanged, left it for him. He showed his appreciation by leaving her a few coins, handkerchiefs, or gloves.[9] The best evidence for her early commitment to writing was later provided by her brother, Karl. In 1866, at a time when her eyesight was failing, he scolded his sister that her eye problems were "foreordained" in her youth because of her "perpetual writing day and night."[10]

When she was a teenager Kathinka's interest in writing was fostered by the literary community of Mainz, especially Friedrich Lehne and Niklas Müller. Both men, it should be stressed in view of Zitz-Halein's later activities, had radical political backgrounds. Lehne (1771–1836) supported the Jacobin movement in Mainz during the French Revolution, worked for the French government, and wrote poems and gave speeches in support of the revolution. Like many other French supporters, he was later integrated into the Hessian regime and eventually became the head of the City Library *(Stadtbibliothek)*. Müller (1770–1851), also a former German Jacobin, was a multitalented individual: playwright, actor, stage designer, poet, editor, and drawing teacher at the gymnasium. He later became Zitz-Halein's drawing instructor and, as editor of the literary journal, *Der Spiegel,* published some of her poetry. Both men aided her when she returned to Mainz in 1829.[11]

Kathinka Halein's first published work was in response to Lehne's letter to the editor of the local newspaper, the *Mainzer Zeitung,* in which he complained about the large hats that women wore to the theater. In an anonymous but humorous response she defended her sisters. The article was well received and the surprise great when it was revealed that a fifteen-year-old girl had written the piece. With this success she began to write poems and do translations for publication, one of which, "La femme" (The Women), won a prize out of sixty-three entries.[12]

By the time she was in her early twenties her poems were appearing in a variety of literary journals and newspapers, such as *Mainzer Zeitung, Rhenus* (Mainz), *Spiegel* (Mainz), *Wöchentliche Unterhaltungen für Stadt und Land* (Frankurt/Main), *Didaskalia* (Frankfurt/Main), *Beobachter am Main und Rhein* (Offenbach), *Charis* (Heidelberg), *Abendzeitung* (Dresden), *Mindner Sonntagsblatt, Rheinische Unterhaltungsblätter* (Crefeld), *Mnemosyne* (Würzburg), *Hermione* (Hamm), *Westdeutscher*

Musenalmanach (Hamm), *Rheinische Erholungsblätter* (Mannheim), and *Mainblüthen* (Hanau). She had also published a volume of poetry. Praised as the "German Sappho," she attracted the attention of Carl Schindel, who included the twenty-one-year-old writer in his biographical lexicon of German female writers. Since there was a large number of journals to choose from, she received some honoraria, and the money gave her a sense of independence. In contrast to some of the writers whom Showalter cites, who appeared to feel guilty about earning money and used it to purchase stained glass windows for churches, the young Kathinka Halein demonstrated concern for her own well-being. She spent her income on her wardrobe and on visits to the theater in spite of her father's opposition. That streak of pride, which was an important part of her character, surfaced as she remembered the "inner pleasure" that the money gave her and that she was "as proud as a queen" about it. Most of all she recalled how she was visited by all the major literary figures who passed through Mainz, a flattering occurrence for an aspiring writer in her early twenties.[13]

In spite of her promising start she never grew from a "lesser light" to a major literary figure of the caliber of Fanny Lewald or Ida Hahn-Hahn. One cannot determine to what degree the unfortunate experiences with her parents, sister, and husband; the need to unite artistic endeavor with domestic work; the requirement to support herself before her marriage; and her straitened circumstances after her separation affected her literary development. She never had the opportunity as a young woman to devote her full time to writing but had to squeeze it into her familial responsibilities, which were heavy. She reported how, after winning the prize for the best translation, she was visited by the editor of the journal, the *Beobachter am Main und Rhein,* who found her cooking dinner for the family. She was not alone in her handicap; in a similiar situation but with more success Louise Otto learned to read and sew at the same time, while Jane Austen and Madame de Staël wrote under the most inhospitable conditions.[14]

More typical, perhaps, of the problem of combining domestic responsibilities with professional aspirations, and thus more indicative of Zitz-Halein's accomplishment, was the example of her lifelong friend and protégé, Emilie Hurst. Born into a well-to-do family around 1815 she, too, developed an early interest in poetry. However, her budding career was damaged by familial problems that forced Emilie to support herself and her parents by "grasping the needle" and by assisting them in running a small inn in Bavaria. Her letter to her mentor in Mainz reflects the difficulties of her situation. While she praises Zitz-Halein for resuming her literary career after the conclusion of her long divorce trial, she contrasts her friend's life with her own depressing situation. Describing life in a miserable farming village, she believes her "poetic vein has completely dried up."

> But no wonder under these conditions. Even Appola would have lost her urge to write poetry and exchanged the lyre for the beer glass. For that is the favorite instrument of the Bavarians. The rattling of the tankards makes the most suitable accompaniment to the so-called folksong (*Schnaderhüpfel*) which they often sing for hours on end. If one asks about literature he is shown the beer mug. Beer, beer, beer, that is entertainment here.

In a poem Emilie had written to Kathinka two years before, describing the latter's marital experience, she referred to "our destiny which is to suffer and endure." This was not her friend's way, and only by comparing Zitz-Halein's fate with those of her friends and contemporaries do we appreciate her achievement.[15] There is certainly a quantitative decline in Zitz-Halein's literary output during her periods of employment and marital troubles. In 1830 during her difficult struggle to earn a living and care for her sister she complained to Schindel that she had no time to write. Years later she made a point of stressing that during her period of cohabitation with Franz Zitz she did not write, but her tone suggests that this is what she was supposed to say in order to prove that she had been a devoted wife.[16]

As a literary figure of secondary rank she had to struggle continuously to find publishers for her works. By the mid-1820s, after the journals that had previously published her works folded, she not only offered her literary products very cheaply but even was willing to accept part of her honorarium in books. Her income from writing was probably never great. The scattered references to honoraria in her correspondence indicate that the eight gulden per 960 lines of printed material from the *Didaskalia* that she mentioned to her lawyer in 1842 represented her maximum. If so, then she never reached what Schenda says was the "average" of eleven gulden for the first half of the nineteenth century. Of course, Schenda's estimate, based on an 1834 work that probably had male writers in mind, may be open to question.[17]

In spite of the increased difficulties Zitz-Halein managed to get her works published, evidence not only of her talent but of her perseverance. It represents a less extreme version of the caricature of a mediocre writer that Hermann Marggräff presented in 1845. He described the progress of the "literary paupers" who "today compose a critical article, tomorrow a correspondence for a journal, in between work on a novel or use up their pen for all seasons on a translation of a foreign book, soon clinging to this, soon to that journal as to the last life preserver."[18] After her initial successes in the early 1820s with her poetry, Zitz-Halein supplemented poetry with Italian and French adaptations and translations, including several of Victor Hugo's plays in the 1830s. After her separation from Zitz she resumed her literary career, and her poems, short stories, and novellas were published in a diverse array of periodicals and newpapers, among others *Didaskalia* (Frankfurt), *Rheinische Blätter* (Mannheim), *Darmstadter Journal*, *Planet* (Leipzig), *Wandelstern* (Grimma), *Rosen* (Leipzig), *Komet* (Leipzig), *Figaro* (Berlin), *Modejournal* (Ulm), *Freimüthiger* (Berlin), and *Musterzeitung* (Stuttgart). In 1844–1845 F. Campe in Nürnberg published collections of her short stories, novellas, and adaptations.[19]

Beyond question Zitz-Halein's most successful work before 1848 was *Herbstrosen in Poesie und Prosa,* which contained a selection of her poetry from the 1820s until 1845; a collection of aphorisms; and an essay on women's emancipation. Both the *Didaskalia* and the *Blätter für literarische Unterhaltung,* two of the most important German literary reviews, praised it. The latter journal called it an example of a "completely mature *(durchgebildet)* poetical talent." She was joyous about the book's reception, believing it had assured her "an honorable place in German literature," and she was proud to report that once again she was visited by the literary community of Germany. This recognition, for the separated woman who lived alone, was no doubt of special importance.[20]

Besides the increasing stream of publications Kathinka Zitz-Halein experienced the rejections that were part of the writer's life. There is little in the surviving correspondence with publishers and editors that indicates that her difficulties were due mainly to her gender. Only Karl Müller, editor of the *Erheiterungen* in Stuttgart, rejected her manuscript with the recommendation that she select material more appropriate for women writers, such as family life. Other reasons for rejections varied from the failure of a periodical to the excessive length of the article submitted, and from the lack of public interest in poems, or among the more original excuses, that men want only "drinking and religious songs" and women are interested in fashion news and cooking recipes, rarely her themes. One editor found her work on Louis XIV unsuitable for his humorous journal, because of the French king's impact on Germany. Robert Blum, the 1848 democrat and martyr, advised her that he could not find a publisher for her work since the "Christmas market" was already filled.[21]

Undeterred by rejection, the clever young woman sought various ways to get her works before the public, for example, by asking friends to find purchasers for her books and by giving them as gifts to her friends and to organizations. The Hessian government sponsored the Association for Assisting Christians in the Orient, to which Zitz-Halein made a gift of her literary works. She also donated copies to German Catholic congregations. Even when she wrote to the masonic lodge to complain about her husband, she proposed that it purchase her books and recommend them to other lodges. The resultant sales, she coaxed, would reduce her dependence on her husband. No opportunity for publicity was untried. She sent the grand duke of Hesse a copy of her translation of Victor Hugo's *Marion de Lorme*, with the plea "Every talent requires encouragement if it is not . . . to be consumed in itself." The ruler paid her eleven gulden for the work even though it was not flattering to royalty.[22]

Learning to accept rejection of her literary submissions was part of Kathinka Zitz-Halein's as well as every writer's education. Nevertheless, she would not tolerate what she regarded as unfair or dishonorable dealings by an editor or publisher. Throughout her career she not only fought privately for just treatment from them; on several occasions, three times between 1840 and 1850 alone, she sought public or legal judgment against them and won. Although the first and third cases are more closely related to her political activities and will be discussed later, the second, even if all the details are not known, provides an insight into her character and her ability to obtain justice. In 1844 she became embroiled in a dispute with the Darmstadt printer and publisher Ernst Bekker (1795–1856), who had previously published some of her works in his *Gutenberg: Unterhaltungsblatt für Stadt und Land*. She sent him copies of her material, which had appeared in another journal. He apparently made disparaging remarks about them as he passed them along to another publisher, who used parts of the stories without her consent. Zitz-Halein demanded payment for the use of her copy as well as a letter of apology. When neither was forthcoming from Bekker she engaged as her lawyer Theodor Reh (1801–1868), a liberal member of the Hessian parliament, later president of the Frankfurt parliament, and a defender of politically persecuted individuals. Again her contacts with the progressive political community in Hesse are evident. Reh pursued her case through the courts for over two years, winning at every level, while she rejected Bekker's compromise proposals. Finally, beaten at the last judicial apppeal, Bekker sent Zitz-Halein a letter of apology, asking "most submissively" for "forebearance and forgiveness" for any unpleasantness that his actions may have caused her. As if Reh were not sure that Zitz-Halein would regard Bekker's *pater peccavi* as sufficient, he urged her to show leniency to the publisher since in his view she had obtained all that could be expected. It was a major victory for her in a life full of legal struggles, and as sign of her pleasure at Reh's handling of the case she presented to him a copy of her *Herbstrosen.*[23]

Her ability to use the legal machinery in the Grand Duchy of Hesse effectively did not mean she refrained from criticizing political and social conditions in the German states. Being a women concerned about civic matters did not make her life easier. If a large part of the public was still skeptical about the literary activities of women, it was even more uneasy about their political and social engagement. Louise Otto complained in the 1840s that a women's interest in the affairs of the fatherland and humanity was denounced as "unfeminine." Kathinka Zitz-Halein also experienced the attempt to exclude her from civic issues. While favorably reviewing her *Herbstrosen,* a critic wondered why the Mainz activist "prattled on in verse about freedom of the press, people's happiness, and princes' virtue." Even as late as 1860 one of her books was reviewed unfavorably in part because the reviewer had no enthusiasm for a woman who wrote about political and religious matters.[24]

Zitz-Halein's views on the proper roles for women are difficult to categorize, although she was clearly in the mainstream of moderate feminism of the first half of the nineteenth century. As Rogers stresses, feminism need not be limited to a "singleminded systematic campaign for women's rights" but should include particular sensibility to their needs and problems. Raised in the age of the "new domesticity" and claiming she was cut out for a traditonal domestic role, the Mainz writer was nevertheless led by circumstance and experience into a more activist stance than she had originally foreseen. Since the thought of any other pursuit outside the home would have been regarded as alien, her affirmations in favor of female domesticity have to be taken with some reserve. Her actions often spoke louder than her words.[25]

Zitz-Halein's writings of the 1840s contain many references to the subject of women's place in society, although her most extensive treatment of it was in an essay, "The Woman Within the Limits of her Destiny," which appeared in her *Herbstrosen.* Its title suggests her point of view. Her ideal of emancipation was nothing other than "the proper acknowledgment of the feminine existence within its own limits." And where these borders seemed to be was clear. The family and the home were a woman's center of gravity, Zitz-Halein argued, and a woman would not find "real and lasting fortune" outside the boundaries of the domestic sphere. In spite of this apparently standard view of separate spheres, which was shared by all but the most radical feminists, such as Louise Aston and perhaps Louise Dittmar, Zitz-Halein did not believe it condemned a woman to a subordinate or inferior position. Rather it should lead to one of respect based on equality. Women, she stressed, should be the "coregent in the realm of domesticity," and female emancipation meant, in Lockean terms, the acknowledgment of her "natural rights" within this sphere. Zitz-Halein defended women's domestic existence. It was the woman's "virtue," rather than shame, she announced, to live within the home and run the house. Domestic management required "demanding qualities," especially since they were demonstrated privately and "seldom acknowledged." "Domestic heroism," she called it, "which, hidden under dark duties, flows and loses itself without having viewed the light. It is something sublime; it is to be compared to a clear source which, hidden under the grass, nourishes and refreshes the plants."[26]

Zitz-Halein saw the ideal relationship between men and women as complementary and based on mutual dependence. Although a woman might need the protection of a man, she in turn civilized him, and the instinct to please each other elevated both. Without this mutual respect, she emphasized in the "The Men's and Women's Republic," mankind would descend to barbarism. In this story the amazons who have used men only for reproductive purposes are helped militarily by them and finally agree that a single bisexual republic is preferable.[27] Unfortunately most men did not accept this principle of cooperation, she moaned, and the "tyranny of their pride, the injustices of their laws" twisted women's virtues into liabilities. Women became mere housekeepers or educators of children. They were condemned for their tenderness, had their talents belittled, and were regarded as incapable of great things. As other observers before and after her, Zitz-Halein noted sarcastically that men claimed a monopoly of all the great virtues but distorted them when they were exhibited by women. "What men in their egoism call character," she cited, "they regard in women as stubbornness and disobedience." Nothing, she called out to her less assertive sisters, was left to the woman; everything worked against her, "often even her indifference to her own fate."[28]

Yet, did recognizing the inequalities under which women had to labor mean that female emancipation was the answer? For Kathinka Zitz-Halein emancipation was relevant only if it was understood in a cultural and "ennobling" sense and embraced a domestic situation. Men should recognize women, Zitz-Halein instructed, as their "faithful companion[s]," as a part of their "own being[s]." What Zitz-Halein did seem to reject out of hand was female emancipation of a more formal political, social, or economic nature.[29] Here her language reached heights of vituperation as she labeled calls for full emancipation an "absurdity" or a "misbegotten creation out of the depths." Those who took part in "Frauenmeetings" *[sic]*, she claimed, wanted women to be eligible to participate in military matters and political questions, hold public office, study at a university, and pursue professional careers as physicians, lawyers, and clergymen: "in short not only to place themselves on the same footing as men in everything, but where possible to try to surpass them in intelligence, understanding and knowledge." This mid-nineteenth-century extremist version of female emancipation, Zitz-Halein rejected. It was "laughable" to think of women in political, professional, or religious roles, she wrote, oblivious of her own interests. In "Shadow Figures on the Wall," she ridicules some of the better known feminists of the day. Her shadow pictures were of the "pants of 'Cavalry Captain' Emilie Lehmann, the cigar supply of Louise Aston, the infamous riding whip of Lola Montez, along with a pack of emancipation-crazed women who take great pains to force their upper lip to produce a moustache, for which they would sacrifice husbands and children."[30] Even if women were in fact denied their rights by men, Zitz-Halein warned, they would not gain them by "distasteful masculine behavior." Zitz-Halein's loathing for these supposed amazonian types may be traced to her experience with the Cavalli family in the 1820s. She paints a very unflattering picture in her memoirs of Dorina, Cavalli's second wife, the "family destroyer," whom she decribes as having a strongly masculine bearing and as being an "amazon." By contrast, Cavalli's innocent first wife epitomized feminine virtues.[31]

Women, in Zitz-Halein's view, were not called upon to be rulers or to lead organizations. Nor were they made for intellectual and scholarly endeavors. Women who devoted themselves to scholarship usually went beyond the "limits of their sex." Nothing, she continued, was more offensive than when a lady "wants to show off through her intelligence. . . . She often falls into a hoydenish tone which wounds the worth of her sex." A woman was most charming, she added, when her "intellectual attainments shimmer through the veil of modesty." She admitted, however, that occasionally women of extraordinary talent do appear, but those should not marry. "Only in this way is it permitted us to stray over into an alien area." She did not draw the implications from this that Louise Otto did in lamenting how "unhappy these few must feel in their isolated position."[32]

There were significant qualifications to Zitz-Halein's almost traditional view of a woman's role in society. Being respected as virtuous, she observed, did not necessarily require spinning and studying cookbooks all day. Like Mary Wollstonecraft, she believed the ideal woman could blend professional, civic, and familial responsibilities.[33] "Lesser lights," according to Zitz-Halein—and she included herself in this category—could be both pianist and housewife or writer and mother. She also acknowledged the right of women to form organizations to deal with the problems of poverty, misery, and moral decline. And although she did not share the desire for full political and social rights for women she did occasionally strike a more emancipated tone, which in fact became the drumbeat to which she marched. In "Mokka di Cheribon," for example, an "emancipated lady" says with apparent approval:

> When the man is ruler of the state and lord of his castle he calls the woman his half; as soon as the wife by virtue of this title wants to share his political or civil powers, the man brings her to a halt with the words: "you are nothing!" . . . One half is everything and the other half nothing. . . . Is there in the world a whole which consists of only one half?

The character goes on to say that the apparent intellectual superiority of men would disappear when women received their rights. Zitz-Halein, like Louise Otto, did in fact emphasize that women should take part in issues concerning the nation, such as the struggle for freedom of the press, judicial reform, and national unification, but, the Mainz writer noted ambiguously, only "passively not actively." It was within the framework of these vague qualifications, but often transcending them, that she would create a role for herself before and during the Revolution of 1848.[34]

Kathinka Zitz-Halein's niche in the German political world was best expressed by the publicist Ludwig Walesrode (1810–1899). In 1845 he described to a female correspondent his view that women could be citizens and active in the struggle for freedom "without surrendering their femininity and morals." He depicted the ideal woman as one who, although growing up in the time of censorship, would be "proud and courageous," rejecting philistinism and all views "which damn women to the same cowardice" that afflicts men. She would refuse to concern herself solely with the hearth or to view the fatherland "only from the window."[35] Zitz-Halein's actions, if not her words, fit this outline.

The content of Kathinka Zitz-Halein's political and social engagement in the 1830s and 1840s was due largely to the influence of the political culture of her native city, Mainz. This Rhenish Hessian town, an integral part of revolutionary and Napoleonic France in 1792–1793 and from 1798 to 1814, received the full impact of France's modernizing legislation. The old aristocratic elite either was expelled by the French or left, and new legal codes were introduced. Moreover, during the brief French occupation of 1792–1793 Mainz had also been the center of a significant Jacobin movement. Annexed by the Grand Duchy of Hesse in 1816 after the defeat of Napoleon, Mainz, with its highly politicized population, remained a democratic and liberal bastion in relation to both Hesse and the German Confederation. The Grand Duchy, although by no means as conservative as several north German states, had one of Germany's earliest constitutions by 1820, was still regarded as retrogressive by the Napoleonic generation of Mainzers and never attracted their loyalty. From 1815 to 1848 the links to French ideals if not to France were strong in Mainz. An active veterans' association of former soldiers of the Napoleonic army functioned throughout the period. Mainzers proudly wore their Legion of Honor awards. At the time of the July Revolution in France in 1830 and the Hambach Festival in 1832 Mainzers, who provided a large contingent for the latter, wore their red, white, and blue rosettes. Otto von Corvin, who was stationed in Mainz as a young officer in the 1830s, described a *Fasching* (pre-Lenten) festivity at which someone appeared as Napoleon and was met with "thunderous jubilation."[36] The government's periodic attempts to unify the law codes for the states exacerbated the tension between Mainz and the Hessian capital, Darmstadt. The Mainzers believed this was merely a device to deprive them of their progressive French law codes, which they had been allowed to keep after being detached from France. By 1840 the mutual hostility created by these issues made the Mainzers advocates of a unified and reformed Germany.[37]

It was in this highly charged political atmosphere that Kathinka Zitz-Halein was raised. She writes in her autobiography that she "inherited" her anti-Prussian, patriotic, and republican beliefs. She mentions learning Greek and Roman history from her mother and hearing of the "noble Washington." Moreover, her family was closely associated with the Jacobin episode in Mainz in 1792–1793 in which her great-grandparents and grandparents played minor roles. Reference has already been made to the formative influence that the former Jacobins Lehne and Müller exercised on her development. Her suitor in Kaiserslautern in the 1820s, Gienant, was from a family identified with the Jacobins. Her husband, Franz, was the grandson of a member of the Mainz Jacobin Club, as was one of her closest acquaintances in Mainz, P. J. Schöppler. Another good friend, the democratic politician Adam Itzstein (1775–1855), was born in Mainz and attended Jacobin Club meetings in 1792–1793.[38]

Her familiarity with and understanding of the Jacobin period of Mainz's history are demonstrated most of all by her novel, *Magdalene Horix*. Named after the daughter of Johann Philipp Horix, a club member, the novel describes the activities of the actual participants in Mainz's Jacobin era. Zitz-Halein was aware of the previously published work by Heinrich König, *Die Klubbisten in Mainz* (The Jacobins in Mainz) (1847), but she believed a more accurate account was necessary. This she provided, as a reviewer recognized when he called the book so realistic that it was "scarcely a novel." As the basis for the work she used the minutes of the Mainz Jacobin Club and the protocols of the Rhenish National Convention, copies of which she owned and later sold to the Mainz City Library. She supplemented these sources with information gained from her family, relatives, and friends such as Lehne and Müller. All of the major figures of the Jacobin era appear in the book, from Baron von Erthal to Georg Foster, and she does not forget to include her friends and relatives. Moreover, when the ordinary people speak they do so in their local dialect.

She possessed a sure grasp of the issues even as they are being discussed today.[39] The scholarly-political dispute centers around the degree of popular support the Jacobins and the French had. Zitz-Halein's attitude, clearly sympathetic to the revolutionaries, was hostile to the electoral regime in Mainz. In describing the pre-1792 scene she stresses the role of the prince's mistresses, and the haughty and spendthrift administration. She notes how the behavior of the French émigrés also helped to alienate the Mainzers, who welcomed the French revolutionaries as liberators. The democratic spirit among the French soldiers and officials, she notes, at first made the Mainzers feel that they had in fact been oppressed by the prince's petty bureaucrats.

At the same time she admits that at least some of the "people," by whom she means the lower middle class and the merchants, were not enthusiastic about revolutionary political and social changes, the increasingly rapacious behavior of the French administration, or a formal connection to France. Her evaluation of the festival of the planting of the freedom tree captures the spirit of her democratic outlook but also indicates that fundamental divisions existed within Mainz society during 1792–1793:

> All this [the festival] had been accomplished in spite of the ill will of many who still cling to the old way of doing things, in spite of the strong aversion to change, in spite of the secret incitement of the aristocratic vermin, and in spite of the secret prayers of the slavish cowards for the return of the old servitude. Even the opponents had to concede, with poison in their hearts, that the festival had been magnificent.[40]

Her account of the Jacobin episode also agrees with some contemporary historians who explain the inconclusive results of the Jacobin attempt to win support for the oath of loyalty to France by stressing the nearness of the monarchical troops. Although she is sometimes critical of the Jacobins, her comments in no way compare to her condemnation of the behavior of the returning German officials after the expulsion of the French. She describes in detail their calculated viciousness toward the revolutionaries and their mistreatment of the insurgents' families, which is confirmed by the diary entries of Kaspar Röth.[41]

Her political sensitivity was illustrated as well in her fictionalized but insightful biographical sketch of the publicist Georg Friedrich Rebmann (1768–1824), who was rediscovered in the twentieth century and is now regarded as one of the most important German Jacobins. In describing his activities Zitz-Halein not only levels criticism at the prerevolutionary Mainz and Saxon aristocracies but, more important, deprecates Rebmann's ability, along with that of other Jacobins, to be reintegrated into both the Napoleonic and restoration governments. As she nicely puts it, the onetime zealous republican died as Herr von Rebmann, a respected judicial official for the Bavarian government.[42]

Besides deriving her political outlook from her city's historical traditions, Kathinka Zitz-Halein had civic attitudes that may have been strengthened by her sympathy for German Catholicism. The German Catholic movement that emerged in the 1840s under the leadership of Johannes Ronge (1813–1887) originally sought to "nationalize" and modernize the Catholic church. Instead it became a new religious sect, which never succeeded in influencing more than a tiny percentage of the population, perhaps seventy thousand at its peak in 1847, strongest in Saxony and southern Germany. Nevertheless, the group had an impact in the 1840s, and especially during the Revolution of 1848, disproportionate to its numbers. About 2 to 3 percent of the representatives to the Frankfurt and Prussian assemblies belonged to this religious community. Politically the German Catholics, including Adam Itzstein, Robert Blum, and Gustav Struve, were generally democratic or Left-liberal.[43]

The German Catholics also tended to be socially progressive, and a number of congregations accorded women important roles in church affairs, often granting them full equality. From the inception of the movement Ronge strongly supported an improved role for women and later their emancipation. On the occasion of his visit to Mannheim in 1845 he announced his happiness that so many women had turned out and stated that they should not remain in the background when important issues of the day were being discussed, "for women, too, were members of the community." In 1849 he wrote that German Catholic women had the duty "to procure for the female sex that position which it should have in society" and to work to "realize the humane ideas of the new age." Women responded to his call, and in cities such as Frankfurt/Main, Hanau, Hamburg, Worms, Heidelberg, Nürnberg, Mannheim, Altenberg, Frankenthal, and Mainz a number of politically active women belonged to or identified with the German Catholic community.[44]

Even as a young girl Kathinka Zitz-Halein had lacked sympathy with the Roman Catholic church and was drawn to the Protestant religion. By the 1840s she had clearly broken with the religion of her birth and adopted what one acquaintance called "very universal religious views." Always influenced by the Enlightenment, she respected people of different religious beliefs. After all, she told a perplexed friend, "We all pray to the same God—even the strictest Catholic, even Jews and Moslems with their different ceremonies." Twenty years later in her biographical novel of Rahel von Varnhagen she still expressed the view that the "form in which one prays to God is without significance." All that mattered was to be "virtuous" and follow the moral law to love one's neighbor.[45]

It is probable that around 1845 she became a member of the Mainz German Catholic community. She wrote for the *Rheinische Blätter,* a journal that was identified with the new movement. She knew many of the most important members of the church, such as Eduard Duller, Heribert Rau, Hugo Krebs, Josef Hecker (Friedrich Hecker's father), Wilhelm Hieronimi, Valentin Streuber, and Josef Brugger, and later worked with several of them during the Revolution of 1848. It is not clear in which direction the lines of influence between Zitz-Halein and German Catholicism traveled. Probably she was attracted to it by her already-formed Voltairean religious views as well as her progressive political and social outlook. At the same time her involvement may have pushed her into a more active public role. Ironically, she who had ridiculed the idea of women heading religious communities now identified with one that most nearly approached this ideal. Her political activism seemed to issue from her changing experiences even if her statements often lagged behind. It is her actions that provide the best clue to her beliefs.[46]

Kathinka Zitz-Halein's youth and adulthood in the highly charged political atmosphere of Mainz, her exposure to German Catholicism, the absence of a family, and her modest but adequate income combined to permit her the political engagement that was so rare for women in mid-nineteenth-century Germany.

4

Before 1848
Women and Politics

*P*olitical opposition in deed in pre-1848 Germany was risky. In 1819 and again in 1832, in response to the assassination of August Kotzebue and to the Hambach rally, respectively, the diet of the Germany Confederation established a central investigating committee to ferret out supposed subversives. This caused Louise Otto to claim that as a surrogate for deeds, "which seldom occur in Germany, one used words and books." Writers regarded themselves, perhaps with more than normal justification, as the "standard-bearers of the most important current issues."[1] But literary work of a political nature was also difficult under the post-1815 laws. Beginning in 1819 all books, journals, and newspapers having fewer than 320 pages (20 *Bogen*) were subject to prior censorship, and longer works faced postpublication censorship. In 1820 a Prussian decree restricted press comment on political affairs and forbade criticism of Prussian ministers, the French king, and ministers of foreign states. It also banned the use of terms such as *ultra* and *liberal*. In the 1830s in reaction to renewed political agitation there was a general toughening of censorship. Baden's liberal press law of 1831 had to be rescinded as the confederation made it possible for a federal state to subject newspapers of neighboring states to monitoring. Prussia began to increase control over the lending libraries *(Leihbibliotheke)*, which were the main source of books for the public. Moreover, potential financial losses due to the fear of confiscation of a printed work tended to make publishers cautious, as did the fact that editors of forbidden newspapers could be prevented from editing a newspaper similar to the one suppressed. Political opponents of the status quo in Germany lost teaching positions, were driven into exile, or were imprisoned, especially after the futile attack on the Frankfurt guardhouse in 1833. Only in the mid-1840s was there some easing of restrictions. Mitigating the formal harshness of the laws, however, was the decentralized system of enforcement that was placed in the hands of the individual states. Southern German states such as Württemberg, Bavaria, Baden, and the Grand Duchy of Hesse tended to be more lenient than northern states like Prussia and Saxony, and publishers operated in the least rigorous states or brought out in one state under a different title a book banned in another state.[2]

The literary opposition in pre-1848 Germany included writers such as Heinrich Heine, Ludwig Börne, Ferdinand Freiligrath, and Georg Herwegh but also included a number of women. Of the latter probably the most wide-ranging in her critique of the status quo was Louise Otto (1819–1895). Born into an upper-middle-class background, she lost her parents as a teenager but developed into a self-reliant woman, who even dared to travel alone through Germany and to attend the meetings of the Saxon legislature. As a contributor to a variety of journals and newspapers as well as a social novelist she called attention both to the subordinate status of the German people vis-à-vis their governments and to the inferior position of women in relation to men. She advocated increased and improved educational opportunities for women. Receiving inferior education, she claimed, women were more likely to remain children their entire lives, mere parrots of others' opinions. Otto also called for a broader concept of cultural history that would include a history of women in society, not just the biographies of famous women. This would lead, she believed, to women's being regarded not merely as wives or mothers but as "half the people themselves." As an important part of achieving self-development and independence, she argued, women should take an interest in the major political and social issues of the day. At the same time she distanced herself from the radical feminist image of the "free woman," which she regarded as the extremist form of what women "themselves call emancipation." More thoughtful and comprehensive in her writings about society than Kathinka Zitz-Halein, she was less as sharp and biting in her criticism of the political and social status quo.[3]

Bettina von Arnim (1785–1859), although from an even more privileged social stratum than Louise Otto, emerged in the 1830s as an outspoken critic of social and political injustice. Although she shared the patriotic enthusiasm generated by the war of liberation, her marriage to Achim von Arnim, which produced seven children, occupied all her time. But with the death of her husband in 1831 and the growth of her children she could "live for a second time." Fifty years old when her first book, *Goethes Briefwechsel mit einem Kind,* was published, she emerged from it as an advocate of reform, which she hoped to see initiated in 1840 by the new Prussian king, Frederick William IV. However, her disappointment with the government's steps regarding new laws on Jewish rights, divorce, and censorship impelled her to warn the king of the impatience of the people. Bearing the inspired title *This Book Belongs to the King* (1843) and dedicated to the Prussian king, the new work slipped by the censor even though it proposed progressive political and social change. She advocated a constitution and freedom of the press; condemned ministerial obscurantism, religious intolerance, and capital punishment; and called attention to the prevalance of poverty in Berlin. Although published in Prussia, the book was forbidden in Austria and Bavaria, whose censors were less intimidated by the title. When Adolf Stahr (1805–1876) tried to publish sections of the lengthy book in plain German, Bettina's style was impressionistic, it was confiscated by the Prussian government. As a result of the "King's" book, she had a running battle with the censor over her later less offensive publications and once was sentenced to two months' imprisonment but pardoned by the monarch. She also used her influence persistently and effectively to intercede on behalf of political prisoners such as Friedrich Wilhelm Schöffel (1800–1870), the Polish revolutionary Ludwik Mieroslawski (1814–1878) (she was always sympathetic to the plight of the Poles), and the Bonn democrat Gottfried Kinkel. She helped the Grimm brothers find a teaching position in Berlin after they were dismissed from Göttingen University for political activities. Although her political goals were vague and she initially expected reform to come from an enlightened monarch, she welcomed the Revolution of 1848, denounced the king as a tyrant, and invited radicals to her salon. Her books and struggles with the authorities made her a well-known personality while her financial security gave her an independence that others lacked. Zitz-Halein expressed it well when she wrote that Bettina's "eccentricity and genius *(Genialität)* displeased many." She would have accepted a recent evaluation of the Berlin writer as an "emancipated writer" who "never aggressively stepped forward as a feminist."[4]

More radical in her social views and life than either of the previous female activists was Louise Aston (1814?–1871), one of the most unorthodox and unique pre-1848 public women. Perhaps more significant for what she symbolized than for what she was, this German "George Sand" was born into a church official's family and married at twenty to a forty-four-year-old British industrialist, Samuel Aston. They were divorced in 1838, remarried in 1841, and divorced again in 1844. After her second divorce she moved to Berlin with her one surviving child and quickly made a name for herself by her unusual behavior. She consorted with the city's radical intellectuals, visiting taverns with them where she smoked cigars and drank, often while supposedly wearing men's clothes. She also carried on affairs with two younger writers, Rudolf Gottschall (1823–1909), who dedicated love poems to her, and August von Szczepanski (1819–1900). The Prussian government, which received regular reports of her unorthodox activities, expelled her from Berlin in 1846. Between then and the outbreak of the Revolution of 1848 several literary works appeared under her name,[5] including a collection of poems, a defense of the behavior that had led to her expulsion, and two semiautobiographical novels that critiqued existing marital relations and defended women's emancipation. These works reinforced and spread her reputation as a radical feminist.[6]

If she was in part a creature of others, Louise Aston did become a celebrated if notorious figure by 1848, one whose literary work, if damned, was taken seriously.[7] Nevertheless, she was disowned by responsible feminists, who regarded her as a liability to the cause of women's rights and democracy. Louise Otto referred to her as an "impure element" and a "forced democrat" who wished to attract attention. In fact she was apolitical, and not even her later nursing activities in Schleswig-Holstein or her book *Revolution und Contrerevolution*, published in Mannheim in 1849, could alter that reality.[8]

Although less radical than Louise Aston and less penetrating in her writings than Louise Otto, and less known than Bettina von Arnim, Kathinka Zitz-Halein was among the small number of women who participated in the political agitation of the time. Furthermore, she was perhaps more effective than any of them in calling attention to social and political abuses. Her earliest political act was her "first visit" in 1825 to the grave of Karl Ludwig Sand, whose assassination of the conservative playwright Kotzebue had been the occasion for the Karlsbad decrees.[9] Decorating the graves of radical political figures was to be a frequent manifestation of women's political activism in later years. Her next and more serious political effort occurred in the early 1830s, when she met the young Prussian officer and aspiring author Friedrich von Sallet (1812–1843) and helped get his first work published in the *Hessische Blätter*. This was not unusual as aiding younger writers, for example, Friedrich Wilhelm Held, who played a role in Berlin during the Revolution of 1848; Friedrich von Asmuth; another Prussian officer; and later Malwida von Meysenbug and Johanna Kinkel, in finding outlets for their literary work was a regular feature of Zitz-Halein's activity. Unfortunately, Sallet's piece, a political satire centering around the activities of a Prussian lieutenant, so offended some of his fellow officers that he was brought before a court of honor. Although Zitz-Halein offered to take the blame by claiming she had the story printed without his knowledge, he refused and ultimately spent two months in fortress confinement, after which he left the army and pursued a literary career until his early death.[10]

This first taste of the political consequences of literary activity did not deflect Zitz-Halein from the inclination to express herself on political and social themes. She used a variety of forms: translations of plays and stories with social or political messages, poems that addressed similar issues, short stories, novellas, newspaper articles, and fairy tales—one of her most frequent literary products—into which one could smuggle criticism of political and social conditions. Her works appeared in at least forty journals and newspapers before 1848.[11] The political and social content of her literary output has to be judged against the backdrop of censorship. Her surviving correspondence with publishers, as well as her statements in the forewords to some of her collected works, which were originally published singly before 1848, refer to problems with the censors. In the period before 1848 she had more difficulty with them than well-known writers such as Louise Otto, Fanny Lewald, and Bettina von Arnim.[12] She expressed herself best on the subject in her "Schattenspiele an der Wand," which appeared at a time of renewed censorship in 1854. Her twenty-fifth picture, which showed the "chained" German press, occasioned the following comment:

> Our work is disfigured by the . . . censor's mark and yet this is not sufficient for its circulation. Works censored today can be censored again next year or forbidden. . . . What becomes of literary property under such circumstances which the authorities protect on paper but confiscate in fact. The little piece of land which the farmer owns . . . cannot be taken from him without the intervention of the judiciary and judicial proceedings. But the fruit of sleepless nights, the holiest property, is arbitrarily destroyed without official judgement, without judicial proceedings, without defense, by the single will, the mood of the censor, who grasps the product of the intellect with a pliers, rips it to pieces and beheads it.

Fortunately, she continued, writers have learned to use "half words," which their readers understand. In this way freedom of the press would not die. "Whoever has a pen in the hand, never will be prevented from saying everything he wishes."[13]

Zitz-Halein's works provide no entirely uniform or integrated view of her political and social views, probably because she had none. She remained the writer of the moment, concerned about entertaining her audience while inserting a political and social message. What emerges is a person who shared the not yet sharply defined or differentiated liberal and democratic views of her progressive contemporaries and who also was sensitive to emerging social problems. As she expressed it in her *Variationen,* the themes of her works were the ever-recurring "pains of life. Oppression from above, passive resistance from below, the arrogance of men and the subordination of women."[14] In fact, in spite of her oft-expressed hostility to so-called feminists her works often featured women as central characters and usually showed them as politically engaged but frequently suffering the injustices of contemporary society. This should make us cautious about reading a too-modern message into her diatribes against "amazons" who were masculine caricatures. She had anything but a passive or "victorian" role in mind for the women of her generation, but she represented instead the cutting edge of mid-nineteenth-century feminine activism. If she still believed that she was not operating outside the boundaries of appropriate female behavior, perhaps our definition of these limits needs to be revised.

Nothing better illustrates Zitz-Halein's attitude than her translations of three of Victor Hugo's plays, *Marion de Lorme* (1833), *The King Amuses Himself* (1835), and *Cromwell* (1835). In the first two, which were banned in France shortly after their opening, women are the main characters and heroines, who overcome experiences of rape and prostitution to emerge as courageous figures, willing to make demanding sacrifices. In *The King Amuses Himself* Blanche ultimately saves the king, who has dishonored her, while Marion De Lorme offers herself to the king and then appeals to the crowd in a vain attempt to save her lover's life. The third play, *Cromwell,* depicts the English ruler as corrupted by his dictatorial power. That she had no qualms about translating works with such strong political and social themes reflects her mature approach to life and women's role in it. Furthermore, in spite of *Marion de Lorme*'s unflattering portrayal of monarchy Zitz-Halein sent her translation to the Hessian ruler, who paid her eleven gulden for the copy. The censors were at best imperfect guardians of political and social standards.[15]

More than in her translations, in her poetry she covered a wide variety of political and social subjects and responded most directly to the issues of the day. Poetry, which was emerging as a separate branch of literature, was the medium with which she seemed most comfortable. The importance of political poetry, especially in the pre-1848 period, has been rated very highly. Poems made statements about immediate events and were the writings of the period most comparable to journalistic articles. In the hands of such skilled writers and political progressives as Georg Herwegh, August Hoffmann von Fallersleben, Heinrich Heine, and Ferdinand Freiligrath, poetry made a significant contribution to the politicizing process in Germany since it could reach the masses in a way that prose works could not. Even poets of lesser renown, the current events poets, *(Tagespoeten)*, had their importance. In 1845 Ludwig Kalisch wrote that the so-called bad poets were the true "people's poets" who contributed to the populace's education. Since their products circulated as broadsides or special inserts in newspapers they were virtually free and the "laborer, for a penny, received his intellectual nourishment." Often they were printed as single sheets and passed out to the people, as in 1848. Viewed in this way, as critics have stressed, political poems should not be judged exclusively by aesthetic standards.[16] Moreover, Louise Otto, whose sensitivity on women's issues was particularly acute, called attention to the significant impact of poetry on women. In an extraordinarily insightful comment, she claimed that political poetry not only was the way to women's hearts but contributed to raising their political consciousness. As a result of the inadequate education that women received, she stressed in the 1840s, they had to use nontraditional means to educate themselves. "Our botany we drew from talking about flowers, our German grammar rules from French grammar, our history from historical novels, our geography from travelogues. Why not our politics from poetry?"[17] In no better statement could one sum up the potential political and social fallout from Kathinka Zitz-Halein's literary activities.

As early as 1822–1823 Zitz-Halein's poems contained expressions of support for Germany's unity and freedom. In "The Soldier" she salutes his "victory and death for the fatherland," and in the "Eighteenth of October," which commemorates the Battle of Leipzig, she celebrates the end of "France's venal yoke."[18] Yet, she praised the Frenchman Lafayette on the occasion of his death as a fighter for freedom. Similarly when a friend of hers died in 1833 she remembered him for his political beliefs.[19]

> With the holy fire of enthusiasm
> You forged the armor of freedom.
> Never did you use your powerful hammer
> To rivet chains of slavery for the German people.
> Only to freedom did you swear an oath. . . .

The opening of an industrial fair in Mainz in 1842 was the stimulous to "A Voice of the Age," a long poem in praise of freedom and unity, which, although respectful to the ruler, makes clear what has to be done.[20] Zitz-Halein wishes to hear a prince proclaim:

> No Austria, no Prussia.
> A single, free German land.
> The Prince is the bulwark of his people
> But only because he grants the loyal multitude
> A constitution and free speech
> And open legal proceedings. . . .
> Away with the obscurantists . . .
> Away with spiritual slavery.
>
> We have men of courage
> Who for justice fear not death. . . .
> The German feels himself highly honored
> Who hears called out the names of Welcker,
>   Itzstein, . . .
> Men who so cleverly stand up for the people's
>   rights.

In this group of praiseworthy individuals she includes her lyrical colleagues.

> A cheer for that band of poets
> Who have given the impulse.
> Now it's a question of pressing forward.
> Listen Germany to the spirit of the age,
> And be strong in unity.

Three years later in "Let There Be Light" she sought to encourage the reawakening reform movement but also to help it avoid self-delusion.[21]

> Many fools dream of Germany's freedom
> And fancy themselves free from slaves' chains.
> Yet their freedom is not yet born,
> It rests in the dark bosom of the future. . . .
> Free speech is kept in chains,
> The rights of the press suffer under pressure
>   and compulsion,
> Legal proceedings in our day continue
> In their old beaten track.
> Instead of prizes we draw only blanks,
> We remained denied the best goods, . . .
> O German land . . .
> When does the day come when your hymn echos,
> No longer mocked by a princely yoke?
> It comes for sure—thus forward brave fighters
> Ever forward on the entered path.
> Do not retreat, press ever forward,
> The victor's laurel will crown you at the end. . . .
> Whoever wants to win cannot avoid the battle.

Although her patriotic feelings occasionally included criticism of France, her national attitudes owed more to Herder than to later nationalists. In 1843 she wrote, "Who insults no nation has best defended his own." And in 1853 she ridiculed excessive expressions of German nationalism in a poem that would lose too much by translation.[22]

> Deutscher, sei deutscher, als deutsche, dann
>   dringet
> die wahre Verdeutschung
> Dir in das deutsche Gebluet, bleibend mit
>   deutschem Bestand.
> Dann lasst durch deutsche Befeindung du nimmer
>   dich feige entdeutschen,
> Sinkest dann ganzlich durchdeutscht, einst in's
>   germanische Grab.

Even her favorite poem, "Farbenwechsel" (Change of Colors), which sums up her life and her refusal to be repressed, reflects her civic spirit. In it she identifies the various phases of her life by the color of her clothing: white for childish innocence, red and green for awakening impulses and hope, blue for the married life "of eternally suffering submissiveness," violet for anger, black for a failed life, and brown for "indifference to a fate for which I am blameless." But when one expects a melancholy or pessimistic conclusion, she finishes instead on a note of activism and defiance, true to her combative nature. "Indifference! Have I forgotten everything / Buried every elevated feeling? / O no! For the fatherland, / For the great issues of the age / My heart will never again be indifferent."[23]

Zitz-Halein also used her poetry to call attention to social and economic abuses. In this regard, the years of deprivation (1829–1833) seem to have had a lasting impact on her. They gave her a new perspective on the less privileged classes and made her ready to protest injustice to others. She later wrote of this period of her life:

> I lived once from the work of my hands; consequently I belong to the proletarian class and consider it an honor to belong to it. I do not feel attracted to the privileged classes but to the people, the poor suffering, oppressed, industrious people, upon whom, nevertheless, the well being of the state rests, and which substitutes for a lack of intellectual culture the culture of the heart.[24]

This sensitivity was reflected in her poetry. In "Number Thirteen," a poem about the notorious gambling dens in the Palais Royal, she pleaded for an end to gambling because it caused the ruination of individuals.[25] She characterized the rich, "the aristocracy of wealth," as "pernicious as the political aristocracy," and in "Thirst for Gold," she damned usurers as those to whom a fatherland and a God were of no value. Although one could read anti-Jewish sentiment into the latter poem, such attitudes were normally not part of her literary or political vocabulary.[26] In "The Taxes of the Poor" the cruelty of poverty is evocatively portrayed.[27] A father and son discuss what to do when faced with the choice of feeding the family or paying taxes.

> (FATHER): The tax collector waits no longer
>   Soon his agent knocks.
>   My last funds are these coins
>   I'll buy you coarse bread with them. . .
> (SON): Pay the taxes good father,
>   We'll eat if it pleases God. . . .
> (FATHER): Oh God! the pale children starve!
>   The agent calls in the taxes.
>   To richly feed the princely servants
>   He must be relentless here.

> With a burden of millions
> Is our poor land weighed down.
> (SON): Pay the taxes, dear father
> We'll eat what God provides us.

The father then condemns the prince and the court who live in the city in great luxury and erect splendid monuments "with the sweat of the poor," who, when the village requires a bridge, build a road to the estate of the provincial official. "The rich only vote the taxes," he explains. The final lines suggest a note of defiance and desperation.

> (SON): Oh father, pay the taxes
> The collector is at the door.
> (FATHER): No! No! To still your hunger
> I'll keep the last coins.
> (SON): Who sleeps eats! Our hovel remains
> There's room enough in it for us.
> Pay, otherwise it's taken from us,
> And then we are really impoverished.
> Pay the taxes good father,
> We'll eat if God pities us.

The same format of father and son is used again to criticize the aristocracy. In "Appearance and Reality" a boy's first visit to the theater is the occasion for the father's lesson in the ways of the world.[28] He cautions the enchanted child not to be fooled by the glitter of the people and scenery.

> Behind it cold reality is hidden.
> The palaces are only painted screens,
> The princesses, so beautiful to look at,
> Are shriveled madeup women,
> And those in royal crowns . . .
> Are pupils who say by heart
> The lessons they have learned.
>
> We all believe too easily.
> We believed that under a prince's cloak
> Goodness was united with power.
> We believed that the princes's conduct
> Was always what it appeared.
> We thought that judges judge
> As their conscience commands. . . .

> That teachers who teach virtue
> Make the effort to practice it.

His son leaves the theater chastened.

Although these poems treated themes that were part of the general democratic-liberal movement, Zitz-Halein transcended its mainstream in "The Negro to the White Woman," which places her in the ranks of the small antislavery movement in Germany. Declaring his love for the white woman the black man asks her to disregard their different skin colors. "For nature," he tells her, "gladly tolerates such a mixture. . . . The Negro is also beautiful. . . . His face is like the night, his eyes like two stars which emit a fiery light out of the distant heavens." He asks her to believe "The black man is good. What does skin color matter if I never cause you pain. The black color does not penetrate to my soul." But it is all to no avail, he realizes. "You do not love me, you flee the black Ali," he laments. Nine years later Zitz-Halein wrote "The Negro Children in the Forest," in which she dealt with the failed attempt of a slave family to win its freedom. The political poets in general supported emancipation of the slaves.[29]

Besides her poems and translations Kathinka Zitz-Halein's stories, especially the fairy tales, provided an effective means of calling attention to existing political and social abuses. Often she wove into the tales experiences from her own life and made her characters resemble too closely her acquaintances in Mainz. Her friend, Caroline Berthold, who grew up in Mainz, derived special pleasure from her works because she could read between the lines.[30] Zitz-Halein's most comfortable literary genres were the novella and the short story. She generally eschewed the full-length novel until later in life, when she focused on biographical novels. It was with short stories and novellas, which were subject to prior censorship, that she experienced difficulties with the censors. Most of her pre-1848 works appeared but were "distorted" by the censor, as she admitted after the revolution made it possible to publish a volume of collected stories. She described them as "wild, at times, ill-bred children who permit themselves crazy leaps into the realm of phantasy, turn somersaults, but never mince words. Nevertheless they are good at heart and completely unpretentious. They do not want to distress anyone but to entertain through harmless jokes or warn through bitter truths."[31] Nevertheless, she managed to make her points, often in a surprisingly explicit manner.

One of Zitz-Halein's most wide-ranging attacks on existing injustices and her personal enemies appears in "Felizian," a German Candide, whose travels and adventures provide the vehicle for her criticism. Orphaned as a teenager, Felizian becomes an assistant to a journalist but one who is willing to serve any party, a capacity that allows her to refer to that variety of journalism as the "disability ward of literature." This reference to her bitter rival, Ludwig Kalisch, who will be discussed later, was not characteristic of her attitude toward the press. Disillusioned, Felizian continues on his way, deciding against a military career because he could not marry without permission unless his wife had a huge pension. This allusion to her own life leads to the remark "[The] novel of love is so beautiful, the history book of marriage so boring." The traveler next stops in Belgium, where he meets many Germans whom the "shameful" law code has forced out of Germany but who, she adds for the sake of the censor, "do not call themselves political refugees." In Russia, the "police state," "the classic land of absolutism," Felizian finds the bootlicking of the courtiers beyond all limits. France is quiet because of the absence of a Mirabeau, Marat, or Camille Desmoulins; this characterization indicates her vague revolutionary ecumenism. Felizian's trip continues to exotic lands. Zitz-Halein notes that although missionaries have sought to eliminate cannibalism, at home "civilized people are always ready to tear their neighbor apart," a clear reference to her personal enemies. Referring to the strange customs of the natives, she calls attention to the equally strange costumes and behavior of the court aristocracy with their golden keys and coat tails. "A person's worth," she insists, "should be based solely on his moral and intellectual stature." And observing the more equal relationship between supposedly uncivilized men and women, she comments: "During five thousand eight hundred and so many years our female ancestors have groaned under the biblical decision which condemned them to original sin." She points out sarcastically that things are different in America, where already a strong minority of Congress rejects the principle of women's responsibility for original sin. Her sisters, she jokes seriously, will soon receive a patent of "wholeness."

Tossed about by a storm at sea, Felizian finally reaches land, where he sees a gallows and exclaims: "'Thank God I am in a civilized country!' He was right; he was in Germany," she added for the benefit of her readers. After more travels he reaches *Dunkelheim* (Home of Darkness), where lanterns are deemed to be a protest against the moon and therefore banned and where nepotism, prison, torture, and an overweening clergy plague the inhabitants. To fight these evils Felizian decides to become a journalist but one who avoids "hypocritical deceitful optimism which only helps the despots." She concludes with an oration of praise for the press, which "enriches the people because it enlightens them," and an uncompromising condemnation of censorship, that "most gruesome institution" which commits "intellectual murder." It is a "blind absolute power which works in insidious ways against authors. . . . Here there is no appeal nor reversal. Everything is done silently in the dark. . . . It takes its pointiest scissors, its sharpest blades, its most penetrating scalpel. It cuts blindly, without understanding, without mercy . . . until [the work] is a skeleton; . . . the little flesh remaining hangs down in bloody pieces." Even then, she adds, the censor did not release his "booty" until shortly before publication.[32]

The Mainz writer's other stories from the 1840s contained similar themes, even if less explicitly stated. In "Master and Slave" a tyrannical regime is overthrown and replaced by a constitutional monarchy, which she calls "libertas nobilitas," while the hero of the story, Populus, goes in search of democracy, "libertas communus." Zitz-Halein makes her point indirectly when she asks whether he has been successful. "The news of it has not reached me. Yet I believe that if he should succeed, . . . it will be possible only in the country of fantasy, for although here on earth [democracy] has many secret supporters, these cannot yet make known their support. The mighty one [most likely a reference to Clemens von Metternich, the Austrian foreign minister] of this earth is and remains in all eternity a hated and feared personnage."[33]

Her preference for a political system seemed to be a constitutional monarchy. Support for a republic was premature in the 1840s, and advocating it openly would have been dangerous. In "Empire of the Stars," which deals with the struggles between the sun and the moon, Queen Sun rules in an enlightened way. She recognizes the need to awaken the "national spirit" in the direction of unity, to be firm with neighboring states, but to tolerate no "national hate" against foreign countries. She permits the progressive spirit of her subjects to develop freely, introducing public judicial proceedings; a state without such a system "must be fled like the plague." A free press emerges; if one suppresses the press, "nothing remains but to go around on all fours and live off acorns." And, she adds, attempts to muzzle the press usually backfire as it becomes a "resounding megaphone." The sun, we are told, introduced these reforms because she wanted to prevent revolution, which arises from a general dissatisfaction with the pressure of the laws. A revolution, Zitz-Halein implied, should be avoided because of the dangers of "anarchy," which would then have to be fought with military power.[34]

In "Hausgenossen" (Lodgers), which in part seems to take a swipe at her husband and his friends, she deals again with the theme of a good political system. An aristocratic government in the land of "Somewhere" aims to pump out the last coin and the last bit of freedom from the people. There ruled the "negative": negative ministers, a negative parliament and a negative freedom. But the strength of a government, she emphasized, rested not on its arbitrariness but on the "intelligent harmony of rights and obligations." To be strong a government did not need to be absolute. "It suffices that it [a government] can do all that is necessary. A strong government should resemble those strong natures who command respect because one recognizes their strength in their powerful constitution. Freedom must be the end of government." It was erroneous to believe, she went on, that authority can be strong only at the cost of freedom. "Nothing is so weak as absolute power; nothing so much like anarchy as dictatorship. The extremes touch." "Under an absolute government by the grace of God," she continued, "the nation is treated as a minor and power is its guardian; under the sovereignty of the people the nation directs, and power is only the executor of its mandate."[35] This explicit advocacy of the principle of popular sovereignty placed her on the cutting edge of the pre-March political opposition in Germany.

Although most concerned with political issues her stories did not ignore women. But Zitz-Halein is ambivalent about their role. "The Tumult in the Empire of the Plants" emphasizes more their passive nature. The king mistreats his wife; when he dies she seizes power and decides to introduce female emancipation. But as with "most women's governments," Zitz-Halein notes, "the queen ruled according to favoritism and not strict justice." An uprising against her occurred, but she is saved by a prince who marries her and in effect takes over the government. However, his unjust rule calls forth a new revolt. The people, now triumphant, nevertheless reject the idea of a republic and return the queen to power on the condition that she governs, not rules; grants civil liberties; and accepts a constitutional consort according to the wishes of the people. Again Zitz-Halein stresses the golden mean of a monarchy bound by a constitution and resting on the will of the people whose civil rights are guaranteed.[36]

In her depiction of the civic-minded woman in "Rumpelstilzchen," which contradicts her previously expressed views about women, the princess, after unhappy marital experiences, no longer believes in matrimony and asks the advice of Rumpelstiltskin. He advises her not to be so slavish; to show less love, more energy, and more strength of character. But as he begins to leaf through her papers he makes one amazing discovery after another. He finds songs by Hoffmann von Fallersleben and copies of the liberal *Rheinische Zeitung,* then edited by Karl Marx. "You take part in politics," he cries. "Why shouldn't I," she proudly responds.

> I am indeed only a woman but I love my fatherland not less than the best man, and if I were one I would be as brave as the Maccabee brothers. . . . I am a child of the century. . . . The instinct to all great things lies in me. But I am no Titan; I do not want to storm the heavens. I am sorry not to have been born a man. If I were, I'd call to my brothers: "Rally around the banner of true freedom. . . . Bury your dead but not your freedom, for as free as we are we are still slaves enough." If I were a man [freedom] would be the mistress to which I would sacrifice blood, life and goods. O my beautiful fatherland which is not only my little principality but all Germany . . . when will the great idea of unity reign in all your districts? And you know I would have become a democrat, for the true democrat . . . must be ready for every sacrifice.

And if this statement of principle were not enough, when Rumpelstiltskin later finds a scientific treatise among the princess's papers and expresses his amazement that a woman dared concern herself with scientific matters, she replies: "And why not. I busy myself with everything I am capable of grasping."[37]

What Zitz-Halein was capable of grasping through the literary medium is well illustrated by one of her numerous quarrels with other writers. Properly labeled the Zitz-Kalisch affair, it is instructive because it offers an insight into her character as well as the social and political milieu in which she operated. Ludwig Kalisch, who had an unsuccessful career as a writer, came to the Mainz area in 1840 and wrote first for the *Rheinland* and then for the satirical journal *Narrhalla.* He quickly made a name for himself as a biting and denigrating satirist. From the start Zitz-Halein found his work needlessly insulting, and already by 1840 she had complained to the provincial governor about him. He advised her not to get involved, but this proved impossible by 1843.[38] Zitz-Halein believed that Kalisch had become a friend of her estranged husband and at the latter's instigation had attacked her in the *Narrhalla.* Although he had not referred to her by name, but only to a "goose covered with poet's feathers," she did not doubt that she was the target. After all, she remarked, she was the only female writer in Mainz. She responded to the attack in another satirical journal, *Narrenzeitung,* on January 14, 1844, and an exchange of open letters followed in which she got the worst because she could not match Kalisch in satirical sharpness. Nevertheless she eventually won the battle because she was willing to use whatever means were at her disposal.[39]

Against the advice of friends she sought to bring government pressure to bear on Kalisch. Twice, on January 21 and 28, she wrote directly to the grand duke of Hesse, complaining of Kalisch's "misconduct." She cleverly tried to frighten the ruler by mentioning that tolerance of Kalisch would hurt his reputation with other German and European rulers. She advised the grand duke that Kalisch had already been disrespectful to the king of Bavaria and the emperor of Russia, quoting certain of his offensive verses. "May such impertinence be tolerated," she charged, "in a state, where there still exists respect for the law?" She also reminded the sensitive ruler that Kalisch's journal had already been forbidden in the Grand Duchy of Baden and the Kingdom of Württemberg. These were strange comments from one who normally was sensitive to acts of censorship. Nevertheless, although while ostensibly advocating censorship, she knew how to cut the Hessian government in a remarkably two-edged statement.

> I believe that in a state where unconditional freedom of the press does *not* [sic] reign, where the censor cuts in so quickly with his thought-killing scissors when an enlightened idea wants to surface, but who shows himself so overly considerate when one endeavors to ruin the fortune and honor of harmless people, I believe that where the censor generally has sway, the life and activity of peaceful citizens must be protected from the attacks of unrestrained insolent caprice.

Apparently concerned by the possible involvement of other German or European governments, the Hessian ministry began to take the matter more seriously. On February 7, it banned *Narrhalla* and forbade Kalisch to edit a similar journal. The prohibition was less than complete and illustrates again how coarse was the sieve of censorship. Someone else took over the journal, changed the name, and hired Kalisch as a writer. Kalisch later became an important political journalist during the Revolution of 1848.[40]

Nevertheless, it was an impressive victory, again demonstrating her personal strengths. She knew how best to activate the authorities while reaffirming her commitment to freedom of expression. The affair was also a striking demonstration of her creed that although loyal to her friends she would be implacable to her enemies: "I do not follow the cowardly biblical injunction to turn the other cheek. Who can do this has no self esteem; he does not respect his own worth. . . . Never do I attack my neighbors first, but who slanders me without my fault, to him I say: An eye for an eye, a tooth for a tooth."[41]

Kathinka Zitz-Halein, this exceptionally strong but unclassifiable woman, followed additional avenues to continue her political activities in the 1840s. She was asked by the editors of *Vaterländische Blätter,* for whom Louise Otto wrote, and *Veilchen* (Bautzen), a "socialistic" journal, to contribute to their periodicals but apparently without results.[42] At the same time she was in contact with South German liberals such as Adam Itzstein, Heinrich von Gagern, Friedrich Daniel Bassermann, and Eduard Duller and had conceived a plan to help political refugees by donating the proceeds from the sale of her literary works. Nothing seems to have resulted from this clever and typical plan of hers to combine patriotism with business and self-promotion.[43]

Zitz-Halein's most important political accomplishment before 1848 was her entry into the field of journalism with the purpose of influencing the citizens of Mainz. In the mid-1840s the Hessian government made a renewed and determined effort to develop and introduce a common legal code for its three provinces. Until then the province of Rhenish Hesse, of which Mainz was the most important city, still used the French legal codes. These so-called Rhenish codes were treasured by the Mainzers and by the Rheinlanders who came under Prussian control in 1815. They saw the French codes as not only providing a measure of autonomy vis-à-vis the central government but giving the inhabitants a degree of legal protection not matched elsewhere. If there was to be any legal unification it was these codes, they believed, that should become the basis of a future German legal system. They feared, however, that their codes would be dismantled in the process of being integrated into a new legal system. The main principles, or Rhenish institutions, embodied in the Napoleonic code included the principles of equality of the citizens before the law, separate spheres for church and state, civil marriage, separation of justice from administration, open court proceedings, and trial by jury in criminal cases. When it became clear that the Hessian government's proposed unified law code would introduce significant departures from the French codes, especially in matters of church-state relations, civil marriage, the role of the state in family questions, and definition of the powers of the police, some of the Mainzers began to organize a campaign of opposition, in which Kathinka Zitz-Halein played a significant part.[44]

The Mainz writer affected this issue by her reports about local affairs in the democratic and widely read *Mannheimer Abendzeitung.* Because of the relatively liberal press laws of the Grand Duchy of Baden, Mannheim was one of the most important newspaper cities in Germany before 1848, with papers of three different political persuasions represented. *Abendzeitung,* published by Moritz Hahner, was the only Baden newspaper that had a supraregional circulation and reported extensively on German affairs. It was strongly democratic in orientation, and because of the sharpness of its attacks on the status quo, other German states such as Prussia pressured the Badenese government to exercise more rigorous censorship.[45]

How Zitz-Halein became involved in the political campaign cannot be determined, but it may have been through her many friends in Mannheim. Her reports in *Abendzeitung* can be identified in several ways. Some newspaper clippings are found in her papers, which give us an indication of the printer's symbols under which she wrote; other articles can be identified with confidence through style and phraseology; and others can be recognized because of comments in her "Skizzen" about the subjects of some of the articles, such as her attacks on Reinhard von Dalwigk, the provincial governor of Rhenish Hesse and later chief minister of Hesse-Darmstadt.

The reports began in September 1846 on the occasion of the Mainz city council election, which she described as a contest between progressives and conservatives ("gentlemen of darkness").[46] She attacked the mayor for censoring election literature because of its liberal phraseology. "Germany now knows," she wrote, "how it will go with all such modern expressions and words when the mayor of Mainz has the exclusive right to decide." But she was also critical of the passivity of the citizens of Mainz, whom she accused of being brave only behind their wine glasses or being united only when it was a question of organizing the pre-Lenten *(Fasching)* carnival. She found a cold indifference in civic life. The Mainzers were too sunk in their carnival revelry to pull themselves out of the "morass of effeminacy." They forgot they had a fatherland, and patriotism, like Barbarossa, was asleep in the Kyffhäuser. She hoped the Mainzers would regain their sense of civic esteem and "manly duty," forget personal considerations, and recognize their obligation to the community. Only a few individuals seemed courageous enough to express liberal views, and she called on this "small band of men," who still had a spark of true patriotism, to continue the work of "progress and enlightenment."[47]

When it became apparent that the principles of the French civil codes would be threatened by the Hessian government's proposals, the Mainzers began to bestir themselves. In October 1846, some members of the city council voiced their opposition to the projected changes in the legal code. A petition with three hundred signatures was addressed to the grand duke. Copies were sent to other Rhenish cities, which circulated their own petitions. In November a similar petition in Mainz received two thousand signatures. Even the Carnival Society decided to forego certain festivities in view of the gravity of the situation, and the women of Mainz began to wear black to protest the threat to the principle of civil marriage.[48]

Kathinka Zitz-Halein's efforts may have helped to stimulate the movement. Several times she attacked the provincial governor, Dalwigk. She reported his attempt to prevent the city council from protesting the proposed legal codes. She also charged him with trying to intimidate electors in Mainz during the elections to the state parliament, as well as being unwilling to recognize the popular will. She added his ban of a performance of *William Tell* and institution of house searches to her catalogue of his misdeeds. Zitz-Halein also pointed out correctly that the major Mainz newspaper, *Mainzer Zeitung*, was controlled by the censor and could not express itself freely. This, she added, made it necessary to publish the truth about Hessian policy outside that state. As for the projected law code, she claimed it would push the Rhenish Hessians back to the Middle Ages. It would be preferable, in her view, to bring the blessings of the Rhenish codes to the other provinces of Hesse. She stressed particularly that it threatened the principle of civil marriage and that the new police regulations would make citizens prey to police offenses. She further charged that Mainz was being exploited by the Hessian government in Darmstadt in the sense that needed local improvements were not being undertaken and that far too many local jobs were in the hands of outsiders ("Darmstadters"). This was a long-heard complaint of the Mainzers.[49]

What impact did her articles have? Buchner confirms the accuracy of Zitz-Halein's charge about the muzzling of the Mainz press and the consequently important role played by the non-Hessian newspapers. Deuchert stresses that the impact of the radical Badenese press was greater outside Baden than inside. Clearly the Hessian government was disturbed. It sued the editor of *Abendzeitung* to force him to identify the correspondent, but he refused and instead paid the fines. Finally, the sale and distribution of the newspaper were banned in Hesse in December 1846. It proved impossible, however, to keep out the newspaper, and *Mannheimer Abendzeitung* continued to be distributed until the outbreak of the Revolution of 1848. Deuchert stresses that articles from *Mannheimer Abendzeitung* would be printed as broadsides and passed from hand to hand in the Grand Duchy of Hesse. He also correctly emphasizes the role that employees of the steamship lines that plied the Mannheim-Mainz route played in delivering the forbidden newspapers to Mainz. It is clear that in 1849 Zitz-Halein used this means to get sensitive material to and from Mannheim. Even one of Metternich's agents in Mainz reported that hundreds of copies of the forbidden *Abendzeitung* were being distributed. Once again the censorship regulations proved relatively ineffective as long as the Badenese government was unwilling to cooperate.[50]

In her memoirs Kathinka Zitz-Halein claims that she wrote about Hessian conditions with "a courageousness such as no man" would have shown at that time; that she attacked Dalwigk "from all sides"; that she called on the Mainzers to rise from the "muck" of the carnival societies, shake off their "wine stupor," and show that "they were men." Perhaps she exaggerated when she claimed that the "spark was lit . . . and to me belongs the credit of having first awakened the slumbering sense of manhood in my hometown."[51] But only a very few had the right to claim that much. Her activities should be ranked alongside Louise Otto's work for *Vaterländische Blätter*, Louise Dittmar's public lectures, and Bettina von Arnim's varied political activities as among the few efforts of this kind before 1848 but one completely in keeping with her long-standing civic outlook.

Whether mainly the result of her initiatives or not, the progressives were now mobilized, and the state elections of 1847 witnessed major gains for the opposition forces and a decided move to the Left. Although the new police code was passed, it became impossible to pass the new legal code before the end of the session because of the efforts of the Mainz delegates.[52] With her appeals to the masculine virtues of her fellow citizens, which betray the female authorship of the newspaper articles, she reminds one of the Germanic women described by Tacitus who encouraged their men in battle, or the Greek and Polish heroines she later celebrated in her poems. It was also the most effective way of stinging the Mainzers into action. Her patriotic courage was real even if she may have been protected by an unwritten law that women were less likely to be punished for their outspoken political behavior than men. She was to test the limits of that tolerance during the next three years.

5

1848

Women in Revolution

*T*he German Revolution of 1848, part of a wave of upheavals that began in France on February 24 and spread to the Italian states and the Austrian Empire, was marked by widespread popular demonstrations, street fighting, and rural violence. The mass disturbances forced the German rulers to dismiss unpopular ministers such as Clemens von Metternich, grant civil liberties, promise constitutional reforms, and progress toward national unity.[1] Revolution, its students have stressed, often makes it possible for previously exploited or neglected groups or individuals to push to the forefront of events. The destruction or even weakening of traditional lines and habits of authority has created sudden opportunities for talented outsiders, whether workers, young people, political radicals, or suppressed nationalities. Although these groups achieved degrees of influence during the revolutionary upheaval that began in the German states in March 1848, perhaps the most unexpected development was the civic activity of women. Although the revolution has been and continues to be studied from a variety of perspectives, the role of women in it has only begun to be examined.[2]

Before the Revolution of 1848 was a month old *Didaskalia,* the widely read literary supplement to *Frankfurter Journal,* caught the spirit of the new era and informed its apparently predominantly female audience of a change in emphasis. Whereas normally women were assumed to immerse themselves in romantic novels and harmless theater criticism, the editor wrote, the revolution had changed matters. Convinced that women would be actively concerned with the cause of Germany's unity and freedom, he believed they would be insulted if

70

the journal sought to withhold reports of the new movements from its pages. Women, the journalist asserted, signaling one of the cardinal principles of the 1848 revolution, did not want to and should not remain in the background when the fate of the fatherland was at stake. Their participation was an imperative of the age, the true meaning of the so often "misconstrued coming of age of women."[3] True to the editor's statement the literary magazine regularly published articles about the revolution and often women's role in it.

That women were intensely interested in the course of the revolution, expressed this attitude in a variety of ways, and saw the relationship between the upheaval and women's rights is no longer open to question. Eugenia Blum, the widow of the executed democratic leader Robert Blum, expressed the new spirit. In February 1849 she advised the Women's Association in Hanau that it was a joyous sign that women "who formerly were regarded as indifferent now are interested in the most important questions of politics and take the most active part in everything . . . that leads to progress and freedom."[4] The small Baden town of Löffingen provided another example of women's commitment to civic issues. There seventeen women claimed to be subscribers to the democratic newspaper, *Volksfreund (People's Friend)*. This, they emphasized, was a sign of their interest in the fate of the nation and an indication that there were many women who cared for more than knitting stockings. In a suggestive comment about the limitations on feminine involvement in civic affairs, they reassured their readers that they did not want to be poetesses or novelists. Citing Rousseau against himself, however, they maintained that as long as they had responsibility for educating children they would properly demand an education appropriate to the task. Even if the woman's hand were "too weak" to carry the sword, "the woman's heart is large enough to share the most intense enthusiasm for freedom, justice and patriotism."[5]

The same theme appeared in Louise Otto's *Frauen-Zeitung* when two articles discussed the question of French and German women's contributions to the revolution. The first article, "Johanna Deroin," argued that Frenchwomen had always participated in public life more than their German sisters. The writer referred to the activities of women during the French Revolution of 1789 in storming the Bastille, encouraging their men to take up arms to defend the revolution, and forming their own organization. She singled out Olympe de Gouges and Madame Roland as individual heroines. She was also familiar with the interest of the St. Simonians in women's emancipation and named a number of women who were involved in the movement. As for the

Revolution of 1848, she called attention to the efforts of Johanna (Jeanne) Deroin, who established women's clubs, edited women's newspapers, advocated women's suffrage, tried to run for political office, was arrested for infringing the laws on association, and finally was forced into exile.[6]

"Helene," one of the many contributors to *Frauen-Zeitung* who used only a first name, responded to the article by arguing that German women did not lag behind their French counterparts in the question of civic participation. She pointed to writers like Bettina von Arnim, Louise Dittmar, Louise Otto, Kathinka Zitz, and Fanny Lewald, who even before 1848 had concerned themselves with public issues and the cause of democracy. According to Helene, during the Revolution of 1848 German women distinguished themselves by founding several short-lived newspapers, such as Louise Aston's *Freischärler*, Dittmar's *Soziale Reform*, and Louise Otto's successful paper.[7] In the area of direct participation in the military struggle *(amazonenhafte)*, Helene stressed that women such as Amalia Struve, Elise Blenker, Emma Herwegh, and Pauline Wunderlich showed more courage than many men. Women also represented socialist views in public, gave speeches on the rights of women, and served as newspaper reporters in the Frankfurt national assembly. Fear of retribution by the authorities prevented Helene from naming more than a few women publicly, but she singled out for special praise Adele Erbe, who had emigrated, as an "ordinary woman," neither writer nor artist, who organized a democratic women's association in Altenburg and in the face of a hostile government openly aided refugees and their families.[8]

Although Helene showed an awareness of a wide range of activities by women she merely touched on the initiatives of the most well known among them. A fuller list can be assembled from the pages of *Frauen-Zeitung, Didaskalia, Fliegende Blätter* (even if often hostile to women), as well as newspapers, posters, letters, memoirs, and novels.[9] It includes fighting on the barricades; decorating graves of executed revolutionaries; collecting money for a German naval force; sewing flags for democratic clubs; writing poems and essays in support of the revolution; establishing their own gymnastic societies; organizing kindergartens; demanding increased rights in marriage, education, and employment; forming organizations to help insurgents, refugees, and their families; and founding the first women's college. Moreover, although most women's rights activists seemed to support left-wing causes, justifying the claim "Reactionaries are above all opponents of women's rights," some women from the Center and Right also cared about politics and were involved in civic activities, even if they did not consciously advocate women's emancipation.[10]

The interest of women in the political events of the day was underscored by the the establishment of a women's section in the spectators' gallery of the St. Paul's Church, where the meetings of the national assembly were held. It was an innovation that regularly provoked comment.[11] The evidence suggests that the women's section in Frankfurt was generally crowded and that women were attentive spectators of the political debates. Luise Zimmermann, wife of the deputy Wilhelm Zimmermann, described the layout of the "Ladies Gallery" on the left side of the chamber, reflecting the sympathy of the great majority of the female spectators with the Left. She stressed how this worked positively on the deputies and with what intense interest the women followed the debate. Luise Zimmermann particularly noted the strong representation of Jewish and Polish women, which probably reflected their interest in full citizenship rights and political independence, respectively.[12] Additional evidence of a desire to attend parliamentary proceedings came from Stuttgart and Baden.[13]

Several delegates to the national assembly called attention to the involvement of women in direct political action. In the spring of 1848 Otto von Keudell described how women in Frankfurt stirred up the crowds against conservatives. In August during the debate on the issue of amnesty for the Badenese revolutionary Friedrich Hecker, unruly spectators in the gallery forced a halt to the proceedings until the visitors' area was cleared. Women were prominently involved in the disturbances and the most difficult to eject, a woman being the last spectator to be forced out.[14] Other observers referred to the role of women in the September 1848 uprising in Frankfurt on the occasion of the acceptance of the truce agreement in the Danish war. "The women were everywhere" during the fighting, noted Julie Pagenstecher, wife of the deputy Alexander Pagenstecher. Of the 3,974 people who were questioned in connection with the uprising, some 15 percent were women. One woman, Margarethe Adams, who was charged with carrying stones for use as weapons and with looking for materials for the building of barricades, supposedly said, "Today one can't stand idly by and fold one's arms." Although she denied the accusations against her, she concluded her testimony with the phrase "One cannot do more than die."[15]

Nor was Frankfurt the only city where women were involved in the fighting. In Berlin on the pivotal days of March 18–19, 1848, when the people seemed to triumph over the army, "women of the lowest social classes," according to Meyerinck, tore up cobblestones to build barricades or carried the stones to the top floors of buildings where they could be used as weapons. They also made bullets. "At a stroke," so it seemed to the writer, "half of Berlin had gone crazy." And not only the male half. Minister of the Interior Ernst von Bodelschwingh could not help commenting on the presence of women among the insurgents. At least seven women died in the fighting. And this was not their first participation in insurgency. The previous year, in April, women initiated the so-called potato riots in Berlin and played an active role during the several days of disturbances. Women constituted 16 percent of the 107 people brought to court.[16] In Vienna during the critical months of August, October, and November 1848 women were involved in the street demonstrations and were among those killed and wounded in the fighting and sentenced to prison. Robert Blum reported from the Austrian capital in October that women demanded that weapons be taken from "hesitant" men and given to them.[17] In Dresden during the spring 1849 uprising women were also at the barricades, causing the revolutionary August Röckel to note their coolness under fire. He related how easily women, in the most unusual, terror-filled situations, "preserve their complete presence of mind. All they needed was an opportunity to demonstrate their courage." One of the most involved barricade fighters was Pauline Wunderlich, who was sentenced to life imprisonment for her efforts. The *Frauen-Zeitung* reporter wondered at the severity of her sentence compared to the more lenient terms meted out to men. It struck her as an attempt to frighten women away from political activity, but she warned that it would only serve to make her a martyr.[18] In other German cities women were punished for their rebellious activities. Several were sentenced to prison for participating in the attack on Waldenburg Castle on April 5, 1848; for taking part in riots in Chemnitz (now Karl-Marx-Stadt) in September 1848; and for being involved in the April 1849 uprising at Rastatt.[19]

Women also demonstrated their civic courage in other ways. They decorated graves of executed revolutionaries at a time when one ran the risk of arrest for doing so. In October 1849 in Freiburg ten women were taken into custody for putting flowers on the graves of those shot after a martial law trial. In Husum, in northern Germany, several servant girls were put on bread and water for five days because they decorated graves of fallen insurgents in spite of repeated prohibitions. In Mannheim a woman was caned for singing a song in honor of the radical Friedrich Hecker. Others were punished for distributing revolutionary propaganda.[20]

The heroic efforts of these unknown and uncelebrated women deserve at least as much attention as the activities of better known women who accompanied their husbands on the military campaigns. Emma Herwegh (1817–1904), perhaps the most resolute of these, was a part of her husband Georg's invasion force in April 1848, which he had organized among Germans living in France. Personally without fear she was motivated not by adventure but principle. Believing that each person should be a "banner for his age," she was determined to assist her husband. Dressed the part of an insurgent with black pantaloons and hat, two pistols, and a dagger, she helped make munitions for the soldiers, served as a messenger, and proved an invaluable support to her less resolute husband.[21] Other women participated in the spring 1849 uprising. Mathilde Anneke (1817–1884) rode with her husband, Fritz, and served as a messenger, and Elise Blenker (1824–1908) and Amalia Struve (1825–1862) accompanied their spouses.[22]

Besides risking their lives and freedom women demonstrated their patriotism in less dangerous ways. They became identified, for example, with the campaign to raise money for a German navy. The navy, untainted by association with repressive measures of the past as was the army, emerged as a symbol of national unity and was regarded as issuing from the people. Moreover, the war against Denmark demonstrated the need for a naval force. Women formed committees, held lotteries, donated jewelry, and sold embroidery work to raise funds for it.[23]

Women also responded to problems caused by economic and social distress. The wife of the deputy Ludwig Schwarzenberg from Kassel described in April 1848 how her daughter had organized other young women and worked from morning to night to collect contributions for the needy. She explained that the poorer citizens must perform guard duty, which took time from employment and caused economic hardship. As the breadwinner the father had to be fed even if it meant that wife and children went hungry. This element of economic distress may cast some light on the little understood problem of the citizens' militia. In Mainz the new freedom was interpreted by some as license to attack new technologies. Female workers were involved in demonstrations aimed at eliminating competition from steam-powered tugboats. It had been customary for ships going by Mainz to be pulled upstream by dockworkers, some of whom were women. For a time traffic around Mainz was threatened as ships were "captured" by male and female workers. In May 1848 *Didaskalia* reprinted Louise Otto's letter to the Saxon minister Martin Oberländer regarding employment problems that women faced. Speaking for those "who did not have the courage to do so," and recognizing that male workers often feared competition from women, she urged the minister not to forget that women too had to support themselves, had few employment opportunities, and had to struggle with wages much lower than men's. Lack of economic security, she stressed, encouraged a decline of morals by making marriage dishonest or driving women to prostitution. The women of Vienna also pointed to the same relationship between work opportunities and prostitution. In that city 44 percent of the workers aided by the public works program were women.[24]

In spring 1848 other women had specific suggestions for reviving the depressed economy, whose problems were exacerbated by the revolutionary disturbances. At the end of March 1848 Elberfelder women announced their decision to buy only German-made products in order to increase demand and help alleviate the misery of the workers. Workers needed employment rather than alms, they asserted. Stressing the need to demonstrate national unity, they asked men to support this initiative, which was particularly necessary at a time when the old bonds of authority were dissolving. Unless the propertied classes demonstrated that they cared, the misery would breed unrest. A "German woman" chastised her "sisters" for their penchant for French fashions. "Be German," she called out, "have pride in buying only German products . . . and doing one's bit to revive German production and to procure food for thousands of people." A group of women from Vienna also called for a boycott of foreign goods, and the women of Giessen stressed the need to restore confidence by not delaying purchases.[25]

As the representatives to the national assembly in Frankfurt and to the legislatures in other German cities debated the future of Central Europe during summer and fall 1848, the revolution was spawning a variety of political and social movements from socialist to conservative, from workers to Junkers, marking the beginning of modern politics in Germany. By far the best organized and largest political movement during the revolution developed among the democratic forces. In hundreds of German cities Democratic Clubs, vehicles for transforming "the people" into a political force, organized the previously excluded lower middle classes. In the Rhenish Hessian area around

Mainz there were 120 clubs by May 1849. They held weekly or bi-monthly meetings at which political and social issues were discussed and reports on the work of the various constitutional assemblies heard. The democratic organizations were also the only ones that evinced any sympathy for women's political and social advancement, and it was from within their ranks that the first tentative openings were made to women. Encouraged by this politicization and the spread of democratic ideas, some German women, not merely content to take part in the upheaval, demanded a new status within the postrevolutionary society.[26]

In July 1848 the Democratic Association of Mainz, which was founded in May and had become the dominant political force in the region, began to admit women to its meetings, reserving the front rows for them. The president, P. J. Schöppler, a friend of Zitz-Halein's, was sensitive to the educational role of the meetings and stressed the importance of spreading political awareness among the female population. Ludwig Bamberger, who was a vice president of the organization, looking back fifty years later, tended to see the move more in terms of propaganda, but he too admitted the seriousness with which women followed the proceedings. Stephan Born, a labor leader during the revolution, confirmed this when he later recalled addressing the Mainz Democratic Association. The filled meeting hall contained a large number of women, and Born remarked that he had never had a more attentive audience. The attendance of the women must have been steady because at the end of September the club limited it to one hundred. However, there is no evidence in Mainz or the other cities that women were permitted to participate in the political discussions. Kathinka Zitz-Halein noted that in spite of her obvious interest in political and social issues she never attended the association's meetings because of fear of running into her husband, who also was a high official in the organization.[27]

Besides attending Democratic Association meetings women were involved in civic affairs in other ways. Mainz, along with many other cities in Germany, had ceremonies in which flags and banners sewn by female groups were turned over to democratic associations, gymnastic organizations, or workingmen's clubs. In these civic ceremonies women participated and often made speeches.[28] The major Mainz ceremony on August 15, 1848, at which the daughter of a hat maker made an unrecorded speech of presentation, involved handing a flag over to the gymnastics society. Attended by one thousand people, the convocation was highlighted by Ludwig Bamberger's surprising speech of acceptance, the second half of which focused on the question of women's role in the emerging democratic society. He obviously took the matter of women's rights more seriously in 1848 than he remembered in his memoirs. Since democracy implied the involvement of the totality in civic concerns, symbolized by women's participation in the flag ceremony, Bamberger pointed out, one needed to define a new status for them. No longer could democrats, he maintained, share the "unreasoning intolerance" and "narrow-mindedness of hate" toward women that had been part of pre-1848 society. No longer could one reject women's participation in political life on the grounds that they would lose the uniqueness of their nature. No longer, he lectured his audience, could it be the destiny of one human being to serve another as a mere object. Agreeing with John Stuart Mill, Bamberger continued: "The narrow range of activity which that outlook grants women issues not from her own essence but from a master, just as with the narrowness of the oriental harem. Limiting women to a life of feeling is nothing but perfumed slavery, a Christian Germanic theory of the harem."[29] It did not matter whether some women were conditioned to feel comfortable in it, he emphasized. It was a result of a one-sided development that denied the wholeness of human beings. The young lawyer understood why women had been advised against politics in the past. It had not been public and was devoid of moral content. But the penetration of democracy into public life would elevate political affairs and make them capable of true beauty. Moreover, he stressed, democracy was built on the feeling of humanity. Thus it was nonsense to oppose the participation of women in the efforts to advance the cause of democracy because of their emotional capacity. Nevertheless, Bamberger hastened to add, as if concerned that his audience might misunderstand him, women's participation had its limits. He assured his listeners that he did not advocate an "equal" involvement of both sexes in public life but an "equable" one.[30] It was "self-evident" to the democratic leader that "each person, each nation, each sex" could do only what was appropriate to its nature.[31]

Even with this qualification Bamberger's speech, which was printed in *Mainzer Zeitung*, represented a major commitment of the Mainz democrats to an improved status for women. It also makes more intelligible the close relationship of women's rights efforts and the democratic movement, in spite of the undeniable hostility manifested by some elements within that camp. Besides the Mainz example female involvement with democratic clubs occurred in Berlin, Bonn, Breslau,

Burg, Hanau, and Worms, and further local research will no doubt turn up other examples.

The Mainz events represent only one example of how the revolution opened the door to feminist ideas. Other men showed sympathetic awareness of the new atmosphere. One male reviewer of a book on education for woman emphasized that it was appropriate to apply a "reasonable (idea) of freedom to the female sex" at a time of general progress toward freedom and independence. Another commentator observed that it was "always women who enter the list for their own freedom" since men usually were "more comfortable with their old mastery." Again the columns of *Didaskalia, Frauen-Zeitung,* and other newspapers bear out both these comments.[32]

The "reasonable idea of freedom" signified to some women an opportunity to use the new situation to advocate reform of the marriage laws to give them a greater degree of equality. This issue, with which Kathinka Zitz-Halein would be sympathetic, was highlighted in an essay by a "German Woman" in May 1848. Although it is unclear whether Zitz-Halein was the author, many of the ideas expressed in it were hers. The writer informed her readers that since the parliamentary delegates were about to draft a new legal and constitutional structure for Germany, this was the time to establish a new marital status for women. Adhering to the commonly held belief that men in gaining their own freedom would not deny it to women, she stressed that women no longer were content to occupy a slavelike position toward men but wished to be their "companions and friends." The idea of companionship appears frequently in the mid-nineteenth-century literature. The degrees of subjection forced on women by the marriage laws of the various German states were clear to her, and she also evinced a knowledge of the widely used French legal codes relating to marriage and regarded them as even more discriminatory toward women. For example, she pointed out that the codes barred a woman from taking possession of an inheritance without her husband's consent. She realized that a marriage contract could protect a woman's property rights but asked why a marriage was something against which a woman had to protect herself. The laws, she pointed out, also virtually permitted if not encouraged men to take mistresses, only requiring them to exercise some discretion. These were issues with which Zitz-Halein was familiar.

The current status of married couples indicated to the "woman" that men not only wanted to dominate the "external world" but also be "master at home" over wife, children, estate, and domestic affairs.

Nothing was left to the wife but the "tiresome details" of housekeeping, child rearing, and cooking. Instead, she advocated much greater equality within marriage. Henceforth, women should only bear the husband's name, share his social standing, and live where he wished. To raise themselves out of their "servitude," she urged women, both single and married, to unite and petition parliament for reform. They must become "free mothers of free sons," she called out, who in the future would proudly say, "I am a woman," instead of resignedly, "I am only a woman."[33]

The marriage reform issue remained alive during 1848.[34] Two newspaper stories from the Baden town of Offenburg reflect the interest in it. A humorous statement by several "country girls" provided evidence of a desire for new social relations between men and women. They complained about the unreasonable demands of the bachelor peasant boys who believed that once one had spoken to a girl he had a sole right to her company. The girls refused to be so bound and demanded the right to have a number of friends without any commitment. "That is culture, you peasant boys," the letter concluded. More serious was the article "Princesses and Middle Class Young Women," which stressed that not only princesses' marriages were arranged but so were those of many ladies of the middle class. "So low does one half of the human race exist under the raw strength of the other half," the article asserted, "that not once does it enjoy its full human rights but is treated like a thing or an object." The female writer wondered whether "in this matter we stand much above the barbarous east."[35]

How the revolution stimulated calls for a new domestic relationship between men and women was amusingly illustrated in a Frankfurt cartoon in 1848. It depicted a wife and four children behind a barricade of furniture and armed with pots, brooms, and stools facing the husband-father on the other side. The wife tells him: "Keep away from the barricade. I don't want you anymore as a domestic tyrant. The children scream, we'll elect another father. Long live the republic; long live Hecker. . . . The red flag is planted. Don't bother me or you'll have trouble." The intimidated husband urges his wife to be calm. "I'll make a new constitution on the spot," he pleads. "Take down the barricade. If parliament hears of this, I'll have a parliamentary investigating committee here. If you are no longer satisfied with me, better that you quietly take a co-regent."[36]

Calls for marriage reform were only one example of an awakening sensitivity to inequality. The organizing of gymnastic societies for women was another. Gymnastic activity in a modern sense took root in Germany in the early 1800s, and during the first half of the nineteenth century gymnastic associations were organized throughout the German states. Although persecuted by the German Confederation from 1820 to 1842 the societies numbered three hundred with ninety thousand members by 1847. Mainz was an active center of the gymnastics movement, and included among the six hundred members of the association in April 1848 were the progressive forces of the city, from future communists to moderate liberals. From their beginnings, and increasingly by 1848, the gymnastics associations were not merely exercise clubs but centers of support for liberalism, democracy, and national unity. Moreover, physical improvement was tied to the moral regeneration of the people, which would make the Germans more self-reliant and better able to defend their country.[37]

The first gymnastic association for females was probably organized toward the end of 1848 in Frankfurt, and it was sensitive to the broader implications of the movement. The membership was brought together in a bond of "true sisterhood" by a yearning for "freedom, strength and simplicity." It saw exercise as a means of achieving equality with men, who should not have the sole privilege of engaging in gymnastic activity. The club subscribed to *Frauen-Zeitung* and Louise Dittmar's short-lived *Soziale Reform* and swore to use only "pure German speech." The Frankfurt group (there may have been two) lasted only until the late spring of 1849, since many of its members seem to have been associated with the delegates to the national assembly, which collapsed at that time.[38]

If the gymnastic club for women in Frankfurt, as well as others in Dresden and Heidelberg, saw broader implications behind their activities,[39] the Leipzig association apparently did not. It was, however, the most successful of the known clubs, lasting at least two years and having ninety members. The reporter attributed its longevity to its modest aims, which were related to the natural capacities of women. It had no other purpose than physical improvement, so that women could bear and raise healthy children. Its exercises could be watched only by women, although they seem to have been led by men. Clothing would be appropriately modest, seemingly neutralizing hostility from "narrow-minded" individuals *(Spiessbürger)*. The Leipzig gymnasts, however, did have a feminist dimension. Rather than blindly copying male gymnastic patterns, women had to devise "uniquely feminine exercise routines," or aerobiclike movements, which would be somewhere between gymnastics and dance.[40] The lack of durability of these

81

first tentative steps by adult women to improve their physical well-being must be measured against the fact that from 1849 to 1859 men's gymnastics societies declined from three hundred to one hundred because of government persecution.[41]

Minna Zimmermann, from Königsberg, who was a regular contributor to *Frauen-Zeitung* on a variety of topics, analyzed the demise of the women's gymnastic societies. According to her, part of the problem was caused by the need to have male teachers, which may have made some women reluctant to become involved. She urged the rapid training of female instructors as a means of attracting more women. In a wider sense, however, this suggested to her the need for increased educational and job opportunities for women, which also emerged as an issue in 1848. One aspect of this issue was the kindergarten movement that developed out of the teachings of Friedrich Fröbel (1782–1852). Fröbel believed that a child's development was inhibited under traditional familial and school situations. In keeping with prevailing liberal ideals he stressed instead that education should liberate and prepare the child for a life of independence and civic responsibility. The newly established kindergartens, which grew rapidly from 1848, when forty-four were established, met with their most enthusiastic response from women. From the outset women made up almost the entire teaching corps. Unfortunately this enthusiasm was matched by the hostility of the German governments, which regarded them as nests of democratic subversion and eventually closed virtually every one. It is true that among the teachers were women whose husbands were in exile or in prison as a result of the spring 1849 uprising. But these women also had to fend for themselves. A report in *Frauen-Zeitung* described one such woman, Auguste Herz, the head of the Dresden kindergarten, which was closed by the police, as someone who had to live off the profits from her school. Her teachers also depended on their salaries to survive. Some of those involved in the movement saw an antifeminist attitude behind the government's policy. An article on the recently closed Breslau kindergarten asked: "Was it not really an unseemly departure from their (women's) normal sphere, a desire . . . to be independent" that led to the schools' prohibition? "The male dominated state has the legal right to punish this [activity] and reject those who encroach on its privileges." The evidence does not yet provide a conclusive answer to this question.[42]

These examples of women's reaching out for a new place in German society were supplemented by more far reaching demands for a new status for women. Although he does not mention it in his memoirs,

Bamberger was also in contact with Louise Dittmar (1807–1884), a writer, lecturer, and proponent of female emancipation. Born in Darmstadt, the child of a high-ranking government official, she as well as her father became known for their progressive views. In the foreword to her *Vier Zeitfragen* (Four Questions of the Day), she compares herself, as a woman, to the captain of a heavily laden ship who has to steer without a compass. She follows instead only her "inner urging," which carries her toward a vague goal, which she defines as "liberation from a pressure which I saw as a gigantic burden pushing down on humanity." This led her from a steady routine of domestic chores, to a path often and "not incorrectly" characterized as "hostile to domesticity and even to feminine destiny."[43] Nothing could have been further from Zitz-Halein's perceptions of a woman's role in society.

Dittmar's writings, which dealt with politics and religion, began to appear, at first anonymously, in the 1840s. Although she was strongly influenced by Hegel, Ludwig Feuerbach, and the utopian socialists, she also possessed the pen of a political pamphleteer. In her first work, *Bekannte Geheimnisse* (Open Secrets), she castigated the classical liberals of her day, ridiculing their symbol of moderation, "Mr. juste milieu." Disdainful of the man of the golden mean, she characterized him as follows: "As a yes man he was a determined legislator; . . . as a Jacobin he never entered the chamber; as an 'I' he has never made his weight felt; . . . as a minority he counts in the chamber; as a minor he lets his government act for him; as an adult he counts for the tax commissioner; as a stomach he can swallow anything."[44]

Although she initially focused on religion and politics, she was concerned about their relationship to the status of women, whose liberation she came to regard as her highest duty. History in her view was a vast conspiracy against women, who were "completely without rights." She believed that "all social institutions" either excluded or subordinated them through religious, economic, and legal relations and made man an "absolute monarch." She claimed that contemporary society denied the "feminine essence," forcing a woman to become what a man imagines her to be. Women, she maintained, had to fight the idea that they were destined to suffer and tolerate everything. She polemicized against the "cooked" *(verkochte)* and "ironed" *(verbügelte)* feminine existence to which all women were condemned, which made one at most a "chief maid" whose life, in her words, was a "mindless degeneration."[45] Marriages, too, were made unhappy by women's economic and political dependence, which relegated them to the propertyless classes. Restricting a woman's right to earn money, she maintained, meant robbing them of their human dignity. She first regarded all men as oppressors but came to realize that they too were social prisoners of the few. Only men's liberation, as part of a revolutionary transformation, would help make women aware of their own subordination and teach them how they could gain their rights. Only then could the "true significance of women's uniqueness" be grasped.[46]

Although encouraged in 1849 when the Frankfurt national assembly passed the Basic Rights of the German People, Dittmar warned that men, even if they spoke of all Germans, meant only themselves and their sons. She called men only the stepfathers of their daughters. The task for women, she emphasized, was not to wait passively for the state to do something for them but to take over the fight for their rights. And this included the right to an education and to child care and the right to establish small businesses dealing in household goods, to undertake artistic and scholarly projects, and to participate in "the totality" of life. Somewhat contradictorily, she expected state financial support for these endeavors.[47]

To achieve these goals, she admitted, would be difficult since it required more decisiveness and self-reliance than women normally possessed. She realized that besides the few "emancipated" women, among whom she presumably included herself, one needed "emancipating women." The task, and it was hers, was to awaken a sense of "self-esteem" in her sisters and lift them out of the "degradation" into which they had fallen. Women must learn to break free of their traditional activities, as she believed George Sand had, and recapture their true natures. Instilling a new consciousness in women involved making them understand how the progressive currents of the day could affect them. In carrying out her self-imposed charge she pioneered the arena of public speaking. Virtually unique in the pre-1848 period she gave at least one public lecture before a male audience, the Monday Club in Mannheim. It met with such opposition that she referred to it as the "Battle of Mannheim." Nevertheless, she continued her public lectures during and after the revolution, speaking in Mainz, Darmstadt, and Hanau to women's clubs and German Catholic groups.[48]

Sometime during 1848 Louise Dittmar delivered a series of lectures on women's emancipation to Mainz's Art Association, which seems to have been a women's organization. The content of her talks remains unrecorded, but clearly she stood for an idea of emancipation that transcended the principle of domestic equality that Zitz-Halein acknowledged. Dittmar refused to give ready credence to the notion of separate but equal spheres but suggested instead that women ought to be permitted to develop freely until truly natural obstacles prevented them from entering a certain field. She also avoided the regular positive references to masculinity that inhabited Zitz-Halein's poetry and prose. Dittmar in fact charged that men refused to grant that there was a more suitable life for women because of fear of surrendering some of their masculinity. It was probably Dittmar's outspokenness that caused Zitz-Halein to respond so negatively to her lectures in Mainz. The memory of Bamberger and Dittmar's striding into the lecture hall together remained etched in her memory and triggered a hostile comment in her "Skizzen." The Mainz poet accused Dittmar of trying to strip women of their essential femininity and of transforming them into hermaphrodites, "which belong neither to the one nor to the other sex." No "genuine woman" could accept this. She also pointed out that the lectures found little favor in Mainz because of both the radical nature of Dittmar's ideas and the politically and socially conservative outlook of the members of the Art Association, whom Zitz-Halein characterized as "true blue aristocrats." Why this supposedly aristocratic group would choose to hear Dittmar, introduced by the democratic radical, Bamberger, is not clear.[49]

Even if the response to Dittmar's talks was negative, it did not discourage Bamberger, who was the editor of *Mainzer Zeitung,* from running a series of articles dealing with the relationships among revolution, democracy, and female emancipation. Whether Bamberger and/or Dittmar was the author cannot be established, but it is likely that both were involved because of the repetition of certain ideas and the Hegelian style of argumentation. Apart from articles in Louise Otto's *Frauen-Zeitung,* this series represents the most serious journalistic discussion of the women's question during 1848–1849. The essays were printed under the titles "Politics and Life" and "On Women's Emancipation." The first involved an exchange of letters between "Maria and Karl," "Louise and Maria," and "Emma and Heinrich." In a reversal of roles it is Maria, the skeptic, who takes Karl to task because of his blindly enthusiastic support for the revolution, which to her seems to signify merely an exchange of masters. Rather than seeing progress in turbulence, she notes the human misery and deaths that it brings in its wake, all for the sake of political principle. The tone of the article is cold and factual even when the writer is mentioning love, hate, and humanity, in a way that might even be referred to as unfeminine.[50]

In fact when Karl replied a week later he first addressed the question of female authorship and tried to weave the issue of woman's character into those of revolution and democracy. He remarked that his friend refused to believe that the letter was written by a woman. Such sharp intellectual powers, such relentless logic, such an absence of warmth or fantasy, his friend argued, could not reside in a woman. For Karl this was evidence of how men judge women, purely on the basis of the caricatures presented in romantic novels. He "knew" that the letter was written by a woman because it betrayed what he called signs of a "feminine incompleteness." But here Karl shifted the argument. The incompleteness was not a product of nature but instead the result of generations of historical conditioning. Although women did not have less intellectual capacity than men, they did incline to one-sidedness, which arose from a lack of intellectual exercise and from restriction to a limited area rather than freedom to experience the universality of life.

Having in a backhanded way accepted Maria as at least potentially his intellectual equal, Karl then proceeded to attack her objections to the revolution. Rather than repeating Karl's rather academic arguments in favor of the revolution, it is worth stressing that he is not deferential to her but treats her opinions, although wrong, as worthy of careful refutation.[51] This exchange of views, although focused more on justifying the revolution than breaking new ground on the question of women's rights, did show a woman as an equal discussant with a man about a serious question.

It was nearly four weeks before a new exchange of letters appeared. A new correspondent, "Louise," enters the exchange and raises the question of how best to achieve women's rights.[52] That is the real issue, according to Louise. She finds in the harsh tone of Maria's letter to Karl a "false" approach to the issue of emancipation. She regards Maria as too critical of men, who individually, Louise emphasizes, are not to be blamed for the liabilities under which women labor. It is not they who are responsible for the deficiencies in female education that make women narrow and one-sided. The fault lies with an immature society. Louise accuses Marie of wanting her rights without running the risks that gaining those rights might entail. Women must defend and support the struggles of men, Louise stresses, because it is "our revolution," not just theirs. The revolution would lead to a democratic society, which Louise defined as "people becoming human." This would create the precondition for women's emancipation, which in Louise's words means "women becoming human." Only when men and women shared a common bond of humanity would their interests become one. But as a final caveat Louise warns Maria that it is foolish to want an identical form of life for both sexes "when nature enjoins something else."[53] This view that a "social" democracy, would, by its very essence, alter male-female relationships while improving the status of women illuminates the ideological dimension of this mid-nineteenth-century political belief. Furthermore, the fact that these serious analyses were presented by real or fictitious women was indicative of a new attitude, even if not necessarily a widespread one.

That every man did not share the expectations of a dawning new relationship betweeen the sexes was clear from the next installment of "Politics and Life." This time it is Emma replying to her brother, Heinrich, who complains that the new demands public life makes on him are difficult to accommodate to other domestic interests, such as business, study, and relaxation. At the beginning of the upheaval, Emma maintains, one did not realize that the changes that the revolution were bringing would penetrate each person's private life. She reminds her brother that even if his wife shares his intellectual tendencies it is difficult for her to adjust to the new demands on his time: the elections, clubs, and committees, "which you men tend to, out of necessity or fancy." Although Emma realizes that unsettled political conditions create additional obligations, she is amazed that Heinrich is using the new situation to demand that he be "more and more emancipated" from his domestic obligations, which of necessity fall to his "self reliant" wife. Under these circumstances, she warns, there might be friendly relations between them but never "a true unity, a merging of one with the other."[54]

This observation leads her to a discussion of the relationship of domestic to public life against the backdrop of the new principles of the day. Following Rousseau, she claims women of her ilk have come to believe in the "conscious participation of the individual in the general," and this transcends beyond merely opening public life to women. In modern terms Emma asks that the "occupational activity of men be joint property or at least comprehensible to us." It is the artificial division of responsibilities that makes women jealous of their husband's additional commitment to public affairs, their increased time spent among their male friends, and their striving for higher cultural attainments. It is no wonder, in Emma's view, that women regard these activities as taking something from them: that they make women's domestic and maternal obligations more distasteful and cause women to be more obstinate, whining, and petulant. In short women are worse wives and mothers because of their restricted sphere of activities. "We want to share [this other world] with you," she calls out.[55]

According to Emma, although men acknowledge that women have a right to a public life, they wonder about what limits this should have. In Emma's view it is like asking what the limits of freedom are. The limit to women's participation in public life, she maintains, should be determined by the capability of the participants. This is the only barrier that one has to respect. In this sense only does she regard emancipation as relative. She rejects any "arbitrary" limitation that men establish and "then have us believe is a limitation set by nature." Whatever limit might exist "can only be determined by our experience." Freedom, she informs him, may be wonderful, but "Do not expect of us what you cannot do yourselves—love this abstraction of freedom. . . . Only life produces life." Women, she points out, can only half experience all that men do, and "Even if you take us to your [Democratic Association] meetings we will never be so completely involved as you" since we "experience freedom only in the figure of a free man." "Make the effort," she pleads, "to share your democratic activity." Only in this way would she become a "good democrat" and not simply a "wife and daughter of a citizen."

In a similar vein Emma reminds Heinrich that men have to be involved in domestic life, and not merely superficially. To ignore this principle would be to countenance a kind of slavery. It is not a question of a specific commitment of time but depends on a variety of factors. Certainly, she admits, there is a limit, as with the participation of women in public affairs. "The modern household," it must be recognized, "relates to the old hearth as the democratic state to a bureaucratic state, as an organism to a machine." She calls on Heinrich to help develop democracy in domestic relations without fear of what his friends might say. Tell them, she advises him, "that they have not studied with sufficient care the chapter on love, marriage and domesticity in the book of democracy."[56]

Emma's letters with their cheerfully resolute tone sought to stake out a new position for women in German society without running the risk of being classified as "amazons" or Louise Astons. Although a new series of letters began two months later, they bogged down in Hegelian dialectics and were discontinued. Whether the exploding political crisis of the spring of 1849 crowded less essential matters from the newspaper or whether public reaction in an increasingly conservative atmosphere was negative is not ascertainable.

Although the public's response to these essays cannot be gauged, the theme of women's emancipation, much of it discussed negatively and with deprecating humor, was a regular subject in the press. *Fränkische Blätter* (Nürnberg) drew the pictorial contrast most directly between the "innocent" and the "emancipated" woman, the former depicted emerging from Adam's rib and the latter, dressed in men's clothing, lecturing a class of male university students in a way that was not flattering to her or without sexual innuendo. In one sense this was an advance. Two years before, the *Fliegende Blätter* had depicted an "emancipated women" merely as a student.[57] Similar uneasy attitudes about the liberating atmosphere of 1848–1849 were expressed in a satirical article, "The Women": "Sentimental women are like roses; they are out of style. The domestic ones are like buttercups; they almost never crop up anymore. The modest are like edelweiss; they are rare and hard to find. The emancipated ones are like daisies; one finds them frequently on country lanes. . . ."[58]

Specific disapproval of the surfacing interest of women in civic affairs was not long in coming. In a story about conditions in Offenbach the reporter described a couple who had lived in harmony until the revolution, but now a fanaticism had taken hold of the wife. "She glows for the republic; she goes to bed with the republic, rises with the republic, visits the Frankfurter parliament, makes eyes at the extreme left, and is in the process of organizing a women's association on the broadest basis." The *Fliegende Blätter*'s illustrations also expressed their disapproval of women's attending parliamentary gatherings, in one case showing a browbeaten and harried husband trying to cope with the children, and in another capturing a woman too exhausted from her parliamentary viewing and from reading about the radicals Hecker and Struve to care for the children.[59] Political activity by a woman could even be grounds for divorce, suggested *Mainzer Tagblatt* in its article "An Anti-social Husband." It described the divorce action by a man whose wife wanted to hear a "socialist apostle preach." Forbidden to go, she attends nevertheless, and makes a toast to the elimination of husbands. The writer, umsympathetic to women's emancipatory strivings, suggests that the case will decide whether husbands can forbid their wives to make speeches at political banquets. This may have been a real issue in Mainz, for in March 1849 the Democratic Association held a huge political banquet to commemorate the revolution, which was probably the spur to the article.[60] More patronizing but equally unsympathetic to women's liberating aims was the poem "To My Little Darling Who Wants to Be Emancipated," in which the husband charges his wife with desiring to "run your affairs by yourself, my pretty little Jacobin, and also have your say in politics." He realizes that she was drawing the logical conclusions from his own teachings of freedom, equality, and human rights. But this time, he explains to her, "My child, let me teach you with kisses; . . . you've understood me so poorly."[61]

Hostility to women's involvement in politics extended to opposition to their organizational activities, which, as will be seen in the next chapter, were quite extensive in 1849. In the "Harangue of a Mainzer (Petty Bourgeois) to His Wife Who Like All Women Is Much Inclined to Agitation," he tongue-lashes his wife for reading the "accursed" democratic *Mainzer Zeitung* rather than the more conservative Catholic *Mainzer Journal.* She sits around all day and bothers herself about politics "instead of darning and housekeeping." He relates that she is busy with the Humania Association, helping political refugees, and dresses up to attend its meetings, even wearing "your brooch." She is the talk of the town, called a republican, making him worried that he will lose all his customers as other republican craftsmen have. Look at the fate of the democrats, he whines: hanged, shot, in exile, or in prison. It will happen to him, he laments, all because of her red ribbon, and so on. The same theme appears in "Jeremiad of a Quiet German Citizen," in which the wife is accused of consorting with "red republicans." The article, which probably appeared first in Munich's *Fliegende Blätter,* was later reprinted in at least Mainz and Hamburg.[62]

Fliegende Blätter on another occasion depicted a "Political Ladies' Club" with Louise Aston presiding and the equally emancipated Emilie Lehmann speaking, calling for an end to darning stockings and a prohibition against men's going out without women. The story was accompanied by an illustration of a disorderly meeting of women. The same negative image is given in a report about the "Club of the Free Women," in which demands for more rights were to be enforced by withholding kisses.[63] In Berlin readers were treated to the "stern lecture" that "Herr Bullrig," a civic guardsmen, delivered to his wife, who wanted to join a democratic women's club. His dressing-down contained suggestions of neglect of domestic responsibilities and of sexual misbehavior at these clubs due to George Sand's immoral influence. Politics, he warns his spouse, are the "affair of us men." There was a similar intimation in a cartoon portraying a "small town communist club," which showed men and women sitting and drinking around a table, demanding an end to marriage. There was some substance to this image in Mainz. In the aftermath of the revolution Philipp Wasserburg, an 1848 democratic radical and later Center party politician, organized a group of young workers and soldiers into a "Communist" discussion club that aimed to collect enough money so its members could migrate to the United States. The statutes, besides rejecting property, money, and parental control, proclaimed that a marriage should last only as long as the love between the two parties. Women attended the meetings, although it is not known whether they were formal members.[64]

To balance these unsympathetic viewpoints there did appear a few positive portrayals of women's new role in the revolution. A frequent theme involved the new consciousness of female servants. As early as April 1848 several stories appeared about a meeting of servants in Leipzig. Although it was labeled a "curiosity" by *Didaskalia* the affair was taken seriously and reported sympathetically by the journal. A servant read a list of demands that included a raise in wages, improved quarters (no longer in the topmost reaches of the attic),[65] better food when there is heavy work to do, permission to retire at 10:00 P.M. if there are no unusual problems, and the right to go out once every four weeks. The demands were voted on and approved in spite of the catcalls from the male spectators. Other stories and cartoons pictured children's maids and cooks reading newspapers and a maid demanding her rights from her employer from behind a barricade. These included greater freedom of speech and time to see her boyfriend. Another shows a cook carrying weapons to her less than conscientious master, who is a member of the civic guard. In Mainz female servants protested against new regulations governing their activities.[66]

Other forms of appropriate behavior by women included the efforts by Leipzig women to organize a Blum Foundation on behalf of his widow and children. The article applauded the efforts to establish a "living monument" to Blum by purchasing his house and turning it into an orphanage for children of patriots. Although the political struggle falls to the men, the reporter emphasized, women have the calling to "pave the way for the social uplifting and resurrection of the nation. . . ."[67]

Typical of the mixed reaction that women's activities provoked was the case of Amalie Struve, whose husband was the radical republican Gustav Struve. She married Struve in 1845 and became his constant companion and political aide, rejecting the notion that a wife was only around to fulfill domestic obligations. In her view what made a woman more than a housekeeper was her sharing the entire life of her husband, including his "patriotic" activity. Being excluded from her husband's political life, as she was once during the 1848–1849 period, made her aware of the "unworthy" position in which the female sex was held. According to a report in *Frankfurter Journal* Struve was often criticized by other republicans because he let his wife attend political discussions and even appear on the field of battle. The report blamed his wife for the fact that Struve had been captured during the September 1848 uprising. It was her presence that gave him away. A caricature of the time portrayed Struve as an owl and his wife as a dove and suggested that because of their different natures they should have no children. It also intimated marital infidelity by Amalie Struve.[68] Her capture and seven-month imprisonment, however, evoked sympathy, at least in Mainz, where one report pointed out that even though women had no political rights they could be branded as political criminals. Also sympathetic toward Amalie Struve's efforts was the reviewer of her *Erinnerungen aus den badischen Freiheitskämpfen* (Memoirs of the Badenese Fight for Freedom). He pointed out, as Zitz-Halein had previously, that whereas men were praised for the virtues of courage, determination, sacrifice, and efforts to transform ideal into reality, when women demonstrated these characteristics they called forth a certain repugnance in men. Their appearance in women suggested that they had left the traditional track of feminine activity and that they risked losing "what we call their femininity." Amalie Struve's book, the reviewer continued, demonstrated that "there are women who are capable of achieving the highest regions of thought and action without for a moment relinquishing the noblest feminine morals." He praised her for attempting to widen the patriotic horizons of women.[69]

A poem best expressed the prevailing ambivalent attitude about women on the eve of the spring 1849 uprising. Entitled "To the Truly German Woman" it sought to strike a balance between the demands of the new age and the constraints of the old tradition.[70] On the one hand, the poet could not suffer a woman who knew only knitting, children's things, and feminine gossip, while having no sense for Goethe, Schiller, and Shakespeare, or did not glow with the same patriotism as he. At the same time he would honor only those women who "did not concern themselves with things which are only for men," who never forgot their tenderness, and who wanted nothing other than to educate children. As for "women with the pen or the paint brush in the hand! O, how miserable and how pedestrian, and how great the stupidity!" The rest of this section continues:

> If the woman succeeded
> To be creative for a time,

> Well! She pulled herself up
> At the price of her femininity
>
> And if she even boasts . . .
> Of wanting to stand, to wield a weapon . . .
> Then femininity is over.
> Or also—She is crazy.

Ultimately women had to know their place.[71]

Among the more novel aspects of the public discussion of women's role in society were the plays written on the subject, of which there were at least three. In Mainz Christoph Dumont was the author of *The Emancipation of Women*. Set in Constantinople in 1848 and early 1849, it concerned the efforts of the women of the sultan's harem to initiate a revolution against him in emulation of the French and German upheavals. The women wished to achieve "personal freedom and emancipation," although part of the motivation is the chief wife's love affair with the French ambassador who plans the revolt. It succeeds and she becomes regent. She then decides to implement female emancipation even though warned against acting too hastily. She abolishes slavery and introduces a "humane" republic. Not only does she free women and abolish polygamy for men, she also decides to right the wrongs done to the female sex over the ages. Only women can vote and hold office; since they mature earlier than men they can vote at fifteen and be elected to parliament at eighteen.[72] The new constitution introduced restrictive laws against men who must be home after dark and can be exiled to Siberia for marital infidelity. Women, on the contrary, are permitted polygamy. Such drastic changes cause the men to revolt, forcing the revolutionary leaders to flee to France and resulting in a restoration of the old regime. Rather than being a play only about women's rights it was a commentary about the German revolution from a moderate liberal point of view. Excesses were spoiling the chances for any progress, leaving the people to suffer for the actions of the radical leaders who fled abroad. The issue of women's rights was the vehicle to make a more general point.[73]

It is thus clear from these examples that women were not only a peripheral element during the revolutionary upheavals but that their initiatives made an impact on the public's consciousness even if society was clearly not yet prepared to accept them in a new role. Nevertheless, there was a perceptible stream, whether main- or otherwise, of women's participation in the revolution, and Zitz-Halein, as much as any woman, was in the middle of it.

6
Zitz-Halein and 1848
Literature and Politics

*B*eginning at the end of February 1848 and continuing for four years, Kathinka Zitz-Halein carried on a wide range of a activities in support of the German Revolution and of those men and women who were committed to it. In doing so she became the center of a network involving hundreds of like-minded people of both sexes throughout Germany who belonged to the democratic camp. Through her literary work, travels, reportage, fund-raising, and organizational accomplishments she did more than virtually any other woman and most men to further the cause of democracy in her native land. These efforts by Zitz-Halein and other women were not simply the product of momentary enthusiasm for the cause; most men were willing to grant this. Women also demonstrated dedication, discipline, tenacity, and organizational talents of a high order. As we have seen, Zitz-Halein had also been one of the most active female protagonists of political and social reform within the German Confederation before 1848. The outbreak of the revolution, with the attendant granting of civil rights, made it possible for her to continue her literary-political efforts without constant concern about the censor.

As a result of the growing political agitation in Mainz between February 28 and March 6 the Hessian government capitulated to the popular movement. The disliked minister, Du Thil, was removed and replaced by the liberal, Heinrich von Gagern, while Grand Duke Ludwig stepped aside designating his son. Freedom of the press and freedom of assembly were granted, as was the right to petition. The powers of the police were restricted and a citizens' militia was organized. The duke made additional promises of a new constitution, a democratic voting law, and the subjection of the military to the framework of the new constitution. These events in Hesse were part of a German-wide trend during the March days, but there too the main task of the revolution became preservation of the March achievements and to translate the promises into laws.[1]

Kathinka Zitz-Halein's participation in the revolutionary movement was in keeping with her pre-1848 actions. Within a few days of the outbreak of the revolution in Paris, but even before the revolutionary disturbances in Germany had had an impact, she captured the spirit of the Mainz revolution in a series of poems. "Out of Favor," the first, attacks the conservative regime by cataloguing the abuses of the pre-March Hessian government.[2]

Who after all is out of favor,
Can't you tell me?
Out of favor is whoever thinks,
Out of favor is whoever speaks,
And who devotes himself
To the interests of the nation.
Yes, he is most disliked,
And remains so for all time.

Out of favor is who demands
Elimination of censorship,
Who intoxicated by freedom of the press
Follows the trail of the new spirit,
Who names reduction of taxes
The duty of the ruler.
O, he is most disliked
And remains so until the end.

Out of favor is who limits
Hunting privileges.
Out of favor is who proposes
Equality before the law.
Do not demand openness
Of judicial proceedings,
Otherwise you're most disliked,
And remain so for all time.

Out of favor is the brazen one
Who has the impudence
To speak against annuities
And against gifts to friends.
And who in budgetary matters
Wants prudent management.
Yes, he is most disliked
And remains so for all time.

Kathinka Zitz-Halein

By contrast, she continues:

> Who holds his tongue
> With slavish patience
> Will always enjoy
> The all highest favor.
> The yes men who nod
> As soon as the state wishes,
> They are in good graces,
> They are worthy of favor.
>
> Who with bent back
> Associates with the court party,
> The puppet whose strings
> The minister holds,
> On him one bestows
> Medals rather than chains,
> Names the conservative
> The bravest man in the land.
>
> One calls him the very best gear
> In the state machine,
> The firm pillar of the throne,
> The wisest head in the state.
> Thus the courtier proceeds
> Along his path.
> But the man of the people remains
> Out of favor for all time.

A few days, later in early March, but still before the initial gains had been won, she sought to encourage the burgeoning popular movement. "It's Fermenting," she chose as the title of a second poem.[3]

> Spring is coming; the sprig of hope is growing.
> The clouds flee, which shroud the light.
> Who does not know how to break his chains,
> He deserves always to be in chains.
> Stand firm you men, be ready for battle,
> Demand the rights which are due the people,
> Don't let yourselves continue like helpless sheep,
> To be led on a leash by those in authority.
> The juice is fermenting; it's turning into clear
>   wine.

> The people have ripened to maturity;
> No longer may they waver or flinch.
> Who seizes the moment knows
> The hour for bold action has struck.
> O, people claim your natural rights. . . .

In the final stanza, however, she cautioned against excesses.

> We want neither pillage nor princely murder,
> We do not want to turn the world upside down.
> We want . . . to fight unjust forces.
> Only what the age requires, that we demand.
> What was promised us many years ago
> As the guarantee of happiness, that we demand. . . .
> You princes, give it, and honor will be yours.
> The juice is fermenting, it's turning to clear wine.

The need to contain the popular demonstrations within peaceful channels and to avoid the lure of demagogues was reemphasized in "True Freedom." It was not "raw, wild freedom" which was needed, Zitz-Halein began, but a "nobler product," which "teaches respect for the laws," "increases morality," "seeks only good," and does not, "inflamed by greed, curse everyone who is rich." Be generous toward the vanquished "great ones," she askes, "let us not make ourselves base through envy." She warned against would-be popular leaders, "the comedians of freedom," "empty shells without a core, who only coquette with freedom." Instead, leaders were needed who not only "cleverly fight abuses, with the holy force of truth" but "also dampen the flames of unrestrained passion." This may have been a criticism of her estranged husband whose inflamatory oratory had galvanized the population of the Mainz area.[4]

Of particular interest to Kathinka Zitz-Halein was the fact that Franz Zitz had emerged as the unchallenged leader of the progressive forces. It was his threat to lead a people's march on Darmstadt, the Hessian capital, that caused the government to proclaim its reforms. In honor of this accomplishment it was he who gave the keynote address at the festivities of March 8 to celebrate the recent gains and herald the coming new age. Zitz-Halein made a special point of hearing his speech. Although no doubt clouded by bitterness, her evaluation of it was astute. His flowery and rather melodramatic oration she characterized as full of empty phrases. Instead of trying to raise the people to a higher level, he lowered himself to theirs, making himself into a "popular buffoon" who "amused the plebes." She later also correctly noted Zitz's need to move to the Left in order to stay in touch with the popular mood and raised questions about the sincerity of his convictions. His discovery of the fatherland and his support for popular rights were in her view of recent vintage, motivated by his need for popular acclaim and his political ambitions. Although there is strong evidence to corroborate her analysis, Zitz, once in the democratic camp, proved to be a sincere and effective leader, even at the cost of later exile.[5]

When the achievement of civil rights in Mainz and Hesse was followed a few days later on March 13 by the dismissal of Metternich, Zitz-Halein's joy increased still more. She rhapsodized in "Autodafé"[6]:

> Three cheers for Austria
> For constitutional rule.
> It's getting light in that land
> The sun of freedom is shining brightly. . . .
>
> The German is a free man,
> And not a Russian slave.

This new freedom was best symbolized by a report that the Austrian troops in Mainz were burning the canes used for administering corporal punishment. She hoped it would be banished from the criminal code.

> Dishonoring to the man is the punishment
> Whose skin must suffer it.
> More dishonoring is it for the one
> Who dictates such punishment.

Even the news from Bavaria seemed to be following the same German trend, although associated with the activities of Lola Montez. The English-born adventuress had managed to win the affection of the Bavarian ruler, Ludwig, and through him aspired to political and social influence. Although Lola failed to become a durable political force in Bavaria and instead served as a lightning rod for popular opposition, Kathinka Zitz-Halein saw her in a positive light. In her poem, "Lola," she portrays the woman as a Judith who, instead of killing with a sword, used a riding whip to free her Bavarian Holophernes from the clutches of "ultramontane slavery" and "priestly obscurantism."

> Scarcely had Lola entered
> She flung suddenly
> The liberal torch
> Into the royal chambers.

Instead of ruining the people as mistresses had in the past, Zitz-Halein concluded, now "Mistresses serve to liberate the people." Lola was saluted as one who had transformed herself from an "emancipated one into an emancipator of the people." "Providence," she called out, "completely unfathomable are your ways." Zitz-Halein's other references to Lola were generally critical because of the latter's unfeminine behavior, but her apparent political accomplishments overrode other considerations. It was a concession she would grant to few women.[7]

The revolutionary process of the early spring retained its momentum. The first steps to create a united German state were taken at the end of March at the meeting of the Preliminary Parliament, which set elections for a national assembly to meet in Frankfurt. Kathinka Zitz-Halein cheered the political progress in her poetry. In April on the occasion of the death of Franz Mämpel, one of the leaders of Mainz's gymnastics movement, which had served as a center of political opposition, she again attacked the old order and celebrated the new. She memorialized the deceased leader and praised the people of Mainz.[8]

> You witnessed the time so serious and stormy
> In which the people have muzzled the princes. . . .
> You experienced the time in which the barriers
>   gave way
> In which soldier and citizen joined hands in
>   brotherhood
> In which bands of love encased the German heart
> And whole battalions went over to the people.

She hailed the citizens of Mainz for their achievement.

> To the people which judges the princes,
> And achieves a place in world history;
> To the people which cleverly drove out the
>   bureaucratic pack
> Which, desirous only of plunder, was cowardly and
>   corrupt;

Kathinka Zitz-Halein

> To the people, whom the government saw as a beast
>   of burden
> Which has now shown that it can stand as one man.

Those who did not favor freedom she wrote off as "bastards, unworthy of our fraternity." Now, she charged her readers, it was time to focus on May 4, the date of the election to the national assembly in Frankfurt, and to elect men who who knew how to "use the freedom to make laws which protect our rights." But if they show themselves hesitant, she warned,

> Then we'll know how to fight, and consecrate our
>   blood
> To the great holy cause which urges us to action.
> Then the last restraints which have restricted us
>   up to now will fall.

This poem, written at the end of April 1848, was the high point of her optimism. The democratic revolt in April led by the Badenese radical Friedrich Hecker and the exiled Georg Herwegh was defeated. The elections to the national assembly failed to produce a democratic majority but instead a moderate liberal one. The first successful step in the postelection counterrevolution occurred in Mainz. There a citizens' militia had been organized with Franz Zitz as the commander and weapons procured. As the guard drilled on a regular basis tension developed between the citizens of Mainz and the Prussian garrison. On the night of May 20, after a series of clashes between Mainz civilians and Prussian soldiers, the military commander demanded the disarming of the guard, threatening to bombard the city if he were not obeyed. Rather than run the risk of large-scale destruction, especially since the Prussian army commanded the heights with its artillery, Zitz convinced the members of the guard to surrender their weapons. A debate over the Mainz Affair in the Frankfurt assembly was inconclusive.[9]

These events constituted a turning point in the revolution, with the more radical elements, among which Zitz-Halein now counted herself, losing control of the situation. In "March Violets," while celebrating the blossoming of the long-suppressed freedom, she captured the changing situation and the outlines of future events. She detected an old spirit[10]:

100

Again authority is pretentiously extending its
    sway.
We're bearing the burden once more.
And what we got provisionally as a prelude
That has already been taken back in Baden
(And since then it has happened in Mainz
    through brutal military force)
....
There sit men imprisoned in dungeons
Who dared let fly the arrow from the bow
....
We have missed the favorable moment.
Now the princes say, "You have dreamed of
    freedom.
We'll send our own kind to the parliament
And make a quick end to the goings on."
Be constantly on guard, my people,
Do not let one intimidate you.
If the violet, happy and fresh, is to transfix you
    again,
You must water it with your life's blood.

She perceived further difficulties in religious issues. The revolutionary year in Mainz brought forth not only a broadly based democratic movement but smaller competing organizations of moderate liberals and Catholics. Some the latter formed themselves into the Pius Association, named for Pius IX, which became the nucleus of political Catholicism throughout Germany during the revolution. Since Mainz had a Catholic majority and a long history as a center for Catholicism, the strength of the association was potentially great. The Pius Association charged the democratic elements with hostility to religion, particularly to Catholicism, and with seeking to undermine religious influence in the schools. The dispute brought Kathinka Zitz-Halein's deep-rooted anticlerical attitude, which had flashed in the "Lola" poem, to the surface in "Party Spirit." She regarded a separate Catholic organization as an attempt to sow discord within the city. Behind it she saw the "forces of darkness," who were "scornful of freedom," and whose electoral slogan was, "It shall remain the same." But the time was past, she claimed, when people would be so easily influenced by appeals to prejudice and religious passions.

You fools you, who mistake the spirit
Because you cling blindly to formalities,

> You fools you who call everyone a heretic
> Whose brighter spirit does not think like yours,
> ....
> The free spirit no longer lets itself be bottled up.
> It celebrates its resurrection.
> ....
> It teaches loudly from pulpit and rostrum
> According to Christ's teachings, that God is love.
> Each prays to him in his own way. . . .
> Whether one calls himself Christian or heathen
> Whether he is Catholic or Protestant
> Whether he confesses to Mohammad's teachings
> Whether he is a Jew—he stands in God's hands.

In her ecumenical way and with the usual masculine overtones she concluded, "We are convinced of the truth that we are a great people of brothers." The Pius Association remained an active force in Mainz during 1848–1849, but it never rivaled the much larger Democratic Association.[11]

Her sensitivity to some of the problems which the democratic movement in Mainz and Germany faced included an awareness of social misery, which had been accentuated by the turmoil caused by the revolution. Kathinka Zitz-Halein added her voice to the previously cited articles in the *Didaskalia,* writing two poems in defense of the textile workers. In "Distress Call" and "Hunger Hurts So Much," she tried to focus attention on the distress in Germany, especially among the Silesian weavers, which she claimed exceeded that of Ireland.[12]

> O hear the laments of the poorest,
> O German land arise and collect
> Donations to strengthen the weak.
> German women, join together and ignore
> The French and English trifles;
> Make it your principle to wear
> From now on only German textiles.

Her attention to political and social problems in Germany included support for the national issue when it emerged immediately in the form of the Schleswig-Holstein question. The attempt by the Danish government to integrate more fully the two predominately German-speaking provinces led to military hostilities between Denmark and the German Confederation that aroused the national consciousness of the German people. Volunteers streamed northward to reclaim German land. In Mainz Kathinka Zitz-Halein organized a collection of supplies for Germans fighting in the north and attached a poem, "To the Schleswig-Holsteiners." Besides praising her compatriots for wishing to "save your Germaness" and to "procure a free existence for yourselves", she also underlined the female nature of her efforts. "That is all our sex can do," she added in an addenda to the poem, "for we do not belong to the hermaphrodites who want to march along and fight. We recognize the calling of women only in feminine endeavors," which she defined as healing, pacifying, and reconciling. "In this way all Germany will constantly find us ready to serve and be useful." How this modest statement fitted in with the inflamatory poetry she was capable of composing only highlights again the need to look behind her self-denying statments at her deeds. The military command thanked Zitz-Halein for her efforts and assured her that her poem would get the widest circulation in the press. The Mainz city librarian, Haas, asked her for a copy of the poem for his institute and noted how popular the piece had become.[13]

This first barrage of poems in spring 1848 represented a continuation and evolution of the political and social themes that she developed before 1848. Politically, however, she moved more decisively to the Left, even if finding the democratic leaders, Zitz and Bamberger, less than her ideal. This suggests the firmness of her principles, rather than personalities. Impressive too, is the wide range of subjects she addressed in her poems. They seem to have had an echo in and beyond Mainz. Most them appeared in broadsheet or pamphlet form as *Volksgedichte* and *Zeitgedichte* or were printed in the *Rheinische Blätter* or the *Didaskalia*. They were also passed from hand to hand or stuck on walls.[14] After this initial outburst of poetry her lyrical voice was relatively silent for the rest of the year, except for a remembrance to the executed revolutionary, Robert Blum.[15]

Although Kathinka Zitz-Halein took advantage of the end of censorship to express herself without inhibition, she remained vigilant for attacks on her reputation. Toward the end of 1848 she became embroiled in another struggle with a publisher, Otto Spamer of Leipzig, because of a supposedly defamatory book that his press issued. Written under a pseudonym, *Ein Tag in der Paulskirche* (A Day in St. Paul's Church) contained a number of attacks on the democratic delegates to the German national assembly, including Franz Zitz. In his biographical sketch of her husband, the author repeated the story that Zitz-Halein had never been his wife in fact but only in name.

According to the writer, Zitz left his wife at the church door immediately after the ceremony and never lived with her. In this depiction the author was merely repeating what Zitz himself had said about his marriage, but now, Zitz-Halein reasoned, this malicious fabrication would get national attention. She reacted in her typically energetic fashion and as with the earlier Bekker and Kalisch affairs became single-minded in pursuit of her perceived defamer. She wrote several newspaper editors who reviewed the book, denying the printed version, and sued Spamer, demanding that he name the author or publicly apologize for the misstatements. Spamer tried to stall and then squirm out of responsibility, but ultimately after activating the Saxon and Leipzig authorities, she forced him to issue the requested apology and retraction. Zitz-Halein believed she knew which "woman" in Mainz had leaked the story to the author, and attacked her enemy in a novella. Later she may have blackmailed the woman, a conservative, into giving financial support to the Humania Association by threatening to reveal her role in the affair publicly. It was both a legal and a personal triumph of which she was proud.[16]

The spring 1849 uprising and its defeat stirred Zitz-Halein to new literary and political efforts. In March after completing its work on the constitution the Frankfurt assembly offered the crown of a united and liberal Germany to the Prussian king, Frederick William IV. When the King refused the call, the majority of the national assembly was unwilling to proceed further and the body began to disintegrate. At the same time, in May, the extreme Left of the parliament issued a call to arms to defend the constitution.[17] The Mainz democracy organized a military contingent of one thousand men under the leadership of Zitz and Bamberger to join other rebel forces in the Palatinate. The unit was soon driven out of its headquarters in Kirchheimbolanden by the Prussians and experienced the general defeat of the insurgent forces.

Kathinka Zitz-Halein now identified completely with the radical democratic forces, as her 1849 poems make clear. They appeared in the Mainz newspapers, often were issued individually as broadsides, and were published later in her collected works. In the earliest poem of this period, "As in Earth So in Heaven," she celebrated the spring uprising as a revolt in the heavens carried out by the "comets with long democratic beards," the clouds, who "run up the red flag," and the Pleiades who tear up the paving stones from the Milky Way to build barricades. The sun, however, threatens those revolting with severe punishment, which Zitz-Halein put in the form of the last names of the Prussian and Austrian military leaders who were suppressing revolts: "Wrangel(n), Jellatschitz(en) and Windischgrätz(en)." In this way "The princes will accomplish it," she warned, "and before you even realize it, bring you back to the old yoke."[18]

When the victory of the counterrevolutionary forces was clear she sought in a series of poems not to deny the victory but to prevent her compatriots from sinking into dispair. In "The Nightmare" she depicted the the impact of the conservative resurgence on the people.[19]

> Head bowed, as if cursed by God
> The people slink by one another
> As if no one any longer trusts his brother;
> Even loved ones are divided,
> Between child and parent anger rules,
> Their hearts long united in love,
> Now torn asunder by politics.
>
> Many stand with sunken courage
> Choking on their quiet fury.
> The flowers reek of shed blood,
> The heavy air murmers treachery.

Not one to wallow in self-pity when it came to public affairs she next lashed out at one of the groups whom she considered was responsible for the triumph of the Right, conservative Catholics. Although a German Catholic, Zitz-Halein always supported progressive elements within the Catholic church, and in "Black Brotherhood" she attacked the religious conservatives around the recently appointed Mainz bishop, Wilhelm Emmanuel Ketteler.[20] "Yes, the moles are mighty, even if at the same time vile," she began, and they "quickly gnaw away at the roots which promise delight to humanity."

> We must strive to root out their brood,
> Chase them out of their narrow
> Artfully designed crooked passageways
> Which they have troubled to bore,
> The straight path is the best.
> Chase out the terrible guests
> So that health and happiness bloom.

If the enemy was not to be left in peace but uncovered, so too were the vanquished not to be forgotten. In response to the defeat at Kirchheimbolanden, which resulted in the deaths of a number of insurgents, Zitz-Halein wrote, "The Baptism of Blood," which was addressed to the women of Mainz. She urged them to help raise funds for a memorial tablet so that the heroic effort would always be remembered.

> Then in future days when we no longer live
> The father will tell his son of you.
> The monument which you have erected
> Tells the entire land
> How the women of Mainz constantly
> Acknowledged and honored great deeds.

Copies of her poem were sold for that purpose.[21]

In August 1849 Zitz-Halein was in Mannheim to witness the trials of the insurgents. Prussia, in contrast to Saxony and Bavaria, dealt harshly with the defeated rebels, utilizing special "martial law courts" to mete out nearly one thousand convictions, including a number of death sentences. Using these experiences, which took place amid a growing reactionary wave, as subjects for her poetry, she paid homage to two executed revolutionaries, the aristocrat, Wilhelm von Trützschler, and the plebian, Carl Höfer. Trützschler from Saxony, was a founding member of the extreme Left faction (*Donnersberg*) of the national assembly. During the spring 1849 uprising he served the revolutionary government of Baden and was taken prisoner when the Prussians occupied Mannheim. Tried and found guilty of treason, he was executed on August 14. Three days later Carl Höfer, a school teacher who had served as a captain in the revolutionary army was also tried, convicted, and executed, leaving behind a wife and small children.[22]

Zitz-Halein's efforts on behalf of the two men were substantial. Besides raising money for Höfer's widow, she reported on the trials in a series of articles. Making sure that the real heroes of 1848–1849 were not forgotten, she tried to immortalize the men as martyrs to the revolution by stressing the widespread support they had from the local population.[23] In her poems, which were printed along with her reports, Zitz-Halein warned the conservatives that the executions would avail them little, for freedom was like a polyp which would grow a new head to replace the one it had lost. Even if it was "one martial law trial after another," and even if Mannheim would "in the future be called Mordheim" (home of murder), she proclaimed, "the dream of Germany's freedom" could not be murdered. The torch of freedom and enlightenment had reached the lowest classes and could no longer be extinguished.[24]

> Fatherland your light is gloomy, your sun is
>   clouded over,
> For the best of your sons are being cruelly
>   slaughtered. . . .
> But you who lie buried under flowers
> You haunt the people's minds, . . .
> To awaken by a heavenly sign the people's sunken
>   courage. . . .
> Many will yet follow you, streams of blood will
>   flow,
> Many prison doors will still close behind victims,
> Long will there be tears, tears and curses,
> But the bloody seed will bear bloody fruit.

The most powerful of this series of poems and certainly the most explicit in its attack on the conservatives was "The Widows." Suggested by her experience in Mannheim, it deals with a dream which an unnamed King [of Prussia], during which he is confronted by the widows of the slain revolutionaries, Robert Blum, Ernst von Biedenfeld, Gustav Tiedemann, Carl Höfer, Wilhelm von Trützschler, and Georg Böhning.

> He [the king] dreams he stood in a sea, yet it was
>   a sea of blood,
> And ever higher climbed the dark red tide
> Until it reached his heart. Then suddenly he saw
>   rising
> Out of the depths, the bullet ridden corpses.
> And on the shore stood many women serious and pale
> Like mournful frightening apparitions out of a
>   distant ghostly realm.
> The mouths remained mutely closed. The eyes shot
>   sparks
> Which burned painfully the swimmer in the dark
>   sea.
>
> "Away you pale skulls!" so calls out, full of fear
>   and dread,
> The man in the sea, trying to ward off the dead.
> "Who are those black clad ghostly figures on shore
> Who rivet me with their angry scornful stares?"

Kathinka Zitz-Halein

A woman speaks, until now quiet and still:
"Listen O exalted butcher of people, I am Eugenia
    Blum.
Look at that pale skull there on the bloody waves
That was my husband Robert, he began it.

"He fell first in the sacred struggle,
For the rights of Germans, he watered the earth
    with blood.
The other skulls, all of them you had shot,
A sea of their blood engulfs you every evening."

The king tries to deny his responsibility, but one after another the widows accuse him. In turn they charge him with being the "massacrer" of their husbands, a "slaughterer of human beings," a "murderer," a "blood drenched person," a "Caligula." Trützschler's widow tells him

What did my husband do to you? Tell me his
    offense.
Had he shed blood? Was he rapacious? Did he
    commit a crime?
You called him a traitor
Merely to excuse your murderous deed—you are the
    evildoer.

The frightened king awakes, shakes off his nightmare as a child's fantasy that does not scare heroes. The people must be kept in the chains of the earthly authorities, he concludes, and he has the judges called to continue the martial law trials.[25]

The poem, when reprinted later in 1849 in the *Kasteler Beobachter,*[26] led the Prussian and Austrian authorities to raid the printer's offices in search of the manuscript and to ban the newspaper. In its original form and when reprinted the poem had appeared anonymously. However, the printer named Zitz-Halein as the author, and, charged with lèse majesté, she faced the prospect of a ten-year prison sentence. According to her, she had told the printer she would take no responsibility for the poem if he printed it. The editor, she believed, was now trying to escape punishment by dragging her in. Thus she officially denied authorship in her confrontation with the investigating magistrate. After leaving the judge's office she had the printer warned by her democratic friends that "he was in a jam" and would not get out of it by implicating her. Even though lying was against her nature, in

108

a case in which she might get a long prison term, she admitted, she "would resolutely deny everything." When confronted with the apparently intimidated printer, it was he, she claimed, "quivering like an aspen leaf," who said he could not identify her because the woman who gave him the poem wore a veil and came in the evening. In a revealing remark about her reputation, he admitted that he had merely assumed it was she since he knew no other woman in Mainz who wrote poetry. Although Kathinka Zitz-Halein asserted that it was an open secret that she was the author, the authorities decided not to pursue the case. It was one of at least three encounters with the police and the prosecutor's office in connection with her political activities in the aftermath of the 1848 upheaval. It was also not the only time she would categorically lie about authorship to avoid a prison term or a fine.[27]

The second anniversary of the start of the revolution, in spring 1850, was the stimulus to another burst of political and social poetry. Most of her outpourings appeared initially in the *Mainzer Anzeiger,* which became the strongest voice of the Mainz democracy until new censorship regulations choked off public dissent. The themes of these poetical works were mainly political, although social and personal concerns are expressed. Politically she saw the need to remind the people what the revolution represented by keeping alive the basic ideas of 1848, as she interpreted them: democracy, a republic, and equality. In a poem devoted to the first named theme, and more prescient than she realized, she asked about the outcome of the revolution.[28]

> Say, who in this stormy time
> Has won, who has lost?
> Against democracy
> Has fate conspired
> Because with main force
> It caused her deep wounds?
> Is it with divine right of kings
> In a blessed union?
>
> Is democracy conquered
> Because martial law bullets
> Hit so many fighters who,
> Murdered, now sleep in their graves?
> Because others in prison darkness
> Strove in vain for freedom,
> And many in flight and impoverished
> Languish away on foreign soil?

Kathinka Zitz-Halein

Did the monarchy supposedly win
Because after the earthquake it
Now believes that tyrants' strongholds
Can be erected more solidly than before? . . .
And because the princes seek
Their power in their armies?

No, No, it is not democracy
Which up until now is losing,
For in the book of life
It is eternally inscribed.
Only thrones are overthrown, and dynasties
When it's a question of the people's happiness.
Nations are not overthrown,
They are transformed.

Democracy reseeds itself,
Out of its own strength renewed,
And new vitality grows out of it,
Out of the death of its fighters.
And new fighters grow up
From the blood of the slain,
For what is to crush them
Fills them with new hope. . . .
Because of that has democracy
Not yet lost its force.

Inseparable from the idea of democracy in 1848 were those of a republic and revolution. For Kathinka Zitz-Halein, this populist poetess, the political form was an outgrowth of revolution.[29]

It is not dead, . . .
It has not yet died, . . .
It is still unspoiled
It's merely catching its breath
For a new resurrection,
Then it blows through Germany
With banners proudly flying.

What is revolution, you ask?
It is like a raging fever,
It is the self help of nature
Against pressure and compulsion from above.
It comes where development
Is unnaturally restricted
Until the spirit of the people
Struggles and makes headway against it.

Aren't there means against it? . . .
These are timely reforms.

....

Through bayonettes and gallows
It does not let itself be killed.

....

Only fools believe they see it
Embedded in a tomb.
It lives on in the realm of the mind
Only to emerge even mightier.

....

Yet when the lightning will strike,
Only the gods know that.

Dynastic self interest, greed . . .
They blind all rulers to people's needs
Yet all states will soon die
Killed by their army and their taxes.
For that reason, my people,
Just learn to be patient.

In "Two Achievements," the third in the series, she used a quick sketch of German history since 1815 to encourage the faithful.[30] She began:

Around the people were spun
Webs of malice and treachery,
And in the center sat
With deception and betrayal in mind
Who long enslaved us—Metternich
The evil old garden spider.

There he sat and wove threads fine
And fear and obedience were paid.
There he sat and looked comfortably about
Fed with Russian gold.
There he sat and practiced book censorship
And wove with busy arms,
And every thought of democracy
He strangled without mercy.

Then came the revolution, which ripped the web asunder and drove the spider away, but without real victory.

> Diplomacy has tied the threads
> Together again and dares
> To glue them with blood, but in vain,
> The glue of dictated power
> Evaporates like fear, and the patchwork
> Badly done will not hold for long.

She claimed to see some rays of hope.

> For overturned was censorship,
> The murderous sword against free thought.
> Freedom of the press, trial by jury,
> O they are two mighty barriers.
> They'll ban the devil of reaction
> Into shackles and heavy chains.
> They are the dearest goods of the age,
> They will save us our freedom.

She miscalculated, at least in the short run. By October 1850 censorship had been reimposed in Mainz.

Her concern for political and civil rights did not mean she ignored the social divisions revealed by the revolution.[31] The call for cooperation among social classes and the need to end social injustice was emphasized in "If I Were a King," in which the good ruler expresses concern for those impoverished and unemployed.[32]

> So long as in my realm beggars still exist,
> So long as workers with strong willing hands,
> Vainly knock on doors in search of work,
> So long would I believe I had done nothing.
> ....
> I would have compassion for girls and women,
> Who beautiful and young of years look around in vain
> For work until misery gradually strips them bare
> And with brutal kicks pushes them to ruin.
>
> For the factory worker I would also have compassion
> And with special zeal think of his betterment,
> For he is the convict, the slave of industry,
> And the liberating bell never sounds for him. . .
> In life only a machine which may not stand still,
> And like the wandering Jew, he must forever go forward.

> And would I succeed in spreading well-being,
> Where now poverty rules, where want and misery
>   contend,
> If I had stilled with soft touch the people's hemorrhaging,
> Only then would I believe I had fulfilled my duty.

The following year, 1851, after the censorship laws were tightened in Mainz, several of Zitz-Halein's poems were published in Louise Otto's *Frauen-Zeitung*. Her "Models from Antiquity" contained the theme of a mother's rejection of her son because of cowardice in the face of the enemy. She used Demosthenes' speech defending the Greeks against Alexander as the theme of another poem, and the conversation between Dia and Thelos, before he goes into battle, as the occasion of a third. The latter portrays a woman in a suitably heroic pose, who exceeds beyond Zitz-Halein's approved limits. Dia encourages Thelos to enter battle without fear: "Fight, Ares will help you fight, so that I am not ashamed of you." When Thelos protests that the sword appears all to short, Dia responds: "Grasp it courageously, your arm will make it longer." When Thelos points to his lack of a shield Dia rejoins: "Does not your courage and my love cover you securely?" When he worries about falling in action, she asks: "Does the fatherland then collapse?" When he expresses concern about her surviving him, she spits at him: "I live as a slave? *Pfui* (shame) Thelos, that maligns me." When Thelos, inspired by Dia, goes to battle without his shield, she now recognizes her patriotic responsibility: "I cannot let him leave this way. Not courage alone, not solely love can give security. . . . Away Dia protect him for the Fatherland and to your Perseus give yourself as a shield."[33]

Her poetry was always her main vehicle for expressing her feelings whether personal or political. Nothing better illustrates this combination than her last poem from this midcentury activist phase, "To a Young Poet," which appeared in the *Mainzer Zeitung* in 1852. The difficult path and responsibility of the poet were sharply stated.[34]

> You want to write poetry! Leave it.
> Only then will you act wisely,
> For the poet, instead of on roses
> Must wander over prickly thorns, . . .
> If he does not want to besmirch
> The golden lyre through flattery.
>
> . . . .
>
> If he does not as a weather vane
> Want to turn toward the favorable wind.

Kathinka Zitz-Halein

If he wants to preserve justice
And call what is bad simply bad.
And in his hymns
Only true greatness praise.

If you subscribe to loyalty and truth . . .
If you demand intellectual clarity,
One wants to repress you.
But call the glitter excellent,
Howl with the wolves, those pious ones,
And if you flatter truly vilely,
O then will you get ahead.

Her poetry usually had a political tip, and in this example she tried to point it at the conservative ruler.

If you find everything good
That the prince found good,
If you wag your tail for bread to eat
Deferential like a cowardly dog,
If you praise each of his acts
To the highest heavens,
If you placate the lord high nose
Daily with sweet incense,

For that the master will reward you, . . .
He bestows on you honored positions
Perhaps even the Councillor's title,
And with a medal decorates your hollow chest,
With the radiance of his grace
Enchants your weak brain.

But if you dare to tell him
What shortcomings you have found,
If you show him with bitter complaints
The deep wounds of the people,
If you show him the court rabble
Which lives off the sweat of the poor,
While in the bare huts
The peasants scarcely feed themselves.

If you show him those classes
Who squeeze out the marrow of the citizenry
In order then in champagne foam
To forget what they have done,
If you show him those sick with hunger
Who like isolated spirits
Stumble miserably through life,
Anger will overcome him.

114

> Obeying his signal without delay
> His guard hurries to grab you,
> And then without delay
> Will drag you along to prison.
> Instead of golden necklaces of honor
> You will wear prisoner's garb.
>
> Leave the poetry or play the hypocrite,
> Become a little sheep of timid soul,
> If you graze with the flock
> You will not lack for food.

It was advice she could not herself follow. The poem represented a potentially dangerous step since censorship had been reimposed, political trials occurred regularly, and the verse could easily be taken to refer to the grand duke of Hesse. To make matters worse, the newspaper's editor had been so imprudent as to print her initials under the poem. She soon received an invitation to visit the examining magistrate, Dael, and the proceedings suggest something of her stature. When confronted with the incriminating poem she denied authorship, explaining in her memoirs that given the prevailing laws she had to play the "cruel mother" and reject her natural child. Although the newspaper editor also denied she was the author, argung somewhat weakly that the initials referred to the *Kölnische Zeitung*, Dael was unconvinced. He pulled out a file on her, which contained poems she had written thirty years before, in order to demonstrate that the incriminating poem was similar in style, construction, and terminology to her earlier work. She denied that the mere accident of similarity of style proved anything since she used a variety of styles. The government tried to find additional proof and questioned the newspaper personnel, but all declared her not to be the author. In the council chamber a majority of the judges reached the decision that the poem did not contain anything directed specifically against the Hessian ruler and declared her no longer under suspicion. "The threatening storm cloud," she remarked, "passed harmlessly by." It was another impressive example of her resoluteness.[35]

Kathinka Zitz-Halein's political and social poetry represented only one aspect of her civic effort during the revolutionary period. Closely related to it and equally important was her prose work. Many of her scattered stories and novellas from the pre-1848 period, several of which have already been cited, were collected and published during the revolution as *Variations in Humorous Fairy Tale Pictures*. Their appearance underscored her improved reputation as a writer and the greater degree of freedom permitted authors. When Louise Otto briefly reviewed the book in 1851 at a time of more rigorous censorship, she stressed that it was only in this veiled form that "all the truths could be said," which one now scarcely dared to utter. After the *Variations* Zitz-Halein's publications appeared at an increasing rate, and between 1849 and 1859 at least twenty volumes, averaging over four hundred pages in length, appeared. The subject matter was either contemporary, set in Mainz, Baden, and Germany, or historical, but with clear allusions to the present. Josef Hecker, Friedrich Hecker's father and a retired Badenese official, who from 1850 until his death regularly corresponded with her, caught the purpose of the prose, as well as her poetry: to keep before the public in every form the memory of "names, the bearers of great ideas, which one would gladly bury."[36]

Donner und Blitz (Thunder and Lightning), Zitz-Halein's first post-1848 publication that contained some new prose, was composed entirely of stories with a political and social orientation. Josef Hecker was impressed but worried. "Where," he asked her insightfully, "with so much noble femininity, do you get such a wicked sense of humor?" He predicted that she would receive a summons from the authorities for her literary impertinence. He failed to understand, however, the relatively freer atmosphere that still reigned in Hesse in comparison to Prussian-occupied Baden. Nevertheless, it did become increasingly difficult to get works with a democratic political message published, as illustrations from her own experience demonstrate.[37] It must have seemed to her that a return to the pre-1848 situation had occurred. Although *Donner und Blitz* was virtually the only one of her prose works to appear in the relatively freer precensorship period, she continued in all of them to express herself in her characteristically forthright manner.

The stories in *Donner und Blitz* were in part used as a means to settle scores with her enemies. The reaction of some citizens was so strong that the publisher had to disclaim responsibility for the book, and she had to announce that she did not intend to depict local persons. The furor must have pleased her.[38] Typical of the collection, "The Democrats' Family" was the Mainz writer's history of the impact of the revolution on an active democratic family. In it she sets out the sins of the moderates and conservatives in an uncompromising fashion and defends her democratic beliefs. Setting the story in postrevolutionary Mannheim, where the spring uprising of 1849 was strongest and the subsequent repression greatest, she paints a picture of destitution: martial law in force, the burden of quartering troops severe, the democratic *Mannheimer Abendblatt* for which she had written before 1848, now renamed and moderate, people fleeing to the United States, and others resigned to poverty. The impact of the Prussian occupation of Baden was severe and a factor in the emigration of approximately eighty thousand Badenese, nearly every eighteenth inhabitant.[39] The story focuses on the Valentini family. He is an artistic painter who had a good living before and during the revolution. But because of his continued allegiance to the revolution's principles and his undisguised democratic attitude, he has suffered financially. The well-to-do no longer desire drawing lessons. His former customers, if they now come to him, only want him to retouch their 1848 portraits so that no symbol of the revolution, such as its black, red, and gold colors, remains. Instead, Zitz-Halein inserts sarcastically, they prefer him to paint into the portrait a book by an acceptable conservative writer. Valentini's elder son, who participated in the uprising, is a political refugee in Switzerland, who requires financial support. The younger son, Alfred, is exposed to taunts at school, and under the "stultifying punishment of papist domination he must regurgitate their sophistries." All of the heroic deeds of the past are "damned as illegal," and any mention of the names of the democratic heroes like Trützschler, Höfer, Böhning, Max Dortu, and Valentin Streuber is forbidden. But worst of all, so the father moans in a litany of injustices, is the "abused fatherland, the powerlessness of the legislature, the lack of food among the people and the resulting usury of the wealthy, the disgraceful [Prussian] military dictatorship, the venal courts, the bribed journalists, and the murderers of freedom in the pulpit and confessional." If only, he laments, one had not had such confidence in moderate liberals such as "[Heinrich von] Gagern and his unprincipled consorts." To make matters worse the daughter, Frederike, is the target of the lecherous advances of the city manager, who threatens the father if he does not get his way. This city official, it should be stressed, represents a new type of conservative, cut in the Bismarckian garb of cynical realpolitik. For him it is not principles that matter. The democratic leaders must be discredited, he claims, and he glories in the newspapers accusations of them as murderers and arsonists. The masses must be manipulated, and their hate directed away from the true source of their misery. Better, he says, that they learn to hate the military so that the conservative civilian governments appear mild by comparison and can wear "the mask of a humane popular governmental system." The parliamentary deputy is his agent and the church too is enlisted to bolster conservative power.[40] In spite of this gloomy picture, she did not advise resignation and the father does not lose faith. Zitz-Halein manages to give the story a hopeful ending with the investigation of the corrupt and cynical official.[41]

Besides focusing on contemporary events she used her fine sense of ancient as well as modern history to find appropriate themes for her aims. *Donner und Blitz* contains a translated work, "Iodine, the Maiden of the Ardennes," which, gave her the opportunity to treat several themes important to her: the patriotic efforts of women, the obscurantism of the Catholic church, and the ultimate victory of democracy. In it she describes the morals and customs of the ancient Gauls in their struggle against the Romans in order to show "with what weight at all times authority presses down on the people, and especially how the accursed priestly domination seeks to maintain itself by the worst means. Blood flowed in streams, every right mocked, every virtue trampled underfoot when it was a question of reaching an intended goal." As people become more enlightened, she believed, "They will rip away the veil of illusions which so long confused their good sense." Iodine, the heroine, in a clear allusion to the failed spring uprising, flees the tyrant and hides herself in the forest, ultimately to emerge from her exile greater and more fearsome than before.[42]

Changing the literary genre, the Mainz writer also concocted a series of amusing definitions of political and social "flora and fauna." which could be turned against her enemies. She describes the "freedom tree" which since 1830 one has tried several times to plant in various countries in Europe. Unfortunately it has been an inferior variety and has not yet taken root nor born healthy fruit. The *Goldregen* (raining gold) tree roots for capitalists, bankers, and speculators but is never seen growing in proletarian soil. The *Heller Kraut* (paupers' money) is found, on the contrary, only in the unfertilized soil of poverty, and the rich despise it as a threat to their fruitful property. But most suggestive of her definitions was that of the *Hungerblümchen* (starving blossom), "found only in the leanest tracts of proletarian soil," which she hoped would be brought to full bloom by a talented "people's gardner."[43]

The following year, 1851, she issued the first of a series of four works set in the Rhineland which trace the history of Mainz and the surrounding area through fictionalized accounts. These *Rheinsandkörner* (Rhenish grains of sand) contain political and social messages regarding civic activism, a muted feminism expressed in women's patriotic roles, and pleas for religious tolerance. The power of the Mainz citizenry is reflected in "Der Sarazenssklave" ("Saracen's Slave") and "Städtebund" ("League of Cities"). The first deals with the eleventh-century struggle for urban rights by the people of Mainz. The princely rulers of the city attempt to break the spirit of the Mainzers by diverting them to participate in a crusade to the Holy Land. This early example of an attempt to export domestic problems fails, and the city gains new freedoms. The latter tale focuses on the thirteenth-century league of Rheinsh cities, which was called into being to rid the Rhine River of robber barons. Besides the antiaristocratic point contained in the piece she correctly emphasizes the important role that an "unpretentious citizen" of Mainz, Arnold Walpod, played in the effort, accomplishing "what so many emperors with all of their power had tried in vain to do." Moreover, this nonaristocratic hero, she stresses, was not sufficiently honored by the Mainzers. A recent history of medieval Mainz confirms this, referring to him, with some wonder, as the "actual originator and the leading personality" of the league, and calls the organization the "greatest political achievement of the citizenry of Mainz in the Middle Ages."[44]

Other stories from this period illustrate how Kathinka Zitz-Halein could strike a modern chord for her social and political beliefs. In "A Witch's Trial", which was contained in the second volume of her *Rheinsandkörner*, she celebrated the ending of witchcraft trials in Mainz. She relates how women were singled out as witches, tortured until they confessed, and finally burned, and "how the plebes cheered." It was in reaction to these trials in the late 1500s, she accurately claimed, that the "dark night of superstition and of the irrational popular mind," at least in Mainz, began to give way to a more enlightened attitude.[45]

A variety of her political and social concerns, including religion, women's emancipation, and democracy are evident in the novella, "Paskaline," as Zitz-Halein blends Mainz's most recent history with autobiographical information. Paskaline, the heroine of the story, embodies, as is often the case with Zitz-Halein's works, those traits with which she identified. Paskaline is a German Catholic who is interested in and knowledgeable about politics, but she never forgets her femininity.[46]

Religion and women's rights, however, are subordinate to the central purpose of the story which is an attack on the pre-1848 regime and a plea for democracy and social equality. The mouthpiece for her views is Theobald, a German American who has recently returned to Germany, with whom Paskaline falls in love. In a long speech to the Democratic Association he depicts America, the "Palestine of the democratic crusades," as a land of human rights where "men" who live in freedom are "masters of themselves." The course of human development, he reiterates, is constantly striving toward freedom, and the purpose of the German revolution was to make possible a common life based on brotherhood and democracy. The latter, he asserts, contains no desire for revenge but only for justice. Democracy stands not for revolutions but elections, a free press, and the greatest possible participation in public affairs. The worst form of tyranny, Theobald proclaims, is the abuse of justice, as laws are made to keep those below in check while the mighty are wealthy enough to obtain their satisfaction through deals outside the law. Theobald points to the corrupting impact of the prison system and the continued use of capital punishment, "this most barbaric of all amputations," which has never served as a deterrent example.

Zitz-Halein's social concern is reemphasized as Theobald announces that it is the lower class whose condition must be improved and which must reclaim its withheld rights. But since power was in the hands of the propertied, the existing laws were incapable of healing the social rifts. Through continual education, as well as "limiting the aristocracy of wealth" who "enrich themselves with the connivance of the government," and permitting the people to participate in elections, can the proletariat's condition be improved. At the present time, the speaker continues, the workers are "prisoners of industry," "human machines" whose bodies are "misshapen" and minds dulled by overwork, who seek to forget their miserable existence by turning to alcohol. Children are deformed by early labor; wives and daughters are driven to prostitution, which usually ends in disease. The solution to the political and social misery of contemporary Germany is not a more efficient police state, which degrades the nation, but a republic, "the work of God," "the living law of humanity," as she calls it. "O German people," the returned exile accuses: "one disparages your name, spits on your history, buries your press, . . . locks up your best writers, confiscates your honor and freedoms, and you put up with everything."[47]

Her commitment to democracy and social reform as represented by the Revolution of 1848 was restated in the final collection of her *Rheinsandkörner* stories. In "Fragments from the Stormy Era (1848–49)," the setting is Mainz during the revolution and the characters real or thinly disguised. She blends in various subplots as she describes very accurately the early rallies in February 1848 out of which Zitz's leadership emerged, the concessions of the grand duke, Zitz's speech of March 8, and the dramatic rally of April 16, where Bamberger pushes Zitz to accept a republic, the word of which "howled like a whirlwind and carried all before it." She goes on to describe realistically the key clash between the Prussian military and the Mainz citizenry on May 21; the memorial service for Robert Blum, where the women are clothed in black; and the armed struggle for the new constitution in spring 1849. The social dimension is expressed through the statements of the deceased gymnastics teacher, Franz Mämpel, who advocates concern for the poor and denounces the rich who have taken everything from them "but their sleep."

Zitz-Halein appears in the story as Selma Busch, the wife of Dr. Busch, who left his newspaper to join the insurgents. She becomes one of the most active members of the Mainz women's organization, the Humania Association, and she is the spokesperson for the democratic adherents against her conservative aunt, Zeiler, who represents Zitz-Halein's stingy aunt who would not help her in the difficult days of the early 1830s. Selma Busch defends the lower classes who, she claims, do not want to seize someone else's property but merely desire equal rights. Instead, it is the greed of the well-to-do that has called forth socialism. Her attempt to reassure the propertied elements that the lower classes do not wish to overturn society suggests the growing fear of the masses of the respectable classes and reflects the increasing social division which aided the conservative counterrevolution and would later help Bismarck. Eventually Selma Busch inherits some money, which she uses to found a colony in America for refugees. The actual heroine of the story, Cölestine, (named after Cölestine Billig, an officer in the Humania Association whose love affair led her to a tragic end in the United States), does not miss any rally or meeting of the democratic forces. Like Paskaline she embodies femininity and civic involvement.

Zitz-Halein's conclusions reflect her personal experiences helping refugees as well as her acquaintanceship with some of the democratic leaders; she praises the faithful, condemns the fainthearted, but expresses some doubts about the future. On the one hand, she asks, "What has become of the men whose lips touched the dish out of which one first sipped hope, then fame, and finally bitterness? They have been eclipsed; they served the fatherland but received ingratitude for it. Now they are back in private life but ready to step forward." But others, she continues, who were "redder than red" in 1848 now reject their former beliefs, and some for measly gain "besmirch the banner for which they fought." In her view "The democracy is well rid of them, those moral cripples." Through her contacts in Mainz and with exile groups in London Zitz-Halein was well informed about the defections from within the democratic ranks. She goes on to imply that at least for the moment it is hopeless to believe in the reality of a republic, especially since a "high monarch [the King of Prussia] wrongly made himself the savior of legitimacy" and "freed the rulers who were guarded by republican dragons." The only hope she could express, at the high point of reaction in the mid-1850s, was for the progress of the human spirit.[48]

Zitz-Halein's extensive written works during the revolutionary epoch put her in the forefront of the literary warriors of the democratic camp. Unwilling to be intimidated by confrontations with the authorities, she sang the praises of democracy and castigated the symbols of conservatism. She attempted to use her talents to embed the progressive principles of the day in her readers' minds and in this sense may have had a long-term impact on her contemporaries. The need to make the events of 1848 part of the popular culture occurred to Fanny Lewald during a stay in Paris in 1848. She visited the theater and was struck by how the French revolutionaries were trying to use it as a means to educate the populace by giving the people their history in a way that was relevant to them.[49] Kathinka Zitz-Halein and other writers sought to do precisely this, and they also placed women in the center of their works. How is one to judge these efforts? Although Zitz-Halein did not consciously write from a feminist viewpoint she made clear in her novels, novellas, and short stories that patriotism and political engagement were not the exclusive preserve of men. Without trying to emphasize women's rights in her prose, she underscored the belief that women were not passive spectators to contemporary events. This was regarded by many who were sympathetic to women's emancipation as the first step in that direction and suggests the need to look beyond the more self-conscious advocates of female emancipation. The Mainz activist demonstrated a similar degree of civic involvement in her unprecedented organizational and fund-raising work.[50]

7

Zitz-Halein and 1848
The Humania Association

*K*athinka Zitz-Halein's contacts with other female political activists during the revolutionary period developed in large measure from her work with the Humania Association. Of all her political activities at that time it spread her reputation farthest, involved the greatest risks, and best reflected her views on women's role in society.

The Humania Association was one of dozens of similar groups founded by women to support the spring 1849 revolt in defense of the Frankfurt assembly's constitution. The uprising that began in April was suppressed by July with the fall of the Rastatt fortress. Nevertheless, the efforts of the women's associations continued and new organizations were formed to aid those now in prison or in exile and to help the insurgents' dependents. It has not been possible to establish the exact number of women's groups or to uncover detailed information about many of them, but the material in Zitz-Halein's papers, in *Frauen-Zeitung*, and in various archives gives sufficient proof of their existence and activities. In terms of its scope as well as the number of women who were involved, this organizational effort represents the most impressive achievement of European women during the revolutionary era. This accomplishment, however, has been largely unnoticed in studies of the revolution or of women in nineteenth-century European history.[1]

The democratic uprising of 1849 generated a number of calls to action by and to German women. One of the most stirring proclamations came from Altenburg, the capital of Saxony-Altenburg, the site of one of the most effective women's organizations. "The task of women in our time," it announced, was not to be excluded from participation in the hour of crisis. "Should women be damned as unworthy or incapable, and thus be spectators or even obstacles in the struggle for human rights," it asked. "Do we not also feel the shame of servitude, doesn't our heart long for freedom?" Simply being bystanders, the female writer stressed, would result in being punished or rewarded without deserving either. "Oppressed, we cannot complain, for we did nothing to lift the oppression; liberated, we could not be joyful because it was not the fruits of our efforts that we harvest." Although the writer assured her audience that women did not think of using physical force, there were other ways to reach one's goals of encouraging and supporting those fighting. She advocated mounting collections to be funneled through "democratic women's associations," which were being formed in every city. Under the leadership of Adele Erbe, whose brother, Hans, was a member of the national assembly and participated in the spring uprising, Altenburg was home of one of the most effective women's organizations. The association lasted until 1851.[2]

The stimulus to organize the Mainz group, however, seems to have come from Mannheim.[3] By May 1849 two women's organizations were set up, the Concordia Association, under the leadership of Therese Canton, and the Germania Association led by Kath. *[sic]* Betz and Kath. *[sic]* Lindenberger. Neither association endured very long since Prussian troops occupied Mannheim on June 23, 1849, and closed all democratic oganizations under the rule of martial law. However, some information about the women and their clubs has survived. Betz, who ran a store, was already known in 1848 as one who "always had funds" for refugees.[4] She and others had drafted an "Appeal" to German women, reminding them of the upheaval that was taking place all over Germany on behalf of the new federal constitution and calling on them to support it in every possible way. This statement was later found during a house search of J. P. Grohe, the editor of *Mannheimer Abendzeitung*, for which Zitz-Halein had written in 1846–1847. Probably because of this document, which clearly identified her political leanings, Betz's organization was banned. Her husband was also in prison, presumably for participation in the armed uprising, and she became a refugee in Strasbourg after her small store was closed by the police. Here was another example of how the revolution gave women an opportunity to demonstrate more self-reliance.[5]

Canton, fifty-four and the mother of two, was the daughter of an army captain and the widow of a businessman. She lived with her mother on a small pension and helped run a school for young children.

During the spring uprising she apparently made "rabble-rousing" speeches on the occasions of handing over flags to the Polish Legion and to the militia contingent from the Mannheim Working Men's Association, as a consequence of which she was questioned and threatened with arrest. The police report identified her as the president of a "republican women's organization." Although she claimed to have headed a legal organization, she had to forfeit her pension and the school was closed.[6]

Both Betz and Canton contacted Zitz-Halein and sent her statutes of their organizations, indicating the Mainz activist's reputation. Betz added the remark that they could not call them statutes but had to refer to them as "rules." Otherwise, she continued, "the police will stick their noses in," and they would have to obtain official authorization. She stressed to her Mainz counterpart the difficulties in founding and even more in holding together such an organization. Nevertheless, she explained, women could no longer be "inactive spectators," and only "unity makes strength." Canton strongly urged the Mainz women to join her Mannheim group as she claimed the Frankfurt women were, in order to help "hungry, imprisoned, exiled republicans." She also mentioned other women's organizations that were being formed in Heidelberg, Kehl, Lahr, and Offenburg.[7]

Offenburg and Lahr, both Badenese towns of less than five thousand, provide examples of the widespread involvement of women in civic activity during the revolution. Even before the spring 1849 uprising there were expressions of female activism, which are recorded in the local newspapers.[8] Thus women were ready to respond to the patriotic call of the leaders of the Badenese uprising who exhorted both men and women to gather supplies for the fortress at Rastatt and to equip the militia contingents from the various towns and cities. In Offenburg, led by Amalia Hofer, a lawyer's wife, and Nannette Rehmann, women organized a collection of clothing, bandages, and money. In Lahr an association of fifty to sixty women was formally constituted to support the "freedom fighters." Even in smaller towns such as Bermersbach and Gengenbach women did their share. However, with the entry of the Prussian troops by the end of June the women's efforts seem to have come to an end. And later histories of women's associations in this area have passed over the 1849 efforts in silence, at least until the last few years.[9]

With many examples of women's initiatives before them, it did not take much to encourage the Mainz women to organize, and by early May two groups were in the process of formation. One newspaper story, probably written by Zitz-Halein, reported that women's associations were forming everywhere to support the politically persecuted and to procure weapons for the fighters. It stressed that the task of women must be more than being inactive visitors at democratic association meetings and rallies or sewing flags. In language that suggests Zitz-Halein's hand, the writer maintained that women, without stepping beyond the bounds of femininity, could be of significant help to the fatherland. It announced a meeting of democratically inclined women to follow the lead of the Mannheim example.[10]

On May 13 Zitz-Halein's group, which was initially called the "Patriotic Support Association," met in the Mainz theater building. The turnout was apparently greater than expected, and the election of a board of directors was postponed until May 15. At the latter meeting the name was changed to the Humania Association. Simultaneously a second organization called the "Women's Association for Patriotic Interests," one of whose leaders was Amalia Bamberger, Ludwig Bamberger's mother, was emerging. Negotiation of a merger between the respective deputations began immediately, and, as the larger of the two, Zitz-Halein's association became the offical organization of the Mainz women. However, the board of directors was enlarged to make room for representatives of the other group.[11]

The statutes reflected careful planning and a democratic philosophy. The purpose of the organization was to help "needy patriots" and their families. Although the regulations did not explicitly limit membership to women, they made clear in the references to the board of directors that only women could serve in those capacities. The board was elected for six months by secret ballot of the membership, and specific elections for the executive officers, such as president, vice president, and treasurer were held. Special provisions placed limits on the power of the president to disburse money without the approval of the board, and on the board without the approval of the general membership. Weekly meetings of the board and monthly meetings of the general membership were specified. The dues were a flexible amount to be determined by the individual member; however, the minimum was three kreuzer per week, equivalent to about one-fifth of the price of a loaf of bread or a pound of butter. Zitz-Halein had announced that it was the intention to make it possible for rich and poor to participate and that no distinction on the basis of class would be recognized.[12]

Kathinka Zitz-Halein became the president of the women's organization and Amalia Bamberger vice president. This reflected not only the leadership of the rival women's groups but also the leadership of the Democratic Association; at least sixteen of the twenty-one women who held board positions appear to have been related to members of the Democratic Association. The overall membership of the Humania Assocation reached 1,647, compared to 2,000 men in the Democratic Association. Unfortunately it was not possible to correlate membership of the two organizations since we do not have full names for all the women and the only surviving membership list for the Democratic Association was compiled in August 1848 when there were only 614 names listed. The 1,647 names represent the largest official participation of European women in civic affairs at midcentury. Moreover, the fact that they supported progressive political developments at the inception of widespread German feminist activity reflects the relationship between the democratic movement and the women's emancipation movement.

Although it is not possible to know the attitude of the membership toward the question of the role of women in German society, we do of course have sufficent information about Kathinka Zitz-Halein's views. She had no reluctance in expressing them before the membership. They seemed to reflect the opinions of the rank and file; at least there is no evidence of any opposition to her pronouncements. Her conception of the proper role of women during the revolutionary crisis could be labeled as realistic but for that reason not necessarily moderate. Characterizing women's activities during times of crises such as war and revolution as timid or courageous assumes a standard of commonly accepted values that in fact does not exist. What can appear as modest by the standards of male participation in political affairs could be regarded as extraordinary for women when one considers the political, legal, economic, and social disabilities with which they had to contend in mid-nineteenth-century Europe. Forming politically oriented organizations like the Humania Association or the Mannheim groups required civic bravery, because there were few precedents.[13]

Zitz-Halein's perception of the role of her organization during the 1849 crisis was in keeping with her previously cited statements about women. In her first speech to the membership of the still unmerged group, she passed in review the names of heroic women of previous epochs whose unique deeds made an imprint on history: from the biblical Judith through Joan of Arc to Charlotte Corday. These were role models that suggest a high degree of political activism and personal courage. And Joan of Arc's distinctly masculine activities as well as dress seemed to exceed the bounds of what the Mainz activist considered proper for women. Nonetheless, she stressed that they had in common the same motivation, a strong sense of patriotism, and that the women of Mainz could do no less than they. "We must cease being merely women and become completely citizens and patriots," she exclaimed, going so far in this first speech as to call for contributions for the purchase of weapons.[14] What this indicates about Zitz-Halein's civic aspirations for women is not easy to ascertain. As we have seen, even though she complained frequently about the ill treatment women received at the hands of men, in part confirmed by her own experiences, she still saw the domestic sphere as women's natural one. How this could be reconciled with leading an army, as Joan of Arc had, or committing political murders is another matter. There is no indication that she expected the success of the revolution to change the status of women in Germany significantly, although it might lead to a new regard for women by men. This had been her major concern before the upheaval.

In her public statements she repeatedly stressed the theme of women's role. Before the Kastel Women's Association she argued that when the fatherland calls all must obey, the men to fight and the women to nurse and sacrifice. If men were given physical prowess and sharper reason, nature gave women mildness and capacity to care. We do not, she warned, want to be "hermaphrodites" who are derided by both sexes. Rather, women should follow the "humane and beautiful call of our hearts" and, working in a "genuinely feminine way," do what the situation requires. At the beginning of July she told the members of the Humania Association, "The task of women in these difficult times . . . is to show our worth in full measure." This would involve getting in touch with prisoners, caring for the wounded, and consoling those left behind.[15] Her description of her meetings with Elise Blenker, the wife of the insurgent general, Ludwig Blenker, who accompanied him on his campaigns, illustrates this attitude. After the first encounter with her Zitz-Halein noted that although "hermaphrodites who go beyond the boundaries of their sex" were "repugnant to her," she believed that Madame Blenker was motivated by a self-sacrificing love for her husband and for that reason deserved respect. But at a second meeting some four weeks later the general's wife appeared smoking a cigar and surrounded by dirty linen, so that Zitz-Halein was "filled with loathing."[16]

The Mainz writer was not alone in condemning the activities of feminists who stepped too boldly into the men's world. Other female activists worried about their impact on the cause of women's rights. Louise Otto, for example, claimed that women who made themselves into caricatures of men brought female emancipation into ill repute, but, she stressed, women still had to find an appropriate way to contribute to the liberation and democratization of Germany. Fanny Lewald also believed that unorthodox behavior such as smoking in public or wearing men's attire would only damage the cause of female emancipation. Malwida von Meysenbug stressed that the aim of female emancipation was not to make women like men but worthier as women.[17] Zitz-Halein's limited view of women's role was for once in agreement with that of her husband. In expressing his thanks for the help the Humania Association gave his men, Zitz praised the Humanians for their ability to enter public life without ignoring their other obligations or "offending the concept of feminine tenderness." This was the framework within which the Humania Association intended to and had to work.[18]

Stepping into the arena of civic affairs at a time of crisis forced Zitz-Halein and the Mainz women to leave their domestic spheres and face a series of problems that tested their political talent, ingenuity, and determination as well as their personal courage. One of the earliest and most serious issues with which they had to deal was caused by the changing political and military fortunes of the insurgency. Because of the military victories of the Prussian-led counterrevolution the Humanians faced the specter of political repression of the civilian supporters of the uprising. The danger was real throughout 1849 and 1850; an ominous example was the Badenese city of Heidelberg. A women's association organized in January 1849 later became the Democratic Women's Association for the Support of Needy Patriots. It was led by Katharina Beck, who was fifty-five, divorced, and an innkeeper. The association collected clothing, bandages, and food for the wounded. It helped needy insurgents who could not outfit themselves when called up for military service, and it also supported refugees.[19] But the Heidelberg women also issued a call to collect funds for weapons and participated in at least one revolutionary event involving a captured cannon. With the Prussian occupation of Heidelberg in June the women's organization was banned. Nevertheless, under the leadership of the president, a part of the membership continued to be secretly active in raising money and supplies for prisoners or their families.[20]

The situation in Heidelberg became more threatening in January 1850 with the arrest of Beck after a search of her dwelling. Incriminating materials were found and, charged with participating in the spring 1849 uprising, she was held for six weeks as a "war prisoner." She was released in March under the assumption she would be dealt with by the appropriate civilian authorities in the Grand Duchy of Baden. As a result of an apparent oversight she was forgotten by them until 1855, at which time she was tried for treason. She was convicted and sentenced to sixteen months' imprisonment but, because of her age, pardoned. The justification for her conviction is worth repeating because it applied to most of the women's associations that were formed in 1849, and certainly to the Humania Association. The judges conceded that occasionally helping a needy patriot was not in itself an act of treason, but in Beck's case it was a question of a "formally constituted association" having as its "main purpose" an "expressed multifaceted participation in activities" that "can no longer be disguised as the product of a well-meaning and benevolent attitude." Rather, "one cannot mistake [seeing] the tenaciously hostile attitude of support for high treason by all those means which the accused has at her disposal by virtue of her sex and age." No other statement better captures the contribution of women to the democratic side in the Revolution of 1848.[21]

The events in Heidelberg, which were duplicated in Mannheim, are good examples of the central role Zitz-Halein was coming to play in 1849–1850. Her contacts kept her informed of the repression in those cities. Zitz-Halein was advised by several people of Beck's arrest the day after it happened, and of her later release. Zitz-Halein was also warned to be prepared for a similar raid since the police had found letters and poems possibly written by the Mainz activist in Beck's abode.[22] In Mannheim her contacts were Nancy Hillebrand and Philipp Heinrich Dressel. The former, one of Zitz-Halein's closest and oldest friends, was a professional singer who was employed on the Austrian stage until she retired. She and her husband then operated a large inn in Mannheim until his death in 1843, when she ran the business herself.[23] Already in 1846–1847 Hillebrand had served as a conduit for Zitz-Halein's newspaper articles in *Mannheimer Abendblatt*. About Dressel, a forty-year-old businessman from Darmstadt, less is known. He apparently came in contact with Zitz-Halein only as a result of their common efforts on behalf of the insurgents. During the 1849–1850 period both reported to Zitz-Halein about the repressive situation in Mannheim and about acts of defiance against the Prussians. Some of their reports about conditions in Mannheim found their way into the Mainz newspapers. Both Dressel and Hillebrand were fund raisers for Zitz-Halein as well as transmitters of money from the Humania Association to needy persons.[24]

As these informants alerted Zitz-Halein to the dangers of political opposition, those dangers were already apparent in Mainz. Already in June one of her friends, Auguste Embdt, a writer and teacher at a girl's school, lost her job as result of her political efforts and German Catholic religious views. She was very active in the Humania Association and later involved in raising funds for Gottfried Kinkel. To survive she began to give private instruction and do embroidery work. Other women were apparently less courageous than Embdt, and Zitz-Halein admitted in July 1849 that some members including one from the board of directors, had resigned because of a rumor that the association's membership list had fallen into the hands of the military authorities.[25]

Moreover, in July 1849 the Hessian authorities gained possession of a chest full of material that gave them information about people in the Mainz area who had aided the spring insurgency. The Hessian officials' examination of the chest's contents led to the arrest of two hundred people, and Zitz-Halein's most dangerous encounter with the authorities. The documents showed that Zitz-Halein had communicated with the insurgents when they were in Kirchheimbolanden. Worse, she had been commissioned by members of the Democratic Association to get the chest, which initially lay undiscovered in Karlsruhe. This attempt failed and she was instead expelled from the city, which seemed to be additional evidence that she was involved with the insurgents. She became one of the 143 who were ultimately accused of high treason, the only woman on the list. She then found herself before the investigating magistrate for questioning. He first accused her of sending gunpowder to the insurgents. When she denied this he produced documents showing that she had sent nonmilitary supplies to them. This she admitted but announced that much of the clothing and bandages had in fact been purchased from the Hessian and Mainz authorities from the supplies of the disbanded citizen's militia. Thus, she explained to the surprised judge, if she was guilty of anything, so were the mayor and the provincial governor who approved the sale. Surely, she told him, the mayor must have known that the items were not for use in a masquerade. Charges against her were in fact dropped for lack of evidence, although the others accused had to stand trial. It was another political triumph.[26]

The preceding events mandated a policy of caution. Whereas in her earliest speech in May 1849 she had called for contributions for the purchase of weapons and had spoken of the "treachery of the bourgeoisie," by July she was at pains to stress the "legality" and nonpolitical nature of the Humania Association's activities. The national assembly had been accepted by the princes of Germany, she explained, and it had constructed the federal constitution that the insurgents now were fighting with all means, even weapons, to uphold. Thus the Humanians' support for them was justified. She reassured her audience, "We are not agitators, not warlike Amazons but rather priestesses of humanity and mercy." Never, she continued, were words of incitement heard in their meetings. She was now publicly critical of the "sister associations" in Baden for departing from the correct path by allowing themselves to exceed the bounds of legitimate feminine activities. The message was clear: as long as the Humanians carefully defined their mission as one of humanity no one could forbid their activities or arrest them. "Even without acting like heroines," she announced, "women can . . . prove how much we collectively know how to value the insurgents' devotion to the fatherland."[27] To emphasize their benevolent purpose the Humanians made contributions to the citizens of Mainz who suffered losses due to flooding, and even to the local poorhouse. Zitz-Halein's strategy, and the absence of a Prussian occupation, made it possible for the Humania Association to function successfully for two years.[28]

The Humania Association attracted a wide following in and beyond Mainz. On occasion it would charge fees for nonmembers to sit in the galleries, without any indication that this was a defense against heckling.[29] It also had extensive contacts with other like-minded individuals and groups throughout Germany. The need for unity or coordination was recognized in many quarters. From Altenburg the activist Adele Erbe described her efforts to involve other Saxon cities in the struggle for freedom. "Georgine," in *Frauen-Zeitung*, echoed her call, and Louise Otto asked that her newspaper be used as a clearinghouse for reports about women's associations. Johannes Ronge hoped to use German Catholic communities as an organizational framework for women's groups, but little seems to have come of this plan.[30]

Even before the calls for cooperation were issued, Zitz-Halein, too, had spoken of the need for a "great network of patriotic women's association's over all of Germany," and she inspired several groups to follow the Mainz example. From the small Nassau town of Diez August Pilgrim described the growth of the local women's association. He had seen a report about the Humania Association in *Demokrat* and was encouraged by it to organize a similar group in his locality. He related how much effort it cost him to keep the spark of interest alive until branch organizations were formed in the surrounding villages and joined with the Diez women. But now, he wrote proudly, the women's association comprised 130 female members, and the "membership was being permeated by the idea of freedom." Yet, he warned, subtle opposition from the "reactionary party" made it necessary to be continually concerned about subversion. To guard against it he urged a closer association with the Mainz women and asked Zitz-Halein to send a copy of Humania's statutes, to give advice on measures to undertake, and to forward a "rousing address" to stimulate the Diezers. This Zitz-Halein did, thereby coming into contact with Bertha Frensdorf, from nearby Oranienstein, who was the activist secretary of the now officially named Democratic Women's Association of Diez. Cooperation developed between the two groups, and the Diez women provided aid in fund-raising activities.[31]

In a similar fashion the Mainz example affected some people in the small town of Osthofen near Worms where a young woman, Sanchen Best, took the lead. She had originally attracted the attention of the public in 1848 because of her speech at the ceremony for presenting a flag to the local gymnastics society. According to the newspaper report her speech was another piece of evidence that "a new sex is emerging." The following year, after reading of Zitz-Halein's appeal for support of the insurgents, she took the initiative in organizing collections for refugees' families and selling copies of the Mainz writer's poem, "The Baptism of Blood." Best wrote to Zitz-Halein of her efforts to found an association, because she believed that only united action could have an impact. She also asked Zitz-Halein to send an appeal that might induce the local ladies to join. There is no indication whether she met with success.[32] Other cities where men and women asked Zitz-Halein to help with organizational efforts or where she worked with such groups include Alzey, Aschaffenburg, Bingen, Bonn, Darmstadt, Frankfurt, Heidelberg, Hessloch, Kastel, Konstanz, Landau, Mannheim, Oppenheim, and Worms.

This web of contacts was part of the Humania Association's broad campaign to aid the insurgents and their dependents, and Zitz-Halein played a key role in it. From June through August 1849 she traveled extensively on behalf of the Humania Association through southwestern Germany, to Switzerland, and to France to give assistance to the rebels. In June, accompanied by two women, while the fighting continued, she visited several cities, including Landau and Germersheim, where captured insurgents were imprisoned, and Karlsruhe. The following month, provisioned with four chests of clothing and a large amount of money, she undertook a more extensive trip, in part alone, which included stops in Strasbourg, Basel, Bern, Zurich, Solothurn, Aarau, and Karlsruhe, visiting some of the cities several times. In August she traveled to Mannheim, ostensibly for a vacation, where in fact she attended the trials of captured revolutionaries. The trips were eventful. Helped along the way by local women's groups, Zitz-Halein negotiated with the military authorities in Landau and Germersheim and was able to oversee the delivery of supplies and funds to incarcerated Rhenish Hessians. In Landau Zitz-Halein provided the inspiration for the founding of a women's association that had to meet in secret because of the Prussian occupation. Some eighty women contributed their "little bit," and Zitz-Halein sent them copies of her speeches and poems. The organization forwarded money and uncensored letters to the prisoners.[33] In Karlsruhe during her first trip she met with the corps commanded by Blenker and described her joy, "among the most beautiful moments of her life," at being able to carry news from Mainz to the troops. As they marched off to Rastatt, the last fortress to surrender to the Prussians, it seemed to her as if "all were my brothers and as if I were separated from my children." She witnessed the entry of the Prussian troops into Karlsruhe and their mistreatment of prisoners. Moreover, she documents the social divisions within Germany as she reports in her newspaper articles how townspeople, especially members of the citizens' militia *(Bürgerwehr)*, turned over tardy rebels to the soldiers. She quotes Blenker and seems to accept his opinion that the rebels were "betrayed by the bourgeoisie." Zitz-Halein also assisted fleeing insurgents.[34]

In the Swiss cities that she visited, the Mainz democrat dealt with the civilian and military authorities in order to dispense aid. When she came across scattered clusters of Mainzers she saw to it that they were moved to larger refugee centers. She aided some in preparing for the return journey to Mainz, for example, seeing to it that they shaved off their beards. She believed that as long as the men who had not been leaders returned home quietly, the Hessian authorities would close their eyes.[35]

Her stay in Mannheim in August, which coincided with the trials and executions of the revolutionary leaders Trützschler and Höfer, galvanized her action. Zitz-Halein and her friends sought to make Höfer and his family the focus of a regional fund-raising campaign. Zitz-Halein's personal success in Mannheim was substantial, especially in view of the demoralization in the wake of the Prussian occupation.

Even donors, Zitz-Halein was told, could be taken into custody. She personally undertook a collection on the day of Höfer's execution, raised one hundred gulden, and reported in detail how she took the money to Höfer's widow and how the widow exhibited bravery in the face of tragedy.[36] Trützschler and Höfer were not the only two revolutionaries whose plight she publicized and for whom she tried to raise funds. For a young imprisoned Mainzer she collected eight hundred signatures in support of a pardon that was later granted.[37] She also conceived the idea of making Robert Blum's children "wards of the nation" and thus ever-present symbols of the revolution.[38]

Kathinka Zitz-Halein's mutifaceted efforts brought her into contact with some of the best-known politically engaged women, among whom were Johanna Kinkel, Malwida von Meysenbug, and Louise Otto. Johanna Kinkel (1810–1859) was a divorcee when she met Gottfried Kinkel, who was a university instructor at Bonn. Their love affair and subsequent marriage caused Kinkel to lose his chance for a permanent university position and was the beginning of many years of struggle for the progressive pair. She was a woman of extraordinary presence and talent. Malwida von Meysenbug, a friend of the Kinkels during their exile in London, described Johanna's "massive figure, strikingly strong almost masculine characteristics." A talented writer who edited her husband's newspaper, as well as a musician and composer, she nevertheless was the devoted if dominant partner, who subordinated her career to his. For Zitz-Halein Johanna Kinkel represented the "complete woman," who raised her four children carefully, excelled at piano playing and composition, and was an effective writer. In other words she was accomplished in both professional and domestic pursuits but operated from a domestic base. During the Revolution of 1848 Gottfried became one of the leaders of the democratic forces in Bonn. Participating in the spring 1849 uprising, he was wounded and captured. Fearlessly and intelligently Johanna effectively orchestrated a national campaign to support her family and keep his case before the public, apparently using the money raised for her family to finance her husband's later escape from prison, which she helped plan.[39]

Zitz-Halein had become acquainted with Johanna Kinkel in the summer of 1849, when the latter apparently wished to enlist the Mainz woman's fund-raising and publicity skills on her husband's behalf. Their friendship was instantaneous, and Zitz-Halein became a tireless fund raiser for the pair. Already in June 1849 in an article in *Mainzer Zeitung* she pointed out how Johanna had been persecuted in Bonn because of her husband's political activities and because she was a democrat. The writer compared her treatment with the sixteenth-century practice of burning as a witch any woman who distinguished herself, a theme about which she had previously written. Johanna herself remarked that she had been denounced as an "anarchist" by her enemies.[40]

It was through her relationship with Johanna Kinkel that Zitz-Halein came to know Malwida von Meysenbug (1816–1903). The daughter of a government official in Detmold (Hesse-Kassel), Malwida grew up as a somewhat withdrawn person, dissatisfied with herself and searching for a "great truth, an overarching principle, a general goal which dominates everything." This she found through her friendship with Theodor Althaus, a young preacher who converted her to his democratic political and social ideals. In spite of familial opposition she continued to see him. When her father died in 1847 she wished to carve out an independent existence but realized how deficient her training had been. The revolution opened the door to civic involvement, and she went to Frankfurt and then to Berlin, where she became interested in working-class problems, associated with radical groups, and attended parliamentary sittings. She tried to educate her maid and distributed copies of the Frankfurt assembly's "Basic Rights of the German People" to the poor.

In part stimulated by the realization of her own inadequate education, she also developed a growing interest in female emancipation, which she saw as a necessary corollary of democracy and as a means to personal fulfillment. How, she asked, could the people regenerate themselves if one-half of them were excluded from participation in the process. As she later wrote to her mother, women no longer wished to have the boundaries of their activity prescribed for them but wanted to be able to pursue any interest to the limit of their capabilities, "without for that reason becoming unfeminine." She especially focused on the need for education, basing it on the Rousseauian ideal that women must educate their children, but adding that woman must be able to share their husband's concern for public affairs.[41]

Inspired by the spring 1849 uprising in Dresden, Malwida von Meysenbug wrote "A Woman's Oath to Democracy," which she sent to Johanna Kinkel in London, who then forwarded it to Zitz-Halein, asking her to find a publisher for it. A few days later it appeared in *Mainzer Tagblatt*. The reformed aristocrat expressed the surge of emotions that she experienced during the revolt, especially the urge to "grasp the sword," and regretted most that the "sisters" must suffer quietly while the "brothers, friends and comrades" were shedding their blood. She encouraged the latter with the thought "Your female friends and companions continue the struggle for freedom in the education of the sons who will finish the struggle." And the conservatives, she warned, should not think that only one of the sexes is capable of resistance and the other dependent and powerless, "a race of slaves." Women "have become different creatures than you think, and their blood has mixed with iron and steel."[42]

The publication of this article and another via Zitz-Halein brought the two women into direct contact. Malwida von Meysenbug saw in the Mainz activist someone with whom she shared similar political and social views, and in March 1851 she sent Zitz-Halein a short report about the Hamburg College for Women. This institution, the brainchild of Emilie Wüstenfeld, Bertha Traun, and the Hamburg Bildungsverein (Educational Association), opened in January 1850 under the leadership of Karl and Johanna Fröbel. Ultimate responsibility for the operation was in the hands of a corporation in which investors bought shares and that was run by a board of directors. Women made up a majority of the membership. The school complex also included a kindergarten, elementary school, and living quarters for the students. The minimum age for the college was sixteen. The official aim of the institution, as announced by Karl Fröbel, was not competition with the university but to educate women for employment without their leaving their traditional cultural and social spheres. This view was clearly not shared by everyone, as lectures were given by some of the leading scholars in Hamburg and increasing attention was paid to science and mathematics courses.

In spite of the enthusiasm of the college's participants, problems developed. The boarding costs were high at four hundred taler, which caused the school to be denounced by democrats as being aristocratic. At the same time the school's close association with the nontraditional Free Religious Community led to its condemnation by the clergy. The fact that Wüstenfeld and Traun were in the process of being divorced also tarnished the reputation of the college. Furthermore, there also seem to have been disagreements over the the purpose of the institution. The attitude of Malwida von Meysenbug, for example, who saw the school as enabling women to become truly independent, was apparently too radical for other members. When increasing government hostility developed, money sources dried up and the school closed.[43]

Little of these facts is apparent in Meysenbug's report to Zitz-Halein. She described her involvement first as a student and then as a member of the staff. In her view the college would make a more collective effort on behalf of women's emancipation possible, whereas in the past individuals had been the pacesetters. It would produce what Louise Dittmar called "emancipating women." Meysenbug believed that the cooperative life of the institute was developing satisfactorily and that the educational pioneers were laying the foundation for something "truly great." She assumed that Zitz-Halein shared her views about the college's purpose and would therefore publicize the institute. She wanted the Mainz activist to recommend the school to "younger girls who want to be trained to teach or otherwise to be independent, or to older ones who are looking for an asylum which offers them simultaneously beautiful and beneficial activity and intellectual enjoyment."[44]

Both von Meysenbug and Johanna Kinkel were sensitive to employment and educational opportunities for women. In exile in England Johanna helped to find employment for the German refugees, especially females. She knew from personal experiences the difficulties that middle-class women faced. For example, a woman with singing talent, Johanna wrote, needed a heavy investment in a piano, clothing, and suitable accommodations to get started and also had to give recitals in private homes.[45] At the same time Johanna was sensitive to the opportunities that British society offered women. She described to Zitz-Halein the private women's colleges that were being founded, claiming that the quality of instruction was good and regretting that nothing like them existed in Germany, at least since the Hamburg College had closed.[46]

Kathinka Zitz-Halein's response, if any, to these observations has not been preserved. Nor has it been possible to determine her reaction to Meysenbug's essay on the Hamburg College. There is no evidence that it was published, at least in the Mainz papers. Perhaps Meysenbug assumed a greater congruity of views than actually existed, particularly regarding the appropriate limits of women's activities. Five years before Zitz-Halein had written disparagingly of women's aspiring to a university education, although in her stories she did permit her characters to express advanced views. Nevertheless, the two women remained on cordial terms.[47]

Kathinka Zitz-Halein's third relationship with female activists, which grew out of the revolutionary period, was with Louise Otto. The latter's major achievement during the midcentury revolutionary era was the founding of Germany's first successful women's newspaper, *Frauen-Zeitung,* which was issued from April 1849 until June 1852.

The Humania Association

The newspaper printed several of Zitz-Halein's poems, regularly recommended her published works, and called attention to the work of the Humania Association. The two women first met in 1851 and remained in contact for at least seven years. They shared similar political aims and to a certain degree had corresponding ideas about women, although Otto had a more comprehensive view of the women's emancipation issue than Zitz-Halein. Their relationship was friendly, and after their first meeting Zitz-Halein conveyed to Johanna Kinkel her pleasure with the Saxon woman's "high intellectual ability" combined with the "noblest femininity, great simplicity, and modesty." These latter characteristics were decisive.[48]

Zitz-Halein's effective leadership of the Humania Association, based in part on her wide-ranging contacts, can be seen in the association's successful fund-raising activities. Although most of the organization's income was produced through dues, the Humanians were especially innovative in seeking funds. Lotteries were held for women's handicrafts; benefit concerts, recitals, and readings where members performed, were staged; plays and poems, including some by Zitz-Halein, Johanna Kinkel, and Louise Otto, were auctioned. The April 1850 concert program contained pieces by Bellini and Meyerbeer, as well as by Kinkel and Zitz-Halein. Further financial support came from the powerful Mainz Carnival Society, which, in spite of opposition from some of its members, was prevailed upon to forego its annual *Fasching* celebration and to donate the contents of its treasury to the Humanians. Money was also raised through gymnastic displays and through collections at baptisms and parties and in taverns and workshops. In addition, as indicated previously, fund-raising efforts were coordinated with those of a number of other cities.[49] It was an impressive array of devices, but it should be noted that Zitz-Halein was no novice in this area. She had previously raised money and supplies for the German volunteers in Schleswig-Holstein and six years before that for aid of the people of fire-torn Hamburg.

The success of these endeavors can be seen in the financial records of the Humania Association. Its bookkeeping was detailed, receipts for expenditures were obtained, and quarterly reports as well as sums of money raised at social affairs were precisely reported in the Mainz newspapers. At the monthly meetings of the membership the books and receipts were available for all members to peruse. From its founding until Kathinka Zitz-Halein's resignation in June 1850 the association collected 5,911 gulden, representing the largest amount of money raised for the refugees. Expenditures totaled 5,837 gulden and can be classified into five main categories. The first clearly indicates a sensitivity to the problems faced by women in wartime. Aid was given to local women whose husbands or fathers were in exile or in prison because of the revolt. These women received one half gulden per week. In addition they were helped by special grants to meet mortgage payments, to redeem pawned items, to obtain medical care for those ill or pregnant, and to pay for nursery care so that mothers could work, "knowing that the child has supervision, fresh air, playmates and nourishment." Support also went to refugees who "passed through" Mainz, to released prisoners who returned to the city, and to those imprisoned or in exile in such places as Bruchsal, Landau, Mainz, Rastatt, Zweibrücken, Basel, Bern, Geneva, Zurich, and Strasbourg. Additional payments were made to a few specific individuals: wives or widows of well-known imprisoned or executed revolutionaries. The most prominent of these was Johanna Kinkel.[50]

In spite of this generally favorable picture the accounts offer evidence of increasing problems that the Humania Association and its founder had to face and that would lead to Zitz-Halein's resignation in June 1850. Income declined steadily. During the first five months the monthly income averaged 618 gulden, for the next three 475 gulden, and from January to June 1850 280 gulden. Although the early meetings of the general assembly heard emotional appeals for additional funds by Zitz-Halein, by November 1849 she had to acknowledge that the organization no longer had the income of the first months. She bemoaned the fact that many who initially were so enthusiastic had "fallen by the wayside."[51]

Although it was to be expected that the great enthusiasm of the first months would wane, the decline in membership support and income seems attributable to other factors. Letters poured in from individuals and groups, each with his or her tale of misfortune, most related to the revolution, some apparently not. Authenticating the requests for aid was difficult enough,[52] but the letters raised a number of questions regarding whom to help and how to disburse assistance. The issue of national versus regional identity proved divisive throughout the revolution and was reflected in the issue of whether all Germans or only Mainzers and Rhenish Hessians should be helped. It was also related to the dispute over the method of disbursing funds: should money be funneled through refugee organizations in Bern, Zurich, and Strasbourg or sent directly to the refugees? Social issues were raised with the question of singling out for support certain individuals or categories of people. And more general personal and political rivalries within the Mainz community came to the fore over whether to expand the scope of the Humania Association to include ordinary welfare activities. These were problems for which the Humanians could find no unified answers, and Kathinka Zitz-Halein's priorities were not always in conformity with those of the membership.

One of the earliest points of disagreement surfaced only five weeks after the association was founded. A letter signed by "several members" asked that the minimum weekly dues of three kreuzer be replaced by monthly dues of the same amount. The writers claimed that since the majority of the insurgents from Mainz had returned, the tasks of the organization were reduced. Moreover, they indicated that as members of the working class they found the dues too high to remain in the organization much longer. The same issue surfaced at least twice thereafter.[53] The issue of financial hardship and/or a weak sense of national solidarity that the letter reflected was difficult to resolve. It was true that the dues for the Humania Association were twice as high as those of the Democratic Association. It was also clear that the departure of about a thousand men from the city and region had caused hardship for many women, and there were references to women who now took in washing and did cleaning. But for those women whose husbands, brothers, or fathers had returned, the crisis apparently was over. Many had returned by the end of June, and those imprisoned in Landau and Germersheim were being released by early August.[54] Kathinka Zitz-Halein had little patience for the women who thought the crisis was over. She charged that it could only have issued from a complete lack of knowledge of the true purposes of the organization. The aim of the association was not to help only women but mainly those men who because of their patriotism were forcibly kept away from their homes. She had in mind not only insurgents from Rhenish Hesse but all German refugees and even Poles.[55]

Zitz-Halein also seemed to single out for special attention certain individuals or groups, who tended to be politically prominent, educated, or wealthy. She was particularly sensitive to the needs of the former members of the Frankfurt assembly, "prominent personalities," she called them, viewing them as people of refinement and education who had lost secure and comfortable existences because of their political beliefs and activities. Now they were being "hunted like wild animals" and would be forced to start anew in America (as her estranged husband soon would). She was in contact with leaders of the democratic party such as Carl Vogt, Franz Raveaux, and Wilhelm Löwe, and funds especially designated for them were sent to Bern.[56]

She also engaged herself strenuously on behalf of the imprisoned democratic leader Gottfried Kinkel and his family. Zitz-Halein raised approximately 220 gulden for the Kinkels through concerts, poetry readings, and special collections. This was 3.75 percent of all money raised by the Humanians. But even this sum was not sufficient, she claimed, for the family's maintenance.[57] Although support for the Kinkels had become a national cause in Germany, her special interest in raising relatively large sums of money for personal friends might not have been accepted with equanimity by the membership.[58]

The issue of whom to support could not be separated from the related question of how to disburse payments. Initially Zitz-Halein believed that she could personally pay out money during trips to refugee centers and prisons. In spite of her apparent satisfaction with the results of her travels, they created many difficulties. They were time-consuming and somewhat disorganized, especially those to the refugee centers in Switzerland and Strasbourg. She often proceeded on the basis of rumors that Mainzers or Rhenish Hessians were in an area, only to find none. In September after she had returned from her stay in Mannheim she had to defend herself against charges of squandering association monies on her travels. She charged that such rumors were being spread by those hostile to the purpose of the organization and urged the membership not to let itself become internally divided. Her offer to resign was not accepted. There is no doubt that her trips filled a need during the chaotic period in the immediate aftermath of hostilities. In the absence of any central refugee organization her personal intervention was the only alternative. For example, Carl Vogt wrote in July 1849 that he did not "have a red cent left" and other parliamentary leaders in exile were waiting for money from him. Four months later Vogt was receiving money on a regular basis and could turn the Humanians' money over to others for distribution.[59]

Nevertheless, to appease the opposition, at the end of July Zitz-Halein announced that the Humania Association was joining a Zurich-based organization for supporting German refugees and would send it a monthly contribution. This step, however, raised another sensitive issue: how to make certain that the funds sent to Switzerland would actually be distributed to Mainzers or Rhenish Hessians. The sense of helping one's own people was strongly ingrained, reflecting in another way the deeply rooted particularism that contributed to the defeat of the revolution. Although Zitz-Halein did not seem to have this attitude, at least not to a significant degree, it was impossible to oppose the strong sense of local or regional identity. Other areas of Germany that sent aid to Switzerland also wanted it to be distributed to specific groups or individuals. Although Zitz-Halein promised that the funds would be targeted for local people, it proved impossible to implement this policy. Even getting funds to the Mainzers in prison in Germany was no easy task, as the correspondence with the Rastatt commander and the prisoners in the Zweibrücken prison demonstrates. Zitz-Halein soon had to defend herself against charges that funds were being given to outsiders, and there were a number of complaints from Rhenish Hessian refugees in Switzerland that they were not receiving support. The official committee in Zurich acknowledged that there were problems but stressed its difficulties. Zitz-Halein could only soothe the membership with the explanation that it was almost impossible to monitor the distribution of funds, but this assurance satisfied few and pressure for a new approach grew.[60]

Finding the committee in Zurich an ineffective means to distribute aid, Zitz-Halein announced at the end of October that henceforth money would be sent to her husband, Franz, for disbursement. Given their history of hostility it was unlikely that this expedient would work. Her husband refused to deal directly with her, and she bypassed him in favor of "local democrats" and other members of the Frankfurt assembly such as Löwe and Vogt. Whoever received payments, the receipts and letters testify, had to account for their use. As she explained to the commandant of the Rastatt prison, the Humania Association "observed accepted rules of procedure."[61]

The difficulties connected with aiding the refugees were not the only ones that precipitated Kathinka Zitz-Halein's resignation. There was apparently a whispering campaign that focused on her affair with Wild and her married life, which she believed was instigated by her well-to-do enemies. These were women, she admitted, for whom she had been "forced to work in the old days" (1829–1836) but who now believed she was ungrateful to her former "benefactors." One can sense the years of accumulated anger of this woman, born into the upper middle class, who was treated as less than equal by her former acquaintances. She responded to the charges in an open letter that amounted to a brief autobiographical sketch. Her defense was complemented by a sharp poetical attack on her enemies.[62] She wanted

> To hold a mirror before you
> In which you see your own shape.
> In spite of your finery, in spite of your
>   musky scent

> In spite of your virtue painted cheeks
> You still equal only a whiten sepulchre
> On the inside rot, on the outside a vain show-
>   ing-off
> You are a Sodom's apple which looks good to
>   the eye
> But deep in the core carries loathsome
>   worms.

This quarrel was related to the controversy with clerical opponents over whether the Humania Association should broaden its mission to become a general relief organization, irrespective of the political views of the recipient. The antidemocratic opposition may have used it as a ploy to dilute the effectiveness of the democratic women's efforts. Adele Erbe reported from Altenburg that the opponents of democracy disguised their attacks against the Women's Association in that city by calling for aid to the poor rather than to the politically persecuted. Although aid was occasionally given to needy women, Zitz-Halein opposed transforming the association into a nonpolitical welfare organization. She and her supporters, she wrote, were not "sisters of mercy," chasing after converts, but remained "children of the world," who aimed to help political refugees and their families. She charged that the pulpit was being used to arouse suspicion of the Humania Association. This was of course nothing new in the highly politicized atmosphere of Mainz, where Catholics had organized their own group and had their own newspaper.[63]

The event that led to Zitz-Halein's resignation remains obscure. Early in 1850, because she lived alone and was less secure against fraudulent claimants, she entrusted the business manager, Josephine Kaufmann, with dispensing support authorization to refugees, without which the treasurer could not pay out money. In Zitz-Halein's view Kaufmann so exceeded her authority that on June 16, 1850, the president and six members of the board of directors resigned. Whether there was a larger point of dispute cannot be ascertained. Zitz-Halein assured her supporters that she had resigned only from the "office" but that she was still committed to the "cause" and would continue in a private capacity to raise money for the refugees.[64] This she did. From the time of her resignation until at least April 1851 Kathinka Zitz-Halein functioned as a one-woman political welfare organization. She scrupulously had printed in the Mainz newspapers the contributions she received and gave an accounting of how the 144 gulden, 40 kreuzer, was distributed.[65]

The Humania Association

Neither did the Humania Association cease its activities. Even Zitz-Halein admitted that the association did not collapse immediately but continued to exist, with a shrunken membership, until September 1851. Its last public accounting was apparently in September 1850, although mention of its activities can be found until the end of the year. In the three months after Zitz-Halein's resignation it raised 591 gulden, a sum that compares very favorably with the previous two quarters' income. Somewhat contradictory reports in *Frauen-Zeitung* indicated that the organization expired in the latter part of 1851, not because of a change of heart by the population but because it had accomplished its purpose. No other families needed assistance for political reasons. It is true that by the end of 1850 only a handful (150) of the 11,000 refugees remained in Switzerland. Furthermore, the main trial of the Mainz participants in the spring uprising had ended in June 1850 with a wholesale acquittal. Perhaps the Humania Association had outlived its usefulness.[66]

The Humania Association was Kathinka Zitz-Halein's major achievement during the 1848 era and one of the most significant accomplishments of German women during that period. The association's 1,647 members represented 9 percent of the entire female population of Mainz. The fact that so many women formally joined a politically oriented and oppositional organization, probably the first group of any kind to which most had ever belonged, should be considered evidence of political courage. The association managed the collection and distribution of more than six thousand gulden to hundreds if not thousands of needy people. Under Zitz-Halein's leadership it adjusted to the changing political atmosphere in the summer of 1849 by carefully redefining its purpose and expressing its sentiments. At the same time the association was more than Zitz-Halein's vehicle. Although the rest of the organization remains shadowy, there was a broad base of active support, as indicated by the disputes over policy and tactics. And the continued existence of the group for at least a year after Zitz-Halein's resignation testifies to the commitment and ability of the membership. These efforts plus the existence of women's associations in more cities than previously known should alter our evaluation of the role of German women in the mid-nineteenth century.

It can be argued that most of these efforts, however heroic, have little relation to feminism, but that is too narrow a view. Kathinka Zitz-Halein, as well as other female leaders, understood the necessity for caution and realized that only through moderation could anything be achieved. Adele Erbe noted how often the female supporters of democracy had been accused of advocating "emancipation," "lacking femininity," or being unchristian. Louise Otto described how even the wives and daughters of democrats were forbidden by their husbands and fathers to join or participate in democratic public activities. Although enthusiasm for the cause of democracy was admirable, it had to be disciplined and kept within acceptable bounds. If carried to an extreme it did more harm than good.[67]

The thousands of women who engaged in public activities around midcentury, these "unintentional feminists," or social feminists as Degler has called them, could not have been completely unaffected by their involvement. Certainly the various German governments that banned political activities by women, passed a law to prohibit women from editing newspapers, and suppressed kindergartens were aware of the implications of female civic activity. At the very least the 1848 experience enlarged women's sphere of socially acceptable activities. The revival of feminist activity in the 1860s should be evaluated against the background of 1848–1851. What had been forcibly driven from the surface of German life now reemerged, even under the old leadership of Louise Otto. And Kathinka Zitz-Halein, for all her traditionalist views, counted among the most effective progressive women of that earlier period. Her work with the Humania Association made her a well-known personality throughout Germany. In Mainz she received two serenades *(Ständchen)* as marks of respect and was honored by the Democratic and the Gymnastic associations. The letters in her papers from midcentury democratic leaders as well as from unknown women and men are a testimony to her reputation. For their efforts during the Revolution of 1848 she, Louise Otto, and Johanna Kinkel were listed in the German police register *(Schwarzes Buch)* as "dangerous writers" who had notoriously close contact with the more infamous individuals of the German revolution. It was a fair statement of Zitz-Halein's activities.[68]

8

Old Beliefs and New Realities

*N*either health, financial, or marital problems, nor the changed political situation after 1849 prevented Kathinka Zitz-Halein from pursuing her literary and civic activities during the 1850s and 1860s. The 1850s were highlighted politically by restrictions on or abrogation of the liberties granted during the initial phase of the revolution. The progressive German constitution, finally completed in early 1849, whose rejection was the cause of the spring upheaval, became a dead letter. The German governments tightened control over printed matter, one new example of which was the Saxon regime's *Lex Otto,* which forbade women from being editors of newspapers and journals. With many of the democratic leaders in exile the political opposition seemed demoralized and divided. A relative political quiet descended over Germany.[1]

As in other areas of Germany, Mainz and Rhenish Hesse experienced a period of political retrogression that reversed some of the early achievements of the revolution. Reinhard Dalwigk zu Lichtenfels, whom Kathinka Zitz-Halein had attacked during the pre-1848 period, was appointed Hessian minister of the interior in June 1850, signifying a new policy. Dalwigk wasted no time in acting. At the end of September the grand duke dissolved the recently (August 1850) elected parliament, in which democrats controlled forty-four of the fifty seats. The following week a series of decrees instituted a new electoral law leading to the election of a conservative legislature, ended freedom of the press and association, and revised the jury selection laws. The Democratic Association and the Workingmen's Educational Club, but not the Humania Association, had to dissolve. Dalwigk also forged a close relationship between church and state, highlighted by the naming of Baron Wilhelm Emmanuel von Ketteler as the bishop of Mainz.[2]

147

Kathinka Zitz-Halein

Despite this backdrop of political repression Kathinka Zitz-Halein remained committed to her progressive beliefs and found outlets for her civic energies. Her political views in the 1850s were clearly expressed in her memoirs. She paid tribute to and defended the defeated revolutionaries as "freedom fighters," who fought and died for a noble and just cause. They did not go as "cattle to the battlefield," bent on plunder and murder, she wrote in their defense, but knew what they wanted: a united Germany based on freedom, rule of law, and protection of property. The emphasis on the last point was to counter criticism by conservatives that the democrats were bent on overturning property relationships. Not the democrats, she announced, suggesting late-nineteenth-century developments, were the gravediggers of the revolution, but rather the standing army, which was turning the citizen into a "shooting machine."[3] It was not easy to remain faithful to one's democratic beliefs. Her friend, Betty Hurst, asked her only half jokingly whether she had not yet become a reactionary. Zitz-Halein reported to the Kinkels about defections of women formerly active in the Humania Association. They were pleased, however, by the firmness with which their friend was withstanding reactionary pressures and by her character as one of the "strong steadfast ones."[4]

Zitz-Halein's correspondence with the Kinkels indicates some of her endeavors on behalf of German democracy. The Kinkels struggled to survive financially as they sought to be the center of the democratic exiles in England. While Gottfried studied English so as to be able to give lectures, Johanna exhausted herself earning money and keeping the family together.[5] Johanna Kinkel valued the Mainz writer's friendship: she remarked that if there ever was something to carry out "that a woman can undertake," it could not be in better hands than Zitz-Halein's. When Gottfried had been imprisoned Johanna had asked her friend to ensure that the prison director was not attacked so harshly in the Mainz newspapers. Later, at Gottfried Kinkel's urging, Zitz-Halein provided regular reports to him about the political mood in the Rheinland. Although these statements have not survived, the Kinkels praised them as insightful and factual. She passed on to the Frankfurt publisher Otto Lüning Kinkel's manuscript that focused on the spring 1849 uprising. She also alerted the Kinkels to the danger of police agents, and they sent her manifestos from the refugee community for further distribution. In spite of her commitment to the democratic and national cause Zitz-Halein remained realistic about people and conditions. She was not deluded by the Kinkels' optimism. "The political refugees in exile still dream of the realization of a unitary

Germany," the Mainz activist wrote. "They do not consider that the slow gradual pressure from above does not rouse the people to rebellion but demoralizes and makes them cowardly." "Want produces hunger," she continued, "and hunger baseness, which lets one be abused and even be grateful for it."[6]

Kathinka Zitz-Halein's assistance to the Kinkels represented only one part of her varied endeavors in the postrevolutionary decade. She maintained contact with the aged democrat Adam Itzstein and kept up her correspondence with Josef Hecker until his death in 1858. He continued to ask her opinion about current affairs. She applauded when she heard that German exiles in the United States such as Friedrich Hecker; Carl Schurz, who became the lieutenant governor of Wisconsin; and Adolf Rösler von Oels, who edited a German newspaper, were successful and that they had remained loyal to their democratic views. "The Americans know how to honor German men who stand out by their moral conduct," she concluded. She continued to be contacted by the politically persecuted such as an unnamed schoolteacher who supposedly lost his position because of his "progressive views." She worked at finding him a new position that would make use of his educational training and apparently was successful.[7]

The limited opportunity for public political action in the German states increased at the end of the 1850s with the outbreak of the war for Italian unification and the start of the so-called liberal era in Prussia. Once again progressive forces inside and outside Germany could reemerge. Kathinka Zitz-Halein, although plagued by ill health and financial problems, did manage a sporadic participation in civic affairs during the subsequent twelve years of the German unification era.

The Austro-French War of 1859 witnessed an outpouring of patriotic sentiment both within the German states and from German exile groups as most Germans rallied to Austria's side against the traditional enemy, France. As a testimony to her reputation as a civic-minded person, Zitz-Halein reported receiving printed appeals "from all sides" directed at German patriots with requests that she see to their distribution. Although she was willing to cooperate, she found this a dubious honor since many of the packages were unfranked, placing on her the cost of the postage. In the future, she wrote in April 1859, she would have to refuse acceptance since her budget did not permit her to assume new financial burdens.[8]

Her patriotic spirit was galvanized to the extent of engaging in war relief work, especially when it appeared that the war might spread to other members of the German Confederation. In spite of her own ill health, she took the lead in organizing assistance for wounded Austrian soldiers because nobody else seemed inclined to do it. Her public announcement, which called for donations of bandages, linen, and money, stressed that it was the mission of women to work for the cause of humanity and to stand above all party disputes. To overcome the significant anti-Austrian feeling that existed at that time in Mainz, especially in her circles, she pointed out that at the time of the munitions depot explosion of 1857 in Mainz it was Austria that delivered the most aid to the stricken city. Privately she had to overcome her strong personal dislike of the Austrian government. "I fundamentally hate the hypocritical Emperor [Francis Joseph]," she admitted, "the protector of priests and spiritual darkness." Only her concern for the "poor devils who are bleeding to death for his unjust cause" impelled her to act. After she had stepped forward the mayor's wife offered to collect supplies, but as Zitz-Halein stressed, virtually all donations still went to her. The Mainz patriot's basic skepticism regarding Austria's motives seemed to be justified by the quick peace that France and the Habsburg monarchy concluded in summer 1859. It was in her eyes a "rotten, shameful peace," because it initially appeared to make the pope the protector of a new Italian confederation, "a true mockery" of national unity, she called it. Nevertheless, she did accept the official thanks of the Austrian government for her efforts during the war.[9]

The sense of disappointment at the outcome of the war and over the lack of progress toward German unity was confirmed toward the end of the year in connection with the Schiller centennial, which led to the establishment of the Schiller Foundation. Designed to pay tribute to a great writer and German patriot, the celebration served to highlight division within German society according to political and religious beliefs. In Mainz, in spite of newspaper support for a citywide illumination and decoration, there was limited response. Much of the city remained in darkness, the Mainz writer remarked, reminding her of the "miserable [state of] German unity." She blamed her old enemies, the "well-to-do and the clerical party," for the poor support and took pleasure in writing down the more amusing anticlerical inscriptions that appeared on the houses of the "good citizens" *[Bürgerstand].*[10]

Because of her reputation as a champion of humanitarian causes, even though as a democrat, people turned to her for support in obtaining amnesties for political refugees. She responded with appeals to German rulers on their behalf. In a letter to the grand duke of

Hesse on behalf of the exile F. Bührmann, she showed her adeptness at argumentation. She downgraded the Revolution of 1848 but only in order to make a more effective case for her candidate. She portrayed him as a youthful enthusiast who had been swept along by events through his love for the fatherland and his desire to help the "afflicted people." There was no denying that he broke the law, she admitted, but she turned this concession into an argument with which the ruler could sympathize. She pointed out that "history teaches" that the greatest statesmen sometimes started out as the most zealous Jacobins but then became the loyalist supporters of monarchy. She pointed to the example of the Jacobin jurist Georg Friedrich Rebmann, who worked for the French Revolutionary government promoting freedom and equality but later entered the Bavarian service and rose to a high position. She assured the grand duke that Bührmann, like most refugees, regretted his earlier activities and now only wanted to live in peace, obey the laws, and be a loyal supporter of the royal house. She apologized for writing directly to the monarch without going through channels but complained that his subordinates could only judge the case as bureaucrats rather than from the standpoint of humanity. She concluded by reminding him that since he had recently pardoned a condemned criminal he should act like the Roman ruler Titus, who considered every day lost that he did not do someone a kindness. Her cleverly written letter was followed a few days later by the granting of amnesty, for which she claimed credit.[11]

A further indication of her reputation is reflected by her relationship with the working class in Mainz. Her friend J. P. Schöppler invited her to hear a speech by the socialist leader Ferdinand Lassalle when he appeared in Mainz on May 20, 1863. Schöppler knew of her interest in seeing such a controversial figure. Whether she attended is not known. She was also contacted by the moderate Workingmen's Educational Association of Mainz, which wished to obtain her support for their endeavors.[12]

The period from 1862 to 1871, the era of Prussian-led unification, were years of irregular political involvement and divided loyalties for Zitz-Halein. The contradictory emotions of a rising sense of German patriotism versus the dislike of Bismarckian Prussia, which seemed best equipped to realize the long desired aim of German unity, affected Kathinka Zitz-Halein as well as other German liberals and democrats. Both she and her friend Caroline Berthold sympathized with the Schleswig-Holsteiners during the Danish-German crisis. Berthold expressed amazement that she, "an old woman," could react like a "teenager" during the patriotic struggle. She regretted that Austria had not sought to lead the patriotic enthusiasm but instead left the initiative to Bismarck, who would do unheard-of harm. Zitz-Halein reported with apparent approval that the Mainzers supported the Austrian rather than the Prussian troops who were fighting in the north. At least this was the implication she drew from the fact that the donations to the Austrian army far exceeded those to the Prussian. It was a clearly a question of the lesser of two evils, and her eye problems permitted her to remain uninvolved in the mobilization of supplies.[13]

The two wars for German unification in 1866 and 1870–1871 found the sixty-five- to seventy-year-old and partially blind Mainz activist again ready to do her part. In answer to an appeal for donations by a local physician, she sent him some of her books that the wounded might appreciate reading. Moreover, she volunteered her services if the need to act occurred, even to the extent of going to the battlefield to tend the wounded. As she explained to Dr. Wenzel in her usual forthright way, "What a sister of mercy can do I will be capable of doing without the nun's garb or having taken vows, for I have a powerful will to act and so I shall be able to act." It was not necessary, since the war never actually reached Mainz. Her reaction to its outcome was not recorded.[14]

Caroline Berthold and Nanni Cavalli Wolf, Kathinka's other long-time friend, both worried about the impending war with France. The Darmstadt friend was pleased when she found out that her son was exempt from military service, but Caroline's two children were called up for the army. For Berthold, the conflict with France, which finally came in July 1870, was an "accursed war." "How human beings could act like wild animals for miserable insignificant reasons," she could not fathom. She saw no battles but only "slaughter" and "pure insanity." The war was the second act of 1866, she believed, and she prophetically wondered where the third act would be played. It would mean, she added, the end of monarchy.[15]

With the outbreak of the Franco-Prussian War Mainz became a center of military planning operations and an area where prisoners and wounded soldiers were brought. The sixty-nine-year-old German patriot, Kathinka Zitz-Halein, in spite of growing financial problems, threw herself into the war effort as if it were again 1848. From July to November she worked continually, preparing quarters for the wounded and then tending the soldiers. And after an illness in November she resumed her work. It was a bittersweet period, her pleasure over Germany's victory tempered by her financial problems. For her humanitarian efforts the Hessian government gave her a commendation and a medal, the fourth time in her long public life that she had been honored by the authorities for humanitarian work. Initially pleased by the recognition, she had herself photographed with the medal. Later she downgraded it, claiming it had lost all value for her when she realized how many had been distributed to supposedly undeserving people.[16]

In keeping with the general atmosphere, she as well as other 1848 democrats were swept along by the tide of patriotism into the Prussian camp. In "Noth der Zeit" (Troubled Times), which she published in July, she rhapsodized over the popular patriotic explosion, from "which Germany arises full of strength." She called on her readers to ignore the accompanying bloodshed since it would lead to a better age. Each had to sacrifice to the utmost. The mothers, she advised, should not hold back their sons but give them "your best blessing" and do their share by aiding the wounded. She noted proudly that the poem had "come off well." In her other war poem she paid effusive tribute to her old enemy, King William of Prussia, soon to be German emperor. No longer the butcher of 1849, he now received her accolade as the ruler who had accomplished great deeds and punished the haughty French. All Germany, she trumpeted somewhat incorrectly, awaited his call to create a united Germany. Women were integrated into the patriotic panorama; they contributed to the creative events not with weapons but with care of the unfortunate. These statements, as the title of the poem makes clear, were "From the Heart to His Majesty, King William of Prussia."[17]

By contrast it was her friend Caroline Berthold who in the blinding glare of the fireworks of war again saw something of the dawning new age. Her brother, a university professor, sent her a clipping containing a report from a philosopher's congress in Prague at which he spoke. What caught her eye, however, was the interesting speech of a Swiss woman. The following year she attended the congress in Frankfurt/Main and was impressed by the speeches by women, especially that of Bertha Marenholz-Bülow (1810–1893), a writer on educational issues. It must have been one of the earliest participations of women at German scholarly conferences. She recalled that the speaker had been involved at the meeting of the *Allgemeiner Deutscher Frauenverein* (General German Women's Association) in Kassel in October 1869. "Things in the world are moving forward wonderfully," she claimed, "and I cannot deny that I share it with heart and soul." Her Mainz friend's reaction to these comments, like the earlier remarks by Kinkel and Meysenbug, is unrecorded.[18]

Kathinka Zitz-Halein was always sensitive to the relationship between politics and literature. The latter could not remain unaffected by the changed political atmosphere of the 1850s and 1860s. According to Horst Denkler, the writers of the postrevolutionary era seemed to lose faith in their ability to carry art over into daily life in order to change reality. Instead they conformed more to the new situation of the 1850s. The increasing popularity of "family magazines" such as *Gartenlaube* signaled a growing depoliticization of German literature.[19]

For German women activists, too, the 1850s appeared to bring either a turning away from politics or one toward a more conservative orientation. Fanny Lewald Stahr became disillusioned with the people's capacity for democracy and focused on the princes as the agents of reform. In 1849 she told Prince Karl Alexander that for the time being all her hopes were centered on the "good princes," for she knew that a republic "was impossible in Germany." World history, she now realized, moved forward "not in days but in centuries." This was national liberalism in the making. Luise Mühlbach no longer wrote the social novels of her earlier career but began to turn out volumes extolling the glories of Frederick the Great. Louise Aston, the enfant terrible of German feminism, gave up her literary and feminist activities. Perhaps the most dramatic conversion was Ida Hahn-Hahn's. The daughter of an eccentric count, raised in isolated Mecklenburg and married to her cousin but divorced within three years, she became internationally known before the revolution through her rebellious writings and travelogues. Although she was never politically oriented before 1848, she did symbolize the principle of freedom and the carving out of a new life-style for women. Frightened by the social and political disorder that accompanied the upheaval of 1848, Hahn-Hahn found security within the Catholic church. Her conversion in 1850 marked a break with her previous existence, and she disowned her earlier writings. For Johanna Kinkel, Hahn-Hahn's experience only proved that one "could not trust anyone who had an aristocratic upbringing. It was like certain poisons which erupt after many years in a healthy body." Hahn-Hahn's new life was well known to Zitz-Halein, since she moved to Mainz.[20]

Kathinka Zitz-Halein swam against this more conservative literary current, as her work in the 1850s and 1860s demonstrates. She continued to turn out a large quantity of poems, short stories, novels, and novellas. In addition, her work showed two new emphases: children's stories and fictionalized biographies of famous people.[21] She continued to utilize historical settings for her stories, even if her interpretation of events was not always accurate by modern standards. She readily admitted that she could be accused of departing from the path of historical veracity, explaining that there was a tendency toward fantasy in her literary makeup. But often it served to make a larger point. For example, in "Lorenzo Medici" she celebrated the Florentine leader, somewhat incorrectly, as the bearer of freedom but only to bemoan the loss of it to the Austrians in the eighteenth century. Again taking liberties with the known facts the Mainz writer has the Greek poetess Sappho attend parliamentary assemblies.[22] Most importantly Zitz-Halein's work continued to reflect her commitment to the German revolution, democracy, and national unity, as well as her advocacy of civic involvement for women and the need to defend their rights.[23]

These latter two themes are much in evidence in her writings during the 1850s. Her major work of the 1850s was the previously discussed *Magdalene Horix,* her personal history of the French Revolutionary era in Mainz. In the novel Zitz-Halein accurately portrays women as performing in patriotic plays, discussing political issues, participating in freedom tree ceremonies, attending Jacobin Club meetings (as paintings attest), acting in the republican theater, and later suffering for their activities.[24] Women appear frequently as the main subjects of her shorter works. In "The Female Patriots of Laval," which she translated and adapted, she emphasized the theme of women's civic responsibility. Set in the same historical era as *Magdalene Horix,* but this time in France during the war years of 1792–1793, it centers around the heroic actions of several young women. But the contemporaneity of their example is made clear. "Let us hope," the writer concludes, "that when the time comes, which is inevitable, Germany too will not lack women who are ready to sacrifice joyfully everything for country and honor like the noble women of Laval." Her biographical sketch of Adam Lux, the Mainz Jacobin who fell victim to the terror in France, provided an opportunity to comment on the heroism of Charlotte Corday and the private bravery of Lux's daughter, Marie.[25]

Other historical analogies serve to make a point about her own society. In "Lukretia," which deals with the period of the overthrow of the Tarquins and the founding of the Roman republic, she suggests, contrary to fact but appropriate to her purpose, that the republic made it possible for women to achieve a more elevated status. "A Victim of Fanaticism," set during the English Reformation, also highlights a woman's bravery. Johanna Boche is brought before Archbishop Cranmer to be interrogated as a heretic. Making use of the "women's right" to speak she attacks the Church of England and the "gospel according to Cranmer" as a new form of Inquisition. I had hoped, Johanna tells him, "We would have nothing more to do with torture and burnings at the stake. . . . From the bottom of my heart I despise you." She was later executed, Zitz-Halein relates.[26]

In her last collection of poetry, *Dur- und Molltöne* (Sharps and Flats), which appeared in 1860, Zitz-Halein continues to treat the theme of women and patriotism. In "Emilie, Countess Platter," she showed her continued support for Poland, at a time when it was declining in Germany, and for her ideal of feminine civic activity. She paid tribute to women who sent their sons into battle during the Polish revolt of 1830 or who, mounted and armed, gave encouragement to the men.

> Tender women also want to sacrifice
> Soft hearts also glow inwardly
> Here the mother sends both her sons
> Into the battle storm, never again to return.
> ....
> But there in masculine outfit
> With sword belt on, high amount a horse
> The naked saber in the white hand
> A beautiful maiden.
> Where she appeared she gave men courage
> Where she commanded, they gave their
>   blood
> There where the struggle burned fiercely, she
>   never failed.
>   ....
> She seemed to be the lofty genius of battle
> The good spirit of the Fatherland.

There was more than poetical truth to the poem. Prussian officials in the nineteenth century repeatedly called attention to the "fanatical Polish women" who "are the chief insurgents and true ringleaders. . . . They suckle and rear their children on hate and rage against the Prussians, and divest themselves of every female virtue to satisfy their most unwholesome fanaticism."[27] Using the French Revolution as her vehicle and this time siding with the Girondins against the Jacobins, Zitz-Halein praised the Girondin leader Madame Roland. The Frenchwoman, in spite of mixing in the affairs of men, still received praise for arousing the flame of patriotism, which Zitz-Halein called "no chimera, no madness," in the hearts of women. Her treatment of Roland again suggests that the Mainz writer was flexible about feminist activities. In her view Roland was that woman who stood astride the two worlds of gender. It was not vanity but desire to be of "use to your people" that motivated the Frenchwoman.[28]

> By word and pen you fought for the people
> Like a swallow raised yourself above your sex.
> You were a man in women's clothes
> A noble clever free man . . .
> You often moved the people . . .
> You acted as a man
> And as a man went to your death.

Several of Kathinka Zitz-Halein's literary efforts, besides praising brave or politically oriented women, focused on the theme of husband-wife relations and the necessity for women to defend their rights within the family. The stories, however, are not clear calls for women's rights; instead they emit ambivalent signals. "Frauenherz" (Women's Heart) concerns the relationship between a wife and her dissolute, lazy, spendthrift and criminal husband. Geraldine, the heroine of the tale, does not resign herself to domestic injustice but defends her rights by denouncing her husband to the sheriff as a thief and testifying against him in court but almost, it seems, for his own good. "True love," the wife explains sternly, "shows itself less through vows than through action," and her husband's warranted the strongest condemnation. Geraldine proceeds to raise her children properly, but Zitz-Halein ends the tale on an ambiguous note, which perhaps suggests her own inner struggle or the need for a socially acceptable conclusion: Geraldine leaves England to search for her husband, who has been transported.[29]

This ambivalence is reflected in more optimistic stories such as "Die Convenienzheirat" (The Marriage of Convenience) and "Männerstreich" (Men's Escapades). The first depicts a marriage between a thirty-eight-year-old man and a seventeen-year-old girl whom he has seen four times previously. Although initially a loveless marriage in which the husband neglects the wife, it ends with a reconciliation. "Men's Escapades," which begins with the husband's cheating on his wife, ends with the Lothario's becoming a model husband.[30]

These two tales, however, are balanced by strong statements against marital injustice found in Zitz-Halein's "Der Geliebter" (The Lover) and "Bilder aus der Eheleben" (Pictures from a Marriage). In the former, set in Prussia in 1813, the period of the War of Liberation against the French, the heroine, Hulda, refuses to agree to an arranged marriage; she condemns marriage as a "connection which thousands reject . . . and no truthful woman praises." She compares love to a mountain that one must descend as soon as one can climb no higher, since there is no plateau. Hulda not only remains true to her principles she unmasks the boyfriend of her friend as a false lover. "Pictures from a Marriage," whose theme is a wife's refusal to submit to a tyrannical husband, was based in part on her experiences with her estranged husband. The husband demands his wife's submission according to the law. She complains bitterly about how the Napoleonic code permits male despotism as long as the wife is not physically assaulted or the husband's mistress is not brought into the household. "You're base and dishonorable in my eyes," she writes to him, "but in the eyes of the law not punishable." She leaves her husband but loses custody of their child. She then sues for divorce but fails and is forced to return to him, whereupon she commits suicide.[31]

In "Johanna Presto," the most interesting of this group, Zitz-Halein presents a two-sided statement regarding female emancipation. The heroine, Johanna, is educated by her father "more to be hero than to be a woman." She meets a man who declares his love for her but asks for a relationship outside the bounds of marriage. Never, he tells her, "will you become my wife in the eyes of the law. . . . The bands of nature are mightier than the chains of the church. . . . Be mine without vows or conditions." Johanna accepts the proposal, although Zitz-Halein suggests that the man was actually unworthy of her. They live together and have a child, but the husband kills someone in an argument over the couple's relationship. They flee from the authorities and when surrounded commit suicide rather than surrender. What is one to make of the tale? It is mainly Johanna's decision that they end their lives. Her strength of will triumphs over his uncertainty but leads to their deaths. Johanna is portrayed sympathetically throughout the story and is depicted as a better person than her husband. Yet her decision to enter into an unorthodox arrangement ultimately ends in tragedy. In the final analysis a woman could not escape her fate.[32]

Although these examples reflect her strong views about women's domestic equality and their civic responsibility, the term *emancipated women* still conjured up unacceptable visions of cigar-smoking, pants-

wearing females who sacrificed their families on the altar of "emancipation" and who readily entered into illicit relations. The fate of a
woman, she admonished, was to be a woman "to the fullest extent."
Even if plagued by men and denied their rights, women would not
gain them by a "distasteful masculine behavior or by an unfeminine
defiance" but only by bringing men to acknowledge their high moral
worth "through the exercise of feminine virtues." In a letter to the
publisher Ernst Keil she referred to herself as an "authentic feminine
being" not an "emancipated women" who "with riding whip in hand
achieves satisfaction for herself." She claimed to be pleased that the
"crazy ideas" of the "free woman" were past, but she was not sure that
the other extreme, of keeping women solely within domestic limits,
had been rejected. Her condemnation of extremists like Aston, who
gave female emancipation a bad name, make her sound more conservative than she actually was. Caring about politics or working in a
political context was, in her view, certainly not unfeminine; standing
up for one's rights against one's husband was proper. Where she
seemed to differ from other moderate femininists was in her apparent
unconcern about educational or employment opportunities for
women. There is little evidence that these issues were of significance
to her, in spite of her personal experience. She ultimately realized that
the French law codes were "bad" for women. But only political issues
roused her to action. Perhaps this was because she never ranged
beyond the specific experiences of her marriage or the political culture
of Mainz.[33] Her friends Johanna Kinkel, Caroline Berthold, and Malwida von Meysenbug were more sensitive to social and economic issues.

Besides her staples of short stories, novellas, novels, and poems,
Zitz-Halein added children's stories and fictionalized biographies of
famous people to her literary repertoire. Both reflected her continued
commitment to political and social progress.

More than twenty titles of children's books appeared between 1844
and 1862 under her real or pen names as she sought to cash in on the
growing popularity of the new literary genre. Children's stories were
regarded as a proper sphere for women's literary activity. Women,
according to one nineteenth-century authority, were thought to have
a special talent for appealing to children, being better able to "speak
the language of the youngest years" than men. Reflecting the general
attitude toward women, he commented that children's stories were
mainly copies of the classics, thus requiring a minimum of creativity.[34]

As expected, Zitz-Halein used children's stories to impart moral
lessons to her young readers. For example, in *Spiegelbilder* (Mirror

Images) she warns against drinking, and in "Juwelenkästchen" (Jewelry Chest) she stresses the importance of hard work, fulfillment obligations, kindness to outsiders, patience, and avoidance of excessive pride. "Das Goldkind" (Cherub) portrays girls and boys in traditional roles: he studying, she sweeping, sewing, and nursing. The poems and stories, however, contain more specific social and political messages. The commitment to religious liberty based on the equality of all religions represented one of her longest and most strongly held beliefs, and it was reiterated in the following poems:

> We all pray to one God.
> God rates a person's deed
> Be they Jew or Christian
> Sunworshipper or Moslem
> Catholic or Lutheran,
> Caring only if he is a good person.
>
> To Him it is the same
> Whether one calls himself
> Christian, Jehovah, Allah, or Brahma
> Whether he serves as bishops or Dalai Lama.
> View every person always as a brother.

She is more explicit in "Judenhass" (Hatred of Jews), in which children attack a Jewish boy and try to take away the coal he is carrying to his father. A man appears and lectures the children:

> A Jew is made in God's image
> Just as the best of Christians.
> The Lord knows no difference.

The children are rueful and one states: "It shall not happen again."[35]

The themes of religious equality and toleration were complemented by more explicit political messages. Schenda points out that censors were slower to focus on children's literature. In "Soldatenspiel" (Playing Soldiers) Zitz-Halein condemns militarism but not fighting for a just cause. When the mother objects to the children's playing soldiers they reply[36]:

Old Beliefs and New Realities

> We practice with weapons
> But take the sword in hand
> To gain freedom for people and country
> And to die for justice.

Her "Geography in Verse" permitted her to take swipes at the enemies of democracy. France under Louis Napoleon is still officially a republic, she notes in 1850, but "soon enough," she predicts accurately, "one hounds it to death." In Switzerland, where "freedom is supposed to reign," she remarks critically but correctly, not all the cantons shared it. In Germany, "Herr Humdrum Way" with his "long pigtail" and "empty head" has resumed his place of importance next to Herr Michel (the symbol of the sleepy indifferent German). In Berlin bureaucrats and soldiers were too numerous to count, and, she relates ironically, "the king rules as the "protector of beautiful Baden."[37]

She continued to stress the theme of the Revolution of 1848. In "Katzenmusik" (literally cats' music, a popular method, involving noisemaking, used by the people to express displeasure of an individual) the cats hold a rally on the roof of the official's house to discuss the "March achievements."[38]

> They want unrestricted freedom of the press,
> They want to live off roast and milk.

The official is alarmed.

> There are democrats
> Who carry on here,
> The counselor cries.
> Where are the gendarmes?
> The pack will murder me
> For it knows no mercy.
>
> And when the torches were brought
> The ghost had quickly vanished.
> Of evil democrats
> There was no trace.
> Only cats.
>
> The lieutenant cried "forbidden" . . .
> That in a state of seige
> One congregates.

> When the cats ignored him
> Thereupon the lieutenant ordered fire.
> Then the whole pack
> With a ridiculing howl
> Ran from the roof.
> ....
> The counselor retired,
> The neighbors continued laughing,
> The cats came again
> And amused themselves further.

In "The Beggar" Zitz-Halein recalls the spring 1849 uprising and the fate of the defeated insurgents. The beggar tells a young girl of his struggle for the constitution, his injury in battle, his capture at Rastatt, and his imprisonment. Finally released, he must find his way home.[39]

> I meant well for the fatherland.
> Loyalty flowed in my veins.
> Now many a man insults me,
> Calls me disloyal, a rebel.
> That hurts me to the core
> When one has given one's blood
> Because one believed
> To serve the fatherland with one's life.

The child helps him. These children's poems retold to the younger generation the meritorious deeds of the true heroes of 1848–1849. Retaining her belief in the pre-1848 principles and the role of the writer, Zitz-Halein would not let the democratic traditions be forgotten.

More ambitious than Zitz-Halein's children's books were the biographical novels of well-known individuals. She followed the literary mode of the 1850s, which witnessed the increasing popularity of this novelistic device. According to Hartmut Eggert it was favored reading matter from 1850 to 1875, constituting as much as 50 percent of all fictional production. He sees the genre as a substitute for an active civic life as readers lived vicariously through the accomplishments of famous people. "Serious writers" and literary critics usually vented their wrath at the practitioners of this literary form. They accused writers such as Theodor Mundt and Zitz-Halein's friend Heribert Rau of making a "mockery of every artistic form," of using the title characters merely as a means of attracting readers to second rate, "contentless," "factory like" products, in which scenes shift without reason and chronology is ignored or deliberately altered. Some critics noted, disapprovingly, the large share that female writers had in producing this literary popularization. It reflected, one wrote, an attempt by women to reach a higher level of literature, but it led only to a corruption of genuine biographies and novels. Women were too hampered by their lack of a broad cultural background and too focused on quick financial gain to produce finished works. Adolf Stern did admit that biographical novels had the potential of elevating the reader, and he acknowledged that in the hands of a Kathinka Zitz-Halein, "the capacity for edifying one."[40]

Kathinka Zitz-Halein always claimed that her writing, particularly her poetry, reflected her current views. Similarly her choices for her biographical novels represented a statement about her social, literary, and political ideals. Not for her the long renditions of the doings of aristocrats and kings à la Luise Mühlbach or the later Fanny Lewald-Stahr.[41] Zitz-Halein's subjects generally identified with progressive ideas during the end of the eighteenth and the first half of the nineteenth centuries, starting with her Goethe biography in 1862 and continuing with those of Rahel Varnhagen von Ense in 1863, Heine in 1864, and Byron in 1867 and the unpublished biography of Clemens von Brentano. These were large-scale projects, the Goethe work twenty-one hundred pages in length and the others each more than thirteen hundred pages long. They suggest at the very least that her eye problems, about which she complained repeatedly in her diary, were not a major hindrance to her professional activity. They also serve to reemphasize the seriousness with which she approached her literary work. She prepared well for her writing. Her correspondence with the director of the Hessian State Library in Wiesbaden, Gottfried Seebode, contains numerous references to books about and by Goethe, Heine, Börne, Gutzkow, Varnhagen, and Gentz that he obtained for her or apologized for being unable to procure.[42] She believed that the novelist just as the historian had the obligation to treat historical persons in a truthful fashion even if the "nimbus of great men, who are only talented persons with weaknesses," suffers as a result. She subscribed to Ranke's dictum, expressed in his *Historisch-politische Zeitschrift,* that it was an "impermissible sensitivity to have reservations about portraying history with all possible accuracy: Certainly deficiencies and human weaknesses will become visible, but should one fear that?"[43] In the Rahel biography, one of the first attempts to present a life and times of that salon woman, she lists the sources that she used. In the Heine work she notes that relatively few biographies have appeared, so that she has had to rely on the original of Heine's and Börne's words where relevant. She allowed herself, as she admitted in the books themselves, to take liberties with the chronology and to invent characters and conversations, but the basic structure of the biographies is accurate. The works were designed for that part of the public who would not read the works of these authors in the original and for whom traditional memoirs or biographies were too "dry or detailed" but who nevertheless desired episodes from the lives of important persons unpretentiously presented. This was done in a novel-like format through which the reader would learn something about the main character while being entertained by minor figures or invented characters who tied the narrative together. The intended audience was the middle-class reader who was amenable to culture presented in a palatable form.[44]

Consequently, despite their length, the works were not especially strong in political and social content. Fiction had become less a medium for political and social protest than an entertaining diversion. Yet her fictionalized biographies did touch on important questions. In the Rahel biography the issue of Jews in German society is raised. Zitz-Halein brought to this problem both knowledge and empathy. Mainz was the center of a large (6 percent in 1849) and old Jewish community whose members had been granted citizenship by the Napoleonic regime. Later through the efforts of the Rhenish Hessian parliamentary representatives full legal emancipation was gained throughout the Grand Duchy in 1847. Jews played an active civic role in Mainz, serving on the city council and being involved in the Revolution of 1848.[45]

In a number of her published works Zitz-Halein mentions Jews, and scattered references also appear in her "Skizzen" and "Tagebuch." Almost always they are portrayed as human beings, not as personifications of greed and immorality. She is among the very few German writers of the nineteenth century who depicted Jews in such a sympathetic light. This is emphasized in the story, "Jew and Christian," which is set in the Mainz area during the anti-Jewish violence issuing from the Second Crusade. It describes the love affair of a Jewish boy and a Christian girl. The boy, Bergmann, refuses to wear his yellow badge of identification, and because of his "untypical Jewish physiognomy" ("he looked like a prince," she notes) he is able to move around freely. After much travail, which includes a description of the burning of the Jews, the girl, Jutta, converts to Judaism. She describes the Jewish wedding ceremony with sympathy, as she had earlier depicted a Passover celebration. Nevertheless, she is not allowed to end the story on this happy note. Bergmann is attacked and killed by robbers; their child dies of disease, and Jutta, now hit by pangs of conscience, reconverts to Christianity and enters a monastery.[46] Six years later in *Magdalene Horix,* the status of the Jews of Mainz at the end of the eighteenth century is described. She portrays them as suffering under discriminatory and demeaning restrictions, victims of a "shameful intolerance." Zitz-Halein shows herself familiar with the Yiddish dialect, which she quotes but without any attempt to ridicule Jews.[47]

In *Rahel* Zitz-Halein describes the milieu in which some Jewish women were torn between emancipation and tradition. The Mainz writer portrays Rahel approvingly as a Voltairean in religious matters, honoring all religions regardless of form. Zitz-Halein emphasizes that the Berlin woman refused marriage to a Jew in order to make her own choice. And when Varnhagen von Ense proposes marriage she agrees to convert. Rahel's Jewish friend Henriette Herz (1764–1847), like Rahel torn between different religious and cultural worlds, is depicted as a high-minded individual who refuses an offer to become the tutor of King Frederick William III's eldest daughter because she will not convert.

The issue of the future of Jews in Germany is discussed in *Rahel* in connection with the anti-Jewish riots of 1819. Zitz-Halein describes a scene in Berlin in which a Jew is followed by a hostile crowd of several hundred, "like a desperate animal." Just as the crowd closes in, a well-to-do person intercedes and lectures the crowd on the equality of Jews as human beings and creatures of God. When the gentleman gives the Jew some money to compensate for his persecution, even Zitz-Halein remarks that the Jew made a "good business." Nevertheless, she characterized the anti-Jewish riots as a plague that the authorities found difficult to control. For many, she opined, the violence might be just fun at the expense of the weaker, rather than hatred of Jews. Yet, she warned, "Misdeeds where they are released from the chains of obedience, easily overstep all moderation and then lead to robbery and murder." Rahel and her friends also discuss the events, and the former predicts that the Jews will be driven out of Germany. A friend disagrees because the authorities will keep the hostility within limits. What limits, Rahel exclaims, "of torture and contempt, of hitting the Jew in the face, of kicks and throwing him down steps" and of forcing him to survive on "wretched peddling."[48]

Zitz-Halein followed the Rahel biography with one of Heinrich

Heine, who came from the same milieu as the Jewish woman. He became what she might have become were she male. There is in the work about Heine less than we might expect to find regarding political and social issues. Even Heine's role as a critic of German society is hardly touched. The most political section of the work does not include Heine but rather his rival, Ludwig Börne, whom Zitz-Halein seems to prefer to Heine because Börne was more politically engaged. In over ten pages she describes in detail the background and course of the 1832 Hambach rally, the most important democratic political meeting in Germany before 1848. She calls attention to the stimulus of the French Revolution of 1830, which, she correctly claims, touched even ordinary people in the Mainz area. She accurately describes the press campaign organized by Johann Wirth and Philipp Siebenpfeiffer as well as the pro-Polish sentiment released by the Polish refugees' passage through Germany. Also well captured by her, but often underemphasized by historians, was the carnival-like atmosphere of the Hambach rally, "like a fair," with booths, portable restaurants, carousels, and the beer, wine and sausage dealers. Recently Karl Wegert has stressed the fairlike and disorganized atmosphere of the rally, but only to play down its political seriousness. Only a fraction of the people, he claims, went to the castle for political reasons; the rest wandered around enjoying the festivities. He seems to have missed the point of political rallies.[49]

The surprisingly prominent role of women at the Hambach Castle is also stressed as Zitz-Halein describes the procession up the hill led by white-clothed women and girls. Siebenpfeiffer, a male feminist, had appealed to women to participate in the rally, calling their exclusion from political life a "mistake and blemish." He wanted women's status to be transformed from a servant's to that of a "free companion of a free citizen," and he advocated their legal equality with men. Zitz-Halein's Börne, whom she celebrates as one of the "great spirits of the German nation," whose name was "mentioned only with respect," defends the participation of women in the event. Three months before the rally, while in Paris, Börne had in fact movingly described the impact on the Polish refugees there of a statement of support from a "Young Women's Association" in Mainz. At the Hambach rally Börne, in Zitz-Halein's words, calls women's involvement a belated recognition that their political exclusion was a great failing in European society. The rally offers them a symbolic role in their own emancipation, and Börne wonders why they were not invited up to the podium. When a stranger takes issue with Börne's feminist utterances, Zitz-Halein has him unmasked as an agent provocateur. Börne's relationship with the married Jeanette Strauss-Wohl is also worked into the narrative. The Mainz writer correctly portrays Madame Strauss as a strong personality who is not afraid to defend the deceased Börne against Heine's attacks.[50] By contrast, according to Zitz-Halein, Heine disliked strong, spirited, and intelligent women.

Zitz-Halein's respect for George Sand is reemphasized. Depicting Heine's visit to the French writer's salon, the Mainz author proceeds to describe her work habits, especially her professional commitment and her ability to "write through the night." One of the fictional female characters whom Zitz-Halein weaves into the story defends George Sand against the criticism of her parents, and clearly the author sides with her. Zitz-Halein also points out that a writer like Sand is less important for what she writes than for the public's perception of her. She functions as "a thermometer of the age," the Mainz writer notes in an expression reminiscent of Charles Fourier's.[51]

The publication of these longer works in the twilight of Zitz-Halein's career with the award of a grant from the Schiller Foundation could be seen as a sign of her growing stature as a writer. Moreover, in spite of the popularity of fictionalized biographies, her publications in the 1860s were during a period of depression in book production, when the printing of books was down nearly 50 percent from the peak years of the 1840s. Her literary career ended before new periodicals such as *Gartenlaube* and *Romanzeitung* revolutionized the literary profession. The record of the last fifteen years of Zitz-Halein's literary activity, however, is mixed. There were compliments from individuals such as Joseph D. K. Brugger, head of *Verein für deutsche Reinsprache*, and Wilhelm Koffka, editor of *Mannheimer Journal*. A local wine dealer came by with a message from the Potsdam writer Galen (Philipp Lange) that he was a great fan of hers and was quoted as saying, "This woman must have considerable talent." "That pleased me very much," she wrote proudly. Equally satisfying was a report from her friend Caroline Berthold, who reported finding a copy of her *Rahel* in a Königsberg lending library, whose owner told her that Zitz-Halein's works were among the library's most popular. Lending libraries *(Leihbibliotheke)* were a major factor in the success of a book, exercising, according to some, a dictatorship over the book market in the 1860s similar to that of book clubs today. The purchase of books by the libraries, which supplied 90 percent of the reading public's needs, was often decisive in the profitability of a literary work.[52]

In spite of some praise Zitz-Halein's literary reputation was never so high that she could be assured of adequate review space in the journals. The reception of her literary work of the 1850s and 1860s, however, must be examined in relation to that of other female writers. The place of women in German literature and the generally hostile reaction to their literary efforts, at least by certain critics and journals, continued into the post-1850 period and affected Kathinka Zitz-Halein. Women were often seen as the main producers of "inferior products," who actually did not produce or initiate anything new but "merely reproduce," in their "dilettantish way," and whose output led to lower honoraria for serious writers.[53] It was difficult for women to escape being labeled as "female" writers, at times criticized for writing like women, at others for not doing so. Luise Mühlbach, one of the most successful writers in the same years, was condemned on the appearance of her *Memoiren eines Weltkindes,* as well as for her earlier novels, such as *Aphra Behn,* for "spreading dirt, of which a woman ought to have no idea, let alone in such detail," and for depicting scenes that "stand in starkest contradiction to the traditions of feminine morals." Her belief in the emancipation of the sexes, which one critic considered the core of her earlier novels, was presented with an "unfeminine brazenness" that made a mockery of all femininity. Her courage was too great for a woman, wrote Prutz; more modesty and discretion would have been better. Yet, when she turned away to her highly profitable biographical novels of Frederick the Great, Marie Antoinette, Prince Eugen, the Great Elector, and the court of Henry VIII she was marked down for writing "factory-like," "petty bourgeois," "anecdotal books," based on undigested material. The gender factor invariably surfaced. Katherina Diez (1809–1882) was complimented because her style deviated "very profitably from the writing of our literary ladies" in not authoring "lending library novels." Louise François (1807–1893) was counted among the few female writers who devoted themselves to "pure intellectual activity." Louise von Gall (1815–1855) was praised for not stepping outside the bounds of "most strict femininity," but when she did try to deal with politics Prutz considered her out of her element. Mathilde Raven (1817–1898) was dismissed for producing "knitting," whereas Luise von Bornstedt's (1807–1870) work represented the "feminine genre" of "*Weltschmerz Literatur.*" Marie Knauff (1842–1895) was credited with writing with "almost masculine energy," as was Fanny Lewald, who could not shake herself of a certain "masculine characteristic." Similarly Louise Otto was praised for turning away from her earlier eccentric fantasies and giving her stories a historical basis, which made her work suitable not only for "women's spheres." She has "knowledge and character," the reviewer concluded.[54]

Against this backdrop it is not surprising that Kathinka Zitz-Halein's reviews were mixed and often demonstrated an antifeminine bias. *Donner und Blitz,* besides rousing the ire of some Mainzers because of its thinly veiled attack on her enemies, was treated roughly in the *Blätter für literarische Unterhaltung.*[55] The reviewer said it contained more fog than thunder from 1848. He admitted that she was "not without talent" but he found her treatment of the anti-democratic characters tending toward caricature and written from the point of view of the "extreme left." He attributed this to the gender factor since women easily absorb the view of their brothers and fathers. For some reason he did not mention husbands. But magnanimously and deprecatingly he did not begrudge her this weakness. Indeed, he wrote, it belonged to the "beautiful privileges of the heart."

The following year in *Didaskalia*[56] Lorenz Dieffenbach praised her *Maikräuter* because of her inexhaustible inventiveness. In 1856 *Blätter für literarische Unterhaltung*[57] reviewed her *Weltpantheon,* which contained two hundred short characterizations of famous men and women from the ancient world to the modern age. It too, illustrated her imagination and inventiveness. The reviewer, while conceding that Zitz-Halein had set a difficult task for herself and complimenting her for her "sound and correct judgment," found many of her sketches neither exhaustive nor marked by pithy points. Most of all he was critical of her choice of poetic style, which he found disconcerting. It was as if, he correctly realized, she were more interested in the substance and thus wrote poetry as prose. It was a fair evaluation of her political and social poetry, with which she later identified. Two months later Hermann Marggräff reviewed her novella collection, *Schiller's Laura,* which was highlighted by the title story, and again stressed gender factors. He found the work "clear, in places almost daringly masculine" in expression and not lacking a humorous conception, "so extremely rare in women."[58]

The most severe criticism for being a female writer that Kathinka Zitz-Halein had to face occurred in 1860 with the appearance of her third volume of poetry, *Dur- und Molltöne.* It triggered an entirely negative review in *Blätter für literarische Unterhaltung.* The anonymous reviewer not only criticized her judgment of individuals whom she memorialized in poetry and her poetic style but made disparaging comments about women who mixed in political activity, which was the male's sphere. In the political sky, so the reviewer lectured, women could aspire to at best glimmer modestly rather than to brighten the sky as he suggested Zitz-Halein wished to do. It was the trite comparison between the moon and the sun. The critic also dredged up her old disputes with Lubojatzky and Hart concerning her marriage. Naturally the Mainz writer was incensed over the personal and professional attack, and she refused to accept the public rebuke. When *Blätter* declined to print her retort she was able to have it published in the *Nordstern*. In it she defended her interest in politics, however modest her role. Lights that only glimmer, she reminded her antagonist, did not leave behind the foul stench of a torch. The collection of poems that occasioned the chastisement contained her patriotic pieces, already cited, from the period 1848–1858. It was these poems that so upset the reviewer, and in her letter of defense she reiterated her old stance on feminism. She denied mixing in the "struggle of the men," pointing out that nobody "hates more than I the emancipation intoxicated women, nobody seeks more than I to work in feminine ways." But this, she strongly stated, reemphasizing her basic philosophy, "never excludes the profound conviction of loyalty to the fatherland." She again outlined her patriotic endeavors of the previous fifteen years, including her more recent efforts during the Austro-French war of 1859, none of which she claimed was unfeminine.

Admitting that in some poems she might not have selected the most appropriate verse, she stood by her old credo of "often preferring to sacrifice the form rather than the thought." The poems were "outpourings of my feelings" that might occasionally send forth "wild sprouts" but also contained "much good fruit." It was a fair response, and her ally, Seebode, called it an "impressive and clever settling of accounts."[59]

Her biographical novels received varied reviews. The work on Goethe was given a favorable evaluation in *Blätter für literarische Unterhaltung*,[60] even though the reviewer admitted his dislike of that type of novel. Later that year the same journal delivered an extremely negative critique of the Rahel Varnhagen von Ense volumes, damning the Mainz writer for paraphrasing Rahel's letters and memoirs and adopting the salon speech of the day, although this was in keeping with the purpose of the novels. Later reviewers found it generally deserving of praise because of her careful preparation and sensitivity to the psychological dimensions of Rahel's existence between the worlds of Jewry and Germandom. Only the volumes' excessive length, often a product of the economics of publishing, might prevent the study from achieving an "honorable place among the works of our women," wrote one critic. Insufficient attention, it should be stressed, has been paid to the pioneering effort of Zitz-Halein's Rahel biography. According to the recent edition of Rahel Varnhagen von Ense's collected works, Zitz-Halein's study was the first attempt at a biographical treatment of her life. The first male biographer of Rahel, Eduard Schmidt-Weissenfels, relegated her to the sphere of the true feminine because she never published her writings or engaged in politics.[61]

The Byron biography also experienced a varied reception. One reviewer defended her against her north German detracters, such as *Blätter für literarische Unterhaltung,* which, he claimed with some justification, seemed to damn everything authored by a woman. He saw it as a concerted effort to drive women out of the literary profession but hoped that Kathinka Zitz-Halein would not be frightened off. The critic praised her ability to transform ordinary biographical scenes into "novelistic depictions," which in the cleverness of their dialogue and the sense for the humorous were the equal of the best of Germany's writers. He also credited her with a devotion to historical accuracy and a willingness to show Byron's weaknesses, instead of filling the pages with gossip. The historical novel, he noted, ceased to be historical when the hero seems superhuman. Perhaps most revealing in the review was the critic's emphasis on gender. Seldom with a woman, he stressed, did one find such a "vigorous (and) at times cheerful writing style," even with those sections that "spoke to the heart." The author's style, he continued, "was a far cry from the usual emotional out-pourings of female writers, and on the contrary strives for a powerful impact." Because of this characteristic, he pointed out, her novels were suitable reading matter for men.

The final volume of Kurz's history of German literature, in attempting an overall evaluation of Zitz-Halein, characterized her as a "not insignificant talent." He praised her ability to express a state of mind or mood and found her love poems "intimate and warm." Criticism was directed at her use of verse, especially in her last volume of poetry, where it failed to "enliven" her politically and socially oriented poems. To this estimation should be added the comments of her fellow Mainzer Ludwig Fränkel, who in a partially hostile evaluation, regretted her need to earn money and to write "en gros" work. Because of it, he believed, our "feminine literature lost a many sided talent who possessed a sure hand in lyrical verse . . . and satire."[62]

The reviews of her books reflected her at best uneven reputation. If success is to be measured by financial gain then Kathinka Zitz-Halein must be counted among the vast majority of unsuccessful writers. For every Berthold Auerbach or Eugenie Marlitt who were paid on the basis of sales and could live well off the proceeds from writing, there were many more Lubojatzkys who died as paupers.[63] It is not certain that Zitz-Halein's income from her extensive literary work did much more than cover the costs of her writing. Her most successful period was probably the 1860s, at least according to the surviving records.[64] Her biographical novels were, nevertheless, semicommissioned works for which she was paid by the quire (sixteen printed pages). But at least she did not have to contribute to printing costs as other writers were forced to do. She did have to insist that her name or a recognizable pseudonym *(Zianitzka)* be used. For the Goethe biography she received 2 taler (3.50 gulden) per quire or 275 taler (476 gulden) for a work of 2,195 printed pages, and for the Byron volumes she was paid 50 percent more per quire. Zitz-Halein's payments of 2 to 3 taler per quire were, according to the estimates of Wittmann and Schenda, 30 to 50 percent below the average paid to ordinary writers, although these figures may refer to shorter works. For the average writer who wished to live from her pen, these figures meant the need to "work like a steam engine and annually manufacture a certain number of volumes." Robert Gisekes, one of the more popular writers in the 1850s and 1860s, who wrote fifteen volumes of novels, earned about 1,100 gulden per year, which Wittmann calculates was enough for the living expenses of a modest bachelor. There must have been some truth to Zitz-Halein's claims that men believed women could live on practically nothing and that the pay of a writer did not compare favorably with that of a clerk.[65]

As low as her rate of compensation was, it was not even easy for the Mainz writer to obtain it. In her negotiations with the Leipzig publisher Kollmann, who brought out her Goethe, Heine, and Rahel series, Zitz-Halein had to fight for her honoraria. She complained to him, "What you offer goes beyond the limits of the possible." It would hardly pay for the costs of paper and light and heat needed to write. "Do you begrudge the writer a small recompense for her sour work," she cajoled. She agreed to do the Goethe work for 3.50 gulden, payable on publication, and demanded twenty-five free copies and the publication of the series under her name or at least an anagram of it. Kollmann accepted her terms, but reaching an agreement over price was only the first step; receiving the money was another matter. Kollmann sought to defer payment as long as he could, finally paying her in installments over a three-month period, and she then found that cashing his checks was difficult.[66] The last of her longer works, with the Mannheim publisher Schneider also ended on a sour note. Although her contract provided her with a higher honorarium, payable on publication, not until several months later did she receive the last of her money.[67]

With the publication of the Byron biography in 1867 her significant literary accomplishments were over. Already during the editing process it was apparent that she could no longer see well enough to proofread her own work. She now wrote only shorter pieces for journals and newspapers and continued to write poems until her death. Her friends honored her with a tribute in 1870 on the occasion of the fiftieth anniversary of her first published poem, "Unhappy Love." Characteristically she dismissed the tribute as twaddle, although well intentioned.[68]

Nevertheless she made a serious effort to have *Didaskalia,* a journal that over the years had published and reviewed her works, take note of her golden literary anniversary. What is most revealing is her complaint to the writer Dieffenbach about the "repeated rejection" of her recent novella manuscripts. "Your father," the forthright woman informed him, "was not so choosy as you. He gladly accepted my things, which cannot be called bad." She pleaded with him unsuccessfully to make allowances "for an old, sick, and nearly blind woman living in wretched conditions." To the end she worked every angle to get her works published.[69]

Some recognition came in the form of interest in her memoirs, "her travails," as she called them, but it smacked too much of "selling her soul." She decided not to provide titillation for "students, seamstresses, and store clerks," as she described her prospective audience. Franz Brümmer, who was compiling a lexicon of German writers, requested information from her, which she was more than ready to supply. Typically for her she tried to interest Brümmer in the work of her friend Emilie Hurst.[70] On her death she left behind a large body of unpublished material, which included two manuscripts of 850 and 600 pages, about thirty works of novella length, and seventeen poems, mainly in honor of her friends. She was a professional writer.[71]

9
After 1850
Personal Struggles

*T*he mid-nineteenth-century upheaval provided an opportunity for German men and women to participate directly in the political issues of the day. Woman no less than men seized the chance, and among the former Kathinka Zitz-Halein stood out. During the two decades following the suppression of the revolution, literature remained her professional activity and politics her avocation. In her private life old patterns continued, while new problems emerged.

Zitz-Halein carried on an active and varied social life. Clearly her position as a de facto single woman never became a significant obstacle to her acceptance in society. She proudly pointed out in the 1850s that she mingled with the "best" families in Mainz, and this seems borne out by her wide circle of friends and correspondents. They included judges, government officials, museum directors, librarians, engineers, newspaper editors, businessmen, actresses, newly discovered relatives, and even a police commissioner's widow, not to mention her many professional contacts with publishers, writers, and book dealers. Most impressive perhaps was her ability not only to retain the friends of her youth but to gain the affection of their children and to make new friends throughout her life. This suggests that although she was occasionally implacable in her hatred this was not the dominant theme of her relationships. Even political disagreements did not prove to be insurmountable obstacles. Her long friendship with the Prussian general Friedrich Aschoff (1789–1850) which began with her teenage years, continued during and after the Revolution of 1848–1849 in spite of his antidemocratic views. She was, as she once expressed it, "surrounded by friends."

Until health conditions prevented her, Zitz-Halein went on outings and picnics in the Rhine-Main area, attended parties and balls, and did charitable work with the local German Catholic women's association. She also made visits to Göttingen to spend time with her girlhood friend Caroline Berthold (born Röder), whom she met in 1853 after a separation of twenty-seven years. She tried to maintain a regular schedule, reserving her morning hours for literary work; in the afternoon she did her embroidery, continually learning new and perfecting old techniques. Keeping busy was almost an obsession with her, she admitted, as well as a way to fight depression. She proceeded on the assumption, as she explained to a despondent acquaintance, that a human being is not permitted to dream away her life in an idle fashion but must strive to "make oneself as useful as possible to the world and to those closest to her." As always she sent along some of her books to cheer up the recipient.[1]

Perhaps the most unexpected of her activities but one that reveals another side not only of Zitz-Halein's character but that of her age was her interest in pseudoscientific endeavors such as fortune-telling, spiritualism, and phrenology. Her basically rationalist frame of mind notwithstanding, she accepted these activities as natural. The involvement began during her Parisian stay. She, the child of the Enlightenment, was cautious and somewhat skeptical as she visited the home of the noted fortune-teller, Mademoiselle Lenormand.[2] She tried to give the Frenchwoman no solid information about her background in the preliminary conversation. Nevertheless, she could not deny her amazement as the medium, using cards and palm reading, evinced knowledge of her earlier life and predicted accurately some future events. Only her prognostication, Zitz-Halein remembered, that she and her estranged husband would be reunited in four years proved inaccurate.[3]

Equally inexplicable to her were her experiences with hypnotism and spiritualism. One form of spiritualism had evolved from the pioneering work in hypnotism done by Friedrich Anton Mesmer (1734–1815), who tried to use his talent to cure various illnesses.[4] Hypnotism also became a means of communicating with spirits, who spoke through the affected person. By the 1800s this "trance speaking" spiritualism was being utilized in Germany and also in England, where Johanna Kinkel said it was a "main interest." In Mainz the chief practitioner was Günzer, an undoubtedly gifted hypnotist *(magnetiseur),* who seemed to specialize in hypnotizing teenagers, who then became the mouthpieces for his "spirits." He claimed that Zitz-Halein had nineteen spiritual guides, among the better known, Jesus and Goethe. His feats left her without a rational explanation but did not erase her doubts. Even when he could conjure up spirits, she noted, her conversations with them were not helpful with specific questions. She realized that the spirits answered to "positive questions" vaguely, if at all. As an example, she related the following conversation between her and the spirit named Florus:

> SHE: How can I improve my situation?
> SPIRIT: It is beneath my dignity to answer such questions.
> SHE: Why is it beneath your dignity?
> SPIRIT: If I answer such a question you will next want to know the winning lottery number.
> SHE: Did Müller-Melchior [her husband's friend] speak with Zitz about me in America?
> SPIRIT: Yes.
> SHE: What did he say?
> SPIRIT: Insignificant.
> SHE: Nevertheless, I would like to know.
> SPIRIT: I won't, not worth it.

The spirit, she remarked, was like the oracle at Delphi. One had to make out of it what one could.[5]

The Mainz writer was also attracted to phrenology, an early science of the brain that had evolved as a result of the work and teachings of Franz Joseph Gall (1758–1828). Widely accepted in Europe, phrenology was based on the belief that the key to understanding human character was to be found in the shape, size, and composition of the human brain as reflected in the configuration of the skull. Since the state of science of the brain was in its infancy, as even the phrenologists admitted, they had to fall back on the external shape of the skull. Phrenology was also utilized by some, most notably the pioneering sociologist August Comte, to demonstrate that women were inferior to men. He claimed that women had smaller and less developed brains, confirming, at least for him, their mental inferiority to men.[6] Zitz-Halein's phrenological chart was worked out in 1853 by Dr. Gustav Scheve, who was a major proponent of the new science. He believed that one could identify the sizes of the key parts of the brain in spite of the thickness of the skull and that they would give an accurate picture of a person's character. His assessment provided a reasonably reliable evaluation of her personality, one that could no doubt have been obtained from their long acquaintance. She received highest marks for love of children, reliability, respectfulness, hopefulness, goodwill, and capacity to make compromises. This last, she noted proudly, Scheve rated as strong, as in the most significant men. She was clearly given an insufficiently high score for fighting spirit, although it was high enough to satisfy her. She received her lowest, meaning weakest, rating for intrigue, and her general temperament was accurately described as "nervous." This phase of her interest seems to have ended during the mid-1850s. She became disenchanted with phrenology when Scheve apparently made a pass at her while in Mainz on a lecture tour.[7]

At a more mundane level the urge to help the less fortunate continued to be a strong factor in Kathinka Zitz-Halein's life. Strangers as well as acquaintances and relatives still turned to her for financial assistance. She did what she could but bemoaned her limited resources, estimating that she would need ten times her income to help all those who requested it. Yet she wrote letters of recommendation as if she were a "business bureau," responding to requests for help from concert performers, poor pregnant women, down-on-their-luck "family fathers," and needy foreigners. She personally assisted several elderly widows, poor writers, and even the brother of her estranged husband and then his widow. When her own resources were not sufficient she could sometimes prevail on the local charitable agencies and individuals to help, interpreting their cooperation as a sign of confidence in her by her fellow citizens. She was able to persuade the Mainz Carnival Association to make a donation to help the poor and the masonic lodge to aid a struggling acting couple.[8]

The urge to help was irrepressible. Characteristic of her efforts was that she served as a reader (of her own works) to the blind publisher von Zabern and tried to console a cousin who had lost a son. Do not surrender to grief, she told the latter, a retired Austrian army officer, "You are a man and fate allots us as a rule our load according to our strength." After Johanna Kinkel's suicide in 1858 she almost volunteered to help Gottfried raise his children. He too recognized the need for help but preferred to remarry. Zitz-Halein desired to do something permanent for humanity. At a time of adequate income in the mid-1850s she conceived the idea of leaving one thousand gulden to the city to establish a foundation that would support a place of refuge for impecunious women from the "cultured class," without reference to religious beliefs. Although she set about calculating how much interest would accumulate after one and two hundred years, nothing seems to have come of this idea. She clearly enjoyed her role as a benefactor, perhaps finding in it the substitute for a family existence.[9]

Letters from female friends, many of whom had suffered misfortune, form a significant part of her correspondence and mirror her own life's experiences. They also indicate something of the often humiliating circumstances in which women found themselves as a result of prevailing social and legal conditions. Auguste Dyrrezstit, an old friend from the 1820s, described how her deceased husband, because of his spendthrift ways, had fallen into debt. Now she and her daughter had to work but still could not adequately support themselves. Closer to home was the Cavalli family, whose existence was so tied up with her own. One of their children, Nanni, whose governess she had been, continued that family's unhappy history. The two women understood each other so well, Zitz-Halein claimed, because they both went through the "school of misfortune." Nanni Cavalli Wolf's life was made miserable by a marriage to a drunkard who ran up significant debts as she tried to raise a family on an income little higher than Zitz-Halein was receiving. The mother of five children, Nanni was made "desperate" by the rise in prices of the late 1850s, which caused her to experience hunger for lengthy periods. Only when her children began to work and to give her rather than their father their earnings did conditions improve somewhat. Compared to her own existence, her friend Kathinka's ability to overcome adversity made the Mainz writer a "credit to all women." Although her friend could do little to help Nanni, she once raised money so Nanni could bury a child. Zitz-Halein agreed with Nanni's brother, who wrote her from America in his broken English, "The down Fahl of Cavalli would maeke a good Novell [sic]."[10]

Probably closest to Kathinka Zitz-Halein was Emilie Hurst, whose promising career was aborted by familial disasters.[11] According to Zitz-Halein the family's financial situation became so precarious that Emilie's father committed suicide in 1856 because he believed he was a burden on her. Emilie survived on what she could earn from her needlework, but she was always on the border of financial ruin. As Kathinka explained in the 1860s to a private philanthropic agency that she approached on Emilie's behalf, her friend could not manage since "the feminine crafts are ever more depressed." She also called attention to the difficulty in inducing customers to pay promptly, and she herself had to intervene to secure payment for Emilie. This was the same problem she had experienced thirty years before. Vowing that she never would abandon her friend, Kathinka several times raised money for the younger woman and tried to assure that Emilie would be remembered in her will. She persuaded her publisher, Scholz, to give Hurst sixty gulden per year, which she could use as she wished, and prevailed on the city council to grant Emilie one hundred gulden.[12] These examples not only serve to demonstrate some of the disabilities that women suffered; they also indicate the significant accomplishment of women like Kathinka Zitz-Halein who were able to carve out modest niches for themselves along the steep wall of obstacles.

Probably the most depressing situation Kathinka Zitz-Halein had to deal with concerned her younger brother, Karl Halein. An unstable individual who seemed to have inherited his father's psychological problems, he needed support throughout his life and often turned to his older sister. Karl Halein's difficulties continued to multiply, and by the 1860s even she had had enough of her sibling. When he eventually entered a hospital pursued by his creditors, she refused him any additional money. She would only write to the authorities, asking for leniency since he was mentally unstable. His death in 1867 was followed by an even more severe blow when his children were arrested for cheating at gambling and imprisoned. Not only the downfall of the Cavalli family was worthy of a novel.[13]

These problems and tragedies that affected Kathinka Zitz-Halein's friends and relatives were only part of a series of misfortunes that plagued her during the last two decades of her life. Financial difficulties, complicated by health problems and continued disputes with her estranged husband, bedeviled her existence until shortly before her death. After the failure of the 1849 uprising Franz Zitz escaped to Switzerland and then immigrated to the United States. There he practiced law in New York state and appeared to prosper.[14] As part of his separation settlement with his wife he had deposited fourteen thousand gulden with his lawyer, Ludwig Herrnsheim, the interest from which provided her with an annual income of five hundred gulden.

Kathinka was also receiving 147 gulden annually as the income from the estate of a deceased relative, the principal of which was under her husband's control. This money had caused an acrimonious dispute between the two in 1849–1850. Franz first had wanted to use the inheritance as an excuse to lower his alimony payments by 100 gulden. She reacted in a predictable way, instituting a legal claim to Zitz's house, which he wished to sell in order to prevent its expropriation by the Hessian government. The German governments regularly seized the property of convicted revolutionaries. Her action delayed the sale, causing, she later wrote with some glee, "great consternation in the enemy camp." Only when she received written assurance from Herrnsheim that she would receive her payment, including the new inheritance, regularly and in full, did she give her consent to the disposal of the property.[15] Although learning how weak her control over her property was, she had won the latest round. Again she knew how to exploit what legal avenues were open to her even when her marriage contract limited her rights. Her associations within the Mainz judicial and legal establishments proved invaluable in these episodes.

By 1857, however, she was beginning to doubt the wisdom of the 1850 financial arrangement. She realized that it rested on a shaky legal foundation. All she in effect had was Herrnsheim's personal commitment, as her husband's agent, to pay her. For seven years this had been enough to ensure regular payments, but as Herrnsheim grew older she began to wonder what would transpire at his death. Correctly she realized that his heirs might not be legally bound to continue the payments. Given the history of the alimony agreement it did not require much for her to convince herself that she had been tricked. She now importuned Herrnsheim for a more binding contract regarding her money but without success.[16] Her financial situation worsened in the following years because of the general increase in the cost of living about which her friend Caroline Berthold also complained, along with additional expenses caused by her eye problems. Of her income of 647 gulden in 1862 about one-fourth went for rent, which was raised 30 gulden in 1863. Her first eye operation in 1861 cost her 84 gulden and a second one at least 50. She began to press her husband, indirectly through his legal partner in America, Friedrich Kapp, for increased support but to no avail.[17]

Her financial situation oscillated greatly in 1863, beginning with the promise of financial improvement but ending with the threat of monetary disaster. To bolster her income the Mainz writer applied for assistance to the recently (1859) established Schiller Foundation, which was to help talented but needy writers and their families. For an applicant to qualify for support other writers had to send in letters of recommendation. One such letter on Kathinka Zitz-Halein's behalf described her as fighting for all that was patriotic and lofty in German society. Nevertheless, the committee was not initially impressed by her application and rejected it. On reconsideration, however, she was granted fifty taler (eighty-five gulden) for 1863. The committee acknowledged that her works were widely read in central Germany. She repetitioned for support in subsequent years and received one hundred thaler in 1864, fifty in 1865 and 1866, and, starting in 1870, she was granted annual payments until her death. The Schiller committee was never enthusiastic about supporting her, fearing that the society would become a "poor relief society." There were complaints about requests for aid from female writers who had scarcely published and whose activities depressed the honoraria of serious writers. Even from the local Mainz branch there was opposition on the grounds that she already received enough income from her husband, her inheritance, and her literary work. The city librarian, Külz, complained that she had an income of fourteen hundred gulden. Zitz-Halein had to explain what her actual income was and to defend her at best erratic literary earnings. The fact that she had recently been paid several hundred gulden for her biographical novel of Goethe and that she had used the income for permanent and visible acquisitions was apparently known. She wondered whether she was expected to squander her money on food and drink. And one can wonder whether a man would have been subjected to such scrutiny.[18]

The issue of her income was raised again in 1863, when Herrnsheim died. The problems she had foreseen surfaced but in a worse form than she had imagined. She learned that he had not only lent out that part of the capital that constituted her inheritance in his own name in a speculative venture but lost some of the funds. Moreover, his heirs initially regarded the money as Herrnsheim's personal possession and thus felt no obligation to make good her inheritance income. This became clear when the heirs paid the 500 gulden but not the additional 147. Threatened with the loss of nearly one-fourth of her income, she carried on a long struggle to ensure a new method of payment. Her exasperation is revealed in a letter to her cousin in Austria in which she complains about the "bad French law," which she had helped the Mainzers defend before 1848, that made the man "master" of her property and left her powerless to do anything. Although that was an exaggeration, it was difficult to reach her husband, who was thousands of miles away. Nevertheless, throughout this period, which lasted nearly five years and was marked by despairing statements about ending her days in a poorhouse or committing suicide and by assorted threats from Zitz, the alimony continued to be paid, even if occasionally late. Finally they seem to have agreed to maintain the old arrangement, and the Mainz lawyer and later National Liberal deputy Joseph Görz, whom she personally hated, became her husband's agent. It appears that his selection was designed to make the alimony process as distasteful as possible for her. After Görz took over, much the same routine continued with her sensitive to any delay in payment and ready to assume evil intentions.[19]

The struggle over money took a new turn as other factors intruded. Her poor eyesight and advancing age made costly medical and nursing care necessary. Beginning in 1857 she began to lose sight in her right eye, eventually being able to see only as if through a "fog," so that by May 1860 it was completely unusable. Her physician diagnosed the problem as a cataract. Her left eye also worsened to the extent that by November 1860 she had to cease her literary activity. Between September 1860 and May 1862 her diary contains no entries. In May 1861 she underwent an eye operation, the first of several, which partially restored her sight in the right eye so that she could recognize people. Her joy was short-lived as another cataract, which necessitated a second operation in November 1861, formed. This was unsuccessful and left her sight worse than before. A third operation in early 1863 apparently restored her sight by removing the cataract. In 1865 she was operated on twice on the left eye, but its vision ultimately was not restored. Sight in the right eye slowly deteriorated so that by 1869 she could "barely read but only sew." She continued her diary entries and correspondence until 1874, although very little of a literary nature was written after 1867. Throughout this series of eye problems she demonstrated anew her courage and her ability to endure pain. She was among the first generation of patients on whom chloroform was used as she subjected herself to the still primitive state of eye surgery. Her friend Charles Galette caught her spirit best when he remarked on the eve of her first operation, "Misfortune has previously found in you an opponent that it must respect."[20]

Zitz-Halein's medical problems, which ate into her limited income, were compounded by new financial burdens caused by the outbreak of the Franco-German War in July 1870. It was the beginning, she expressed ironically, of "terrible times, not to mention the war." With Mainz a military center for the German forces prices rose sharply, hurting people such as she on a fixed income. Moreover, the inhabitants of Mainz, a fortress city, were expected to quarter soldiers or pay for their upkeep elsewhere. It is also clear that the next three years were generally inflationary, fueled by the 5-billion-franc French indemnity. Even her friend Caroline Berthold complained again of the "unprecedented increase in prices." To make matters worse when Zitz-Halein went to see Görz in August to collect her quarterly installment he refused her payment on the grounds that the necessary authorization from America had not arrived. Considering that a war was in progress, some problems with communication could have occurred. Zitz-Halein believed that Görz was acting out of deliberate malice. She could not refer to him in her diaries without calling him a "thug" or an "ape" and claimed that going to his office to pick up her money was like going to one's "execution." She experienced hunger and cold and was forced to sell some of her silver in order to purchase food. Only in September did she receive her alimony payment.[21]

Desperate, the seventy-year-old woman considered going to America to claim a fair share of her husband's wealth. She wrote to a lawyer, F. Wagner, who encouraged her to travel to America, assuring her that during the life of the husband the wife had easily enforcable rights to alimony. This became unnecessary as the alimony was once again paid regularly. In fact, after Franz returned to Germany from America in 1872 he personally sent her the payments, leaving her thrilled to be free of the "infamous" Görz. Nevertheless, the experience left her, she remarked bitterly, with a feeling of "powerlessness which comes in the wake of poverty."[22]

Her basic problem, of insufficient income, Kathinka Zitz-Halein wished to resolve by having her alimony increased by two hundred gulden. The reaction to her request by her lawyer, the democratic leader Franz Dumont, suggests the limits she faced and other women in her position perhaps confronted. He apparently thought her request excessive and would ask her husband for only an additional one hundred gulden, and she was not even sure he would do that. "The coward," she called him for his caution. "Men in general," she went on, "believe that women so to speak require nothing to live on." It only confirmed her belief, going back to the divorce proceedings, that "men stick together" and "a lone woman," she claimed with less than complete accuracy, "has no one on whom she can rely." There is no doubt that Zitz, with his social and political connections, still commanded considerable influence in Mainz. Since she could not rely on Dumont to contact Zitz she had to try another way to reach him. The ever-resourceful and tenacious woman turned to Zitz's widowed sister-in-law, for whom she had previously done a favor. Her initiative apparently led to Kathinka and Franz Zitz's first direct contact in more than thirty years.[23]

Through all of this thirty-year struggle for alimony Franz Zitz was both an albatross and an inspiration to her. She hated him one moment, declared her eternal love for him the next, and repeatedly bemoaned her fate as a woman. As early as 1853 Johanna Kinkel was trying to bring her out of her sympathetic preoccupation with her husband. "Can't you learn to hate with intensity," the sturdy and practical woman advised the Mainzer, instead of having "compassion for the man who embittered half your life. Put him out of your mind." Kathinka Zitz-Halein could not. Her sensitivity about her relationship with Zitz was evident when it again received publicity. In 1855 a book by Franz Lubojatzky (1807–1887), written six years before and entitled *1848: Oder Nacht und Licht* (1848: or Night and Light), came to her attention. It contained the old and false story of her wedding day abandonment by Zitz that had originally appeared in the 1848 book *Bilder aus der Paulskirche.* Lubojatzky was at times a moderately successful writer who ultimately ended his life in poverty, living off payments from the Schiller Foundation. Zitz-Halein was incensed by the reappearance of the insulting tale and initially believed that he also must have been the author of the 1848 work. Taking the offensive in her customary way, she wrote to the publisher demanding an immediate retraction and threatening to press criminal charges. She also contacted two prominent editors, Karl Gutzkow and Ernst Keil, the later editor of *Gartenlaube,* trying to enlist their support. To them she described her marriage and proper social life as well as commitment to progressive political views and actions. She was proud of her efforts in 1848–1850 and never missed an opportunity to call attention to them.

The innocent and well-meaning Lubojatzky, who admitted taking the story from the earlier publication, was as embarrassed by developments as she was angered. They finally settled on a private apology from him, one that would be issued in *Frankfurter Journal.* When it was clear that Lubojatzky was innocent of malicious intent, her tone changed. He flattered her by informing her that the material she sent him about the background of the affair gave him several ideas for characters for future novels. She intimated that he might want to cast her life in fictional form and proposed sending him material. The affair ended with Lubojatzky's contributing a poem about the writer and moral responsibility to her album.[24]

There is no doubt that her estranged husband remained at the center of her life. Her diary entries continually contain references to her feelings about him as she oscillated between hostility and sympathy. She called him "overrated," a "complete Parsifal," and noted his affair with a woman who followed him to America and bore their child. While she led an "unblemished, virtuous" life, and lived "like a good woman," for whom infidelity was akin to "disbelief by a priest," she lamented, he "lives like a man." Nevertheless her love for Zitz was still present. "I loved him too exclusively, I loved him like no other man in the world was loved, and this love covered my whole life with a mourning veil. I preserve the memory of my love as others preserve ashes in memorium, and time which destroys and ruins everything has no influences on ashes." In her poem "Feminine Love" written in 1853, the same theme had sounded:

> It cannot die, no it lives
> Even if betrayal strives . . .
> To blow out the loyal flame.

She always noted the anniversaries of their engagement and marriage. She reported what she had heard about his excellent financial status, his love affairs, and his travels. When she heard he was returning to Germany she worried about his boat trip; once again had her fortune told, hoping in vain for a favorable prediction; reported on his activities; spied him from afar; noted how fat he had become; and offered to nurse him when she heard he was ill. She even sent him a friendly greeting, which he returned with thanks but signed himself simply "Addressee." Her friend Caroline Berthold warned her against expecting any goodwill from her estranged husband. "Woman," she lectured Zitz-Halein, "after all that's happened, how can you expect an iota of unselfish action?" Zitz-Halein realized it, too, and wondered how she could still love the "loudmouth who had brought misfortune" to her name.[25]

The answer she gave in various ways made her reflect not only on her own life but on the role of women. Although there is excessive pathos and self-pity in her writings, in the style of the mid-nineteenth century, she never gave up her struggle against adversity. She repeatedly returned to the themes "a woman's heart feels things differently than a man's heart" and men did not understand "how we lose ourselves in the heavens which are not accessible to evil passions."[26] This drew her again and again back to Zitz. As she lamented to her diary: "O cowardly revolting female heart, in spite of all insults I cannot free myself from this unworthy person. If once a deeply held love is firmly attached to the feminine existence, even one's personal pride is not capable of rooting it out. . . . Women are always ruined by their greatness. Their greatness is love and they die of it."[27] As her financial condition worsened in the late 1860s she surrendered more and more to self-pity but never completely. Her diary abounds with statements that she was "predestined to misfortune"; that she always strove for the "beautiful, true and good" but the "baseness of the world stood in the way"; that she had the characteristics to be a happy spouse but she was persecuted by envy and wickedness. Why, she wondered, did she have to be made of a "tender, poetical essence" that would never "understand the material side of life?" Zitz might have disagreed. Her life had for her a sense of tragedy that, nevertheless, may have given her the will to carry on. She expressed this in 1869: "Elevated souls find a bitter enjoyment to suffer for a great cause. They spread their wings out in the limitless space of misfortune and lift themselves above a world which they despise and which is not capable of understanding them." Through all her lamentations and even musings about suicide, her desire to spite fate held firm. Her inner toughness is apparent in her admission that although the years burdened her body her spirit was "fresh and vigorous."[28]

The subject of a large part of her memoir and diary entries, Franz Zitz, finally responded in 1872 to his wife's requests for an increase in alimony and even entered into an exchange of letters with her. Although she regarded Zitz's letter as a "certificate of honor," their correspondence was not without the expected friction and was solely concerned with financial matters. He wanted to gain ownership of her inheritance for his grandchild even if he predeceased her. According to French law if he survived her, he would have ownership of the inheritance, but if the reverse occurred the inheritance as well as the interest from it would be hers. Kathinka had the idea of bequeathing the interest from her inheritance to her friend Emilie Hurst and tried to offer the ultimate ownership of her inheritance to her husband as bait. She proposed to surrender her rights to it if he would increase her alimony to seven hundred gulden annually and provide iron-clad guarantees that the interest on the inheritance would be paid to Emilie after her death. Equally tenacious as a negotiator Zitz saw no need to pay for something that might be his for nothing. All that Kathinka could achieve was an increase in her alimony payment to six hundred gulden per year. Behind all of her complaints about her alleged weaknesses she demonstrated anew a clear perception of her interests, aided as needed by her judicial acquaintances. For her husband his wife's behavior only confirmed an old pattern: that she wanted to remain "mistress of your actions and not act in conformity with traditional inheritance laws nor to subordinate yourself to any alien will." Her attitude reminded him of the saying "A potato over which I have taken great pains would taste better, at least to me, than a pineapple which I was ordered to eat." Her "unfeminine" sense of independence and pride had always been difficult for her husband to accept.[29]

In her experiences with Franz Zitz, Kathinka Zitz-Halein suggests a woman in whom a feminist consciousness was struggling to be born. However, she was unable to draw the conclusions from her own experiences because of the social and psychological baggage that she bore. She recognized that "only those women who were forgiving and self-sacrificing holies . . . who swallow the consecrated wafer in the temple of the Lord" were given recognition by society. She was beyond this deferential conduct but could not move to the next stage.

10
Conclusion

*T*he last five years of Kathinka Zitz-Halein's life passed quietly. Her financial situation improved somewhat after Zitz increased her alimony to six hundred gulden annually. She also received help from an unnamed person. Now she did not have to order the twelve kreuzer (one-fifth of a gulden) special meal but could order a half portion for twenty-four kreuzer, which at least was "minimally sufficient." Yet she complained about the humid air in her apartment, and her diary contains increased references to ailments, besides her eyes, that seemed to be related to nerves. In March 1873 she lost consciousness but was fortunately found by a friend. Her physician, Dr. Hess, advised her to avoid "excitement" and to find less damp quarters. New lodgings and the need for a full-time nurse, who would require a separate room, raised the specter of expenses beyond her means. She calculated she would need three hundred gulden additional income. The only other alternative was to enter a nursing home or take lodging with a family. The decision she ultimately arrived at was unexpected.[1]

In April 1873 she moved into the Catholic St. Vincent's hospital, whose nursing home was staffed by the Sisters of Mercy *(Barmherzigen Schwester)*. The decision to move into the nursing home was difficult for two reasons. It was the most expensive one in Mainz, costing 638 gulden for basic room and board, plus at least another 100 gulden for extras. Given her annual income of 600 gulden alimony and 147 gulden from her inheritance she barely had enough for basic expenses, requiring her to "sell" her furniture and linen to the home. A more serious problem involved the reversal of a lifetime of antipathy to the Catholic establishment and of identification with the German Catholic religious community. Even as a sixty-five-year-old she expressed this alienation, as well as her basic self-confidence. "Happy are those who believe in an after life; unfortunately I am without [such a] faith and hover between unbelief and the desire to believe as a bird between heaven and the sea. And yet, my nature was never ignoble; goodness predominated in me and material considerations never ruled me." In her unpublished biography of Clemens von Brentano Bettina von Arnim speaks what were certainly Zitz-Halein's thoughts: "Even all research is religious. I do not fail to recognize God, I recognize him in another way. . . . I believe in God and love Him. I hurt no one nor do I do wrong. How will you find a better religion?"[2]

Her lack of strong formal religious beliefs was supplemented by a continuing intense dislike of the Catholic church as an institution. In the early 1860s there was an outcry against the activities of the Sisters of Mercy in the city's old-age home, who supposedly persuaded senile patients to bequeath their estate to the Catholic church. An anonymous anticlerical pamphlet, "Sister Adolphe," which appeared in 1863, elicited a favorable reaction from Zitz-Halein. In her view it displayed the activities of the "pious horde" in the right light. The thought that she might come under the care of the Sisters of Mercy, these "intellectually stupid and hypocritical nuns," was "repugnant" to her nature and another reason initially to reject that alternative.[3]

Not only did she have to put a lifetime of prejudices behind her to enter a Catholic nursing home she also had to sever her connection with the German Catholic religious movement. Throughout the 1850s Kathinka Zitz-Halein continued her work for the Mainz German Catholic Association. She raised money for the needy, embroidered items that were auctioned, sold tickets for lotteries, and wrote short verses that could be used in the religious services. In 1859 she noted with pride that she had donated forty-eight books and sold 350 lottery chances among her acquaintances. During the 1860s there is no indication whether she continued to be an active member of the community, but shortly after entering the Catholic nursing home she remarked in one of her last diary entries that for a long time she had seen that German Catholicism had become a "negation" and "not a religion." Beyond that she never explained herself.[4]

She never regretted her decision to enter the nursing home. She was treated royally by the sisters and visited regularly by her friends, but what pleased her most was her reception by the male Catholic dignataries of Mainz. Professor Hundhausen, the head of St. Vincent's administrative council and a "very learned man," provided her with books, which, she discovered, were not especially religious in subject matter but historical and belletristic. The head of the Catholic seminary in Mainz and later Reichstag deputy, Franz Christoph Moufang, visited her, and she had to admit that he was a "completely different man than I expected based on the depiction in the newspapers and public opinion." Most satisfying of all was a visit by Bishop von Ketteler, who she also discovered was not a "fanatical priest" but a "cultivated man of the world," who deserved praise for his support of the "journeymen houses" *(Gesellenhäuser)*. His visit was an especially significant sign of her good reputation, she believed. He had come even though he knew that "I am not an excessively pious woman *(Betschwester)* since I have no talent for it." So happy was she in her new situation that on November 5, 1873, she "quietly returned to the bosom of the Catholic Church." Yet the irony of it all did not escape her. Who would have thought it possible, she confided to her diary, that "I would end my life in a nuns' convent and feel very comfortable with the pious sisters."[5]

She died in the nursing home on March 8, 1877, a few weeks after her husband, outliving virtually all of her contemporaries. During the last ten years of her life her diary reads like an obituary column. In death as in life she was unyielding to her enemies. She was buried in the Mainz city cemetery. Zitz-Halein composed her own epitaph[6]:

> All of you down here
> Who often grieved me so intensely
> Now in death don't begrudge me peace
> And don't slander me any more.
>
> Joyless you made my life
> Coldly you trampled upon my good fortune
> My revenge was forgiveness,
> I leave no anger behind.

Another poem, one of the last she wrote, captures instead the benevolent and civic side of her personality. Her "New Years Wishes" of 1874 contained the following resolutions[7]:

> Sharpened sight, open ears to the sovereign
> And public spirit to the ministers and advisers.
> Understanding, a good conscience to all those
> Who support themselves on Themis' weak staff.
> To the clergy harmony and goodwill
> To fulfill what reason enjoins.
> To the soldiers humanity and cool temper,

Conclusion

To the authors intellect, integrity, and courage,
To the people laws, freedom, upright conduct,
To the maidens men, to the women loyalty
Which preserves them against an all-too-soon
   remorse.

Kathinka Zitz-Halein's life cast a broad shadow across nineteenth-century German political and cultural history. Favored by a patrician birth during the reign of Napoleon, she died in genteel poverty during the first decade of Germany's unity. Her gilded early years were undermined by her father's mental instability and her mother's death, which left her penniless by the time she was twenty-three. Adding to her financial woes were unhappy relations with the two men in her life. The first, an inexplicable ten-year attachment to a mediocre army officer, ended in disappointment. The second, a tempestuous five-year engagement and marriage to the lawyer and politician Franz Zitz, left her separated and dependent on her estranged husband for financial support. More than merely financially dependent on him, she clung to the legal relationship with him to preserve her respectability and perhaps to punish him.

Forced by circumstances to live independently, Zitz-Halein was saved from despair by her tenacity, training, and talent. She was not a person who would accept her destiny but one whose pride compelled her to rebel against misfortune. The fate of many of her friends casts her accomplishments into sharp relief. Her education made it possible for her to find employment as a teacher and to earn money from her embroidery. She was also a born writer, although rarely ever better than a mediocre one. Her literary efforts ranged from poetry to detective novels; whatever the market might absorb she produced. Like most writers she struggled to find publishers, and even though producing a large body of published works, she never gained financial security from it. Nevertheless, she found in literary activity a stabilizing element in her life. Her writings, published and unpublished, closely mirrored her personal experiences and, because of her wide circle of acquaintances, provide an excellent source for the unwritten social history of Mainz. It suggests a less inhibited gender relationship than we normally envision. Victorian prudery was a concept that seemed irrelevant to the lives of many of Zitz-Halein's contemporaries.

Her status as a professional writer also placed her in a select company of women. Achieving adulthood at a time when the first feminist outcries were being heard, Zitz-Halein, nevertheless, resisted any far-reaching change in women's status. Carl Degler's point regarding Eleanor Roosevelt could be applied to the Mainz writer: she "asserted no feminist ideology or outlook."[8] Explicit feminism, tantamount in her mind to aping men's actions, she considered a form of exhibitionism. She accepted the norms of a male-dominated society and sought approval of her conduct by men. Although this was not unusual for middle-class women, considering her personal experiences she might have been more sympathetic to calls for increased educational or employment opportunities for women. Nevertheless, her call for a moral transformation in domestic attitudes between men and women was potentially more revolutionary than the pronouncements of her more radical sisters. She was correct in sensing that a moral change in the home must precede more extensive changes in society. Moreover, and again following Degler, through her militant defense of her rights against her husband and male publishing and literary figures, as well as her political activities, she demonstrated that women had to be counted as adults.

Zitz-Halein's literary efforts were closely tied to her civic initiatives, which she regarded as appropriate to women. Her political accomplishments before and during the midcentury upheaval, along with other women's efforts, should make us rethink our standard for rating civic involvement. Comparing what men and women could potentially accomplish in a given situation, even if difficult to measure, should not be ignored altogether. How many men were more effective than Zitz-Halein in spreading the progressive ideas of the pre-March period? Did all those hundreds of delegates to the Frankfurt parliament contribute more to the revolution than Kathinka Zitz-Halein or Louise Otto? Wasn't far more talent required to manage an organization of seventeen hundred members or to edit a newspaper than to sit in parliament? Was serving in the civic guard more demanding than raising money for a German navy, sewing flags, or decorating graves of executed insurgents? Should we highlight the bravery of the insurgents in the failed 1849 uprising but ignore the equally courageous efforts by women to aid the fighters? Women's helping the sick and wounded was certainly not without precedent, but never before had the effort been so political and been done in the face of a hostile government. Never before had it involved the possibility of arrest and punishment. It was civic courage of a high order that was shown in Mainz, Mannheim, Heidelberg, Altenburg, and other cities.

Although this activity lacked a conscious feminist ideology, it showed what women could accomplish in the world while remaining technically within their sphere. Some women grasped the larger issues generated by 1848 and sought to apply the revolution's principles to achieve women's emancipation. Most did not, at least in a conscious sense, and Kathinka Zitz-Halein belonged to this much larger group. Yet she acted as if she understood the liberating message of the revolution. She identified with the democrats, and it was they, or at least some of them, who saw the relationship between political and social reform and a new status for women. In her political and religious views she represented what was most progressive and humane in German society.

Notes
Bibliography
Index

Notes

Introduction

1. Gerda Lerner, "New Approaches to the Study of Women in American History," and "Placing Women in History: Definitions and Challenges," in her *The Majority Finds Its Past: Placing Women in History* (New York, 1979), 355–58; Estelle C. Jellinek, *The Tradition of Women's Autobiography: From Antiquity to the Present* (Boston, 1986); Nona Glazer-Melbin, "Housework," *SIGNS* 1 (Summer 1976): 905–22.

2. Kay Goodman, "German Women and Autobiography in the Nineteenth Century" (Ph.D. diss., University of Wisconsin-Madison, 1978) and "Die grosse Kunst nach innen zu weinen," *Die Frau als Heldin und Autorin* ed. Wolfgang Paulsen (Bern, 1979), 124–35.

3. Her "Tagebuch" is also inthe Wiesbaden State Library.

4. Elaine Showalter, *A Literature of Their Own: British Women Novelists from Brontë to Lessing* (Princeton, N.J., 1977), 6–7; Anton Maria Kein, "Rheinsandkörner: Erinnerungen an Kathinka Zitz-Halein," March 8, 1964, 9 p., mog m:4/1700 Stadtbibliothek Mainz; hereafter cited as Stabi Mz.

1. Early Life

1. Ute Gerhard, *Verhältnisse und Verhinderungen: Frauenarbeit, Familie und Rechte der Frauen im 19. Jahrhundert* (Frankfurt/Main, 1978); Margrit Twellmann, *Die deutsche Frauenbewegung im Spiegel repräsentativer Frauenzeitschriften: Ihre Anfänge und erste Entwicklung 1843–1889,* 2 vols. (Meisenheim/Glan, 1972); Ruth-Ellen Boetcher Joeres, "Louise Otto and Her Journals: A Chapter in Nineteenth Century German Feminism," *Internationales Archiv für Sozialgeschichte der deutschen Literatur* 4 (1979): 100–29; Renate Möhrmann, *Die andere Frau: Emanzipationsansätze deutscher Schriftstellerinnen im Vorfeld der Achtundvierziger-Revolution* (Stuttgart, 1977); Eda Sagarra, "Echo oder Antwort: Die Darstellung der Frau in der deutschen Erzählprosa 1815–1848," *Geschichte und Gesellschaft* 7 (1981): 394–411; Stanley Zucker, "German Women and the Revolution of 1848: Kathinka Zitz-Halein and the Humania Association," *Central European History* 13 (September 1980): 237–54.

2. Fritz Böttger, ed., *Frauen im Aufbruch: Frauenbriefe aus dem Vormärz und der Revolution von 1848* (Berlin, DDR, 1977); John Fout, ed., *German Women in the Nineteenth Century: A Social History* (New York, 1984); Catherine M. Prelinger, "Religious Dissent, Women's Rights, and the Hamburger Hochschule für das weibliche Geschlecht in Mid-Nineteenth Century Germany," *Church History* 45 (March 1976): 42–55, and her *Charity, Challenge and Change: Religious Dimensions of the Mid-Nineteenth Century Women's Movement in Germany* (New York, 1987).

3. The account is based mainly on the two drafts of Kathinka Zitz-Halein's autobiography, "Skizzen aus meinem Leben," 1ab, 2a, 53ab, 54a, 55b, 56a, 60a, Kathinka Zitz Nachlass HS 122, Hessische Landesbibliothek, Wiesbaden (hereafter cited as "Skizzen," KZN-W). Kathinka Zitz-Halein to ?, July 5, 1850, KZN-W. All future references to her in the footnotes will be abbreviated KZH. One draft is numbered 1–52, the other 53–120. Since she wrote, in a very small script, on both sides of a sheet but numbered only one side, I have designated the front as "a" and the reverse as "b." See also KZH, "Prost Neu Jahr," in her *Neueste Rheinsandkörner* (Mainz, 1853), 297, and "Felizitas und ihr Feier," in her *Neue Rheinsandkörner* (Mainz, 1852), 289–365, which contain references to this early period of her life. Karl Georg Bockenheimer, *Geschichte der Stadt Mainz während der französischen Herrschaft 1798–1814* (Mainz, 1890), 333, 338–43, 365; "Landtagswählen 1820–1831," 70 (122), Stadtarchiv, Mainz.

4. "Landtagswählen 1820–1831," 70 (121–23), Stadtarchiv, Mainz; "Skizzen," 3a, 6a, KZN-W.

5. "Skizzen," 1ab, 2a, 4a, 53a, 54a, 55b, 56a, KZN-W.

6. KZH, "Klagen," *Abendzeitung* (Dresden) 1 (1822, no. 5): 49.

7. Kathinka Halein to the grand duke, September 6, 1821, Hessisches Staatsarchiv, Darmstadt, Abt. D 12, no. 697 (3–5); hereafter cited as HSA-D.

8. "Skizzen," 4b, 8a–10b, 58a–62a, KZN-W.

9. "Skizzen," 55ab, KZN-W; Karl Georg Bockenheimer, *Geschichte der Stadt Mainz in den Jahren 1813–1814* (Mainz, 1886), 124–33.

10. "Skizzen," 53a, KZN-W.

11. "Skizzen," 60a, KZN-W; Otto Brunner, "Das ganze Haus," *Neue Wege der Verfassungs- und Sozialgeschichte*, 2d ed. (Göttingen, 1968).

12. "Skizzen," 60b, KZN-W.

13. Ibid., 54ab, KZN-W.

14. For the material on her education see "Skizzen," 2ab–3ab, 53b–54b, 56a, 62a, 69b, 102b, KZN-W; Bockenheimer, *Geschichte der Stadt Mainz*, 277–304; Karl Bachem, *Vorgeschichte, Geschichte und Politik der deutschen Zentrumspartei*, 9 vols. (Cologne, 1927–1932), 1: 285–87; Achill Wenzel, *Die Schule zwischen Kurstaat und Säkularstaat: Eine Studie über die Mainzer Volksschule um 1800* (Wiesbaden, 1963), 4–19; Otto Schlander, *Der Aufbau des Schulwesen im Grossherzogtum Hessen-Darmstadt nach 1815* (Frankfurt/Main, 1978), 77–78; W. Lexis und Gertrud Bäumer, *Das Unterrichtswesen im Deutschen Reich*, Vol. 2., *Die höheren*

Lehranstalten und das Mädchenschulwesen (Berlin, 1904), 258–75; Elisabeth Blockmann, *Das Frauenzimmer und die Gelehrsamkeit* (Heidelberg, 1966) and Jürgen Zinnecker, *Sozialgeschichte der Mädchenbildung* (Weinheim, 1973).

15. Ruth-Ellen Boetcher Joeres, *Die Anfänge der deutschen Frauenbewegung: Louise Otto-Peters* (Frankfurt/Main, 1983), 42–48, 78.

16. Carl von Schindel, *Die deutschen Schriftstellerinnen des neunzehnten Jahrhunderts,* 3 vols. (Leipzig, 1823–1825), 1: 187, 3: 144–49.

17. "Skizzen," 9b–10b, 60b–63b, KZN-W, *Herbstrosen in Poesie und Prosa* (Mainz, 1846), 40ff; Zitz-Halein's description of the Cavalli family agrees with the surviving data in the Hessisches Staatsarchiv and the Stadtarchiv; letter from archivist to author, June 30, 1987. According to Showalter, *A Literature of Their Own,* 48, this is less than the twenty to forty-five pounds that British governesses received.

18. K. Halein to the grand duke, March 19, 1827, HSA-D, Abt D 12, No. 697, 6–9.

19. For the Kaiserslautern phase see "Skizzen," 10b, 63b–66a, KZN-W; Marianne Burkhard, "Love, Creativity and the Female Role: Grillparzer's 'Sappho' and Staël's 'Corinne' Between Art and Cultural Norm," *Jahrbuch für Internationale Germanistik* 16 (1984): 128–46; Madelyn Gutwirth, *Madame de Staël, Novelist* (Urbana, 1978), 154–200; Halein to the grand duke of Hesse, January 1, 1828, HSA-D, Abt. D 12, no. 697, 10–14; K. Halein to C. von Schindel, July 25, 1830, Carl von Schindel Nachlass, Oberlausitzische Bibliothek der Wissenschaften, Görlitz, DDR. For a humorous but perhaps accurate depiction of the exploitation of female teachers see *Neue Mainzer Narrenzeitung,* January 14, 1844, 29.

20. "Skizzen," 12a, 66ab, 76b–77b, KZN-W. On the reputation of middle-class German women as hard workers see Priscilla Robertson, *An Experience of Women: Pattern and Change in Nineteenth-Century Europe* (Philadelphia, Pa., 1982), 139–40.

2. Love and Marriage

1. "Skizzen," 1b, 3ab, 56a, 62a–64b, 71ab, 75ab, 76ab, 103b–104a, 107a, KZN-W. Again the data in the Hessian archives confirm the outlines of Zitz-Halein's account; letter from archivist to author, June 30, 1987.

2. KZH, "Entgegnung an die Redaktion. . . ," *Nordstern,* no. 38, June 23, 1860, KZN-W.

3. The preceeding citations from her poems and aphorisms are found in KZH, *Phantasieblüthen und Tändeleien* (Mainz, 1825), 40–41, 47–48 and *Herbstrosen,* 253, 257, 261, 271, 289, 292, 295.

4. On the life of a young officer in Mainz, one who was certainly wealthier than Wild, see Otto Corvin-Wierbitski, *Erinnerungen aus meinem Leben,* 2 vols., 3d ed. (Leipzig, 1880), 1: 158–91, 213–61.

5. On the Wild affair see "Skizzen," 5b, 6a, 11b, 12ab, 57ab, 58ab, 60a, 61a, 62a, 65a–69a, 72b–73b, KZN-W; "Tagebuch," 4a–5a (July 6, 7, 1854), 54a (June 16, 1865), KZN-W; Robertson, *An Experience of Women*, 61–63, 70–71, on the financing of a marriage and the importance of the engagement. Detlev Schinachen, *Das Rheinische Recht in der Gerichtspraxis des 19. Jahrhunderts* (Stuttgart, 1969), 53, 57.

6. "Skizzen", 68b–71a, KZN-W; Ludwig Bamberger, *Erinnerungen* (Berlin, 1899), 27–31, gives a good sketch of Zitz and mentions his interest in the opposite sex; Ludwig Frankel, "Zitz, Kath. und Franz," *Allgemeine Deutsche Biographie*, vol. 45, 373–79; *Actes de Naisscenses*, vol. 12, no. 130; *Guide de la Ville de Mayence* (Mainz, n.d.), 119; *Wegweiser der Stadt Mainz für das Jahr 1825* (Mainz, 1825), D 107; Luise Zimmermann, "Bilder aus dem Frankfurter Parlamentsleben," 01006, Nachlass Wilhelm Zimmermann, F Sg 1/215, Bundesarchiv (Aussenstelle Frankfurt); hereafter cited as BAF.

7. KZH, *Herbstrosen*, 259, 264; K. Halein to Franz Zitz, September 16, 1833 (copy), KZN-W; "Skizzen," 12b, 69b–71a, KZN-W.

8. According to the story Zitz spread he was coerced into the engagement and marriage by her threat to commit suicide. On Zitz's version of the affair see Bamberger, *Erinnerungen*, 28–29; Friedrich Hart, *Ein Tag in der Paulskirche: Skizzen und Porträts aus dem Reichstag in Frankfurt am Main*, 2 vols. (Leipzig, 1848). She claimed she was ill and took too much opium, which her enemies later transformed into a suicide attempt. She maintained that Zitz came by and of his own free will proposed. She supposedly even gave him a chance to back out. Opium was not an uncommon sedative. Showalter, *A Literature of Their Own*, 129–30, and Nanni Wolf to KZH, November 11, 1849, KZN-M; "Skizzen," 69b–71a, KZN-W.

9. "Skizzen," 12a, 73b, KZN-W.

10. KZH, *Herbstrosen*, 159–60, 168–69, 182; K. Halein to F. Zitz, May 24, 1834, KZN-W; KZH, *Einige Worte an das Publikum im Allgemeinen und an Diejenigen, die es angeht, ins Besondere* (Mainz, 1850), mog m3163, Stabi Mz.

11. "Skizzen," 13a, 70b, 71a, 74ab, 77b–78a, KZH to Franz Zitz, May 29, 1834, February 22, 1837, KZN-W; *Heiratsregister*, 1837, 57, Stadtarchiv Mainz.

12. "Skizzen," 12b–13b, 19b, 78a, 78b–79b; K. Halein to F. Zitz, May 24, 1834, KZN-W. In his study of French divorces, Phillips cites several examples in which husbands could compel their wives to tolerate their mistresses, even introducing them as servants and lodgers. Roderick Phillips, *Family Breakdown in Eighteenth Century France: Divorces in Rouen 1792–1803* (Oxford, 1980), 125–29, 136.

13. "Skizzen," 79a–81a, KZH to Franz Zitz, November 8, 1838, KZN-W.

14. "Skizzen," 13b–20a, 78a, 83ab, 84b, 85b, 86ab, 89b, KZH to Judge Weiss, February 1, 1839, and "Notizen e," KZN-W. The Notizen were notes that she prepared for the use of her lawyer during the divorce trial; I have labeled the Xerox copies of the slips in my possession alphabetically.

15. KZH, "Calpurnia," *Herbstrosen*, 190–92. See also in "Domestic Conversations," KZH, "Häusliches Gespräch," *Herbstrosen*, 183–84.

16. "Skizzen", 86b–87b, 88b–89b; KZH to Eugenia Liffreing, December 8, 1838, KZH to Franz Zitz, November 8, 1838, KZN-W. Zitz-Halein's description of this Kaiserslautern family, Liffreing agrees with the surviving material in the Stadtarchiv; letter to the author, August 4, 1987. The father of Zitz's paramour fathered a child with a woman forty years his junior and then married her.

17. J. G. Kaufmann to KZH, May 9, 1842, Marie Kaufmann Fuchs to KZH, April 19, August 16, 1846, July 19, 1847, KZN-M; KZH to Bertha Henrich, November 23, 1839, KZN-W.

18. KZH to F. Zitz, November 8, 1838, "Skizzen," 73b, 89b–90b, KZN-W. Unfortunately a copy of the marriage contract has not survived. She claimed that Zitz at the time of their marriage had fixed the value of his estate at an artificially high amount to mask his future gains. Some wealthy women could protect their property, as Wild's experience proved. When his wife inherited a large sum of money she was able to establish separate estates so that in Kathinka's words, "the poor Tantulus (Wild) was surrounded by his wife's moneybags but not master of a cent." According to Robertson, *An Experience of Women*, 278, only 9 percent of the marriages had a separation of goods clause.

19. H. Weiss to KZH, KZN-M; January 7, 1839, F. Zitz to KZH, January 10, 1839, "Skizzen," 20b, 90ab, KZN-W.

20. K. Halein (*sic*) to F. Zitz, copy, January 11, 1839, KZN-W. The fact that in a fit of anger she had signed the letter with her maiden name was later used against her by Zitz in the divorce trial.

21. "Skizzen," 22b, 23a, 94a, KZH to F. Zitz, February 5, 1839, KZH to Haas, February 5, 1839, KZH to Heinrich Zitz (Franz's half-brother), February 5, 1839, Dr. Forch to KZH, January 8, 1839, KZN-M; Judge Weiss to KZH, January 31, 1839, KZN-W.

22. KZH to Weiss, February 1, 1839, Henriette Weiss to KZH, January 31, 1839, KZH to F. Zitz, February 5, 1839, KZN-W. The French law code was in force in Mainz.

23. "Skizzen," 21a, 90b, KZH to F. Zitz, February 9, 1839, KZN-W; KZH to Haas, February 5, 1839, Weiss to KZH, February 16, 1839, Amalie Bruck to KZH, January 17, 1839, KZN-M. These letters suggest the course of the negotiations.

24. "Skizzen," 91a, 92a, 93b, Judge Weiss to KZH, February 16, August 15, 1839, H. Weiss to KZH, May 15, 1839, KZN-W.

25. Pappenheim to KZH, July 27, 1839, Karl Benedict Hase to KZH, July 31, 1839, KZN-M; KZH, *Dictionaire des Gallicismes* (Leipzig, 1841, 1860); "Skizzen," 24a, 92a, KZN-W; Kirchheim (Mainz publisher) to KZH, September 29, 1839. As late as 1848 French women were demanding the right to use the National Library.

26. François Illig to Franz Zitz, January 3, 1839, with marginalia by KZH, "Skizzen," 21b, 90b, 91a, 91b, KZN-W. Illig was Franz Zitz's intermediary with his wife in Paris.

27. Franz Zitz to François Illig, n.d. (September–October 1839), KZN-W; Robertson, *An Experience of Women*, 304.

28. "Skizzen," 21b, 25ab, 93b–95a, KZN-W. The Napoleonic Code (article 213) did give the husband the right to control his wife's domicile.

29. KZH to Bertha Henrich, April 1, 1839, KZN-W.

30. *Der Reisende* no. 24, June 11, 1843, 95, contains an article that appears to have been written by Zitz-Halein about a physician who sexually abused a female patient while she was under sedation, KZN-W.

31. B. Henrich to KZH, May 6, 1839, "Skizzen," 21a, 25ab, 71a, 71b, 72a, 94a, KZN-W.

32. KZH to Bertha Henrich, October 7, 27, 1839, KZN-W.

33. B. Henrich to KZH, November 12, 1839, "Skizzen," 96a, KZN-W.

34. KZH to B. Henrich, November 23, 1839, KZN-W.

35. "Skizzen," 25b, 26a, 95ab, KZH to Lehne, December 17, 1839, KZN-W. Zitz also delayed as long as possible returning her furniture; according to Phillips, *Family Breakdown*, 139–40 this situation was not uncommon.

36. KZH to Lehne, December 17, 1839, KZN-W; Lehne to KZH, December 20, 1839, Weiss to KZH, December 19, 1839, KZN-M.

37. "Skizzen," 26a, 62a–64b, 96ab, KZH to Lehne, December 28, 1839, KZN-W; Lehne to KZH, January 5, 1840, KZN-M.

38. Lehne to KZH, January 5, 1840, KZH to B. Henrich, January 14, 1840, KZN-M; "Skizzen," 25b–26a, 95ab, 96a, KZN-W.

39. Ernst Wolf, Gerhard Luke, and Herbert Hax, *Scheidung und Scheidungsrecht* (Tübingen, 1959), 31–73, 112–19, 381–87; Robertson, *An Experience of Woman*, 241–46; *Mainzer Wochenblatt*, January 1839–1849; Phillips, *Family Breakdown*, 1–4, 47, 52; Hans Hesse, *Evangelische Ehescheidungen in Deutschland* (Bonn, 1960), 112–15. A good modern historical work on divorce is lacking, although Dirk Blasius, "Scheidung und Scheidungsrecht im 19. Jahrhundert: Zur Sozialgeschichte der Familie," *Historische Zeitschrift*, 241 (October 1985): 329–360, is preparing one. [Publisher's Note: This research has been included in an expanded version by the author. Dirk Blasius, *Ehescheidung in Deutschland 1794–1945: Scheidung und Scheidungsrecht in historischer Perspektive* Kritische Studien zur Geschichtswissenschaft, vol. 74. Göttingen: Vanderhoeck & Ruprecht, 1987.] During this period divorces were forbidden in France and almost impossible to obtain in Great Britain.

40. James Traer, *Marriage and the Family in Eighteenth Century France* (Ithaca, 1980), 175–78, 188–89; *Code Napoleon or the French Civil Code* (New York, 1841), articles 227–68. During the divorce proceedings the wife had to reside in a house approved by the court. Failure to do so could prejudice her position

41. KZH to B. Henrich, January 14, 1840, Lehne to KZH, January 25, 1840, "Skizzen," 26ab, 95b–96b, KZN-W.

42. Lehne to KZH, February 8, March 21, 23, April 4, 9, 20, May 13, 1840, KZN-M; KZH to Lehne, January 22, February 17, 20, March 6, 9, 1840, Prof. Spring to KZH, March 12, 1840, KZN-W.

43. Lehne to KZH, June 11, 1840, KZN-M; KZH to Lehne, June 20, 1840, "Skizzen," 96ab, KZN-W.

44. "Skizzen," 26ab, 96b–97a, Lehne to KZH, December 4, 1840, KZN-W. Lehne delayed as long as possible in returning the documentary evidence that she had supplied to him.

45. "Skizzen," 23b, 24ab, 92a–93b, 94a, KZN-W.

46. Captain Grallmann to KZH, January 23, 1841, Madam Kees to KZH, January 26, 1841, KZH to Appeals Court President Pitschaft, January 26, 1841, "Skizzen," 97b–98b, KZN-W.

47. KZH to Krämer, January 31, 1841, KZN-W.

48. KZH to Krämer, April 8, 1841, Krämer to KZH, April 10, 1841, Müller to Zitz, September 23, 1841, "Skizzen," 27b–28a, 98b–99a, KZN-W. Pitschaft to KZH, July 17, 1841, KZN-M. She never forgot Krämer's effort on her behalf. On his death she wrote: "Here lies a human being in the highest sense, . . . whom we without envy call the best." Handschriftenabteilung II, 41 O, KZN-Stabi Mz.

49. KZH to Krämer, May 19,1842, "Notizen q," KZN-W. Better known writers such as Fanny Lewald and Ida Hahn-Hahn earned considerably more according to Möhrmann, *Die andere Frau,* 2, but these were the tip of the literary iceberg. See Chapter 3 for further discussion.

50. Robertson, *An Experience of Women,* 244; KZH to Dernburg, December 29, 1841, May 29, 1842, KZH to District Court Mainz, February 19, 1842, KZH to (Mainz city government, 1842), KZH to Meister vom Stuhl (masonic lodge), (1842), KZH to Krämer, April 19, 20, May 23, August 15, 1842, "Skizzen," 28ab, 99b–100a, KZN-W.

51. "Skizzen," 100a, KZN-W.

52. KZH, *Herbstrosen,* 306, and also 203, 302, 305, 323, 327.

53. KZH, *Herbstrosen,* 196–97.

54. *Rheinische Telegraph,* September 14, 1842, 296; KZH, "Notizen t," KZN-W; Mayor Nack to KZH, June 11, 1842, KZN-M; "Skizzen," 100a, KZN-W. Of another friend in a similar situation Zitz-Halein wrote, "She understood nothing nor learned anything." "Tagebuch," 15b (February 28, 1856), KZN-W.

3. Becoming a Political Activist

1. "Skizzen," 29ab, 52a, 95a, 120b, KZN-W; *Didaskalia,* no. 85, March 26, 1846, and *Blätter für literarische Unterhaltung,* no. 144, May 24, 1847, 575, contain reviews of *Herbstrosen.* Zitz-Halein's friend Ferdinand Kurz wrote to her after reading the manuscript of one of her short stories that he could not wait to find out who the persons really were. Kurz to KZH, September 28, 1846, KZN-M; Phillips, *Family Breakdown,* 179; Katharine Rogers, *Feminism in Eighteenth Century England* (Urbana, Ill., 1982), 89, claims that there was prejudice against separated women.

2. Rainer Rosenberg, *Literaturverhältnisse im deutschen Vormärz* (Munich, 1957), 27–41; Rudolf Schenda, *Volk ohne Buch* (Frankfurt/Main, 1970), 305; Friedrich Winterscheidt, *Deutsche Unterhaltungsliteratur der Jahre 1850–1860* (Bonn, 1970), 55–56.

3. Schindel, *Die deutschen Schriftstellerinnen,* 3: vi, xv; Schenda, *Volk ohne Buch,* 147–48; Möhrmann, *Die andere Frau,* 2–9; Olympe de Gouges, *Schriften,* ed. and trans. Monika Diller, Vera Mostowlansky, and Regula Wyss (Frankfurt/Main 1980), 26; *Frauenbriefe der Romantik,* ed. Katja Behrens (Frankfurt/Main, 1981), 449; Eduard Fuchs, *Die Frau in der Karikatur* (Munich, 1906), 27, 466, 467, 469; *Fliegende Blätter,* 4, no. 89 (1846–1847), 135; Reinhard Wittmann, *Buchmarkt und Lektüre im 18. und 19. Jahrhundert* (Tübingen, 1982), 162–63, 202; Robertson, *An Experience of Women,* 416–17. Ruth-Ellen Boetcher Joeres, "1848 from a Distance: German Women Writers on the Revolution," *MLN* 97 (April 1982): 594–95; Ilke Frederiksen, "Deutsche Autorinnen im 19. Jahrhundert: Neue kritische Ansatze," *Colloquia Germania* 14, no. 2 (1981): 99–100; Friedrich Sengle, *Biedermeierzeit: Deutsche Literatur zwischen Restauration und Revolution 1815–1848,* 2 vols. (Stuttgart, 1971–1972) I: 815; *Blätter für literarische Unterhaltung,* February 1, 1841, 124–25; *Mainzer Tagblatt,* December 30, 1849.

4. Showalter, *A Literature of Their Own,* 21, 42–43, 67, 73–76, 82, 84–85, 101; "Die deutsche Schriftstellerin," *Didaskalia,* no. 106, April 28, 1858; Rogers, *Feminism in Eighteenth Century England,* 23; Sandra Gilbert and Susan Gubar, *The Madwoman in the Attic* (New Haven, Conn., 1979), 45–56, 59–61, 69, 74.

5. "Skizzen," 4a, KZN-W; see the material relating to Annette Droste-Hülshoff, Mathilde Franziska Anneke, and Erica Jong in Maria Wagner, *Mathilde Franziska Anneke* (Frankfurt/Main, 1980), 29–30; Uwe Schweikert, " 'Am Jungsten Tag, hab ich recht': Rahel Varnhagen als Briefschreiberin," in Rahel Varnhagen, *Gesammelte Werke,* ed. Konrad Feilchenfeldt, Uwe Schweikert, and Rahel E. Steiner, vol. 10 (Munich, 1983), 41.

6. KZH, "Ulrike," in her *Donner und Blitz* (Mainz, 1850), 29–30; KZH, *Magdalene Horix* (Mainz, 1858), 132; KZH, "Harpar und Tulisant," in her *Variationen in humoristischen Märchenbildern* (Mainz, 1849), 405; KZH, *Weltpantheon* (Mainz, 1856), 134; Showalter, *A Literature of Their Own,* 102.

7. Rogers, *Feminism in Eighteenth Century England,* 26, 242–43; Bettina von Arnim to Clemens von Brentano, July 31, 1834, Böttger, *Frauen im Aufbruch,* 125–28; Joeres, *Die Anfänge der deutschen Frauenbewegung,* 85–86; Germaine Goetzinger, *Für die Selbstverwirklichung der Frau: Louise Aston* (Frankfurt/Main, 1983), 42–44.

8. KZH, "Die Schriftstellerin," in her *Quodlibet* (Mainz, 1857), 47–71.

9. "Skizzen," 4b, KZN-W; Showalter, *A Literature of Their Own,* 57–64; Sophie Pataky, ed., *Lexikon deutscher Frauen der Feder,* 2 vols. (Berlin, 1898), 1: vii, although for a later period, stresses that women wrote in response to financial need. This was certainly true of Zitz-Halein later in life.

10. Karl Halein to KZH, June 30, 1866, KZN-W.

11. "Skizzen," 7ab, 56a, 66b, KZN-W; Friedrich Lehne, *Gesänge der freien Deutschen in Mainz* (Mainz, 1793), and his *Gesammelte Schriften*, 5 vols. (Mainz, 1836–1839); Niklas Müller, *Der Aristokrat in der Klemme* (Mainz, 1792). On the Jacobin period in Mainz history see *Deutsche Jakobiner, Mainzer Republik und Cisrhenanen, 1792–1798*, 3 vols. (Mainz, 1981); Heinrich Scheel, ed., *Die Mainzer Republik*, 2 vols. (Berlin, DDR, 1975), 1: 384, 420–25, 487–89, 710; Schindel, *Die deutsche Schriftstellerinnen*, 3: 146.

12. "Skizzen," 4b, 56ab, KZN-W.

13. "Skizzen," 2b–4b, 5a–7b, 56ab, 61a, 65a, KZN-W; KZH, "Als mich P & F Sappho nannte," in her *Phantasieblüthen und Tändeleien*, 185–86. Schindel, *Die deutsche Schriftstellerinnen*, 1: 187, 3: 144–149 contains the most complete list of her early writings. K. Halein to Schindel, May 10,1823, June 8, 1824, Schindel Nachlass, Görlitz; Karl Goedke, *Grundriss zur Geschichte der deutschen Dichtung* (Dresden, 1938), 13: 296–98; KZH to Brümmer, August 1, 1875, Brümmer Nachlass, Briefe II (Kathinka Zitz), Deutsche Staatsbibliothek, Berlin, Frederiksen, "Deutsche Autorinnen," 98–101; Showalter, *A Literature of Their Own*, 48, 57; Rogers, *Feminism in Eighteenth Century England*, 17. On Friederich see Wilhelm Kosch, *Deutsches Literatur-Lexikon*, 5 vols. (Bern, 1978), V: 673–74.

14. "Skizzen," 6b, 7a KZN-W; Böttger, *Frauen im Aufbruch*, 246–92; Rogers, *Feminism in Eighteenth Century England*, 25; Joeres, *Die Anfänge der deutschen Frauenbewegung*, 63, 87–90; Louise Dittmar to Lorenz Dieffenbach, July 30, 1847, Nachlass Dieffenbach, Universitätsbibliothek, Giessen.

15. "Skizzen," 85b, KZN-W; Emilie Hurst to KZH, n.d. (1842), and her poem to KZH, n.d., KZN-M.

16. K. Halein to Schindel, July 25, 1830, Schindel Nachlass, Görlitz; KZH to Brümmer, August 17, 1874, Nachlass Brümmer, Briefe II, Berlin, BRD.

17. KZH to Leonhard Schrag, December 10, 1826, Sig. Schragiana I (Halein), Bayerische Staatsbibliothek, Munich; Schenda, *Volk ohne Buch*, 159; Schenda cites J. C. Gädicke, *Zur Statistik der deutschen Literatur* (Berlin, 1834), 8; Showalter, *A Literature of Their Own*, 46–52.

18. Originally appeared in the *Beilage* to the *Augsburger Allgemeine Zeitung*, February 10, 1845, 345 as cited in Wittmann, *Buchmarkt und Lektüre*, 157; another critic, Hermann Hauff, compared a writer to a "factory" who delivers "all sorts of literary yard goods, all produced according to the newest rococo model" (cited in Max Bucher, Werner Hahl, Georg Jäger, and Reinhard Wittmann, eds., *Realismus und Gründerzeit: Manifeste und Dokumente zur deutschen Literatur 1848–1880*, 2 vols. (Stuttgart, 1976), 1: 591.)

19. KZH (trans.), *Marion de Lorme* (Mainz, 1833); *Blätter für literarische Unterhaltung*, no. 141 (May 21, 1834), 578; KZH (trans.), *Cromwell* (Stuttgart, 1835); KZH, *Sonderbare Geschichten aus den Feenländern*, 2 vols. (Nürnberg, 1844); KZH, *Erzählungen und Novellen*, 2 vols. (Nürnberg, 1845); the best list of her journal publications is the one she prepared for Brümmer in 1875, Brümmer Nachlass, Berlin, BRD.

20. *Didaskalia,* no. 85, March 26, 1846; *Blätter für literarische Unterhaltung,* no. 144, May 24, 1847, 575; KZH to Schindel, June 8, 1824, Schindel Nachlass, Görlitz.

21. Friedrich to KZH, December 20, 1845, editor, *Gutenberg,* to KZH, December 2, 1842, C. Wipfler to KZH, July 12, 1840, Karl Müller to KZH, July 12, 1843, Robert Blum to KZH, September 13, 1845, KZN-M. More examples can be found in the folder marked "Verhandlungen mit Verleger."

22. KZH to Nanni Hillebrand, February 6, 1847, Klick to KZH, June 11, 1844, Luise von Ploenies to KZH, May 8, 1846, KZN-M; KZH to grand duke, July 28, 1833, Abt D 12, no. 697, Bl. 15, 16, HSA-D.

23. Bekker to KZH, October 31, 1843, July 20, 1847, Reh to KZH, May 18, 1845, January 17, June 19, August 18, December 8, 1846, July 28, 1847, KZN-M. Information from the Stadtarchiv Darmstadt, March 9, 1985.

24. Gilbert and Gubar, *Madwoman,* 544, cite the hostile reaction, perhaps unrepresentative, to Elizabeth Barrett Browning's political poetry in 1860; Joeres, *Die Anfänge der deutschen Frauenbewegung,* 79; *Blätter für literarische Unterhaltung,* no. 183 (June 30, 1836): 774, no. 144 (May 24, 1847): 575; *Nordstern,* no. 38, June 23, 1860, KZN-W.

25. "Skizzen," 2a, KZN-W; Rogers, *Feminism in Eighteenth Century England,* 4; Robertson, *An Experience of Women,* 11–13.

26. KZH, "Die Schriftstellerin," 61; Rogers, *Feminism in Eighteenth Century England,* 246.

27. KZH, "Die Männer- und Frauenrepublik," in her *Kaiserin Josephine* (Mainz, 1855), 443–48; see also Robertson, *An Experience of Women,* 30–32.

28. John Stuart Mill, in an article in the *Westminister Review* (1824), wrote that what is considered meritorious in men, such as independence and courageousness, is considered inappropriate in women. The English suffragette Annie Kenney, *Memoirs of a Militant* (London, 1924), expressed this monopolization of virtue as follows: "Our (Women's Social and Political Union's) discretion and secrecy were looked on as cunning. Our loyalty was spoken of as slavish, our devotion was called fanaticism."

29. As Dengler stresses for the United States, women who were primarily concerned about establishing their moral authority in the home were not interested in the feminist argument. Carl Degler, *At Odds: Women and the Family in America* (New York, 1980), 282–84.

30. KZH, "Schattenspiele an der Wand (1847–1848)," *Letzte Rheinsandkörner* (Mainz, 1854), 381–84. Emilie Lehmann was supposed to have taken part in the Polish Revolution of 1831 and spent several months as a prisoner, during which time she became an emancipated woman. After her release she generally wore men's clothing and was pictured in military uniform. Ulla Wischermann, *Frauenfrage und Presse: Frauenarbeit und Frauenbewegung in der illustrierten Presse der 19. Jahrhunderts* (Munich, 1983), 89, 91, 198.

31. KZH, "Skizzen," 63a–64a, KZN-W; Louise Otto also expressed her horror at the "free women" associated with the St. Simonians. Joeres, *Die Anfänge der deutschen Frauenbewegung,* 72.

32. Ibid., 112.

33. Mary Wollstonecraft, *Vindication of the Rights of Woman* (England, 1975), 255.

34. For the above material on her views about women see KZH, "Das Weib in der Grenzen seiner Bestimmung," in her *Herbstrosen*, 330–41 and also 257, 258, 271; KZH, "Aus den Papieren einer Unglücklichen," *Der Rheinische Telegraph*, no. 29, April 10, 1842, 114; KZH, "Schattenspiele an der Wand," *Letzte Rheinsandkörner*, 359, 381–84; KZH, "Mokka di Cheribon," *Variationen*, 72–76.

35. L. Walesrode to Marie Pinder, June 23, 1845 (September 1845, no. 151) Nachlass J. Pinder, BAF. Ludwig Walesrode, "Über das Proletariat: In Briefen an eine Dame," *Königsberger Taschenbuch* (Königsberg, 1846), 248–53.

36. Corvin-Wierbitski, *Erinnerungen*, 1: 221, 286–92; Johannes Bühler, *Das Hambacher Fest* (Ludwigshaven, 1932), 100, 113; *Mainzer Wochenblatt*, April 4, 1820, May 30, 1832.

37. Karl W. H. du Bois Du Thil, *Denkwürdigkeiten aus dem Dienstleben des hessen-darmstädtischen Staatsminister Freiherrn du Thil* (1921, reprint, Osnabrück, 1962), 204–6, 365–68; Walter Grab, "Eroberung oder Befreiung? Deutsche Jakobiner und die Franzosenherrschaft im Rheinlande 1792–1799," *Archiv für Sozialgeschichte* 10 (1970): 7–94; Karl-Georg Faber, *Die Rheinlande zwischen Restauration und Revolution* (Wiesbaden, 1966), 10, 118, 263–65, 306–12; Werner Schubert, "Der Code Civil und die Personenrechtsentwürfe des Grossherzogtums Hessen-Darmstadt von 1842 bis 1847," *Zeitschrift der Savigny Stiftung fur Rechtsgeschichte: Germanistische Abteilung* 88 (1971): 110–71.

38. "Skizzen," 76a, KZN-W; Helmut Haasis, *Morgenröte der Republik: Die linksrheinischen deutschen Demokraten* (Frankfurt/Main, 1984), 214, 218, 230; Scheel, *Mainzer Republik*, 1: 499, 2: 265, 350, 415, 446, 450, 503, 563, 582, 656; Friedrich Schütz, "Der Vormärz in Mainz und Rheinhessen," *Geschichtliche Landeskunde* 24 (1984): 83–89, 99.

39. The debate over the significance of 1792–1793 was reopened with the publication by Heinrich Scheel of the records of the meetings of the Jacobin Club and the Rhenish National Convention. He uses Zitz-Halein's *Magdalene Horix* for descriptions of several events. In 1981 when the city mounted an exhibit to commemorate the Jacobin period it generated a lively controversy. Scheel, *Mainzer Republik*, 1: 116, 305–7, 2: 660; *Deutscher Jakobiner*, 3 vols., 2d ed. (Mainz 1982).

40. Scheel, *Mainzer Republik*, 1: 54; KZH *Magdalene Horix*, 358.

41. "Skizzen," 57ab, KZN-W; KZH, *Magdalene Horix*, iv, 229–41, 247, 289–91, 362, 368, 439, 452–69; *Mainzer Zeitung*, June 16, 1858; Winfried Dotzauer, *Freimaurer Gesellschaften am Rhein* Geschichtliche Landeskunde, vol. 16 (Wiesbaden, 1977), 73. The recent work by T. C. W. Blanning, *The French Revolution in Germany: Occupation and Resistance in the Rheinland 1792–1803* (Oxford, 1983), presents significant evidence for the negative impact of the French occupation and thus for the thin layer of support for the Jacobins. See also Karl Wegert, "Patrimonial Rule, Popular Self Interest, and Jacobinism in

Germany, 1763–1800," *Journal of Modern History* 53 (September 1981): 440–62; Walter Grab, *Ein Volk muss sein Freiheit selbst erobern: Zur Geschichte der deutschen Jacobiner* (Frankfurt/Main, 1984).

42. KZH, "Der Verfasser des grauen Ungeheurs," *Neueste Rheinsandkörner,* 79–128; *Allgemeine Deutsche Biographie,* 27: 483–85; R. R. Palmer, *The Age of the Democratic Revolution,* 2 vols. (Princeton, N.J., 1964), 2: 442–43; Fritz Valjavec, *Die Entstehung der politischen Strömungen in Deutschland, 1770–1815* (Munich, 1951), 218–23.

43. Günter Kolbe, "Demokratische Opposition in religiösen Gewand: Zur Geschichte der deutschkatholischen Bewegung in Sachsen am Vorabend der Revolution von 1848/49," *Zeitschrift für Geschichtswissenschaft,* vol. 20, no. 9 (1972): 1102–12; Jacques Droz, "Die religiösen Sekten und die Revolution von 1848," *Archiv für Sozialgeschichte,* vol. 3 (1963): 109–18; Friedrich Graf, *Die Politisierung des religiösen Bewusstseins: Die bürgerliche Religionsparteien im deutschen Vormärz: Das Beispiel des Deutschkatholiken* (Stuttgart-Bad Cannstatt, 1978), 57–59; Prelinger, *Charity, Challenge and Change,* 57–61.

44. Graf, *Die Politisierung des religiösen Bewusstseins,* 35–37, 103, 120–55, 177 n. 65a, 182 n. 22; *Mannheimer Abendzeitung,* February 10, 1848; *Rheinsche Blätter,* October 16, 1845, 495–96; Ronge to Frau ?, March 6, 1847, no. 37, Ronge to Geehrte deutsche Schwester, August 1, 1849, no. 55, Johannes Ronge Nachlass, Sächsische Landesbibliothek, Dresden; Catherine M. Prelinger, "The German Catholic Church: From National Hope to Regional Reality" in *The Consortium on Revolutionary Europe, Proceedings 1976,* ed. Lee Kennett (Athens, Ga., 1978), 88–91, and her *Charity, Challenge, and Change,* 113–14, 118–21; *Literarische Geheimberichte,* 2: 120.

45. Gross to KZH, June 29, 1842, June 13, 1843, February 20, 24, 1845, KZH to Gross, February 22, 1845, KZN-M; KZH, *Rahel oder dreiunddreissig Jahre,* pt. 2, vol. 2, (Leipzig, 1864), 52.

46. See the material in her folder, "Beziehungen zu Deutschkatholizismus [*sic*]," KZN-M; "Skizzen," 44a, 54b, 104ab, KZN-W; Josef Pirazzi to KZH, January 11, 1848, M. Zoebel to KZH, November 11, 1848, Fl. Gulde to KZH, January 21, 1848, Heribert Rau to KZH, February 6, 1848, Lizius to KZH, June 18, 1849, KZN-M. Her papers contain the application for membership in the German Catholic community in Mannheim. On Duller, who was sympathetic to female emancipation, see *Allgemeine Deutsche Biographie,* 5: 457–58.

4. Before 1848: Women and Politics

1. Joeres, *Die Anfänge der deutschen Frauenbewegung,* 83; Wittmann, *Buchmarkt un Lektüre,* 155; Rosenberg, *Literaturverhältnisse,* 79–85; Peter Hohendahl, *Literarische Kultur im Zeitalter des Liberalismus, 1830–1870* (Munich, 1985), 124–28.

2. Heinz-Dietrich Fischer, ed., *Deutsche Kommunikationskontrolle des 15. bis 20. Jahrhundert* (Munich, 1982), 75–113; Ute Radlik, "Heine in der Zensur

der Restaurationsepoche," in *Zur Literatur der Restaurationsepoche 1815–1848*, ed. J. Hermand and M. Windfuhr (Stuttgart, 1970), 463–65, 479; for individual cases see Heinrich Houben, *Verbotene Literatur von der klassischen Zeit bis zur Gegenwart*, 2 vols. (Berlin, 1924), who cites only one example of censorship involving a female writer: Bettina von Arnim. Rosenberg, *Literaturverhältnisse*, 38–39, 41–43; Alfred Oehlke, *100 Jahre Breslauer Zeitung 1820–1920* (Breslau, n.d.), 42–46, 102; Bucher et al., *Realismus und Grunderzeit*, 2: 633–35.

3. Joeres, *Die Anfänge der deutschen Frauenbewegung*, 33–99; Ruth Gotze, "Louise Ottos Beziehungen zum Proletariat im Vormärz und in der Revolution von 1848/49," *Sächsische Heimatblätter* 27, no. 4 (1981): 154–56.

4. Karl Heinz Hahn, *Bettina von Arnim in ihrem Verhältnis zu Staat und Politik* (Weimar, 1958), 9–12, 18, 26, 28–35, 52–53, is the best treatment of her political activities and views. Wilhelm Frels, *Bettina von Arnims Königsbuch* (Schwerin/Mecklenburg, 1912); Houben, *Verbotene Literatur*, 1: 33–39; Böttger, *Frauen im Aufbruch*, 147–57, 530–31; Bettina von Arnim, *Armenbuch* (Frankfurt/Main, 1969), 24–30, 74–75; Günter Jäckel, ed., *Das Volk braucht Licht: Frauen zur Zeit des Aufbruchs 1790–1848 in ihren Briefen* (Darmstadt, 1970), 606–18, 742; *Der Briefwechsel Bettine von Arnim mit den Brüder Grimm, 1838–1841*, ed. Hartwig Schultz (Frankfurt/Main, 1985), 19; Bettina von Arnim, *Clemens Brentanos Frühlingskranz* (Leipzig, 1985), 303–07; *Literarische Geheimberichte*, 2: 187, 240, 245.

5. Although there is no doubt that Aston believed in complete social equality for women and men, there is some doubt as to whether she wrote the works attributed to her or whether they were produced in an early "as told to" format. Karl August Varnhagen von Ense claimed that when Aston was to be expelled from Berlin, Gottschall proposed that she pass herself off as a writer who needed to stay in Berlin to complete her literary work. Her lover then wrote *Wilde Rosen* as well as *Meine Emanzipation*, whereas the later works were written by others. Statement in Varnhagen von Ense Collection, Jagellonian University Library, Cracow; Goetzinger, *Für die Selbstverwirklichung der Frau*, 49, 52, 65, 168; Goetzinger, whose book gives us a documentary-biography, is too uncritical in her use of material.

6. Louise Aston, *Wilde Rosen* (Berlin, 1846); ———, *Meine Emanzipation, Verweisung und Rechtfertigung* (Brussels, 1846); ———, *Aus dem Leben einer Frau* (Hamburg, 1847); ———, *Lydia* (Magdeburg, 1848); for the biographical details see Goetzinger, *Für die Selbstverwirklichung der Frau*, and Nachlass Brümmer, Briefe II, Aston, 63, Handschriftenabteilung Deutsche Staatsbibliothek, Berlin, BRD; Louise Aston to Rudolf Gottschall, n. d. (1851), Varnhagen von Ense Collection, Jagellonian Library, University of Cracow.

7. The first three works cited in the preceding note were favorably reviewed by *Blätter für literarische Unterhaltung*, but the fourth, *Aus dem Leben einer Frau*, left the supposedly sympathetic reviewer with a feeling of "revulsion." No. 353 (December 12, 1846): 1412, no. 82 (March 23, 1847): 328, no. 260 (September 17, 1847): 1039–40, and no. 304 (November 30, 1848): 1215.

8. *Frauen-Zeitung*, September 9, 1849, January 5, 1850.

9. KZH, *Rahel*, pt. 3, vol. 6: 85n**.

10. "Skizzen," 11a, KZN-W; on Sallet see *Allgemeine Deutsche Biographie* 33: 717–26; Veit Valentin, *Geschichte der deutschen Revolution 1848–1849*, 2 vols. (Berlin, 1930–1931), 1: 49–50, 2: 57–58, 236, 254, 256. KZH's version of the Sallet affair is confirmed by Corvin-Wierbitski, *Erinnerungen*, 1: 196–99.

11. The best collection of her works is in the Stadtbibliothek, Mainz; see also Goedke, *Grundriss zur Geschichte der deutschen Dichtung*, 13: 295–98 and the list she prepared for Brümmer (Nachlass Brümmer, Briefe II, Zitz), Deutsche Staatsbibliothek Handschriftenabteilung, Berlin, DDR.

12. Auguste Schmidt and Hugo Rosch, *Louise Otto-Peters: die Dichterin und Vorkämpfer für Frauenrecht* (Leipzig, 1898), 38; Fanny Lewald-Stahr, *Erinnerungen aus dem Jahre 1848*, 2 vols. (Braunschweig, 1850), 2: 345; Friedrich to KZH, November 11, 1835, ? to KZH, October 8, 1840, Retmer to KZH, March 16, 1843, Dr. Lasker to KZH, December 12, 1844, Rau to KZH, February 6, 1848, KZN-M; KZH, *Variationen*, Vorwort.

13. KZH, "Schattenspiele an der Wand," *Letzte Rheinsandkörner*, 384–85.

14. KZH, *Variationen*, Vorwort.

15. *Blätter für literarische Unterhaltung*, May 21, 1834, 578, June 30, 1836, 774; Hessisches Staatsarchiv, Darmstadt, Abt. D 12, no. 697, Bl. 15–17.

16. Rosenberg, *Literaturverhältnisse*, 211–17; the collections of pre-1848 and 1848 poetry, which contain only a few examples by female poets such as Louise Otto, Louise Dittmar, Louise Aston, and Wilhelmine Müller, are Bruno Kaiser, *Die Achtundvierziger: Ein Lesebuch* (Weimar, 1958), 11–13, 213–15; Ernst Volkmann, *Um Einheit und Freiheit, 1815–1848* (Leipzig, 1936), 210–12; Elfriede Underberg, ed., *Die Dichtung der ersten deutschen Revolution* (Leipzig, 1930); Hans-Georg Werner, *Geschichte des politischen Gedichts in Deutschland von 1815 bis 1840* (Berlin, DDR, 1949), 10, 12, 255; and Christian Petzet, *Die Blütezeit der deutschen politischen Lyrik von 1840 bis 1850* (Munich, 1903); Ludwig Kalisch, "Die schlechten Dichter," *Didaskalia*, vol. 23, no. 22, January 22, 1845.

17. Joeres, *Die Anfänge der deutschen Frauenbewegung*, 81–82.

18. Kathinka Halein, *Phantasieblüthen und Tändeleien*, 48–51, 176–77, 180–81, 252–53.

19. KZH, "Todtenkranze," for Peter Paul Metzger, HS 122, KZN-W.

20. KZH, "Eine Stimme der Zeit," *Herbstrosen*, 221–23; see also her "An das Volk von Spanien," 227–29.

21. KZH, "Es werde Licht," *Herbstrosen*, 242–43.

22. KZH, "Für einen übertreibenden Deutschtümler," *Deutsche Dichterinnen vom 16. Jahrhundert bis zur Gegenwart*, ed. Gisela Brinkler-Gabler (Frankfurt/ Main, 1978), 217.

23. KZH, *Herbstrosen*, 243–44; Susan Cocalis, ed., *The Defiant Muse: German Feminist Poems from the Middle Ages to the Present* (New York, 1986), 30–33.

24. KZH, *Dur- und Molltöne* (Mainz, 1859), 59–61; KZH, *Einige Worte*.

25. Balzac's *Old Goriot* indicates that the casino was still active in the 1830s.

26. KZH, *Herbstrosen*, 230–33, 238–41, 296–97. See Chapter 10.

27. KZH, "Die Steuern des Armen," *Herbstrosen*, 234–36.

28. KZH, "Schein und Wirklichkeit," *Herbstrosen*, 236–38.

29. KZH, *Dur- und Molltöne*, 19–20, 162–64; for other poems of a political and social nature see 16–17, 273–75, and KZH, *Herbstrosen*, 227–29, 296–97; on the issue of slavery see R. Koch, "Liberalismus, Konservatismus und das Problem der Negersklaverei," *Historische Zeitschrift* 222, no. 3 (June 1976): 532, 572–73. Some of the poems that she wrote during the Rhein crisis in 1840 have not survived in an identifiable form.

30. C. Berthold to KZH, February 14, 1855, KZN-W.

31. KZH, *Variationen*, Vorwort.

32. KZH, "Felizian," in her *Donner und Blitz*, 225–77; in her "Narziss der Wandelbare," *Variationen*, 201–51, she uses a similar format to attack the censor, to support a free press, and to stress the necessity of parliamentary opposition in a representative system.

33. KZH, "Herr und Sklav," *Variationen*, 1–34.

34. KZH, "Das Reich der Sterne," *Variationen*, 177–200.

35. KZH, "Hausgenossen," *Donner und Blitz*, 400–99. Similar themes are developed in "Adler Eier," "Der Metallkönig," "Schattenspiele an der Wand," "Chikander," and "Die heilige Schafer und sein Assistant," in *Variationen*.

36. KZH, "Die Aufruhr im Pflanzenreich," *Variationen*, 34–52; see also "Die Königen der Geizigen," and "Bärenpratz," *Variationen*, 278–335.

37. KZH, "Rumpelstiltzchen," *Variationen*, 150–76.

38. Julius Schoeps, "An der seite der Unterdrückten: Ludwig Kalisch (1814–1882) im Vormarz, in der Revolution und im französischen Exil," in *Juden im Vormärz und in der Revolution von 1848* ed. Walter Grab (Stuttgart, 1983), 331–51; Josef Heinzelmann, "Ludwig Kalisch," *Neue Deutsche Biographie*, 11: 59–60; Baron von Lichtenberg to KZH, October 8, 1840, KZN-M.

39. *Narrhalla*, 1844, 14, 39–44, 81–83; *Neue Mainzer Narrenzeitung*, January 14, 1844, 28–29.

40. "Skizzen," 102b–103a, which contain no mention of the letters to the grand duke, KZN-W; N. Müller to KZH, February 6, 1844, E. E. Hoffmann to KZH, December 18, 1843, E. Reis to KZH, January 22, 1844, KZN-M; Alexander Burger, "Aus der Geschichte des Mainzer Karnevals: Kathinka Zitz und die Mainzer Karnivalszeitung von 1844," *Heim und Welt*, no. 73, March 1, 1924; Fritz Saurmann, "Ein karnevalistisches Literategeplänkel aus Alt-Mainz und seine Folgen," *Mainzer Warte*, nos. 5, 7, 8 (February 2, 16, 23, 1929).

41. KZH, "Glaubensbekenntniss," in her *Dur- und Molltöne*, 59–61.

42. Götze, "Louise Ottos Beziehungen," 154–56.

43. "Skizzen," KZN-W, 83b; Itzstein to KZH, December 3, 1844, KZN-M; Josef Rosskopf, "Johann Adam von Itzstein" (Ph.D. diss., Johannes Gutenberg University, Mainz, 1951), 134–40; Siegfried Schmidt, *Robert Blum* (Weimar, 1971), 58–63; *Literarische Geheimberichte* 1: 58; B. Theobald to KZH, July 11, 1846, KZN-M; Karl Marx and Friedrich Engels, *Werke*, 4 vols. (Berlin, DDR, 1977), 4: 268–70; Sybille Obenaus, *Literarische und politische Zeitschriften 1830–1848* (Stuttgart, 1986), 73–74.

44. Rüdiger Schütz, *Preussen und die Rheinlande: Studien zur preussischen Integrationspolitik im Vormärz* (Wiesbaden, 1978), 5, 250; Elisabeth Fehrenbach, "Rheinischer Liberalismus und gesellschaftliche Verfassung," in Wolfgang Schieder, ed., *Liberalismus in der Gesellschaft des deutschen Vormärz* (Göttingen, 1983), 272–94.

45. Norbert Deuchert, *Vom Hambacher Fest zur badischen Revolution: Politische Presse und Anfänge deutscher Demokratie 1832–1848/49* (Stuttgart, 1983), 159–68, 228–31; Kurt Koszyk, *Deutsche Presse im 19. Jahrhundert* (Berlin (BRD), 1966), 100, 104, 117, 329; Eberhard Naujoks, "Der badische Liberalismus im Vormärz in Kampf für Pressefreiheit und gegen Zensur (1832–1847)," *Zeitschrift für die Geschichte des Oberrheins* 131 (1983): 362–65, 368.

46. She had used the phrase in a poem a year before.

47. *Mannheimer Abendzeitung*, September 1, 4, 22, October 4, 7, November 10, 1846, pp. 946, 958, 1029, 1078, 1091, 1226.

48. "Allerdurchlauchtigster Grossherzog . . . ," October 1846, mog m: 4/443, Stabi Mz; "Bürger von Frankenthal . . . ," November 1846, 66: 2/30, Stabi Mz; Ronge Nachlass, Mscr Dresden, App 131, Bl 39–40, Sächsische Landesbibliothek Dresden; *Mannheimer Abendzeitung*, November 29, December 1, 1846, 1301, 1309; Veit Valentin, *Geschichte der deutsche Revolution,* 2 vols., 1: 171–80; Schütz, "Der Vormärz in Mainz und Rheinhessen," 96–99; Paul Wentzcke and Wolfgang Klötzer, eds., *Deutscher Liberalismus im Vormärz, Heinrich von Gagern: Briefe und Reden 1815–1848* (Göttingen, 1959), 337, 345–48.

49. *Mannheimer Abendzeitung*, October 21, 23 25, 26, November 29, December 5, 23, 31, 1846, September 28, 1847, 1145, 1153, 1162, 1166, 1301, 1326, 1398, 1425, 1053.

50. Karl Buchner, *Das Grossherzogtum Hessen in seiner politischen und sozialen Entwicklung von Herbst 1847 bis zum Herbst 1850* (Darmstadt, 1850), 8; *Grossherzoglich Hessisches Regierungsblatt*, no. 42, December 30, 1846; *Mainzer Zeitung*, January 1, 1847; Sicherheitspolizei, 1846, XVIII/1 no. 968, 2220, 2269, Stadtarchiv Mainz; the Hessian foreign ministry files, Acta ministeriale betrd. die Versendung und Verbreitung der *Mannheimer Abendzeitung* und des *Deutschen Zuschauer* innerhalb des Grossherzogtum 1848, Abt G 1/Konv. 156/6, Hessisches Staatsarchiv, Darmstadt; Deuchert, *Vom Hambacher Fest*, 165, 230–32, 366; *Literarische Geheimberichte*, 1: 184; Ilse Spangenburg, *Hessen-Darmstadt und der Deutsche Bund 1815–1848* (Darmstadt, 1969), 12–16, 124–26.

51. "Skizzen," 104b, KZN-W; on reading Madame de Staël's *Corinna* she commented negatively on Lord Arthur because of his lack of manly virtues. "Skizzen," 65, KZN-W.

52. Büttner, *Die Anfänge des Parlamentarismus in Hessen-Darmstadt*, 218–23. Her husband and her former lawyer, Lehne, were both elected in 1847.

5. 1848: Women in Revolution

1. Good recent bibliographical treatments of the revolution are Franzjörg Baumgart, *Die verdrängte Revolution: Darstellung und Bewertung der Revolution*

von 1848 in der deutschen Geschichtsschreibung vor dem Ersten Weltkreig (Düsseld-
orf, 1976), which covers the pre World War I literature; Dieter Langeweische,
"Die deutsche Revolution von 1848/49 und die vorrevolutionäre Gesellschaft:
Forschungsstand und Forschungsperspektiven," *Archiv für Sozialgeschichte* 21
(1981): 458–98, and Donald Mattheisen, "History as Current Events: Recent
Works on the German Revolution of 1848," *American Historical Review* 88
(December 1983): 1219–37. Langewiesche, *Die deutsche Revolution von 1848/
49* (Darmstadt, 1983), has also edited a collection of articles on the German
revolution. Theodore S. Hamerow, *Restoration, Revolution, Reaction: Economics
and Politics in Germany, 1815–1871* (Princeton, N.J., 1958), provides the most
convincing analysis of the upheaval, and Valentin, *Geschichte der deutschen
Revolution* remains a mine of reliable information. Wolfram Sieman, *Die
deutsche Revolution von 1848/49* (Frankfurt/Main, 1985) is the best recent account.

2. Langewiesche takes note of this literature in his bibliographical essay,
but he neglects to include any examples in his edited volume of essays. Besides
the works listed at the beginning of Chapter 1, see Anna Blos, *Die Frauen der
deutschen Revolution von 1848* (Dresden, 1928), which contains profiles of ten
women, and Gerlinde Hummel-Haasis, ed., *Schwestern zerreisst eure Ketten* (Munich, 1982) which is a collection of documents, dealing especially with south
German women's activities. Prelinger, *Charity, Challenge, and Change* analyzes
the significance of religion as a factor in women's activism.

3. *Didaskalia,* no. 74, March 14, 1848.

4. *Didaskalia,* no. 49, February 26, 1849.

5. *Offenburger Wochenblatt,* July 14, 1848, 386; hereafter cited as *OW.*

6. *Frauen-Zeitung,* August 23, 1851, 227–28; on the role of French women
in public affairs during the first half of the nineteenth century see Claire
Goldberg Moses, "The Evolution of Feminist Thought in France, 1829–1889"
(Ph.D. diss., George Washington University, 1978), 150–73, and her *French
Feminism in the Nineteenth Century* (New York, 1984), 127–50.

7. She neglected to mention the journalistic activities of Mathilde Anneke,
who took over her husband's newspaper, *Neue Kölnische Zeitung,* when he was
imprisoned and ran it successfully for several months, even briefly issuing a
Frauenzeitung until it was suppressed.

8. Helene, "Seitenstuck zu den Aufsatz uber Johanna Dorvin," (*sic*) *Frauen-
Zeitung,* December 28, 1851, 358–59; Wagner, *Mathilde Franziska Anneke,* 42–
57; Gustav Otruba, "Zur Frauenfrage im Revolutionsjahr 1848 im Spiegel
Wiener Flugschriften," *Wirtschafts- und sozialhistorische Beiträge* (Vienna, 1979),
395, mentions a Viennese women's newspaper. See Chapter 7 for further
references to Adele Erbe.

9. The most extensive collection of published material relating to women's
activities during the revolution appears in Hummel-Haasis, *Schwestern.*

10. *Frauen-Zeitung,* May 31, 1851, 136. See also the papers of Marie Pinder
in the Julius Pinder Nachlass, F Sg 1/152, Bundesarchiv Aussenstelle Frankfurt; hereafter cited as BAF.

11. Before 1848 women could view meetings of the Saxon legislature as

Louise Otto relates, and women did attend the Offenburg meeting of the democratic radicals under Friedrich Hecker. Amalie Struve, *Erinnerungen aus den badischen Freiheitskämpfen* (Hamburg, 1850), 15.

12. "Erinnerungen Luise Zimmermanns aus dem Frankfurter Parlament," 28–29, Nachlass Zimmermann, F Sg 1/25, and Karl Streymayer to Berta von Gudenus, June 24, 1848, Streymayer Nachlass, F Sg 1/179, both in BAF. The material in the Aussenstelle contains the correspondence, diaries, and memoirs of the wives, mothers, and daughters of the representatives of the national assembly in Frankfurt.

13. *Didaskalia,* no. 294, November 4, 1848; *Frauen-Zeitung,* May 31, 1851, 136; Amalie Struve, *Erinnerungen,* 15, 21, relates that women attended the Baden chamber's session in February 1848.

14. Women's groups in such cities as Mannheim and Constance had previously demonstrated their interest in the issue by sending petitions to the national assembly requesting amnesty for Hecker and his followers. Even if women were accorded no direct share in politics, the Constance appeal stressed, they still followed with great interest the "struggle for human rights." *OW,* April 21, June 13, July 28, 1848, 204, 314, 419–20.

15. Wilhelm Schweidler to his wife, August 2, 1848, Schweidler Nachlass, F Sg 1/168, Frau Pagenstecher to her son Carl, August 8, September 18, 1848, F Sg 1/148, Friedrich Albert to his mother, August 9, 1848, F Sg 1/74, Otto Keudell to R. Keudell, May 22, 1848, F Sg 1/121, all in BAF; "Acta Criminalia 1848. Übersicht der Akten . . . Aufruhr am 16, 17, 18 September. Verzeichnis der vernommenen Personen" and "Acta Criminalia 1848, D 62," Stadtarchiv Frankfurt; Frank Eyck, *The Frankfurt Parliament, 1848–49* (London, 1968), 247–53.

16. Hubert Meyerinck, *Die Strassenkämpfe in Berlin am 18 und 19 März 1848* (Leipzig, 1911), 5, 21, 24; Tim Klein, ed., *1848: Der Vorkampf deutscher Einheit und Freiheit* (Munich, 1914), 88–89, 155, 159, 162; Valentin, *Geschichte der deutschen Revolution,* 1: 445.

17. R. John Rath, *The Viennese Revolution of 1848* (Austin, Texas, 1957), 292–93, 324; Otruba "Zur Frauenfrage," 398–99, 402; Hummel-Haasis, *Schwestern,* 100–130; Eduard Fuchs, *Die Weiberherrschaft in der Geschichte der Menschheit,* 2 vols., (Munich, 1913), 393, 418, 420; R. Blum to Jenny Blum, October 17, 1848, Robert Blum Nachlass, F Sg 1/52, BAF, reprinted in Ludwig Bergsträsser, *Das Frankfurter Parlament in Briefen und Tagebücher* (Frankfurt/Main, 1929), 406. At least forty-two women were killed and wounded; Siemann, *Die deutsche Revolution,* 169.

18. Röckel cited in Karl Obermann, *Einheit und Freiheit* (Berlin, DDR, 1950), 289. 815–17; Hummel-Haasis, *Schwestern,* 130–43; *Mainzer Kurier,* December 28, 1851; *Frauen-Zeitung,* May 26, 1849, no. 12, March 23, 1850; according to Claire Moses this deterrent intention may have been a factor in the sentencing of Jeanne Deroin. Moses, "Evolution," 170–73.

19. *Frauen-Zeitung,* December 17, 1849, 352, April 21, 1852, 116; *Mainzer Abendpost,* nos. 12, 14, January 14, 18, 1851; Otruba, "Zur Frauenfrage," 402.

20. Hummel-Haasis, *Schwestern,* 130–52; "Adolf Kohn: Politische Tage-bucher 1848–1851," *Denkwürdige Jahre 1848–1851,* Nobert Conrads and Günter Richter, eds., (Cologne, 1978), 252–53; Obermann, *Einheit,* 825; *Frauen-Zeitung,* November 17, 1849, November 9, 1851, 341, December 7, 1850; *Mainzer Kurier,* October 2, 1851; *Mainzer Tagblatt,* June 18, 1850, February 5, 15, April 12, 1851; H. P. Dressel to KZH, January 13, 1851, KZN-M.

21. "Emma Sigmund jetzt Mad. Herwegh," *Rheinische Telegraph,* no. 86, October 25, 1843; Emma Herwegh to Georg Herwegh, November 28, Decem-ber 4, 1842, Böttger, *Frauen im Aufbruch,* 208–09, 215, 217–18; Emma Her-wegh, *Zur Geschichte der deutschen demokratischen Legion aus Paris* (Grünberg, 1849); Hummel-Haasis, *Schwestern,* 185–202; Corvin-Wierbitski, *Erinner-ungen,* 2: 358–59, 411–12.

22. Mathilde Anneke, *Memoiren einer Frau aus dem badisch-pfälzischen Feldzuge 1848/49* (1853, Newark, N.J.; reprint, Munster, 1982), 72–73. In one town Anneke was thought to be Robert Blum's daughter and viewed with awe by the local women; Hummel-Haasis, *Schwestern,* 203–20 (Struve), 235–239 (Blenker); Wolfgang Dressen, ed., *1848–1849 Bürgerkrieg in Baden* (Berlin, BRD, 1975), 96–97; Henriette Feuerbach to Sophie Heydenreich, July 15, 1849, Böttger, *Frauen im Aufbruch,,* 202–3; Fuchs, *Weiberherrschaft,* 390, 393, 418, 420; *Die neue Zeit,* July 15, 1849; Barton C. Hacker, "Women and Military Institutions in Early Modern Europe: A Reconnaissance," *SIGNS,* 6, no. 4 (1981): 643–71.

23. *Didaskalia,* no. 148, May 28, 1848, no. 158, June 9, 1848, no. 223, August 25, 1848, no. 234, August 26, 1848, no. 272, October 10, 1848 no. 312, November 25, 1848, no. 18, January 20, 1849; Valentin, *Geschichte der deutschen Revolution,* 2: 25–27.

24. Frau Schwarzenberg, to Franziska Sattler, April 19, 1848, Schwarzen-berg Nachlass, F Sg 1/167, BAF; Bamberger, *Erinnerungen,* 49–50; *Didaskalia,* no. 149, May 29, 1848; Otruba, "Zur Frauenfrage," 400; Siemann, *Die deutsche Revolution,* 166.

25. *Didaskalia,* no. 100, April 9, 1848, no. 118, April 28, 1848, no. 121, May 1, 1848; Otrube, "Zur Frauenfrage," 399–401.

26. Joachim Paschen, *Demokratische Vereine und preussischer Staat* (Munich, 1977), 11, 42; *Mainzer Tagblatt,* no. 109, May 8, 1849; *Neue Zeit* (Worms), December 17, 1848; "Hanauer Chronik," vol. 2 (1846–1851), 525, Stadtarchiv, Hanau.

27. *Mainzer Zeitung,* July 31, September 27, 1848; Bamberger, *Erinnerungen,* 80, 132, Stephan Born, *Erinnerungen 1848* (Leipzig, 1898), 195; KZH, "Skiz-zen," 107a, KZN-W; *Fliegende Blätter,* 6, no. 141 (1848): 116; *Mainzer Tagblatt,* March 18, 1849.

28. References to them can be found in *Didaskalia,* no. 228, August 19, 1848 (Weimar), no. 266, October 3, 1848 (Heidelberg), no. 276 (Idstein), no. 291, Novemeber 5, 1848 (Darmstadt), no. 295, November 6, 1848 (Eisenach); *Neue Zeit* (Worms), April 2, May 19, 24, September 24, 1848, February 27,

1849; *Mainzer Zeitung,* October 10, 1848, January 17, 1849; *Mainzer Tagblatt,* January 10, 1849; Friedrich Battenberg and Eckhart G. Franz, *Darmstadts Geschichte* (Darmstadt, 1980), 341.

29. Mill had used the phrase, pampered slavery. Bernard Semmel, *John Stuart Mill and the Pursuit of Virtue* (New Haven, Conn., 1984), 74, 76–77. Similar phraseology also appears in an article by the Königsberger radical, Ludwig Walesrode, who will be discussed later. Walesrode, "Über das Proletariat," 252.

30. Thirty years later the French feminist Leon Richer also made a distinction between "equality" and "equivalence." The latter term implied differences between the sexes but not inferiority. Moses, *French Feminism,* 202; see also Karen Offen, "Ernest Legouve and the Doctrine of 'Equality in Difference' for Women: A Case Study of Male Feminism in Nineteenth Century Thought," *Journal of Modern History* 58 (June 1986): 452–84.

31. Bamberger, *Erinnerungen,* 114–22; *Mainzer Zeitung,* August 17, 18,1848; Hummel-Haasis, *Schwestern,* 147–48, cites a second statement in favor of women's rights by the Mainz Democratic Association.

32. *Didaskalia,* no. 126, May 28, 1849, no. 166, June 17, 1848.

33. *Didaskalia,* nos. 140, 141, May 20, 21, 1848, no. 186, July 7, 1848.

34. *Didaskalia,* no. 329, December 16, 1848, no. 334, December 21, 1848; Otruba, "Zur Frauenfrage," 401; *Frauen-Zeitung,* no. 24, June 15, 1850. There is no evidence that petitions demanding marriage reform were sent to the Frankfurt Parliament.

35. *OW,* May 26, June 9, July 28, 1848, 273, 305, 419. See also Prelinger, *Charity, Challenge, and Change,* 64–66, 116–18.

36. Fuchs, *Die Frau,* 108.

37. "Namensverzeichnis der Mitglieder des Mainzer Turnvereins Anfangs April 1848," *Anschlagzettel 1848,* no. 82, Stabi Mz; Louis Snyder, *German Nationalism: The Tragedy of a People* (Harrisburg, Pa. 1952), 21–43; Norbert Heise, "Demokratischer Turnerbund und Deutscher Turnerbund," *Die bürgerlichen Parteien in Deutschland* (Leipzig, 1968), 1: 274–77; Dieter Düding, *Organisierter gesellschaftlicher Nationalismus in Deutschland 1808–1847* (Munich, 1984), 233 n. 917, 235, 246 n. 981; Deuchert, *Vom Hambacher Fest,* 237–40.

38. *Didaskalia,* no. 289, October 30, 1848; *Frauen-Zeitung,* July 6, 1850, no. 28, July 18, 1851, 187–89.

39. *Frauen-Zeitung,* no. 32, August 16, 1851, p. 220.

40. *Frauen-Zeitung,* no. 14, April 12, 1851, 77–78, no. 36, September 27, 1851, 249–50, no. 38, October 5, 1851, pp. 270–71, no. 43, November 9, 1851, 311–12.

41. Eberhard Jean, "Deutsche Turnerschaft," *Die bürgerlichen Parteien in Deutschland,* 1: 607. The issue of women's sports was raised in the 1850s as a result of concern about the too-sedentary life of middle-class women. Ulla Wischermann, *Frauenfrage und Presse,* 78–79, 195.

42. *Frauen-Zeitung,* no. 47, December 7, 1851, 338–41, no. 1, January 11, 1852, 6–7; see also no. 14, April 14, 1852, 106–8 and no. 15, April 21, 1852,

113–15; Ann Taylor Allen, "Spiritual Motherhood: German Feminists and the Kindergarten Movement, 1848–1911," *History of Education Quarterly* 22, no. 3 (1982): 319–39, and her "Gardens of Children, Gardens of God: Kindergartens and Day-Care Centers in Nineteenth Century Germany," *Journal of Social History* 19 (Spring 1986): 433–50; Prelinger, *Charity, Challenge, and Change,* 139–44, 161–63.

43. Louise Dittmar, *Vier Zeitfragen* (Offenbach/Main, 1847), I, II.

44. Louise Dittmar, *Bekannte Geheimnisse* (Darmstadt, 1845), 44.

45. Louise Dittmar, *Wesen der Ehe* (Leipzig, 1849), 14, 66–70, cited in Renate Möhrmann, *Frauenemanzipation in deutschen Vormärz: Text und Dokumente* (Stuttgart, 1978), 55–57, 62–64.

46. Dittmar, *Wesen der Ehe,* 47–63, 113–18, cited in Möhrmann, *Frauenemanzipation,* 94–103, 129–44.

47. Dittmar, *Wesen der Ehe,* 47–63, 106–18, cited in Möhrmann, *Frauenemanzipation,* 94–103, 126–48, 216–19.

48. Louise Dittmar, *Skizzen und Briefe aus der Gegenwart* (Darmstadt, 1845), 55; Dittmar, *Vier Zeitfragen,* V, 22–26; see also Alfred Bergmann, ed., "Funfzehn Briefe Carl Volkhausens an Malwida von Meysenbug aus den Jahren 1849–1852," *Mitteilungen aus der lippischen Geschichte und Landeskunde* 23 (1954): 221–23 and Louise Dittmar to Lorenz Dieffenbach, July 30, 1847, October 2, 1852, Lorenz Dieffenbach Nachlass, Universitätsbibliothek, Giessen.

49. KZH, "Skizzen," 107b, KZN-W.

50. *Mainzer Zeitung,* November 23, 24, 1848.

51. Ibid., December 2, 9, 1848.

52. Ibid., January 5, 1849.

53. Ibid., January 5, 6, 1849.

54. Ibid., February 7, 1849.

55. Ibid., February 8, 1849. Moses, *French Feminism,* quotes Flora Tristan's remark that women begrudge their husbands time with politics because of ignorance of public affairs.

56. *Mainzer Zeitung,* February, 8, 9, 1849.

57. *Fränkische Blätter,* 1848, 10, 11; *Fliegende Blätter,* 4, no. 89 (1846–1847): 135.

58. *Mainzer Tagblatt,* no. 77, March 28, 1849; see also *Mainzer Tagblatt,* no. 17, January 20, 1849; *Fliegende Blätter,* 5 (1848–1849): 145–48, 7 (1850–1851): 6, 20; *Didaskalia,* May 27, 1848. Other negative views of women, particularly those expressed in the Berlin area, have been evaluated by Sigrid Weigel, *Flugschriftenliteratur 1848 in Berlin: Geschichte und Öffentlichkeit einer volkstümlicher Gattung* (Stuttgart, 1979), 76–90, 158.

59. *Didaskalia,* no. 259, September 25, 1848; *Fliegende Blätter,* 7 (1849–1850): 143–52.

60. *Mainzer Tagblatt,* March 18, 1849.

61. Ibid., March 18, December 30, 1849, October 9, 1850.

62. *Fliegende Blätter,* 5 (1848–1849): 2; *Hamburger Beobachter,* June 6, 1849, 177; *Mainzer Anzeiger,* December 8, 1849.

63. *Fliegende Blätter,* 5 (1848–1849): 14–15, 17, 31; Fuchs, *Weiberherrschaft,* 388.

64. Fuchs, *Die Frau,* 472–73; Philipp Wasserburg, "Ums 1848," *Mainzer Anzeiger,* September 25, 1897. Transcript of Wasserburg's trial in *Mainzer Anzeiger,* no. 278, November 11, 1855, 1087.

65. For a description of the grim servants' quarters in Paris around 1850 see Edmond and Jules de Goncourt, *Germinie Lacerteux* trans. (Middlesex, England, 1984), 155.

66. *Didaskalia,* April 26, 1848; *Hamburger Beobachter,* April 29, 1848; *Fliegende Blätter,* 5 (1848–1849): 17, 7 (1850–1851): 48, 55; *Fränkische Blätter,* 1848, 2; *Mainzer Tagblatt,* June 15, 1849.

67. *Mainzer Zeitung,* no. 338, December 25, 1848.

68. *Frankfurter Journal,* October 3, 1848; Hans Blum, *Die deutsche Revolution 1848–49* (Leipzig, 1894), 321; Hummel-Haasis, *Schwester,* 219; Struve, *Erinnerungen,* esp. 1, 5, 27, 35–36, 40, 69, 72, 77–85.

69. *Mainzer Anzeiger,* April 21, 1850.

70. *OW,* May 8, 1849.

71. Another story, about Louise Aston's efforts as a nurse in Schleswig-Holstein, although praising her work concluded, "A woman remains a woman in spite of all emancipation." *OW,* October 10, 1848, 591–92.

72. The issue of votes for women surfaced briefly in Frankfurt during the debate on the electoral law. Franz Edlauer, who called attention to efforts for political emancipation for women, worried that female suffrage would introduce political disputes into the family; Karl Mathy, the Badenese parliamentarian, argued that the logical consequence of letting women vote would be to permit minors to vote. When Konrad Matthies asked jokingly why women should not vote, he was answered by cheers from the Left and then general "levity." *Stenographischer Bericht über die Verhandlungen der deutschen constituirenden Nationalversammlung 1848/49,* vol 7, February 15, 19, 20, 1849, 5236, 5292, 5298; Gerhard Schilfert, *Sieg und Niederlage des demokratischen Wahlrechts in der deutschen Revolution 1848–49* (Berlin, DDR, 1952), 16, 318.

73. Christoph Dumont, *Die Emanzipation der Frauen* (Mainz, 1848); *Mainzer Tagblatt,* April 21, 26, 1849. This incident is in some ways similar to the debate over the role of women's salons in late seventeenth-century France, which were a means to discuss major political, social, and economic issues of the day. Carolyn Lougee, *Paradies des Femmes* (Princeton, N.J., 1976). *Ambisexia, the Land of the Unyoked Women* by "justice for women," was apparently performed in Leipzig. The reviewer noted that the piece was serious although not without humor and not without criticism of women. *Didaskalia,* June 17, 1848; Weigel, *Flugschriftenliteratur,* 89.

6. Zitz-Halein and 1848: Literature and Politics

1. For the events in the Mainz area during the Revolution of 1848 see Karl Georg Bockenheimer, *Mainz in den Jahren 1848 und 1849* (Mainz, 1906);

Mathilde Katz-Seibert, *Der politische Radikalismus in Hessen während der Revolution von 1848/49* (Darmstadt, 1929); and the Nazi-oriented but still useful Carlo Buckler, *Die politischen und religiösen Kämpfe in Mainz während des Revolutionsjahre 1848–1850* (Giessen, 1936).

2. KZH, "Missliebigkeit," *Zeitgedichte* (n.p., n.d.), Mog m/104, Stabi Mz.

3. KZH, "Es gahrt," *Zeitgedichte*, Mog m/1044, Stabi Mz.

4. KZH, "Wahre Freiheit," *Zeitgedichte;* this poem later appeared in *Didaskalia*, no. 93, April 3, 1848.

5. "Skizzen," 30a, 102b, 104b–108a, 116b, KZN-W; KZH to FZ, March 8, 1848, KZN-W. Zitz's role in Frankfurt is treated in Gunther Hildebrandt, *Parlamentsopposition auf Linkskurs* (Berlin, DDR, 1975) and *Opposition in der Paulskirche: Reden, Briefe und Berichte kleinbürgerlichdemokratischer Parliamentarier, 1848/49* (Berlin, DDR, 1981). Someone issued a condemnation of Franz Zitz, accusing him of being a poor husband, a shyster lawyer, and pro-French, and signed her name to it. Their relations certainly did not improve at this time. "Betrogene arme Mitbürger," *Anschlagzettel*, nos. 40, 41, Stabi Mz.

6. KZH, "Autodafé," *Zeitgedichte*, KZN-M.

7. KZH, "Lola," *Zeitgedichte*, KZN-M; perhaps the most reliable source for Lola Montez is Valentin, *Geschichte der deutschen Revolution*, 1: 115–22, 125–29, 131–40, 392–93; Eduard Fuchs, *Ein vormärzliche Tanzidyl: Lola Montez in der Karikatur* (Berlin, 1905), 87, and his *Weiberherrschaft*, 2: 207; Ishbel Ross, *The Uncrowned Queen: Life of Lola Montez* (New York, 1972), 108, 116, 120, also emphasizes that Lola acted as a liberal influence on King Ludwig.

8. KZH,"Dem am 20. April 1848 heimgegangen Turnwart Franz Mämpel," Mog m/992, Stabi Mz.

9. Hildebrandt, *Opposition in der Paulskirche*, 15–18, 21–22; Valentin, *Geschichte der deutschen Revolution*, 2: 18–20.

10. KZH, "Märzveilchen," folder 4, no. 282, KZN-M. Two years later her friend Nanni Wolf remarked the "prophetic spirit" contained in the poem. Nanni Wolf to KZH, December 31, 1850, KZN-M.

11. Eleven years later she still chose to reprint the poem, "Parteigeist," in her *Dur- und Molltöne*, 57–59; Heribert Pauly, "Zur soziale Zusammensetzung politischen Institutionen und Vereine der Stadt Mainz im Revolutionsjahre 1848," *Archiv für hessische Geschichte und Altertumskunde*, N.F. 34 (1973): 44–81.

12. *Didaskalia*, March 31, April 28, May 1, 1848; KZH, "Notruf" and "Hunger tut so Weh," *Dur- und Molltöne*, 34–46. The latter poem was set to music later that year by Peter Garisch. KZN-Handschriftenabteilung, III, 36, Stabi MZ.

13. KZH, "An die Schleswig-Holsteiner," KZN-M, and also reprinted in her *Dur- und Molltöne*, 37–39; Haas to KZH, June 21, 1848, KZN-M; A. M. Brackel to KZH, June 14, 1848, *Anschlagezettel 1848*, nos. 174, 175, Stabi Mz; Louise Aston did serve as a nurse in Schleswig-Holstein. See *Offenburger Wochenblatt*, October 10, 1848, 593, and Nachlass Brümmer, Briefe II, Aston 63, Handschriftenabteilung, Deutsche Staatsbibliothek, Berlin, BRD.

14. Haas to KZH, June 21, 1848, Friedrich Müller to KZH, February 8,

1850, KZH-M; *Didaskalia,* no. 93, April 3, 1848; Keim, "Rheinsandkörner: Erinnerungen an Kathinka Zitz-Halein;" Rosenberg, *Literaturverhältnisse,* 56, mentions that poetry was circulated in the form of posters and handbills and thus made available to the people.

15. "Robert Blum," *Die neue Zeit* (Worms), December 6, 1848, KZN-M.

16. (Friedrich Hart), *Ein Tag in der Paulskirche,* 1: 37–42; Spamer to KZH, January 30, March 14, 1849, Agnes Leo (the woman in question) to KZH, May 18, 1849 with KZH's marginalia, and other material relating to her relations with publishers in folder labeled, "Verhandlung mit Verleger", KZN-M. See also "Skizzen," 47b, 52a, 103b, 109a, KZN-W.

17. Christoph Klessmann, "Zur Sozialgeschichte der Reichsverfassungskampagne von 1849," *Historische Zeitschrift,* 218, no. 2 (1974): 283–337.

18. KZH, "Wie auf Erde, so im Himmel," *Dur- und Molltöne,* 41–43.

19. KZH, "Der Alptraum," *Demokrat,* no. 67, September 9, 1849, 285, reprinted in *Dur- und Molltöne,* 44.

20. KZH, "Schwarze Brüderschaft," *Demokrat,* no. 66, September 6, 1849, 283.

21. KZH, "Die Bluttaufe im Garten zu Kirchheimbolanden," *Mainzer Tagblatt,* July 28, 1849; Paul Seemann to KZH, September 18, 1849, Chrafer to KZH, September 23, 1849, Therese Rauch to KZH, January 4, 1850, KZN-M; KZH, "Die Verbannte," *Dur- und Molltöne,* 44–45.

22. Valentin, *Geschichte der deutschen Revolution,* 2: 536–42; *Allgemeine Deutsche Biographie,* 38: 691–92; Hildebrandt, *Parlamentsopposition auf Linkskurs,* 199–239; Hildebrandt, ed., *Opposition in der Paulskirche,* 375.

23. This did not prevent her from beng scornful of some women, "creatures in female shape," at Trützschler's trial who did not show the proper respect.

24. KZH, Am Grabe Wilhelm Adolph's von Trützschler," "Carl Höfer," "Noch ein Standgericht," *Demokrat,* August 26, 30, 1849, 270, 273.

25. KZH, "Die Wittwen," *Der Demokrat,* September 2, 1849, 281; "The Widows" was not reprinted in KZH, *Dur- und Molltöne,* 44–47 for reasons that will become clear in the next paragraph.

26. Kastel is directly across the Rhein from Mainz.

27. KZH, "Skizzen," 46b–48a, 117b–118a, KZN-W; "Erscheinungsbefehl," November 7, 1849, KZN-M.

28. KZH, "Die Demokratie," *Mainzer Anzeiger,* 1850, 236, and Mog m/1825, Stabi Mz.

29. KZH, "Die Republik," *Mainzer Anzeiger,* 284, and Mog m/1828, Stabi Mz.

30. KZH, "Zwei Errungenschaften," *Mainzer Anzeiger,* 1850, 326, and Mog m/1826, Stabi Mz.

31. KZH, "Gleichheit der Stände," *Mainzer Anzeiger,* 1850, 306, and Mog m/1827, Stabi Mz.

32. KZH, "Wenn ich ein König wäre," *Mainzer Anzeiger,* 1850, 268 and Mog m/1829 Stabi Mz; KZH, *Dur- und Molltöne,,* 49–51. The poem was reprinted

in 1851 in *Märzbluthen!*, ed. T. Haffner (Grossenhain, 1851), a collection of democratic literature to commemorate the 1848 revolution, and in Louise Otto's *Frauen-Zeitung*.

33. KZH, "Vorbilder aus der Alterthume," *Frauen-Zeitung*, December 17, 28, 31, 1851. See also "Die Kraft des Menschenswillens ist gebunden," *Dur- und Molltöne*, 61–63, a protest against newly imposed restrictive voting laws.

34. "Skizzen," 119ab, KZN-W.

35. "Skizzen," 48ab, 119a–120a, KZN-W.

36. Hecker to KZH, November 21, 1850, KZN-M. Her poetry in honor of Blum, Trützschler, Höfer, and those who fell at Kirchheimbolanden served this purpose.

37. Hecker to KZH, November 2, 1850, KZN-M. The editor of the Stuttgart *Eulenspiegel*, although accepting her manuscript, warned that it was not exactly "beneficial" to him since it brought with it the prospect of a censorship trial. Becker, the editor of the *Teutsche Zeitung* in Cologne, accepted two poems from her but rejected a novel because one "must be cautious," especially since the former editor had been expelled. Schmidt to KZH, March 10, 1851, Becker to KZH, June 5, 1850; see also Dr. AD . . . (Leipzig) to KZH and Thomas Haffner to KZH, July 18, 1851. All of the above in KZN-M.

38. *Mainzer Abendpost*, nos. 21, 23, December 13, 15, 1850.

39. Valentin, *Geschichte der deutschen Revolution*, 2: 540–42.

40. KZH, "Eine Demokratenfamilie," in *Donner und Blitz*, 154–57.

41. KZH, "Eine Demokratenfamilie," *Donner und Blitz*,, 119–224, KZN-M; it originally appeared in the *Mainzer Tagblatt*, July 1850.

42. "Iodine," *Donner und Blitz*, 278–449.

43. KZH, "Aus der Flora des Lebens," *Donner und Blitz*, 450–66. Among her anticlerical definitions were "Jesuits' weeds" (pernicious plants), the "Church festival tree" at which one got "caning soup," and "cloister berries," which purged one of hertical ideas.

44. KZH, "Der Sarazenssklave," and "Der Städtebund" in her *Rheinsandkörner*, 175–247, 387–415. She also makes women responsible for the spread of Christianity (ibid., 1–28, 29–50). Their roles will be discussed later. Ludwig Falck, *Geschichte der Stadt Mainz* (Düsseldorf, 1972), 8–10, 105–8.

45. KZH. "Ein Hexenprozess," *Neue Rheinsandkörner*, 141–74.

46. KZH, "Paskaline," in her *Süss und Sauer*, (Mainz, 1851), 367–68, 392; Anastasias Schnüffler, *Der Aufhebung des demokratischen Frauenclubbs oder das schreckliche Ende* (Berlin, 1848); Weigel, *Flugschriftenliteratur*, 85, 89.

47. KZH, "Paskaline," *Süss und Sauer*, 367–409; in the same collection see also "Der Usupator von Schottland," 51–162.

48. KZH, "Fragmente aus der Sturmperiod," *Letzte Rheinsandkörner*, 392–475.

49. Fanny Lewald-Stahr, *Erinnerungun aus dem Jahre 1848*, 1: 221–26, 2: 87; Horst Denkler, ed. *Der deutsche Michel: Revolutionskomödien der Achtundvierziger* (Stuttgart, 1971), and Denkler, "Revolutionäre Dramaturgie und revolution-

äres Drama im Vormärz und Revolution," *Gestaltungsgeschichte und Gesellschafts-geschichte* ed. by Helmut Kreuzer (Stuttgart, 1969), 306–37 cites a number of 1848 plays.

50. Joeres has sought to give a feminist analysis of how such authors as Fanny Lewald, Louise Aston, and Louise Otto treated the Revolution of 1848 in their novels. It suggests that women's activities were still regarded as circumscribed but that there was a cautious going beyond these limitations. Joeres, "1848 from a Distance: German Women Writers on the Revolution," 590–614.

7. Zitz-Halein and 1848: The Humania Association

1. See, for example, Langewiesche, *Die deutsche Revolution von 1848/49.* The Humania Association is mentioned in Karl Georg Bockenheimer, *Mainz in den Jahren 1848 und 1849,* 12, 103, 164, but incorrectly.

2. *Altenburger Volksblatt,* June 22, 29, 1849, 231–32, 240–41; "Zuruf württembergischen Frauen und Jungfrauen an unseren deutschen Krieger," and other calls in *Die neue Zeit* (Worms), May 15, 19, 1848. The "Zuruf" seems to have had a wide circulation as it was posted on "every street corner" in Frankfurt. It called on women to have no association with men who did not join the spring uprising. Bergsträsser, *Frankfurter Parlament,* 138, 432. See also Twellmann, *Deutsche Frauenbewegung,* 2: 68–70, and the *Frauen-Zeitung,* June 16, August 11, 1849, and August 30, 1851. In Bremen women were involved in the organization of a committee to help political refugees in Switzerland. Werner Biebusch, *Revolution und Staatsstreich: Verfassungskämpfe in Bremen 1848–1854* (Bremen, 1973), 134; Prelinger, *Charity, Challenge, and Change,* 162–63.

3. Already in August 1848 in that Badenese city a women's association had been formed that gathered signatures for a petition in favor of an amnesty for political refugees. Composed mostly of wives and daughters of members of the democratic Volksverein (People's Association) it collected over seven hundred, which it presented to the deputy, Adam von Itzstein. The group appears to have undertaken no initiatives thereafter, and its possible connection to later groups is not known. "Politische Vereine" (Report on a Damenvereinigung im Mannheimer Volksverein, October 12, 1848, 70), 236/8201, Generallandesarchiv, Karlsruhe; hereafter cited as GLA-K.

4. Georg Böhning, who was later executed, to J. Hecker, October 10, 1848, KZN-M. Hecker forwarded the letter to Zitz-Halein.

5. "Aufruf" of the Germania Association signed by Betz, Lindenberger, and others, 276/3404, GLA-K.

6. "Polizei Verhör," of Therese Canton, June 6, 1850, Stadtarchiv Mannheim; "Skizzen," 41a, KZN-W.

7. Kath. Betz to KZH, April 30 or May 1, 1849, Therese Canton to "Liebe Schwester," May 1, 1849, KZN-M.

8. See the 1848–1849 issues of the *Offenburger Wochenblatt* and the *Lahrer Wochenblatt*. Several examples have been cited in Chapter 5.

9. *OW*, June 1849 issues, August 3, 1849, 511; *Lahrer Wochenblatt,* June 1849 issues and October 10, 1849, 401; *Ortenauer Rundschau,* January 25, February 22, 1936 (90 Jahre Offenburger Frauenvereine).

10. Both clippings, the second of which appeared in *Mainzer Tagblatt,* are found in Zitz-Halein's papers in Mainz. The internal evidence indicates her authorship.

11. Landler to KZH, May 11, 1849, KZN-M; *Mainzer Zeitung,* May 12, 13, 1849; *Mainzer Tagblatt,* May 15, 20, 1849; *Der Demokrat,* May 17, 1849; KZ-H's speech to the Humania Association, May 24, 1849, KZN-M.

12. *Statuten des Humania-Vereins,* KZN-M; *Der Demokrat,* May 17, 1849, 153–55.

13. See the essays in Carol R. Berkin and Clara M. Lovett, eds., *Women, War and Revolution* (New York, 1980), and Sheila Rowbotham, *Women, Resistance and Revolution* (New York, 1972).

14. KZH's speech of May 13 or 15, 1849, printed in *Der Demokrat,* May 17, 1849, pp. 153–55, and *Kasteler Beobachter,* May 18, 1849.

15. *Kasteler Beobachter,* May 31, 1849; KZH's speeches July 1, 27, November 27, 1849, KZN-M; KZH, "Skizzen," 41a, KZN-W.

16. KZH, "Skizzen," 33a, 35a, 107b, 112a, KZN-W; Hans Blum, *Die deutsche Revolution 1848–49,* 413, has a portrait of Madame Blenker in uniform. Several years later after the Blenkers and her husband had immigrated to the United States she recounted Zitz's efforts to obtain money from them. Zitz-Halein described how Frau Blenker had reacted as an "aroused tigress" and thrown him out. Now the former hermaphrodite was a "resolute women." KZH, "Tagebuch," 29b–30a (October 12, 1859), KZN-W.

17. Gertrud Bäumer, *Gestalt und Wandel: Frauenbildnisse* (Berlin, 1939), 328–31; Jutta Schoers Sanford, "Origins of German Feminism" (Ph.D diss., Ohio State University, 1976), 143; Malwida von Meysenbug, *Memoiren einer Idealisin,* 2 vols. (Berlin, 1916), 1: 244; Gerlinde Geiger, "Die befreite Psyche: Emanzipationsansätze in Früwerk Ida Hahn-Hahn" Ph.D. diss., University of Massachusetts, 1984), 42.

18. Franz Zitz to the Humania Association, November 11, 1849, all in the KZN-M.

19. The women's association in Lahr in Baden also helped "equip" the military contingent that participated in the insurgency. *Lahrer Wochenblatt,* June 23, 1849, 259, Stadtarchiv Lahr.

20. *Frauen-Zeitung,* June 16, 1849; H. P. Dressel to KZH, September 9, 1849, all in KZN-M; several former members of the Frauenverein in Heidelberg to the Humania Verein (December 30, 1849); Ph. Schaaf to KZH, September 14, 1849; transcript of the trial of Katherine Beck, February 28, April 13, 1855, 240/1373, GLA-K; on the revolution in Heidelberg see Herbert Derwein, *Heidelberg im Vormärz und in der Revolution 1848/49* (Heidelberg, 1958). In Landau the women's association continued to function and raise money with-

out public sittings because of the military occupation. Therese Rauck (Landau) to KZH, October 25, 1849, KZN-M.

21. Beck's trial transcript, 240/1373, GLA-K.

22. Beck's trial transcript, 240/1373, GLA-K; Therese Bomer to KZH, January 16, 1850; Nancy Hillebrand to KZH, September 1, 1849, n.d., March 1850; Nanni Hurst to KZH, n.d.; Willigis Letzniser to Humania Association, April 11, 1850, all in KZN-M.

23. "Skizzen," 38a, KZN-W; KZH, "Tagebuch," 9b–10a, 19b–20a (November 12, 1855), KZN-W.

24. Nancy Hillebrand to KZH, August 2, 1846, February 6, 1847, September 1, November 16, December 22, 1849, February 24, 1850, Dressel to KZH, September 9, 20, 1849, April 3, 1850, January 13, 1851, KZN-M.

25. *Mainzer Zeitung,* June 20, 21, 29, 1849, *Mainzer Tagblatt,* June 21, 1849, November 17, 1850, which contains Embdt's poem in honor of Kinkel's escape; KZH's speech, July 1, 1849, KZN-M; "Skizzen," 115b, KZN-W.

26. Zitz-Halein's speech to the Humania Association, July 1, 1849, KZN-M; "Skizzen," 36b–38a, 44b–45a, 113ab, 118ab, KZN-W; KZH, "Meine Ausweisung aus Karlsruhe," *Kasteler Beobachter,* July 24, 26, 1849; *Mainzer Zeitung,* April 27, 1850, which reported the dropping of charges against her.

27. "Speeches to the Humania Association," May 15, July 1, 27, 1849, February 24, 1850, KZN-M; "Skizzen," 36ab, 41a, 118b, KZN-W; "Verzeichnis der Mitglieder der am 24 Mai 1849 in Mainz von Frau Kathinka Zitz gegründeten Frauenverein Humania" (Ms), 1, KZN-M.

28. Receipts from Mayor Nack, February 6, 1850, and Müller, January 15 and February 24, 1850, KZN-M.

29. *Mainzer Anzeiger,* November 22, 1849, March 6, 1850.

30. *Frauen-Zeitung,* August 11, 1849, January 19, February 2, March 16, 1850; Ronge to "geehrte deutsche Schwester, August 1, 1849, Ronge Nachlass, no. 55, Sächsische Landesbibliothek, Dresden; Ronge to Emilie Wüstenfeld, May 27, 1851, Paulaner Stiftschule 26, Staatsarchiv Hamburg.

31. Speeches of KZ-H, February 24, July 1, 1849, August Pilgrim to KZ-H, June 20, 1849, Bertha Frensdorf to KZ-H, December 10, 1849, March 12, April 1, 1850, KZN-M.

32. *Die neue Zeit* (Worms), September 3, 1848; Sanchen Best to KZH, July 17, November 26, December 2, 1849, KZN-M.

33. Therese Rauck to KZH, October 25, 1849, January 4, 1850, KZN-M.

34. "Skizzen," 31a–34b, 111b–112a, KZN-W; KZH, "Eine Missionsreise nach Baden und der Pfalz," *Demokrat,* July 5, 8, 1849, 209–10, 213–14.

35. "Skizzen," 34a–38a, 112a–113a, KZN-W; KZH, "Meine Ausweisung," *Kasteler Beobachter,* July 24, 26, 1849. Annie Claussen, wife of the parliamentary deputy Hans Claussen, also visited refugee centers. Annie Claussen to Frau Hildebrand, July 30, 1849. Nachlass Hildebrand, F Sg 1/111, BAF.

36. KZH, "Mannheimer Briefe," *Demokrat,* August 26, 30, 1849, 269–71, 273–75; J. Lichterfeld to Democratic Association, n.d., Hillebrand to KZH, September 1, 17, 1849, Dressel to KZH, September 20, October 29, 1849, KZN-M.

37. KZH, "Mannheimer Briefe," *Demokrat,* September 9, 13, 1849, 285–86, 290–91; Dressel to KZH, September 13, 1849, October 19, 1849, August 4, 1851, Hillebrand to KZH, February 2, 1850; she also tried to help the exiled revolutionary Gustave Struve. Kath. Lindenberger to KZH, September 13, 1850, May 29, 1851, KZN-M; "Skizzen," 44ab, KZN-W.

38. KZH to Frau Robert Blum, n.d., KZN-M.

39. Hans Trefouse, *Carl Schurz* (Knoxville, 1982), 29–36; "Skizzen," 113b–115b, KZN-W; KZH, "Johanna Kinkel," *Die deutsche Frau,* 1859 (no. 18): 141–42; Johanna Kinkel to Leopold von Henning, October 11, 1841, Böttger, *Frauen im Aufbruch,* 401–6, and 382–437, where Johanna's letters describe her love affair with Kinkel and the political and social attitudes in Bonn. Meysenbug, *Memoiren,* 1: 266.

40. "Skizzen," 37a, 38a, 44b, 47b, 113b, 114a, KZN-W; *Mainzer Zeitung,* June 14, 1849; Johanna Kinkel to Emilie von Henning, May 18, 1848, Böttger, *Frauen im Aufbruch,* 427–28; most of the Kinkel-Zitz-Halein correspondence has been published by Rupprecht Leppla; see Leppla, ed., "Johanna und Gottfried Kinkel's Briefe an Kathinka Zitz, 1849–1861," *Bonner Geschichtsblätter* 12 (1958): 7–82.

41. There is no better source for Malwida von Meysenbug than her *Memoiren einer Idealistin,* originally published in French in 1869, and in 1875 in German. Since then they have been reprinted many times. For the preceding material see vol. 1: 139–48. The biography of her by Berta Schleicher, *Malwida von Meysenbug* (Berlin, 1916), is unsatisfactory.

42. Johanna Kinkel to KZH, September 12, 24, 1850, KZN-M; Malwida von Meysenbug, "Ein Frauenschwur zur Demokratie," and "Die Wahl des Genius," *Sonntagsblätter,* supplement to *Mainzer Tagblatt,* September 22, October 13, 1850; Meysenbug, *Memoiren,* 1: 175–76.

43. Prelinger, "Religious Dissent and Women's Rights," 42–55, and her *Charity, Challenge, and Change,* 95–100, 135–36, 163–64; Christiane Hartwig, "Frauenburger und Frauenbewegung in Hamburg während und nach der Umbruchzeit von 1848–49" (unpublished ms., 1981), Handschriftensammlung, Staatsarchiv Hamburg; Eduard Spranger, *Die Idee einer Hochschule für Frauen und die Frauenbewegung* (Leipzig, 1916), 23–40; Meysenbug, *Memoiren,* 1: 187–236.

44. Meysenbug to KZH, November 17, (1850), March 8, (1851), KZN-M; and her contribution to Zitz-Halein's "Album" in KZN-W; Meysenbug, *Memoiren,* 1: 244; Marie Schwarzenberg, the thirty-year-old daughter of a deputy to the Frankfurt assembly, after hearing favorable reports about the college, was looking forward to attending it. Marie Schwarzenberg to Julius Schwarzenberg, October 13, 1850, Ludwig Schwarzenberg Nachlass, F Sg 1/167, BAF.

45. On this subject see George Eliot, *Daniel Deronda.*

46. J. Kinkel to KZH, May 31, July 18, August 5, September 25, 1851, August 5, 1852, January 17, June 6, 20, 1853, May 31, 1854, January 23, 1856, G. Kinkel to KZH, August 7, 1852, KZN-M; Rosemary Ashton, "The

Search for Liberty: German Exiles in England in the 1850s," *Journal of European Studies* 13, no. 51 (September 1983): 194–96.

47. Johanna Kinkel to KZH, July 25, 1856, KZN-M; Leppla, "Johanna und Gottfried Kinkels Briefe," 58.

48. KZH to Johanna Kinkel, August 27, 1851, Sig S2663, Gottfried Kinkel Nachlass, Universitätsbibliothek, Bonn; "Skizzen," 47b, 48a, KZN-W; Joeres, *Die Anfänge der deutschen Frauenbewegung*, 160–64.

49. M. E. to KZH, March 16, 1850; the best overview of the Humania Association's varied fund-raising activities is gained from the announcements in *Mainzer Anzeiger* and *Mainzer Zeitung* between November 1849 and June 1850.

50. For the best overview of expenses see the statement of account of June 1850 contained in "Verzeichnis" (Ms), last page, KZN-M; see also Zitz-Halein's speeches, July 29, September 2, November 25, 1849, KZN-M and "Skizzen," 41b, 110b, 115b, KZN-W.

51. KZH's speeches, November 25, 1849, January 1850, Elizabeth Grob to KZH, n.d., KZN-M; "Skizzen," 34a, 112ab, KZN-W.

52. See "Skizzen," 116a, KZN-W, for the problem of dealing with those who tried to pass themselves off as refugees, and Wolf to KZH, attesting that the father of a claimant had indeed been one of the insurgents.

53. "Mehrere Mitglieder to KZH," July 1, 1849, KZH's speeches of October 28, November 25, 1849, February 24, 1850, KZN-M.

54. *Demokrat,* August 2, 1849, 244.

55. KZH's speeches, July 1, October 28, 1849, KZN-M.

56. KZH's speech, November 25, 1849, Carl Vogt to KZ-H, November 16, 1849, Wilhelm Löwe to Humania Verein, January 8, March 5, April 19, 1850, KZN-M; Paul Neitzke, *Die deutschen politischen Flüchtlinge in der Schweiz 1848–1849* (Charlottenberg, 1926), 58–60; "Skizzen," 41b, 42a, 44ab, 11b, KZN-W.

57. Hans Kersken, *Stadt und Universität in den Revolutionsjahren 1848–1850* (Bonn, 1931); Leppla, "Johanna und Gottfried Kinkels Briefe," 7–82; KZ-H's speech, February 24, 1850; see the *Mainzer Zeitung,* April 23, 1850, for a description of these concerts and poetry readings in which Zitz-Halein performed.

58. There is a hint of this in Leppla, "Johanna und Gottfried Kinkels Briefe," 20 and "Skizzen," 115b, KZN-W.

59. KZH's speeches, July 29, September 2, 1849, Vogt to KZH, November 16, 1849, KZN-M; Carl Vogt to Carl Meyer, July 7, 1849, in Hildebrandt, *Opposition in der Paulskirche,* 369–70.

60. KZH's speeches, July 29, September 2, 1849; "Thirty Mainzer" to Cuny, November 28, 1849, KZH to the Rastatt Fortress Commander September 25, 1849, Bittong to KZH, December 12, 1849, Therese Weismandel (a cook at Rastatt who helped to distribute money to prisoners) to KZH April 4, 1850, Commander to KZH, October 6, 24, 1849, Regnier (Zweibrücken) to KZH, June 9, 1850, Franz Moritz Fourie to Deutsche Frau, July 17, September 1, November 11, 1849, Bauwart to Humania-Verein, August 24, October 10,

1849, Pet. Hinkel to KZH, n.d., Hilfskomitee für die deutsche Flüchtlinge to KZH; Refugee Committee of Neukirch to Humania-Verein, November 11, 1849, KZN-M; *Mainzer Tagblatt,* July 28, 1849; *Mainzer Zeitung,* August 2, 1849; Neitzke, *Die deutschen politischen Fluchtlinge,* 59–60, confirms the haphazard and disorganized way money was distributed.

61. "Skizzen," 116b, KZN-W; F. Zitz to Humania Association, December 3, 1849, January 31, 1850, C. Vogt to KZH, November 16, 1849, W. Löwe to KZH, February 21, April 19, 1850, Sauerland to KZH, February 1, 1850, KZN-M; Otto Corvin-Wierbetski to KZH, July 22, 184 (9), Raveaux to the Democratic Association, (September 1849), Raveaux to KZH, (early December 1849), December 27, 1849, Strasbourg Refugee Committee to KZH, October 3, 1849, KZH's speech, November 25, 1849, KZN-M; Otto Wiltberger, *Die deutschen politischen Fluchtlinge in Strassburg vom 1830–1849* (Berlin, 1910), 74–83.

62. KZH, *Einige Worte;* KZH, "Glaubensbekenntnisse," *Dur- und Molltöne,* 159–61.

63. Tina Knorr to KZH, December 31, 1849, January 24, 1850, J. Daub to KZH, n.d. (December, 1849), KZH, "Einige aufklärende Worte zu dem Streite über die arme Frau in der Goldene Luft," *Mainzer Anzeiger,* January 1850, 98–100, 108, KZN-M; *Frauen Zeitung,* August 11, 1849; Prelinger, *Charity, Challenge, and Change,* 163.

64. *Mainzer Anzeiger,* June 27, July 9, 1850; *Mainzer Zeitung,* July 2, 7, 9, 1850.

65. *Mainzer Wochenblatt,* April 10, 1851, 367.

66. *Mainzer Anzeiger,* September 12, 1850; "Verzeichnis" (Ms), 2, KZN-M; *Frauen Zeitung,* October 26, December 17, 1851, 292–93, 350–51; Neitzke, *Die deutschen politischen Flüchtlinge,* 55.

67. *Frauen-Zeitung,* August 4, 11, September 8, 1849, January 5, 1850. *Die Fackel*'s editor included "Fraülein Zitz" among those women who had given up sewing for politics.

68. "Skizzen," 44ab, 115b, 116b, KZN-W; Carl Degler, *At Odds,* 311; *Anzeiger für die politische Polizei Deutschlands auf die Zeit vom 1 Januar 1848 bis zum Gegenwart* (1855; reprint, Hildeshein, 1970), 50, 212, 252; KZH, "Tagebuch," 15b, (April 20, 1856), KZN-W.

8. Old Beliefs and New Realities

1. Ernst Huber, *Dokumente zur deutschen Verfassungsgeschichte* (Stuttgart, 1964), 2: 2–6.

2. Gerhard Schult, "Die hessische Innenpolitik unter dem Minister von Dalwigk 1850–1859" (Ph.D diss., Johannes Gutenberg University, Mainz, 1953); Anon., "Hessen-Darmstadt in den Jahren 1850–1866," *Unsere Zeit* 3 (1867): 1–24, 81–104; Philipp Stöhr to KZ-H, July 8, 1853, KZN-M (Stöhr, who was a secretary to Blenker, described how he was harassed by the police and forced to leave Mainz; "Tagebuch," 5b (March 16, 1854), KZN-W.

3. "Skizzen," 42b–43a, KZN-W.

4. Betty Hurst to KZH, December 18 (1852 or 1853), J. Kinkel to KZH, July 18, August 27, 1851, August 5, 1852, KZN-M.

5. When Zitz-Halein asked her to write articles for the *Frauen-Zeitung*, Gottfried informed Zitz-Halein that it would be difficult for Johanna to submit anything since she was responsible for managing the household; educating the children; earning money by giving German, music, and singing lessons; and managing their demanding responsibilities to the refugee community. Johanna described to her Mainz friend the "superhuman strength" required to raise a family in London on one's own work. "Who wants to know slaves," she wrote, "must come to London. Who does not work night and day does not make it." J. Kinkel to KZH, May 31, July 18, August 5, September 25, 1851, August 5, 1852, January 17, June 6, 20, 1853, May 31, 1854, January 23, 1856, G. Kinkel to KZH, August 7, 1852, KZN-M.

6. J. Kinkel to KZH, September 8, 1850, March 18, July 18, 1851, January 17, 1853, February 3, May 31, December 22, 1854, KZH to J. Kinkel, November 4, 1849, August 27, 1851; Lüning to KZH, November 26, 1850, KZN-M; "Tagebuch," 5ab (July 6, 1854), 9a (August 6, 1855), KZN-W.

7. "Tagebuch," 7a (December 9, 1854), 7b, 8a–9a, 10a (February 15, July 23, August 6, November 25, 1855), 15ab (January 11, April 10, 1856), 20a (October 18, 1857), 28b (October 12, 1859), Hecker to KZH, December 15, 1856, January 9, 1857, March 16, 1858, KZN-W; Stöhr to KZH, July 8, 1853, KZN-M.

8. "Tagebuch," 26b (April 30, 1859), KZN-W.

9. "Tagebuch," 27b–28b (June 16, July 17, 1859), Adolf Braun (Austrian representative in Frankfurt) to KZH, June 16, 1859, KZN-W.

10. "Tagebuch," 29a (November 12, 1859), KZN-W; *Rheinhessisches Volksblatt*, no. 123, November 22, 1859; *Rheinische Handelszeitung*, no. 264, November 13, 1859; Rainer Noltenius, *Dichterfeier in Deutschland* (Munich, 1984), 71–85, 244–45.

11. KZH to grand duke of Hesse (1862), KZH to King of Württemberg, August 8, 1863 (A plea on behalf of a widow of military orchestra conductor), "Tagebuch," 34ab (May 17, 1862), KZN-W.

12. P. J. Schöppler to KZH, May 20, 1863, A. Muller to KZH, January 14, 1865, "Tagebuch," 86b (July 15, 1870), 108b (March 15, 1873), KZN-W.

13. Caroline Berthold to KZH, February 17, 1863, KZH to Frau Haradauer, February 25, 1864, KZN-W.

14. KZH to Dr. Wenzel, June 30, 1866, "Tagebuch," 62a (May 20, 1866), 62b (June 29, 1866), 63ab (July 30, 1866), 64ab (December 30, 1866), KZN-W. Not so her friend, Caroline Berthold, who complained bitterly from Göttingen about how cruelly the Prussians were treating the Hanoverians. One wanted the French back, she maintained, but in any event, "We won't be Prussians for a long time yet." C. Berthold to KZH, May 17, 1867, KZN-W.

15. C. Berthold to KZH, July 21, August 19, 30, 1870, Nanni Wolf to KZH, October 21, 1868, KZN-W.

16. "Tagebuch," 87a (July 27, 1870), 87b (September 18, 1870), 92ab (November 27, 1870), 103a (June 10, 1872), KZN-W.

17. "Tagebuch," 87a (July 27, 1870), KZN-W. The poems are also in KZN-W.

18. C. Berthold to KZH, January 21, 1869, January 20, 1870, KZN-W.

19. Denkler, "Revolutionäre Dramaturgie und revolutionäres Drama in Vormärz und Revolution," 336; Wittmann, *Buchmarkt und Lektüre*, 149–52.

20. Böttger, *Frauen im Aufbruch*, 359–60, 371; Möhrmann, Die *andere Frau*, 88–112, 151–57; Winterscheidt, *Deutsche Unterhaltungsliteratur*, 190–99; Bucher et al., *Realismus und Gründerzeit*, 2: 83–87; on Aston see the material in Sammlung Varnhagen, Uniwersytet Jagiellonska, Biblioteka Jagiellonska, Cracow, Poland; Ida Hahn-Hahn, *Faustine* (Berlin, 1919), 9–52; J. Kinkel to KZH, August 5, 1851, KZN-M.

21. "Tagebuch," 101b (March 18, 1872), KZN-W.

22. KZH, "Lorenzo Medicis," in her *Strohfeuer* (Mainz, 1855), 334–411; KZH, "Sappho," *Ernste und heitere Lebensbilder*, 3 vols. (Berlin, 1854), 2: 265–368.

23. KZH, *Ernste und heitere Lebensbilder* 1: 199.

24. KZH, *Magdalene Horix*, 262, 289–90, 329, 350–58, 394–401, 452–69; "Tagebuch," 35a (May 20, 1862), KZN-W: Scheel, *Mainzer Republik*, 1: 530, 532, 540.

25. KZH, "Die Patriotinnen von Laval," *Kaiserin Josephine*, 359–62 and "Angeline," ibid., 151–91; KZH, "Adam Lux und seine Tochter Marie," *Neueste Rheinsandkörner*, 175–214. The biographical sketch of Marie Lux in *Hessische Biographien*, 3: 230–33, uses Zitz-Halein's article as a source. On Marie Lux see also Ludwig Bamberger, *Charakteristiken* (Berlin, 1894), 37–40.

26. KZH, "Lukretia," in her *Maikräuter* (Mainz, 1852), 201–3; KZH, "Ein Opfer des Fanatizismus," *Beiträge zur Unterhaltungsliteratur* (Mainz, 1856), 320–31; KZH, "Ulrike," *Donner und Blitz*, 16.

27. KZH, "Emilie, Gräfin Platter," *Dur- und Molltöne*, 221–23; the Prussian reference is from William Hagen, *Germans, Poles and Jews: The Nationality Conflict in the Prussian East, 1772–1914* (Chicago, 1980), 69, 88.

28. KZH, *Dur- und Molltöne*, 214–15, and in general 198–235, where she deals with "Frauen Charaktere" and pays tribute to Florence Nightingale and Latitia Bonaparte.

29. KZH, "Frauenherz," *Maikräuter*, 325–37; a similar plea for female self-reliance is found in her "Uhrmacher Clärchen," *Kaiserin Josephine*, 203.

30. Both in KZH, *Beiträge*, 1–43, 189–202.

31. KZH, "Der Geliebter" in her *Beiträge*, 332–40; KZH, "Bilder aus der Eheleben," in her *Hausbibliothek der Mainzer Volkszeitung* (Mainz, 1854), 385–414.

32. KZH, "Johanna Presto," *Beiträge*, 271–77.

33. KZH, "Ulrike," *Donner und Blitz*, 16; KZH to E. Keil, December 12, 1855, copy in her "Tagebuch," 13a, KZN-W; KZH, "Schriftstellerin," *Quodlibet*, 61; KZH, "Schattenspiele," *Letzte Rheinsandkörner*, 381–82.

34. A. Merget, *Geschichte der deutschen Jugendliteratur*, 3d ed. (1882; reprint, Leipzig 1967), 99, 121–22, 216, 225. Zitz-Halein often selected male pseudonyms (Johann Golder, August Eggers, D. Schmitt, and Theophyl Christlieb).

35. KZH, *Juwelenkästchen* (Mainz, 1862), 15–17; KZH, *Spiegelbilder* (Mainz, 1861), 211–23; KZH, *Das Goldkind* (Mainz, 1851).

36. KZH, *Spiegelbilder*, 46–47; Rudolf Schenda, "Zensur der Kinder- und Jugendliteratur," in *Lexikon der Kinder- und Jugendliteratur* (Weinheim, 1979), 3: 847–49.

37. KZH, *Geographie in Versen* (Leipzig, 1850), 3–4, 18, 21–22, 33.

38. KZH, *Spiegelbilder*, 40–47. "Katzenmusik" is clearly a direct reference to a method of expression used during the revolution.

39. KZH, *Spiegelbilder*, 18–22.

40. Hartmut Eggert, *Studien zur Wirkungsgeschichte des deutschen historischen Romans 1850–1875* (Frankfurt/Main, 1971), 7–12, 25–27, 37–38, 45; Bucher et al., *Realismus und Gründerzeit*, 2: 297–304, 635–39.

41. Winterscheidt, *Deutsche Unterhaltungsliteratur*, 156–98.

42. Gottfried Seebode correspondence, KZN-W.

43. The preceding statements appear at the beginning of two of her unpublished works, "Schloss Lilienstein und dessen Bewohner," pt. 1, 1, and "Clemens von Brentano," 1, both in KZN, Handschriftenabteilung, III, 37, 39 Stabi Mz.

44. Winterscheidt, *Deutsche Unterhaltungsliteratur*, 73–77; KZH, *Heinrich Heine, der Liederdichter*, vol. 3, pt. 6, (Leipzig, 1864), 129; Kay Goodman, "The Impact of Rahel Varnhagen on Women in the Nineteenth Century," in *Gestaltet und Gestaltend: Frauen in der deutschen Literatur*, ed. Marianne Burkhard (Amsterdam, 1980), 150.

45. K. A. Schaab, *Diplomatische Geschichte der Juden in Mainz und dessen Umgebung* (Mainz, 1855); Falck, *Geschichte der Stadt Mainz*, 104, 111–18, 125–27, 158–60; Ludwig Falck, *Mainz in frühen und hohen Mittelalter* (Düsseldorf, 1972), 118–42.

46. KZH, "Jude und Christin," *Rheinsandkörner*, 248–321.

47. KZH, *Magdalene Horix*, 39–52, 122–31. For other examples see KZH, "Schinderhannes," *Neueste Rheinsandkörner*, 262; KZH, "Die ewige Judin," *Champagner Schaum* (Mainz, 1854), 316–54.

48. KZH, *Rahel*, sect. 1, vol. 1, 40, 72–75, 143, 151–54; vol. 2, 43–46, 50–52, 150; sect. 2, vol. 2, 52, 89, 94; sect. 3, vol. 6, 54–58.

49. Karl H. Wegert, "Ideologie und Aktion," *Liberalismus und Gesellschaft des deutschen Vormärz*, ed. Walter Schieder (Göttingen, 1983), 167–93.

50. Helmut Mathy, "Die freien Genossin des freien Burgers! Das Hambacher Fest und die politische Rolle der Frau im 19. Jahrhundert," *Geschichtliche Landeskunde* 24 (1984): 239–44; Böttger, *Frauen im Aufbruch*, 10–55; Bühler, *Das Hambacher Fest*, 80, 95–99, 102, 124.

51. KZH, *Heinrich Heine*, vol. 1, pt. 2, 89–91; vol. 2, pt. 1, 131, 163–76; vol. 2. pt. 2, 42–64, 76–80, 130–35; vol. 3, pt. 1, 40–41, 45–49; vol. 3, pt. 5, 197, 199–201; vol. 3, pt. 6, 2–5, 34, 54; see also "Tagebuch," 86b (July 15, 1870), KZN-W.

52. Josef Brugger to KZH, January 14, 1859, KZN-M; "Tagebuch," 52–53a (April 27, 28, 1865), KZN-W; Wilhelm Koffka to KZH, n.d., KZN-W; Wittmann, *Buchmarkt und Lektüre*, 115–19, 142–45; Georg Jäger, "Die deutsche Leihbibliothek im 19. Jahrhundert: Verbreitung, Organisation, Verfall," *Internationales Archiv für Sozialgeschichte der deutschen Literatur* 2 (1977): 96–133; Eva Becker, "'Zeitungen sind doch das Beste': Bürgerliche Realisten und der Vorabdruck ihrer Werke in der periodischen Presse," *Gestaltungsgeschichte und Gesellschaftsgeschichte*, ed. H. Kreuzer (Stuttgart, 1969), 390–92; Bucher et al., *Realismus und Gründerzeit*, 2: 635–39.

53. Reinhard Wittmann, "Literarisches Leben 1848 bis 1880," *Realismus und Gründerzeit*, ed. Bucher et al., 1: 202.

54. Wittmann, *Buchmarkt und Lektüre*, 162; Rudolf Goehler, *Geschichte der Deutschen Schillerstiftung 1859–1909*, 2 vols. (Berlin, 1909), 2: 17, 24, 36–37, 45–47, 64, 116; Heinrich Kurz, *Geschichte der neuesten deutschen Literatur von 1830 bis auf die Gegenwart*, vol. 4 (Leipzig, 1872), 406–07, 665–66; Winterscheidt, *Unterhaltungsliteratur*, 235; Robert Prutz, *Die deutsche Literatur der Gegenwart*, 2 vols. in 1 (Leipzig, 1859), 2: 252, 256–57, 264.

55. *Blätter für literarische Unterhaltung*, no. 85, April 9, 1851, 340.

56. *Didaskalia*, no. 13, January 15, 1852.

57. *Blätter für literarische Unterhaltung*, no. 25, June 19, 1856, 459–60.

58. *Blätter für literarische Unterhaltung*, no. 32, August 7, 1856, 590.

59. *Nordstern*, no. 38, June 23, 1860; "Tagebuch," 30b (April 10, 11), 31a (May 20, 1860), KZN-W; Seebode to KZH, October 10, 1860, KZN-W.

60. *Blätter für literarische Unterhaltung*, 1864, 147–48.

61. Goodman, "Impact of Rahel," 150.

62. For the preceding two paragraphs see Bouffier to KZH, June 6, October 10, 1867, KZN-W; Ludwig Fränkel, "Kath. und Franz Zitz," *Allgemeine Deutsche Biographie*, 45: 377; review clippings in the Mainz Stadtbibliothek copy of her *Lord Byron*, 55/221; Varnhagen, *Gesammelte Werke*, 10: 454; Kurz, *Geschichte der neuesten deutschen Literatur*, 61.

63. Wittmann, *Buchmarkt und Lektüre*, 163; Bucher et al., *Realismus und Gründerzeit*, 1: 211.

64. Around the 1848 period she tried to get ten gulden per quire but always had to settle for less. Emil Rollherz to KZH, January 13, 1848, Lizius to KZH, June 12, 1848, Englert to KZH, January 21, February 2, March 6, 1850, J. Scholz to KZH, July 28, 1851, KZN-M.

65. Wittmann, *Buchmarkt und Lektüre*, 145–46, 157, 166–74, 207–12; Schenda, *Volk ohne Buch*, 159; Winterscheidt, *Deutsche Unterhaltungsliteratur*, 31, 238; Frederick Betz, "Fontane Scholarship, Literary Sociology and Trivialliteraturforschung," *Internationales Archiv für Sozialgeschichte der deutschen Literatur* 8 (1983): 201; Becker, "'Zeitungen sind doch das Beste,'" 392–93; Bucher et al., *Realismus und Gründerzeit*, 1: 188, 206–13. Louise Otto also depended on payment from the Schiller Foundation.

66. KZH to Kollmann, February 17, 1862, Kollmann Nachlass, Landesbibliothek, Wiesbaden; Kollmann to KZH, March 25, November 21, December 6, 12, 1862, "Tagebuch," 52a, (January 31, 1865), KZN-W.

67. J. Schneider to KZH, February 28, 1866, August 2, October 24, 1867, KZN-W.

68. Bouffier to KZH, September 22, 1867, KZN-W; "Tagebuch," 67b (December 31, 1867), 78b (December 30, 1868), 84b (February 19, 1870), 87a (July 30, 1870), 101b (January 28, 1872), KZN-W; *Mainzer Anzeiger*, July 31, 1870, August 1872, KZN-W; Werner to KZH, October 18, 1872, KZH-W.

69. KZH to L. Dieffenbach, March 21, April 12, 15, 1870, Nachlass Dieffenbach, Universitätsbibliothek, Giessen.

70. "Tagebuch," 86a, (May 29, 1870), KZN-W; Karl Ebernau to KZH, October 16, 1873, KZN-W; KZH to Brümmer, August 17, 1874, August 1, 1875, Brümmer Nachlass, Briefe II, Deutsche Staatsbibliothek, Berlin BRD.

71. KZN, Handschriften Abteilung III, 36–39, 41a–41o, Stabi Mz.

9. After 1850: Personal Struggles

1. For the preceding two paragraphs see KZH, "Tagebuch," 1ab (February 16, 1854), 3a (March 16, 1854), 5b–6b (July 16, 1854), 7ab (December 9, 12, 1854, February 25, 1855), 17b (February 20, 1857), 18a (September 1, 1857), 20a (September 18, 1857, KZH to Frau Haradauer), 28b (July 25, 1859), 35a (June 29, 1862), 43a–44b (January 30, 1864, KZH to Friedrich Kapp), KZN-W.

2. For a contemporary reference to Mademoiselle "Le Normand" see Anne Tyler, *Searching for Caleb* (New York, 1976), 132.

3. "Skizzen," 21ab, 22ab, 91ab, KZN-W.

4. "Skizzen," 71a, 72ab, KZN-W.

5. "Skizzen," 48b–51a; "Tagebuch," 2a (February 16, 1854), 3b–4a (March 26, 1854), 5b (July 6, 1854), KZN-W; Geoffrey Nelson, *Spiritualism and Society* (New York, 1969), 8–15, 17–18, 29, 48–52; Dotzauer, *Freimaurer*, 256.

6. Semmel, *J. S. Mill and the Pursuit of Virtue*, 63–71, 78.

7. "Skizzen," 48b–49b, KZN-W; Gustav Scheve, "Phrenologische Charakteristik," Gehrig to KZH, June 9, August 14, 1844, KZN-M; J. F. Volrad Deneke, "Die Phrenologie als publizistisches Ereignis: Galls Schädellehre in der Tagespublizistik des 19. Jahrhunderts," *Medizinhistorisches Jahrbuch* 20 (1985): 83–108; Showalter, *A Literature of Their Own*, 77.

8. See, for example, Charles Galette to KZH, December 10, 1852, Hobart Ulitzsche to KZH, July 23, 1853, Babette Wolf to KZH, April 15, 1850, KZN-M; Louise Schneider to KZH, November 23, 1861, May 19, September 19, 1867, November 17, 1868, June 4, 1870, K. Schneider to KZH, June 24, December 21, 1873, KZN-W.

9. For her philanthropic efforts see "Tagebuch," 1a (February 16, 1854), 10b (November 25, 1855), 15b (April 10, 1856), 16a (May 10, 1856), 17b (February 26), 17b–18a (March 9), 18ab (September 7), 21a (December 23, 1857), 30b (April 6, 1860), 32 (September 24, 1860), 34b (May 18, 1862), 38a

(February 10, 1863), KZN-W; KZH to G. Kinkel, September 11, 1859, Kinkel Nachlass, Universitätsbibliothek Bonn; Nanni Wolf to KZH, October 3, 1854, KZN-M; KZH to Herr Haradauer, January 24, 1864, KZN-W.

10. Auguste D. to KZH, July 1, 1863, "Skizzen," 10a, KZN-W; "Tagebuch," 1ab (February 16), 6b (August 24, 1854), 17b (September 3, 1857), 28ab (July 25, 1859) 79b (May 31, 1869), 84b (February 19, 1870), 85b (May 22, 1870), KZN-W; Nanni Wolf-Cavalli to KZH, November 1853, December 16, 1853, January 30, 1854, November 1854, November 24, 1855, KZN-M; Nanni Wolf to KZH, November 24, 1856, February 9, 1857, December 13, 1864, February 16, 1865, Hugo Cavalli to KZH, November 18, 1855, KZN-W.

11. See Chapter 3.

12. "Tagebuch," 1a, 2a (February 16, 1854), 15b–16a (September 16, 1856), 17b (March 9, 1857), 66a (August 25, 1867), 67a (November 27, 1867), KZH to Mainz City Council, n.d., KZN-W; Emilie Hurst to KZH, March 29, May 11, 1852, October 7, 1872, KZN-M.

13. "Tagebuch," 54b (September 1, 1865), 60ab (September 5, 1865), 61ab (September 10, 1865), 57a (September 12, 1865), 58–59 (September 25, 1865), 64b–65a (March 13, 15, 1867), 67b–68a (January 20, 1868), KZN-W.

14. Criminalia 1848. General Akten: Verzeichnis der Gefangenen und Angeschuldeten, Folder A, 103, Stadtarchiv Frankfurt.

15. "Skizzen," 46ab, 117b, 118b, KZN-W; KZH to F. Zitz, December 26, 1849, Dumont to KZH, December 12, 1849, Herrnsheim to KZH, August 3, 1850, KZN-W.

16. KZH to Herrnsheim, September 24, 1857, "Tagebuch," 20a (September 29, 1857), KZN-W.

17. Caroline Berthold to KZH, January 18, 1858, KZH to F. Kapp, December 23, 1862, "Tagebuch," 36a (December 23, 1862), KZN-W.

18. Rudolf Gottschall, *Die deutsche Nationalliteratur des neunzehnten Jahrhundert,* 5th ed. (Breslau, 1881), 4: 245–46; see KZH's file in the Akten der Deutschen Schillerstiftung, no. 96, 9: Kathinka Zitz, Deutsche Staatsbibliothek, Handschriftenabteilung/ Literaturarchiv, Berlin, DDR; Goehler, *Schillerstiftung,* 1: 97; "Tagebuch," 36a–37b (December 31, 1862, January 10, 1863), 109a (March 13, 1873), KZN-W; Tony Kellen, "Die Honorare deutscher Dichter und Schriftsteller," *Nord und Süd,* 93 (1900), 173.

19. "Tagebuch," 48a, 49a (December 2, 1863), 51b (January 18, 1864), 52b (February 12, 1864), 57a (January 23, 1865), 62a (January 18, 1866), 96a (May 6, 1871), KZH to Cousine, February 25, 1864, Emilie Hurst to Doktor Zitz (December 1865), Görz to KZH, February 25, 1868, KZN-W.

20. Her somewhat contradictory comments about her eyes are found in "Tagebuch," 23b, 24ab, 31b, 33a, 34a, 35a, 36a, 52a, 53a, 54ab, 55a, 61b, 62a, 64b, 81a, 113b, KZH to Friedrich Kapp, April 2, 1862, Caroline Berthold to KZH, December 12, 1859, August 18, 1860, February 3, 1861, recommended eyewash. KZN-W; Galette to KZH, February 27, 1859, KZN-W.

21. "Tagebuch," 87b, 90a (KZH to FZ, November 28, 1870), 92a (September

18, 1870), Caroline Berthold to KZH, January 20, 1873, Lotte Haradauer to KZH, March 20, 1871 (Zitz-Halein had asked her for a loan of one hundred gulden), KZN-W.

22. "Tagebuch," 90a–91b, November 27, 1870 (KZH to Madam Gorz), 92ab, November 28, 1870 (KZH to FZ), 93b (March 19), 94a (May 6, 1871) 96b (May 23, 1871), 98a (November 8, 1871), 100b (November 9, 1871), 101a (May 12, 1872), F. Wagner to KZH, May 30, 1871, KZN-W.

23. "Tagebuch," 22a (January 3, 1858), 102a–103a (August 3, 1872, August 4, 1872, KZH to Frau Zitz), KZN-W.

24. Johanna Kinkel to KZH, August 9, 1853, KZN-M; "Tagebuch," 10b–15b, F. Lubojatzky to KZH, December 12, 18, 1855, January 1, 1856, KZH to Karl Gutzkow, December 12, 1855, KZH to Ernst Keil, December 12, 1855, KZH to Lubojatzky, December 14, 20, 1855, January 11, 1856, KZN-W; Goehler, *Schillerstiftung*, 2: 82–84; Winterscheidt, *Deutsche Unterhaltungsliteratur*, 238, 287–89. In the eighteenth century, according to Rogers, *Feminism in Eighteenth Century England*, 36, female writers had to be exceptionally careful to avoid being the subject of gossip.

25. "Tagebuch," 3b (March 16, 1854), 27ab (May 18, 1859), 70ab (May 21, June 24, 1868), 73b–75a (August 25, October 5, 1868), 76a (October 9, 1868), 78b (February 17, 1869), 97a–97b (May 6, 14, 1871), 108b (March 15, 1873), KZN-W; KZH, "Weibliche Liebe," *Dur- und Molltöne*, 140; Nanni Wolf to KZH, December 23, 1851, August 7, 1852, November 1854, KZN-M; C. Berthold to KZH, January 1, 1869, KZN-W.

26. Meysenbug echoed this regarding her first love Theodor Althaus: I loved him like a woman while he loved me like a poet. Meysenbug, *Memoiren*, 1, 189.

27. "Tagebuch," 27a (May 15, 1859), 27b (May 20, 1859), 70a (June 13, 1868), 79a (April 14, 1869), 81a (June 15, 1869), 81b (July 26, 1869), KZN-W.

28. "Tagebuch," 81b (July 25, 1869), 83b (December 3, 1869), 85a (May 22, 1870), 93b (January 30, 1871), 94b (April 16, 1871), 98b (May 24, 1871), 105b (January 4, 1873), KZN-W.

29. "Tagebuch," 104b (October 2, 1872), 106ab (March 9, 1873), 109a (March, 15, 1873), KZH to FZ, October 2, 7, 12, 1872, FZ to KZH, October 6 (two letters), November 15, 1872, January 1, 1873, KZN-W.

10. Conclusion

1. "Tagebuch," 71a (June 30, July 9, 1868), 92a (November 20, 1870), 104a (October 25, 1872), 106b–109a (March 1873), KZN-W.

2. "Tagebuch," 65a (April 10, 1867), 108b–109a (March 14, 15, 1873), KZN-W; KZH, "Clemens von Brentano," Handschriftenabteilung III 39n, KZN-Stabi Mz.

3. J. Kinkel to KZH, July 31, 1855, KZN-M; "Tagebuch," 35b (July 22,

1862), 38a (February 10, 1863), KZN-W; KZH to Friedrich Kapp, April 2, 1862, KZN-M; *Mainzer Journal,* August 2, 3, 6–8, 1862; Heinrich Brück, *Geschichte der katholische Kirche in Deutschland im neunzehnten Jahrhundert* (Mainz, 1896), 3: 312–16.

4. Heribert Rau to KZH, March 16, 1851, KZN-M; "Tagebuch," 7a (December 9, 1854), 16b–17a (December 31, 1856), 28b–29a (October 12, 1859), 113a (November 6, 1873), KZN-W; Fritz Vigener, *Ketteler: Ein deutsches Bischofsleben des 19. Jahrhunderts* (Munich, 1924), 314–15; *Deutschkatholisches Sonntagsblatt,* September 7, November 16, 23, December 14, 1851, Stabi Mz.

5. "Tagebuch," 109a (July 29, 1873), 113a (November 6, December 29, 1873), 113b–114a (January 14, 26, February 9, 14, 1874), KZN-W.

6. Reprinted in *Mainzer Nachrichten,* January 1, 1893.

7. "Tagebuch," 113b (January 1, 1874), KZN-W.

8. Degler, *At Odds,* 437.

Bibliography

Works by Kathinka Zitz-Halein

Lists of her works can be found in Fränkel, Godeke, Pataky, and Schindel.

"Der Alpdruck." *Demokrat.* No. 67, September 9, 1849.
"Am Grabe Wilhelm Adolph's von Trützschler." *Demokrat.* No. 63, August 26, 1849.
Beiträge zur Unterhaltungsliteratur. Mainz, 1856.
"Betty Muller Melchiors." n.p., n.d., mog m:4°/733 Stabi Mz.
Die Bluttaufe im Garten zu Kirchheimbolanden: An die Mainzer Frauen. n.p., n.d. mog m99 Stabi Mz.
"Carl Höfer." *Demokrat.* No. 64, August 30, 1849.
Champagnerschaum. Mainz, 1854. (Vol. 1 of *Hausbibliothek*).
Corallen-Zinken. Mainz, 1855.
Cromwell. Stuttgart, 1835. Trans from the French of V. Hugo.
"Dem am 20 April 1848 heimgegangenen Turnwart Franz Mämpel." n.p., n.d. mog m992 Stabi Mz.
"Eine Demokratenfamilie." *Mainzer Tagblatt.* Nos. 199, 200, July 23, 24, 1850. (Also *Donner und Blitz,* 119–225.)
"Die Demokratie." n.p., n.d. mog m/1825 Stabi Mz.
"Deutsche Hymne." n.p., n.d. 66:2°/24 Bl. 19 Stabi Mz.
Dictionnaire des Gallicismes. Leipzig, 1841.
Donner und Blitz. Mainz, 1850. Also printed as *Novellenstrauss.* Mainz 1851.
Dur- und Molltöne. Mainz, 1859.
"Edelmann und Burger." *Didaskalia.* May 12 - June 30, 1868.
"Eduard Duller." Mainz, n.d. mog m4°/732 Stabi Mz.
"Einige aufklärende Worte zu dem Streite über die arme Frau in der Goldene Luft." *Mainzer Anzeiger.* January 1850.
Einige Worte an das Publikum im Allgemeinen und an Diejenigen, die es angeht, ins Besondere. Mainz, 1850, mog m3163 Stabi Mz.
"Entgegen die Redaktion." *Nordstern.* June 23, 1860.
Ernste und heitere Lebensbiblder. 3 vols. Mainz, 1854.
Erzählungen und Novellen. 2 vols. Nürnberg, 1845.

Bibliography

Folget mir nach!. Mainz, 1849.

"Die Frauen- und Jungfrauenverein Humania in Mainz." No. 34, May 17, 1849.

Die Fremde. Mainz, 1826. Trans. from the French.

Geographie in Versen. Leipzig, 1850.

"Gleichheit der Stände." n.p., n.d. mog m/1827 Stabi Mz.

Das Goldkind. Leipzig, 1851.

"Gottfried Kinkel." *Demokrat.* No. 58, August 9, 1849.

"Grosses europäisches Concert." *Mainzer Anzeiger.* May 1850.

Hausbibliothek der Mainzer Volkszeitung. 3 vols. Mainz, 1854–1855.

"Heinrich Frauenlob." *Rheinische Blätter.* November 6–December 12, 1845.

Heinrich Heine, der Liederdichter. Leipzig, 1864.

Herbstrosen in Poesie und Prosa. Mainz, 1846.

"Herr Anton und die schöne Adelheid." *Mainzer Anzeiger.* 1871, nos. 93–118.

"Humoristische Spielerei mit Namen, Strassen und Hausbenennungen." *Mainzer Anzeiger.* 1859, Nos. 279–284.

"Jermak Timofejew." *Hausbibliothek der Mainzer Zeitung* 1853/54, 4, 360–88.

"Johanna Kinkel." *Die deutsche Frau.* (1859): 141–42.

Jugend-Bibliothek. Mainz, n.d.

Juwelenkästchen. Mainz, 1862.

Kaiserin Josephine. Mainz, 1855.

"Kinkels Retter." *Mainzer Wochenblatt.* No. 327, December 10, 1850.

"Knud, der Laward, König der Wenden, Herzog von Schlewig." *Rheinische Blätter.* October 2–30, 1845.

Letzte Rheinsandkörner. Mainz, 1854.

Lord Byron. Mannheim, 1866–67.

"Luther, Schiller, Robert Blum." Mainz, n.d. mog 1082, no. 4 Stabi Mz.

Magdalene Horix. Mainz, 1858.

Maikräuter. Mainz, 1852.

"Mannheimer Briefe." *Demokrat.* Nos. 63–68, August 26- September 13, 1849.

Marion de Lorme. Mainz, 1833. Trans. from the French of V. Hugo.

"Meine Ausweisung aus Karlsruhe." *Kasteler Beobachter,* July 24, 26, 1849. Also in *Demokrat.* No. 53, July 22, 1849.

"Menschliche Gerechtigkeit." *Hausbibliothek* 1855, 2, 1–46.

"Eine Missionsreise nach Baden und der Pfalz." *Demokrat,* July 5, 8, 1849.

Die Najade des Soolsprudels zu Nauheim. Mainz, 1854.

Naturgeschichte des gesammten Thierreichs in Versen. Leipzig, 1851.

Neue Rheinsandkörner. Mainz, 1852.

Neueste Rheinsandkörner. Mainz, 1853.

"Noch ein Standgericht." *Demokrat.* August 30, 1849.

"Paul Estuart, Graf von St. Megrin." *Rheinische Blätter.* 1844–1845.

"Der Pechkönig." *Didaskalia.* September 25–October 6, 1849.

Phantasieblüthen und Tändeleien. Mainz, 1825.

Ein Quodlibet. Mainz, 1857.

Rahel oder dreiunddreissig Jahre. Leipzig, 1864.

"Die Republik." n.p., n.d. mog m/1828 Stabi Mz.

Rheinsandkörner. Mainz, 1851.

"Robert Blum." Mainz, 1848. mog 861, no. 9 Stabi Mz.

Robinson Crusoe. Mainz, 1849.

Der Roman eines Dichterlebens. Leipzig, 1863.

"Schillers Laura." *Hausbibliothek* 1 (1855): 1–87.

"Die schwarze Brüderschaft." *Demokrat.* No. 66, September 6, 1849.

"Skizzen aus dem Privatleben Ludwigs XIV." *Hausbibliothek* 1853/54, 4, 1–26.

"Skizzen aus meinem Leben." Nachlass Kathinka Zitz-Halein. Hessische Landesbibliothek Wiesbaden.

Sonderbare Geschichten aus den Feenländern. 2 vols. in 1. Nürnberg, 1844.

Spiegelbilder. Mainz, 1861.

Strohfeuer. Mainz, 1855.

Süss und Sauer. Mainz, 1851.

"Tagebuch." Nachlass Kathinka Zitz-Halein. Hessisches Landesbibliothek Wiesbaden.

Triboulet (Le Rois' amuse). Mainz, 1835. Trans from the French of V. Hugo.

Variationen in humoristischen Märchenbildern. Mainz, 1849.

"Die Verbannten." *Demokrat.* No. 67, September 9, 1849.

"Vermählungsfeier des Herrn Franz Joseph Usinger mit Fraulein Sophia Weiland." n.p., n.d. mog m/1878. Stabi Mz.

"Vorbilder aus der Alterthume." *Frauen Zeitung,* December 17, 28, 31, 1851.

Weihnachtsblümchen. Mainz, n.d.

Weltpantheon. Mainz, 1856.

"Wenn ich ein König wäre." n.p., n.d. Stabi Mz.

"Die Wittwen." *Demokrat.* No. 65, September 2, 1849.

Zeitgedichte. Mainz, 1848. mog m/1044. Stabi Mz.

"Zwei Errungenschaften." n.p., n.d. mog m/1826. Stabi Mz.

Archival Sources

Altenburg, DDR: Stadtarchiv. *Altenburger Volksblatt.* 1849.

Berlin, BRD: Deutsche Staatsbibliothek, Handschriftenabteilung Nachlass Brümmer, Briefe II (Kathinka Zitz-Halein and Louise Aston).

———: Staatsbibliothek Preussischer Kulturbesitz, Handschriftenabteilung, Zentralkartei der Autographen.

Berlin, DDR: Akten der Deutschen Schiller Stiftung, No. 96, 9 (Kathinka Zitz-Halein).

Bonn, BRD: Universitätsbibliothek, Handschriftenabteilung. Nachlass Gottfried Kinkel (Kathinka Zitz-Halein letters).

Cracow, Poland: Biblioteca Jagiellonska, Uniwersytet Jagiellonska. Sammlung Varnhagen von Ense (Louise Aston material).

Darmstadt, BRD: Hessisches Staatsarchiv and Stadtarchiv. Bestand D 12, Konv 697 (Kathinka Zitz-Halein letters). Bestand G 1, Konv 156, Fasz 6 (Mannheimer Abendblatt). Letters to author, June 30, September 29, 1987.

Bibliography

Dresden, DDR: Sächsische Landesbibliothek. Nachlass Johannes Ronge. *Frauenzeitung*, 1849–1850. (R K Z D.13, Ephem Lit. 236).

Düsseldorf, BRD: Heinrich Heine Institut. Nachlass Julius Campe.

Frankfurt/Main, BRD: Bundesarchiv Aussenstelle Frankfurt. Nachlässe of deputies to the Frankfurt Assembly.

———: Stadtarchiv Akte Criminalia 1848.

———: Stadt- und Universitätsbibliothek. Nachlass Johannes Rau.

Giessen, BRD: Universitätsbibliothek. Nachlass Lorenz Dieffenbach (Louise Dittmar and Kathinka Zitz-Halein letters).

Görlitz, DDR: Oberlausitzische Bibliothek der Wissenschaften. Nachlass Carl von Schindel.

Hamburg, BRD: Staatsarchiv. Nachlass Emilie Wüstenfeld. Polizei Kriminalwesen, Serie V, Lit I, No. 2332.

Hanau, BRD: Stadtarchiv and Historisches Museum. Hanauer Chronik des Johann D. W. Ziegler. *Hanauer Zeitung*.

Heidelberg, BRD: Universitätsbibliothek. Heid.Hs2120 (Poems by Kathinka Zitz-Halein).

Kaiserslautern, BRD: Stadtarchiv. Letter to author, June 6, 1987.

Karlsruhe, BRD: Generallandesarchiv. Untersuchungakten über Katharina Beck and Aufruf for "Germania" Association.

Lahr, BRD: Stadtarchiv. *Lahrer Wochenblatt*, 1849.

Mainz, BRD: Stadtarchiv. Nachlass Kathinka Zitz (mainly correspondence).

———: Stadtbibliothek. Handschriftenabteilung. Nachlass Kathinka Zitz (mainly unpublished manuscripts).

Mannheim, BRD: Stadtarchiv. Meldebogen. *Mannheimer Abendblatt*. Polizeiverhör.

Marbach, BRD: Schiller-Nationalmuseum, Deutsches Literaturarchiv. Handschriftenabteilung. Nachlass Berthold Auerbach.

Merseburg, DDR: Zentrales Staatsarchiv Nachlass Robert von Keudell.

Munich, BRD: Bayerische Staatsbibliothek. Nachlässe Leonhard Schrag and Rümpler.

Offenburg, BRD: Stadtarchiv. *Offenburger Wochenblatt*.

Weimar, DDR: Goethe- und Schiller-Archiv der Nationalen Forschungs- und Gedenkstätten der klassicher deutschen Literatur in Weimar. Nachlass Nicolaus Meyer.

Wiesbaden, BRD: Hessische Landesbibliothek. Nachlass Kathinka Zitz-Halein HS 122 (Memoirs, diary, letters).

———: Hessisches Hauptstaatsarchiv. Nachlass Habel-Conrady.

Worms, BRD: Stadtarchiv. Local newspapers.

Other Sources

Actes de Naisscenses. Vol. 12, no. 130.

Adler, Hans, ed. *Literarische Geheimberichte*. 2 vols. Cologne, 1981.

————. *Soziale Romane im Vormärz: Literatursemiotische Studie.* Munich, 1980.

"Adolph Kohn: Politische Tagebucher 1848." *Denkwürdige Jahre 1848–1851.* Norbert Conrads and Günter Richter. Cologne, 1978. Pp. 97–316.

Allen, Ann Taylor. "Gardens of Children, Gardens of God: Kindergartens and Day-Care Centers in Nineteenth Century Germany." *Journal of Social History* 19 (Spring 1986): 433–50.

————. "Spiritual Motherhood: German Feminists and the Kindergarten Movement, 1848–1911." *History of Education Quarterly* 22, no. 3 (1982): 319–39.

Allgemeine Deutsche Biographie. Vols. 5, 27, 33, 38, 45.

Altenburger Volksblatt. 1849.

Anneke, Mathilde. *Memoiren einer Frau aus dem badisch pfälzischen Feldzuge 1848/49.* Newark, N.J., 1853; reprint, Münster, 1982.

Anon. "Hesse-Darmstadt in den Jahren 1850–1866." *Unsere Zeit* 3 (1867).

Anzeiger für die politische Polizei Deutschlands auf die Zeit vom 1 Januar 1848 bis zum Gegenwart. Dresden, 1855; reprint, Hildesheim, 1970.

Arnim, Bettina von. *Armenbuch.* Frankfurt/Main, 1969.

————. *Clemens von Brentanos Frühlingskranz.* Leipzig, 1985.

Ashton, Rosemary. "The Search for Liberty: German Exiles in England in the 1850s." *Journal of European Studies* 13, no. 51 (September 1983): 187–98.

Aston, Louise. *Aus dem Leben einer Frau.* Hamburg, 1847.

————. *Lydia.* Magdeburg, 1848.

————. *Meine Emancipation, Verweisung und Rechtfertigung.* Brussels, 1846.

————. *Wilde Rosen.* Berlin, 1846.

Bachem, Karl. *Vorgeschichte, Geschichte und Politik der deutschen Zentrumspartei.* 9 vols. Cologne, 1927–1932.

Bamberger, Ludwig. *Charakteristiken.* Berlin, 1894.

————. *Erinnerungen.* Berlin, 1899.

Battenberg, Friedrich, and Eckhart G. Franz. *Darmstadts Geschichte.* Darmstadt, 1980.

Bäumer, Gertrud. *Gestalt und Wandel: Frauenbildnisse.* Berlin, 1939.

Baumgart, Franzjörg. *Die verdrängte Revolution: Darstellung und Bewertung der Revolution von 1848 in der deutschen Geschichtsschreibung vor dem Ersten Weltkrieg.* Düsseldorf, 1976.

Becker, Eva D. "'Zeitungen sind doch das Beste': Bürgerliche Realisten und der Vorabdruck ihrer Werke in der periodischen Presse." *Gestaltungsgeschichte und Gesellschaftsgeschichte.* Helmut Kreuzer. Stuttgart, 1969. Pp. 382–408.

————, and Dehn, Manfred. *Literarisches Leben: Eine Bibliographie.* Hamburg, 1975.

Behrens, Katja, ed. *Frauenbriefe der Romantik.* Frankfurt/Main, 1981.

Bergmann, Alfred, ed. "Fünfzehn Briefe Carl Volkhausens an Malwida von Meysenbug aus den Jahren 1849–1852." *Mitteilungen aus der lippischen Geschichte und Landeskunde* 23 (1954): 221–23.

Bergsträsser, Ludwig, ed. *Das Frankfurter Parlament in Briefen und Tagebücher.* Frankfurt/Main, 1929.

Berkin, Carol, and Clara M. Lovett, eds. *Women, War and Revolution*. New York, 1980.

Berliner Strassenecken-Literatur. Berlin, 1977.

Betz, Frederick. "Fontane Scholarship, Literary Sociology and Trivialliteraturforschung." *Internationales Archiv für Sozialgeschichte der deutschen Literatur*. Sonderdruck, 8B (1983): 200–20.

Biebusch, Werner. *Revolution und Staatsstreich: Verfassungskämpfe in Bremen 1848–1854*. Bremen, 1973.

Biographisches Lexikon. Berlin (DDR), 1966.

Birke, Adolf. *Bischof Kettler und der deutsche Liberalismus*. Mainz, 1971.

Blanning, T. C. W. *The French Revolution in Germany: Occupation and Resistance in the Rhineland 1792–1803*. Oxford, 1983.

Blasius, Dirk. *Ehescheidung in Deutschland 1794–1945: Scheidung und Scheidungsrecht in historischer Perspektive*. Kritische Studien zur Geschichtswissenschaft, No. 74, Göttingen, 1987.

———. "Scheidung und Scheidungsrecht im 19. Jahrhundert: Zur Sozialgeschichte der Familie." *Historische Zeitschrift* 241 (October 1985): 329–60.

Blätter für literarische Unterhaltung. Leipzig, 1831–1859.

Blochmann, Elisabeth. *Das "Frauenzimmer" und die Gelehrsamkeit*. Heidelberg, 1966.

Blos, Anna. *Die Frauen der deutschen Revolution von 1848*. Dresden, 1928.

Blueher, Hans. *Frauenbewegung und Antifemininismus*. Lauenburg/Elbe, 1921.

Blum, Hans. *Die deutsche Revolution 1848–49*. Leipzig, 1894.

Bockenheimer, Karl Georg. *Geschichte der Stadt Mainz in den Jahren 1813–1814*. Mainz, 1886.

———. *Geschichte der Stadt Mainz wahrend der französischen Herrschaft, 1798–1814*. Mainz, 1890.

———. *Mainz im Jahre 1866*. Mainz, 1907.

———. *Mainz in den Jahren 1848 und 1849*. Mainz, 1906.

Boldt, Werner. *Die württembergische Volksvereine 1848–1852*. Stuttgart, 1979.

Börckel, Alfred. *Aus der Geschichte eines Altmainzer Kaufmannshauses 1787–1907*. Mainz, n.d.

———. *Frauenlob*. Mainz, 1880.

———. *Hessens Fürstenfrauen*. Giessen, 1908.

———. *Mainzer Geschichtsbilder*. Mainz, 1890.

Born, Stephan. *Erinnerungen 1848*. Leipzig, 1898.

Böttger, Fritz, ed. *Frauen im Aufbruch: Frauenbriefe aus dem Vormarz und der Revolution von 1848*. Darmstadt, 1979.

Brandon, Ruth. *The Spiritualist*. London, 1983.

Brinkler-Gabler, Gisela, ed. *Deutsche Dichterinnen vom 16. Jahrhundert bis zur Gegenwart*. Frankfurt/Main, 1978.

Brück, Heinrich. *Geschichte der katholischen Kirche in Deutschland im neunzehnten Jahrhundert*. Vol. 3. Mainz, 1886.

Brümmer, Franz. *Lexikon der deutschen Dichter und Prosaisten von Beginn des 19. Jahrhunderts bis zum Gegenwart*. 6th ed. Leipzig, 1913.

Brunner, Ludwig. *Politische Bewegungen in Nürnberg 1848/49*. Heidelberg, 1907.

Brunner, Otto. "Das ganze Haus." *Neue Wege der Verfassungs- und Sozialgeschichte.* 2d ed. Göttingen, 1968.

Bry, Gerald. *Wages in Germany 1871–1945.* Princeton, N.J., 1960.

Bucher, Max, Werner Hahl, Georg Jäger, and Reinhard Wittmann, eds. *Realismus und Gründerzeit: Manifeste und Dokumente zur deutschen Literatur 1848–1880.* 2 vols. Stuttgart, 1976.

Buchner, Karl. *Das Grossherzogtum Hessen in seiner politischen und sozialen Entwicklung von Herbst 1847 bis zum Herbst 1850.* Darmstadt, 1850.

Buckler, Carlo. *Die politischen und religiösen Kämpfen in Mainz während der Revolutionsjahre 1848/50.* Giessen, 1936.

Bühler, Johannes. *Das Hambacher Fest.* Ludwigshafen, 1932.

Burger, Alexander. "Aus der Geschichte des Mainzer Karnevals: Kathinka Zitz und die Mainzer Karnivalszeitung von 1844." *Heim und Welt,* no. 73, 1 March 1924.

Burkhard, Marianne. "Love, Creativity and the Female Role: Grillparzers 'Sappho' and Staël's 'Corinne' between Art and Cultural Norm." *Jahrbuch für Internationale Germanistik* 16, no. 2 (1984): 128–46.

———, ed. *Gestaltet und Gestaltend: Frauen in der deutschen Literatur.* Amsterdamer Beiträge zur neueren Germanistik Vol. 10 (1980). Amsterdam, 1980.

Büttner, Siegfried. *Die Anfänge der Parlamentarismus in Hessen-Darmstadt und das du Thilsche System.* Darmstadt, 1969.

Cocalis, Susan L. *The Defiant Muse: German Feminist Poems from the Middle Ages to the Present.* New York, 1986.

———, and Kay Goodman, eds. *Beyond the Eternal Feminine.* Stuttgart, 1982.

Code Napoleon or the French Civil Code. New York, 1841.

Corvin-Wierbitski, Otto. *Erinnerungen aus meinem Leben.* 2 vols. 3d ed. Leipzig, 1880.

Damen Konversations-Lexikon. Vol. 5, 1846.

Degler, Carl. *At Odds: Women and the Family in America.* New York, 1980.

Deneke, J. F. Volrad. "Die Phrenologie als publizistisches Ereignis: Galls Schädellehre in der Tagespublizistik des 19. Jahrhunderts." *Medizinhistorisches Jahrbuch* 20 (1985): 83–108.

Denkler, Horst, ed. *Der deutsche Michel: Revolutionskomödien der Achtundvierziger.* Stuttgart, 1971.

———. "Politik und Gesellschaft" *Internationales Archiv für Sozialgeschichte deutscher Literatur* 5 (1980): 94–126.

———. "Revolutionäre Dramaturgie und revolutionäres Drama im Vormärz und Revolution." *Gestaltungsgeschichte und Gesellschaftsgeschichte.* Helmut Kreuzer. Stuttgart, 1969. Pp. 306–37.

———. "Volkstümlichkeit, Popularität, und Trivialität in den Revolutionslustspielen der Berliner Achtundvierziger." *Popularität und Trivialität.* Ed. Reinhold Grim and Jost Hermand. Frankfurt/Main, 1974. Pp. 77–100.

Derwein, Herbert. *Heidelberg im Vormärz und in der Revolution 1848/49.* Heidelberg, 1958.

Desai, Ashok. *Real Wages in Germany 1871–1913*. Oxford, 1968.

Deuchert, Norbert. *Vom Hambacher Fest zur badischen Revolution: Politische Presse und Anfänge deutscher Demokratie 1832–1848/49*. Stuttgart, 1983.

Deutsche Jakobiner, Mainzer Republik und Cisrhenanen, 1792–1798. 3 vols. Mainz, 1981.

Didaskalia (Frankfurt). 1845–1850.

Dittmar, Louise. *Bekannte Geheimnisse*. Darmstadt, 1845.

———. *Skizzen und Briefe aus der Gegenwart*. Darmstadt, 1845.

———. *Vier Zeitfragen*. Offenbach/Main. 1847.

Dotzauer, Winfried. *Freimaurer Gesellschaften am Rhein*. Geschichtliche Landeskunde, Vol. 16. Wiesbaden, 1972.

Dressen, Wolfgang, ed. *1848–1849: Bürgerkrieg in Baden*. Berlin (BRD), 1975.

Drewitz, Ingeborg. *Bettine von Arnim*. Düsseldorf, 1969.

Droz, Jacques. "Die religiösen Sekten und die Revolution von 1848." *Archiv für Sozialgeschichte* 3 (1963): 109–18.

Düding, Dieter. *Organisierter gesellschaftlicher Nationalismus in Deutschland (1808–1847)*. Munich, 1984.

Dumont, Christoph. *Die Emanzipation der Frauen*. Mainz, 1848.

Du Thil, Karl W. H. du Bois. *Denkwürdigkeiten aus dem Dienstleben des hessen-darmstädtischer Staatsminister Freiherr du Thil 1803–1848*. Stuttgart, 1921.

Eggert, Hartmut. *Studien zur Wirkungsgeschichte des deutschen historischen Romans 1850–1875*. Frankfurt/Main, 1971.

Estermann, Alfred. *Die deutschen Literatur-Zeitschriften*. 10 vols. Nendeln, 1981.

Evans, Richard, and W. R. Lee. *The German Family: Essays on the Social History of the Family in 19th and 20th Century Germany*. London, 1980.

Eyck, Frank. *The Frankfurt Parliament, 1848–49*. London, 1968.

Faber, Karl-Georg. *Recht und Verfassung: Die politische Funktion des rheinischen Rechts im 19. Jahrhundert*. Cologne, 1970.

———. *Die Rheinlande zwischen Restauration und Revolution*. Wiesbaden, 1966.

———. "Die rheinschen Institutionen." *Hambacher Gespräche*. Wiesbaden, 1964. Pp. 20–40.

Falck, Ludwig. *Geschichte der Stadt Mainz*. Düsseldorf, 1972.

———. *Mainz im frühen und hohen Mittelalter*. Düsseldorf, 1972.

———. *Mainz in seiner Blütezeit als freie Stadt (1244–1328)*. Düsseldorf, 1973.

Fehrenbach, Elisabeth. "Rhenischer Liberalismus und gesellschaftliche Verfassung." *Liberalismus in der Gesellschaft des deutschen Vormärz*. Wolfgang Schieder. Göttingen, 1983. Pp. 272–94.

Fischer, Heinz-Dietrich, ed. *Deutsche Kommunikationskontrolle des 15. bis 20. Jahrhunderts*. Munich, 1982.

Fliegende Blätter (Munich). Vols. 1–7 (1845–1848).

Fout, John., ed. *German Women in the Nineteenth Century: A Social History*. New York, 1984.

Fränkel, Ludwig. "Zitz, Kath. und Franz." *Allgemeine Deutsche Biographie*. 45 (1900): 373–79.

Frankfurter Journal. 1848.

Bibliography

Frankfurter Oberpostamtszeitung. 1849.

Fränkische Blätter (Nürnberg). 1848.

Frauen-Zeitung. 1849–1852.

Frederiksen, Elke. "Deutsche Autorinnen im 19. Jahrhundert: Neue kritische Ansätze." *Colloquia Germania* 14, no. 2 (1981): 97–113.

———. "Die Frau als Autorin zur Zeit der Romantik: Anfänge einer weiblichen literarischen Tradition." *Gestaltet und Gestaltend: Frauen in der deutschen Literatur.* Amsterdam, 1980. Pp. 83–108.

———. "German Women Writers in the Nineteenth Century: Where Are They?" *Beyond the Eternal Feminine.* S. Cocalis, and K. Goodman. Stuttgart, 1982. Pp. 177–201.

Frels, Wilhelm. *Bettina von Arnims Königsbuch.* Schwerin/Mecklenburg, 1912.

———. *Deutsche Dichterhandschriften von 1400 bis 1900.* Leipzig, 1934.

Fricke, Dieter, et al. *Deutsche Demokraten: die nichtproletarischen demokratischen Kräfte in der deutschen Geschichte 1830–1945.* Berlin (DDR), 1981.

Friedrichs, Elizabeth. *Die deutschsprachigen Schriftstellerinnen des 18. und 19. Jahrhunderts.* Stuttgart, 1981.

Fuchs, Eduard. *Die Frau in der Karikatur.* Munich, 1906.

———. *Ein vormärzliche Tanzidyll: Lola Montez in der Karikatur.* Berlin, 1905.

———. *Die Weiberherrschaft in der Geschichte der Menschheit.* 2 vols. Munich, 1913.

Gay, Peter. *The Bourgeois Experience: Victoria to Freud.* Vol. 1. New York, 1984.

Geiger, Gerlinde. "Die befreite Psyche: Emanzipationsansätze im Früwerk Ida Hahn-Hahn." Ph.D. dissertation, University of Massachusetts, 1984.

Geiger, L. *Das junge Deutschland und die preussische Zensur.* Berlin, 1900.

Geiger, Ruth. *Zeitschriften 1848 in Berlin.* Hamburg, 1977.

Geisel, Karl. *Die Hanauer Turnerwehr.* Marburg, 1974.

Gerhard, Ute. *Verhältnisse und Verhinderungen: Frauenarbeit, Familie und Rechte der Frauen im 19. Jahrhundert.* Frankfurt/Main, 1978.

Gerhard, Ute, Elisabeth Hannover-Drück, and Romina Schmitter, eds. *"Dem Reich der Freiheit werb' ich Bürgerinnen": Die Frauenzeitung von Louise Otto.* Frankfurt/Main, 1980.

Gilbert, Sandra, and Susan Gubar. *The Madwoman in the Attic.* New Haven, Conn., 1979.

Glazer-Melbin, Nona. "Housework." *SIGNS* 1 (Summer, 1976): 905–22.

Goedke, Karl. *Grundriss zur Geschichte der deutschen Dichtung.* Dresden, 1938. Vol 13. Pp. 295–98.

Goehler, Rudolf. *Geschichte der Deutschen Schillerstiftung 1859–1909.* 2 vols. Berlin, 1909.

Goetzinger, Germaine. *Für die Selbstverwirklichung der Frau: Louise Aston.* Frankfurt/Main, 1983.

Goncourt, Edmond, and Jules de. *Germinie Lacerteux.* Trans., Middlesex, England, 1984.

Goodman, Kay. "German Women and Autobiography in the Nineteenth Century." Ph.D. dissertation, University of Wisconsin- Madison, 1978.

————. "Die grosse Kunst nach innen zu weinen." *Die Frau als Heldin und Autorin.* Ed. Wolfgang Paulson. Bern, 1979. Pp. 124–35.

————. "The Impact of Rahel Varnhagen on Women in the Nineteenth Century." *Gestaltet und Gestaltend: Frauen in der Deutschen Literatur.* Marianne Burkhard. Amsterdam, 1980. Pp. 125–53.

Gottschall, Rudolf. *Die deutsche Nationalliteratur des neunzehnten Jahrhunderts.* 5th ed. 4 vols. Breslau, 1881.

Götze, Ruth. "Louise Ottos Beziehungen zum Protetariat im Vormärz und in der Revolution von 1848/49." *Sächische Heimblätter* 27, no. 4 (1981): 154–56.

Gouges, Olympe de. *Schriften.* Ed. and trans. Monika Diller, Vera Mostowlansky, and Regula Wyss. Frankfurt/Main, 1980.

Grab, Walter. "Eroberung oder Befreiung? Deutsche Jakobiner und die Franzosenherrschaft im Rheinlande 1792–1799." *Archiv für Sozialgeschichte* 10 (1970): 7–94.

————. *Ein Volk muss sein Freiheit selbst erobern: Zur Geschichte der deutschen Jakobiner.* Frankfurt/Main, 1984.

Graf, Friedrich W. *Die Politisierung des religiösen Bewusstseins: Die bürgerliche Religionsparteien im deutschen Vormärz: Das Beispiel des Deutschkatholiken.* Stuttgart-Bad Cannstatt, 1978.

Gross, Heinrich, ed. *Deutsche Dichterinnen und Schriftstellerinnen in Wort und Bild.* 3 vols. Berlin, 1885.

Grossherzoglich Hessisches Regierungsblatt. Darmstadt, 1846.

Guide de la Ville de Mayence. Mainz, n.d.

Gutwirth, Madelyn. *Madame de Staël, Novelist.* Urbana, Ill., 1978.

Haasis, Helmut. *Morgenröte der Republik: Die linksrheinischen deutschen Demokraten.* Frankfurt/Main 1984.

Hacker, Barton C. "Women and Military Institutions in Early Modern Europe: A Reconnaissance." *SIGNS* 6, no. 4 (1981): 643–71.

Hagen, William. *German, Poles, and Jews: The National Conflict in the Prussian East, 1772–1914.* Chicago, 1980.

Hahn, Karl Heinz. *Bettina von Arnim in ihrem Verhältnis zu Staat und Politik.* Weimar, 1958.

Hahn-Hahn, Ida Marie. *Faustine.* Berlin, 1919.

Hamburger Beobachter. 1848–1849.

Hamerow, Theodore S. *Restoration, Revolution, Reaction: Economics and Politics in Germany, 1815–1871.* Princeton, N.J., 1958.

Hanauer Chronik 2 (1846–1851).

Hanauer Zeitung. 1848–1850.

Hänsel, Markus. *Elise von Hohenhausen (1789–1857).* Frankfurt/Main, 1984.

Hart, Friedrich. *Ein Tag in der Paulskirche: Skizzen und Porträts aus dem Reichstag in Frankfurt am Main.* 2 vols. Leipzig, 1848.

Hartwig, Christiane. "Frauenbewegung und Frauenbildung in Hamburg während und nach der Umbruchzeit von 1848–49." 1981, Handschriftensammlung, 1122, Staatsarchiv Hamburg.

Heinzelmann, Josef. "Ludwig Kalisch." *Neue Deutsche Biographie.* Vol. 11. Pp. 59–69.

Heiratsregister, 1837. Stadtarchiv, Mainz.

Heise, Norbert. "Demokratischer Turnerbund und Deutscher Turnerbund." *Die bürgerlichen Parteien in Deutschland.* Vol 1. Leipzig, 1968. Pp. 274–77.

Helps, Arthur, and Elizabeth J. Howard. *Bettina: A Portait.* New York, n.d.

Hermand, Jost, ed. *Der deutsche Vormärz: Texte und Documente.* Stuttgart, 1967.

———, and M. Windfuhr, eds. *Zur Literatur der Restaurationsepoche 1815–1848.* Stuttgart, 1970.

Herwegh, Emma. *Zur Geschichte der deutschen demokratischen Legion aus Paris.* Grünberg, 1849.

Hesse, Hans G. *Evangelische Ehescheidungsrecht in Deutschland.* Bonn, 1960.

Hessische Biographien. 3 vols. Darmstadt, 1918.

Hessische Hausfreund (Darmstadt). 1828, 1843, 1844, 1846.

Hildebrandt, Gunther. *Parlamentsopposition auf Linkskurs.* Berlin (DDR), 1975.

———, ed. *Opposition in der Paulskirche: Reden, Briefe und Berichte kleinbürgerlich demokratischen Parlamentarier 1848/49.* Berlin (DDR), 1981.

Hirsch, Helmut. "Carl Heinrich Marx als Prediger der Krefelder Deutschkatholiken (1847–1851)." *Archiv für Sozialgeschichte* 3 (1963): 119–39.

Hohendahl, Peter U. *Literarische Kultur im Zeitalter des Liberalismus 1830–1870.* Munich, 1985.

Houben, Heinrich H. *Verbotene Literatur von der klassische Zeit bis zur Gegenwart.* 2 vols. Berlin, 1924; reprint, Hildesheim, 1965.

Huber, Ernst. *Dokumente zur deutschen Verfassungsgeschichte.* Stuttgart, 1964.

Hummel-Haasis, Gerlinde, ed. *Schwestern zerreisst eure Ketten.* Munich, 1982.

Jäckel, Günter, ed. *Das Volk braucht Licht: Frauen zur Zeit des Aufbruchs 1790–1848 in ihren Briefen.* Darmstadt, 1970.

Jäger, Georg. "Die deutsche Leihbibliothek in 19. Jahrhundert. Verbreitung, Organisation, Verfall." *Internationales Archiv für Sozialgeschichte der deutschen Literatur* 2 (1977): 96–133.

Jean, Eberhard. "Deutsche Turnerschaft." *Die bürgerlichen Parteien in Deutschland.* Vol 1. Leipzig, 1968. Pp. 605–19.

Jelinek, Estelle C. *The Tradition of Women's Autobiography: From Antiquity to the Present.* Boston, 1986.

Joeres, Ruth-Ellen Boetcher, ed. *Die Anfänge der deutschen Frauenbewegung: Louise Otto-Peters.* Frankfurt/Main, 1983.

———. "1848 from a Distance: German Women Writers on the Revolution." *MLN* 97, no. 3 (April 1982): 590–614.

———. "Louise Otto and her Journals: A Chapter in Nineteenth Century German Feminism." *Internationales Archiv für Sozialgeschichte der deutschen Literatur* 4 (1979): 100–29.

———, and Mary Jo Maynes, eds. *German Women in the Eighteenth and Nineteenth Century: A Social and Literary History.* Bloomington, Ind., 1986.

Kaiser, Bruno. *Die Achtundvierziger: Ein Lesebuch.* Weimar, 1955.

Kalisch, Ludwig. "Die schlechten Dichter." *Didaskalia* 23, no. 22 (January 22, 1845).

"Karl Friedrich Hempel: Die Breslauer Revolution." *Denkwürdige Jahre 1848–1851*. Norbert Conrads and Günter Richter. Cologne, 1978. Pp. 3–94.

Kasteler Beobachter. 1849.

Katz-Seibert, Mathilde. *Der politische Radikalismus in Hessen während der Revolution von 1848/49.* Darmstadt, 1929.

Keim, Anton Maria. "Rheinsandkörner: Erinnerungen an Kathinka Zitz-Halein." March, 8, 1964. (Typewritten). Stadtbibliothek, Mainz.

Kellen, Tony. "Die Honarare deutscher Dichter und Schriftsteller." *Nord und Süd* 93 (1900): 164–75.

Kenney, Annie. *Memoirs of a Militant.* London, 1924.

Kerksen, Hans. *Stadt und Universität in den Revolutionsjahren 1848–1850.* Bonn, 1931.

Kern, Bernd-Rüdiger. "Das Darmstädter Hoftheater und Rossini." *Archiv für hessische Geschichte und Altertumskunde* 42 (1984): 149–83.

Kirschstein, Eva-Annemarie. *Die Familienzeitschrift.* Leipzig, 1937.

Klein, Tim, ed. *1848: Der Vorkampf deutscher Einheit und Freiheit.* Munich, 1914.

Klessmann, Christoph. "Zur Sozialgeschichte der Reichsverfassungskampagne von 1849." *Historische Zeitschrift* 218, no. 2 (1974): 283–337.

Klötzer, Wolfgang, ed. *Clothilde Koch-Gontard an ihre Freunde: Briefe und Erinnerungen.* Frankfurt/Main, 1969.

Knapp, Ulla. *Frauenarbeit in Deutschland.* 2 vols. Munich, 1984.

Koch, R. "Liberalismus, Konservatismus und das Problem der Negersklaverei." *Historische Zeitschrift* 222, no. 3 (1976): 529–77.

Koepcke, Cordula. *Geschichte der deutschen Frauenbewegung von den Anfängen bis 1945.* Freiburg im Breisgau, 1979.

———. *Louise Otto-Peters.* Freiburg im Breisgau, 1981.

Kolbe, Günter. "Demokratische Opposition in religiösen Gewande: Zur Geschichte der deutschkatholischen Bewegung in Sachsen am Vorabend der Revolution von 1848/49." *Zeitschrift für Geschichtswissenschaft* 20, no. 9 (1972): 1102–12.

Kosch, Wilhelm. *Deutsches Literatur-Lexikon.* Vol. 5. Bern, 1978.

Koszyk, Kurt. *Deutsche Presse im 19. Jahrhundert.* Berlin (BRD), 1966.

Kraus, Alexander. *Die Garantie der französischen Einrichtungen in der Provinz Rheinhessen.* Darmstadt, 1847.

Kühn, Hans. "Politischer, wirtschaftlicher und sozialer Wandel in Worms 1798–1866." *Der Wormsgau*, Beiheft 26.

Kurz, Heinrich. *Geschichte der neuesten deutschen Literatur von 1830 bis auf die Gegenwart.* Vol. 4. Leipzig, 1872.

Lahrer Wochenblatt. 1849.

"Landtagswählen, 1820–1831." 70, 121–23.

Lange, Helene. "Louise Otto und die erste deutsche Frauenzeitung." *Die Frau* 34, nos. 5, 6 (1927): 257–67, 321–32.

Langenbucher, Wolfgang. "Das Publikum im literarischen Leben des 19. Jahrhunderts." *Der Leser als Teil des literarischen Lebens.* Bonn, 1971. Pp. 52–84.

Langewiesche, Dieter. "Die deutsche Revolution von 1848/49 und die vorrevolutionäre Gesellschaft: Forschungsstand und Forschungsperspektiven." *Archiv für Sozialgeschichte* 21 (1981): 458–98.

———, ed. *Die deutsche Revolution von 1848/49.* Darmstadt, 1983.

Legge, J.G. *Rhyme and Revolution in Germany.* London, 1918; reprint, New York, 1970.

Lehne, Friedrich. *Gesammelte Schriften.* 5 vols. Mainz, 1836–1839.

———. *Gesänge der freien Deutschen in Mainz.* Mainz, 1793.

Leppla, Rupprecht, ed. "Johanna und Gottfried Kinkels Briefe an Kathinka Zitz 1849–1861." *Bonner Geschichtsblätter* 12 (1958): 7–82.

Lerner, Gerda. "New Approaches to the Study of Women in American History." In her *The Majority Finds Its Past: Placing Women in History.* New York, 1979. Pp. 349–56.

———. "Placing Women in History: Definitions and Challenges." in her *The Majority Finds Its Past: Placing Women in History.* New York, 1979. Pp. 357–65.

Lewald-Stahr, Fanny. *Erinnerungen aus dem Jahre 1848.* 2 vols. Braunschweig, 1850.

Lexis, W., and Gertrud Bäumer. *Das Unterrichtswesen im Deutschen Reich.* Vol. 2. *Die höheren Lehranstalten und das Mädchenschulwesen.* Berlin, 1904.

Lougee, Carolyn. *Paradies des Femmes.* Princeton, N.J., 1976.

Lück, Andreas. *Friedrich Hecker.* Berlin (BRD), 1979.

Mainzer Abendpost. 1850.

Mainzer Anzeiger. 1849–1850, 1855.

Mainzer Kurier. 1851.

Mainzer Tagblatt. 1849–1850.

Mainzer Wochenblatt. 1843–1850.

Mainzer Zeitung. 1847–1850.

Mannheimer Abendzeitung. 1846–1848.

Martini, Fritz, *Deutsche Literatur im bürgerlichen Realismus 1848–1898.* Stuttgart, 1962.

Martino, Alberto. "Die deutsche Leihbibliothek und ihr Publikum." *Literatur in der soziale Bewegung.* Tübingen, 1977.

Marx, Karl, and Engels, Friedrich. *Werke.* Vol. 4. Berlin (DDR), 1977.

Märzblüthen! Eine Sammlung volkstümlicher Aufsätze, Novellen und Dichtungen. 2d ed. Grossenhain, 1851.

Mathy, Helmut. "Die freien Genossin des freien Bürgers! Das Hambacher Fest und die politische Rolle der Frau im 19. Jahrhundert." *Geschichtliche Landeskunde* 24 (1984): 238–52.

Mattenklott, Gert, and Klaus Scherpe, eds. *Demokratisch-revolutionäre Literatur in Deutschland: Vormärz.* Kronberg im Taunus, 1974.

Mattheisen, Donald. "History as Current Events: Recent Works on the German Revolution of 1848." *American Historical Review* 88 (December 1983): 1219–37.

Merget, A. *Geschichte der deutschen Jugendliteratur*. 3d ed. Berlin, 1882.

Meyerinck, Hubert. *Die Strassenkämpfe in Berlin am 18. und 19. März 1848*. Leipzig, 1911.

Meysenbug, Malwida von. *Memoiren einer Idealistin*. 2 vols. Berlin, 1916.

Möhrmann, Renate. *Die andere Frau: Emanzipationsansätze deutscher Schriftstellerinnen in Vorfeld der Achtundvierziger-Revolution*. Stuttgart, 1977.

————, ed. *Frauenemanzipation im deutschen Vormärz: Texte und Dokumente*. Stuttgart, 1978.

Morgenstern, Lina. *Die Frauen des 19. Jahrhunderts*. 3 vols. Berlin, 1888–1891.

Moses, Claire Goldberg. "The Evolution of Feminist Thought in France 1829–1889." Ph.D. dissertation, George Washington University, 1978.

————. *French Feminism in the Nineteenth Century*. New York, 1984.

Mosse, George L. "Was die Deutschen wirklich lasen." *Popularität und Trivialität*. Ed. R. Grimm and J. Hermand. Frankfurt/Main, 1974. Pp. 101–20.

Müller, Niklas. *Der Aristokrat in der Klemme*. Mainz, 1792.

Narrhalla (Mainz). 1843, 1844.

Naujocks, Eberhard. "Der badische Liberalismus im Vormärz in Kampf für Pressefreiheit und gegen Zensur (1832–1847)." *Zeitschrift für die Geschichte des Oberrheins* 131 (1983): 347–81.

Naumann, Ursula. *Charlotte von Kalb*. Stuttgart, 1985.

Neitzke, Paul. *Die deutschen politischen Flüchtlinge in der Schweiz 1848–1849*. Charlottenburg, 1926.

Nelson, Geoffrey K. *Spiritualism and Society*. New York, 1969.

Neue Mainzer Narrenzeitung. 1844.

Die neue Zeit (Worms). 1848, 1849.

Noltenius, Rainer. *Dichterfeier in Deutschland*. Munich, 1984.

Obenaus, Sybille. *Literarische und politische Zeitschriften 1830–1848*. Stuttgart, 1986.

Obermann, Karl. "Die deutsche Einheitsbewegung und die Schillerfeier." *Zeitschrift für Geschichtswissenschaft* 3 (1955): 705–34.

————. *Einheit und Freiheit*. Berlin (DDR), 1950.

————. *Flugblätter der Revolution*. Berlin (DDR), 1970.

Oehlke, Alfred. *100 Jahre Breslauer Zeitung 1820–1920*. Breslau, n.d.

Oehlke, Waldemar. *Bettina von Arnims Briefromane*. Berlin, 1905; reprint New York, 1970.

Offen, Karen. "Ernest Legouvé and the Doctrine of 'Equality in Difference' for Women: A Case Study of Male Feminism in Nineteenth Century French Thought." *Journal of Modern History* 58 (June 1986): 452–84.

Offenburger Wochenblatt. 1848, 1849.

Ortenauer Rundschau. 1936.

Otruba, Gustav. "Zur Frauenfrage im Revolutionsjahr 1848 im Spiegel Wiener Flugschriften." *Wirtschafts- und sozialhistorische Beiträge*. Vienna, 1979. Pp. 395–409.

Pagenstecher, Heinrich Karl Alexander. *Lebenserinnerungen*. Vol. 2. *Als Abgeordneter in Frankfurt im Jahre 1848*. Leipzig, 1913.

Palmer, R. R. *The Age of the Democratic Revolution*. 2 vols. Princeton, N.J., 1964.

Paschen, Joachim. *Demokratische Vereine und preussischer Staat*. Munich, 1977.

Pataky, Sophie, ed. *Lexikon deutscher Frauen der Feder*. 2 vols. Berlin, 1898.

Pauly, Heribert. "Zur socialen Zusammensetzung der politischen Institutionen und Vereine der Stadt Mainz im Revolutionsjahre 1848." *Archiv für hessische Geschichte und Altertumskunde* N.F. 34 (1976): 44–81.

Peiser, Jürgen. *Gustav Struve als politischer Schriftsteller und Revolutionär*. Frankfurt/Main, 1973.

Petzet, Christian. *Die Blütezeit der deutschen politischen Lyrik vom 1840 bis 1850*. Munich, 1903.

Pfütze, Curt. "Heribert Rau." *Allgemeine Deutsche Biographie*. 27 (1888): 376–78.

Phillips, Roderick. *Family Breakdown in Late Eighteenth Century France: Divorces in Rouen 1792–1803*. Oxford, 1980.

Prelinger, Catherine M. *Charity, Challenge and Change: Religious Dimensions of the Mid-Nineteenth Century Women's Movement in Germany*. New York, 1987.

———. "The German-Catholic Church: From National Hope to Regional Reality." *The Consortium on Revolutionary Europe: Proceedings 1976*. Ed. Lee Kennett. Athens, Ga., 1978. Pp. 88–101.

———. "Religious Dissent, Women's Rights, and the Hamburger Hochschule für das weibliche Geschlecht in Mid-nineteenth Century Germany." *Church History* 45 (March 1976): 42–55.

Prutz, Robert. *Die deutsche Literatur der Gegenwart*. 2 vols. Leipzig, 1859.

———. "Über die Unterhaltungsliteratur insbesondere der Deutschen." *Schriften zur Literatur und Politik*. Ed. B. Hüppauf. Tübingen, 1973.

Puckett, Hugh Wiley. *Germany's Women Go Forward*. New York, 1930. reprint ed. New York, 1967.

Pulz, Waltraud. "Lola-Montez-Darstellungen als Indikator für Sexualstrukturen im bayrischen Alltagsleben der Mitte des 19. Jahrhunderts." *Oberbayerisches Archiv für vaterländische Geschichte* 107 (1982): 303–30.

Quataert, Jean H. *Reluctant Feminists in German Social Democracy, 1885–1917*. Princeton, NJ, 1979.

Radlik, Ute. "Heine in der Zensur der Restaurationsepoche." *Zur Literatur der Restaurationsepoche 1815–1848*. J. Hermand and M. Windfuhr. Stuttgart, 1970. Pp. 460–89.

Rath, R. John. *The Viennese Revolution of 1848*. Austin, Texas, 1957.

Der Reisende no. 24, June 11, 1843.

Rheinhessisches Volksblatt (Mainz). 1859

Rheinische Blätter (Mainz). 1843, 1845.

Rheinische Handelszeitung (Mainz). 1859.

Der Rheinische Telegraph (Mainz). 1842–1843.

Robertson, Priscilla. *An Experience of Women: Pattern and Change in Nineteenth Century Europe*. Philadelphia, Pa, 1982.

Rogers, Katharine M. *Feminism in Eighteenth Century England*. Urbana, Ill., 1982.

Bibliography

Rosenberg, Rainer. *Literaturverhältnisse im deutschen Vormärz.* Munich, 1975.

Ross, Ishbel. *The Uncrowned Queen: Life of Lola Montez.* New York, 1972.

Rosskopf, Josef. "Johann Adam von Itzstein." Ph.D. dissertation, Johannes Gutenberg University, 1951.

Rowbotham, Sheila. *Woman, Resistance and Revolution.* New York, 1972.

Rudolf, Maria. *Die Frauenbewegung in Frankfurt am Main.* Frankfurt/Main, 1978.

Sagarra, Eda. "Echo oder Antwort: Die Darstellung der Frau in der deutschen Erzählprosa 1815–1848." *Geschichte und Gesellschaft* 7 (1981): 394–411.

Sanford, Jutta Schoeres. "Origins of German Feminism." Ph.D. dissertation, Ohio State University, 1976.

Saurmann, Fritz. "Ein karnevalistisches Literatengeplänkel aus Alt-Mainz und seine Folgen." *Mainzer Warte,* nos. 5, 7, 8, February 2, 16, 23, 1929.

Schaab, K. A. *Diplomatische Geschichte der Juden zu Mainz und dessen Umgebung.* Mainz 1855.

Scheel, Heinrich. *Die Mainzer Republik.* 2 vols. Berlin, (DDR), 1975.

Schenda, Rudolf. *Volk ohne Buch.* Frankfurt/Main, 1970.

———. "Zensur der Kinder- und Jugendliteratur." *Lexikon der Kinder- und Jugendliteratur.* Vol. 3. Weinheim, 1979. Pp. 847–49.

Scherpe, Klaus. *Poesie der Demokratie.* Cologne, 1980.

Scherr, Johannes. *1848: Ein weltgeschichtliches Drama.* Vol. 2. Leipzig, 1875.

———. *Geschichte der deutschen Frauen.* Leipzig, 1860.

Schieder, Wolfgang, ed. *Liberalismus in der Gesellschaft des deutschen Vormärz.* Göttingen, 1983.

Schilfert, Gerhard. *Sieg und Niederlage des demokratischen Wahlrechts in der deutschen Revoultion 1848–49.* Berlin (DDR), 1952.

Schinachen, Detlev. *Das Rheinische Recht in der Gerichtspraxis des 19. Jahrhunderts.* Stuttgart, 1969.

Schindel, Carl von. *Die deutschen Schriftstellerinnen des neunzehnten Jarhhunderts.* 3 vols. Leipzig, 1823–1825. reprint ed. Hildesheim, 1978.

Schlander, Otto. *Der Aufbau des Schulwesen im Grossherzogtum Hessen-Darmstadt nach 1815.* Frankfurt/Main, 1978.

Schleicher, Berta. *Malwida von Meysenbug.* Berlin, 1916.

Schmidt, Auguste, and Hugo Rösch. *Louise Otto-Peters: die Dichterin und Vorkämpfer für Frauenrecht.* Leipzig, 1898.

Schmidt, Siegfried. *Robert Blum.* Weimar, 1971.

Schneider, Franz. *Pressefreiheit und politische Öffentlichkeit.* Neuwied, 1966.

Schnüffler, Anastasias. *Der Aufhebung des demokratischen Frauenclubbs oder das schreckliche Ende.* Berlin, 1848.

Schoeps, Julius. "An der Seite der Unterdrückten: Ludwig Kalisch (1814–1882) im Vormärz, in der Revolution of 1848 und im franzosischen Exil." *Juden im Vormärz und in der Revolution von 1848.* Walter Grab. Stuttgart, 1983. Pp. 331–51.

Schönert, Jorg. "Kriminalgeschichten in der deutschen Literatur zwischen 1770 und 1890." *Geschichte und Gesellschaft* 9 (1983): 49–68.

Schubert, Werner. "Der Code Civil und die Personenrechtsentwurfe des Grossherzogtums Hessen-Darmstadt von 1842 bis 1847." *Zeitschrift der Savigny Stiftung für Rechtsgeschichte. Germanistische Abteilung.* 88 (1971): 110–71.
———. *Französische Recht in Deutschland zu Beginn des 19.Jahrhunderts.* Cologne, 1977.
Schult, Gerhard. "Die hessische Innenpolitik unter dem Minister von Dalwigk 1850–1859." Ph.D. dissertation, Johannes Gutenberg University, 1953.
Schulz, Hartwig, ed. *Der Briefwechsel Bettine von Arnim mit den Brüdern Grimm, 1838–1841.* Frankfurt/Main, 1985.
Schumann, Clara, and Robert. *Briefwechsel: Kritische Gesamtausgabe.* Vol. 1. 1832–1838. E. Weissweiler. Frankfurt/ Main, 1984.
Schütz, Friedrich. "Der Vormärz in Mainz und Rheinhessen." *Geschichtliche Landeskunde* 24 (1984): 77–99.
Schütz, Rüdiger. *Preussen und die Rheinlande: Studien zur pressischen Integrationspolitik im Vormärz.* Wiesbaden, 1978.
Schweikert, Uwe. "'Am jungsten Tag hab ich Recht.' Rahel Varnhagen als Briefschreiberin." *Rahel Varnhagen: Gesammelte Werke.* Vol 10. Konrad Feilchenfeldt, Uwe Schweikert, and Rahel E. Steiner. Munich, 1983. Pp. 17–42.
Scriba, H. E. *Biographisch-literärisches Lexikon der Schriftsteller des Grossherzogtums Hessen im neunzehnten Jahrhundert.* Pt 2. Darmstadt, 1843.
Seitz, E. *Die rheinhessischen Rechtsinstitutionen in ihren Verhältniss zu allgemeinen Codification des Grossherzogtums Hessen.* Regensburg, 1847.
Semmel, Bernard. *John Stuart Mill and the Pursuit of Virtue.* New Haven, Conn., 1984.
Sengle, Friedrich. *Biedermeierzeit: Deutsche Literatur zwischen Restauration und Revolution 1815–1848.* 2 vols. Stuttgart, 1971–1972.
Showalter, Elaine. *A Literature of Their Own: British Women Novelists from Brontë to Lessing.* Princeton, N.J., 1977.
Siemann, Wolfram. *Die deutsche Revolution von 1848/49.* Frankfurt/Main, 1985.
Snell, John L. *The Democratic Movement in Germany, 1789–1914.* Chapel Hill, N.C., 1976.
Snyder, Louis L. *German Nationalism: The Tragedy of a People.* Harrisburg, Pa. 1952.
Spangenberg, Ilse. *Hessen-Darmstadt und der Deutsche Bund 1815–1848.* Darmstadt, 1969.
Spiessbürger, Abraham. *Katzenmusikalische Notenblätter.* Sonderhausen, 1848.
Spranger, Eduard. *Die Idee einer Hochschule für Frauen und die Frauenbewegung.* Leipzig, 1916.
Stauten des Humania-Vereins für vaterländische Interesse gegründet zu Mainz am 24 Mai 1849. n.p., n.d.
Stein, Peter. "Vormärz." *Wirkendes Wort* 22, no. 6 (1972): 411–26.
Stenographischer Bericht über die Verhandlungen der deutschen constituirenden Nationalversammlung zu Frankfurt am Main. Frankfurt/Main, 1848/1849.

Struve, Amalie. *Erinnerungen aus den badischen Freiheitskämpfen.* Hamburg, 1850.

Tapp, Alfred. "Hanau im Vormärz und in der Revolution von 1848–1849." *Hanauer Geschichtsblätter* 26 (1976).

Toop, Hans. *Ehescheidung und Aufhebung der ehelichen Gemeinschaft nach dem Bürgerlichen Gesetzbuch.* Leipzig, 1908.

Traer, James. *Marriage and the Family in Eighteenth Century France.* Ithaca, N.Y., 1980.

Trefousse, Hans. *Carl Schurz.* Knoxville, Tenn., 1982.

Twellmann, Margrit. *Die deutsche Frauenbewegung im Spiegel repräsentativer Frauenzeitschriften: Ihre Anfänge und erste Entwicklung 1843–1889.* 2 vols. Meisenheim/Glan, 1972.

Tyler, Anne. *Searching for Caleb.* New York, 1976.

Underberg, Elfriede, ed. *Die Dichtung der ersten deutschen Revolution.* Leipzig, 1930.

Valentin, Veit. *Frankfurt am Main und die Revolution 1848–1849.* Stuttgart, 1908.

———. *Geschichte der deutschen Revolution 1848–1849.* 2 vols. Berlin, 1930–1931.

Valjavec, Fritz. *Die Entstehung der politischen Strömungen in Deutschland 1770–1815.* Munich, 1951.

Varnhagen, Rahel. *Gesammelte Werke.* Vol 10. Konrad Feilchenfeldt, Uwe Schweikert, and Rahel E. Steiner. Munich, 1983.

Vigener, Fritz. *Ketteler: Ein deutsches Bischofsleben des 19. Jahrhunderts.* Munich, 1924.

Volkmann, Ernst. *Um Einheit und Freiheit, 1815–1848.* Leipzig, 1936.

Wagner, Maria. "A German Writer and Feminist in 19th Century America." *Beyond the Eternal Feminine.* Ed. S. Cocalis and K. Goodman. Stuttgart, 1982. Pp. 159–72.

———. *Mathilde Franziska Anneke.* Frankfurt/Main, 1980.

Walesrode, Ludwig. "Über das Proletariat." *Königsberger Taschenbuch.* Königsberg, 1846. Pp. 247–97.

Wasserburg, Philipp. "Ums 1848." *Mainzer Anzeiger,* September 25, 1897.

Wegert, Karl H. "Ideologie und Aktion." *Liberalismus in der Gesellschaft des deutschen Vormärz.* Ed. Walter Schieder. Göttingen, 1983. Pp. 167–93.

———. "Patrimonial Rule, Popular Self Interest and Jacobinism in Germany 1763–1800." *Journal of Modern History* 53 (September, 1981): 440–62.

Wegweiser der Stadt Mainz für das Jahr 1825. Mainz, 1825.

Weigel, Sigrid. *Flugschriftenliteratur 1848 in Berlin Geschichte und Öffentlichkeit einer volkstümlicher Gattung.* Stuttgart, 1979.

Weiland, Daniella. *Geschichte der Frauenemanzipation in Deutschland und Österreich.* Düsseldorf, 1983.

Wentzcke, Paul, and Wolfgang Klotzer, eds. *Deutscher Liberalismus im Vormärz, Heinrich von Gagern: Briefe und Reden 1815–1848.* Göttingen, 1959.

Bibliography

Wenzel, Achill. *Die Schule zwischen Kurstaat und Säkularstaat: Eine Studie über die mainzer Volksschule um 1800.* Wiesbaden, 1963.

Werner, Hans-Georg. *Geschichte des politischen Gedichts in Deutschland von 1815 bis 1840.* Berlin (DDR), 1969.

Wiltberger, Otto. *Die deutschen politischen Fluchtlinge in Strassburg vom 1830–1849.* Berlin, 1910.

Winterscheidt, Friedrich. *Deutsche Unterhaltungsliteratur der Jahre 1850–1860.* Bonn, 1970.

Wischermann, Ulla. *Frauenfrage und Presse: Frauenarbeit und Frauenbewegung in der illustrierten Presse des 19. Jahrhunderts.* Munich, 1983.

Wittke, Carl. *The German Language Press in America.* Lexington, Ky., 1957.

Wittmann, Reinhard. *Buchmarkt und Lektüre im 18. und 19. Jahrhundert.* Tübingen, 1982.

————. "Literarisches Leben 1848 bis 1880." *Realismus und Gründerzeit: Manifeste und Dokumente zur deutschen Literatur 1848–1880.* Ed. Max Bucher et al. Vol. 1. Stuttgart, 1976. Pp. 161–257.

Wolf, Ernst, Gerhard Luke, and Herbert Hax. *Scheidung und Scheidungsrecht: Grundfragen der Ehescheidung in Deutschland.* Tübingen, 1959.

Wollstonecraft, Mary. *Vindication of the Rights of Woman.* England, 1975.

Wormser Zetiung. 1839, 1841–1843.

Zahn-Harnack, Agnes von. *Die Frauenfrage in Deutschland: Strömungen und Gegenströmungen 1790–1930.* 2d ed. Tübingen, 1960.

Ziegler, Johann. "Hanauer Chronik." Vol. 2 (1846–1851). Historisches Museum Hanau.

Zimmermann, Ludwig. *Die Einheits- und Freiheitsbewegung und die Revolution von 1848 in Franken.* Würzburg, 1951.

Zimmermann, Wilhelm. *Die deutsche Revolution.* 2d ed. Karlsruhe, 1851.

Zinnecker, Jürgen. *Sozialgeschichte der Mädchenbildung.* Weinheim, 1973.

Zucker, Stanley. "Female Political Opposition in Pre–1848 Germany," in *German Women in the Nineteenth Century: A Social History.* Ed. John Fout. New York, 1984. Pp. 133–50.

————. "German Women and the Revolution of 1848: Kathinka Zitz-Halein and the Humania Association." *Central European History* 13, no. 3 (September 1980): 237–54.

Index

255

*S*tanley Zucker received his doctorate in history from the University of Wisconsin in Madison and was Professor of History at Southern Illinois University at Carbondale. He is the author of *Ludwig Bamberger: German Liberal Politician and Social Critic, 1823–1899*. His previous publications and conference papers focus on the mid-nineteenth-century revolution in Germany, political Catholicism, anti-Semitism, and women's history.